The Outdoor Survival Handbook

For my parents, who made my learning possible and suffered piles of sticks, bundles of bark fibres, wood shavings, smelly skins and decaying fungi for too long.

The Outdoor Survival Handbook

RAYMOND MEARS

ILLUSTRATED BY PAUL BRYANT

St. Martin's Press
New York

Warning
None of the outdoors activities and techniques described in this book should be performed on private land without the consent of the landowner. In all cases you should check the ownership and any by-laws relating to a piece of land before you start.

 For information, address St. Martin's Press, 175 Fifth Avenue, New York, N.Y. 10010.

Library of Congress Cataloging-in-Publication Data

Mears, Raymond.
The outdoor survival handbook / Raymond Mears.
p. cm.
ISBN 0-312-09359-4
1. Wilderness survival—Handbooks, manuals, etc. I. Title.
GV200.5.M33 1993
613.6'9—dc20 93-9683
CIP

First published in Great Britain under the title *The Complete Outdoor Handbook* by Random Century Group Ltd.

10 9 8 7 6 5

About the author

Raymond Mears grew up near the North Downs in England. A master of primitive technology and a specialist in the living skills of native peoples, he regularly teaches and lectures on the outdoors to private groups, schools and societies. He has traveled in the rainforests of Equatorial Africa, living in the villages with local peoples, sharing their foods and learning their traditional ways.

Acknowledgments

To Tessa Strickland for conceiving the project and bringing together the team.

To Mark Lucas for guiding me so well through the business thickets.

Special thanks to Paul Burcher for designing the book, patiently translating things that I take for granted into layperson's terms, to Paul Bryant for his superb illustrations that bring to life the subject and to Miles Litvinoff who tidied and polished my somewhat rustic text. Also to the rest of the team at Rider for their support and encouragement: Teresa Wilkinson, Cécile Landau and the production, sales and marketing teams.

Personal thanks to my friends and aquaintances who have offered their opinions and comments: Ffyona Campbell, James Locke, David Shepherd, Robert Craigie, Christopher James, Joe Pratt. Also to Turrka Aaltonen for his background information on the Scandinavian use of birch bark, and Lars Falt for introducing me to the Roycraft snow-shoe which has kept me from sinking into many snow-drifts. Also to Gillian Wynn Ruffhead and Dr Derek Reid for equipping me with the knowledge to explore the world of fungi, one of my greatest pleasures.

Finally, my gratitude to all the students who have passed through the Woodlore courses in the last few years, who have been my best teachers.

Contents

AUTUMN 142

WINTER 176

Introduction

This morning I walked up the steep trail on to one of my favourite ridges. There is an old yew tree there with low sheltering branches under which I often sit. It is now autumn; with the year coming to a close, the trees are decked in their late-season best, and the scent of decay is in the air. As the sky pulled back its curtains and allowed the early-morning sunlight in, two roe deer in the field below began their retreat to the cover of nearby woodland.

Unusually it has been a long time since I last sat under that special tree. There have been many changes there – the trail was the most overgrown I have ever seen it. Yet, from the tree's far longer time-perspective, I had hardly been gone at all. Sitting there with my back against the gnarled old grandfather trunk, in the wild again for the first time for many months, I felt truly alive.

Writing this book has enabled me to return to places and experiences like these after too long an absence. Now, more than ever before, I appreciate the refreshment brought by the sobering rain, the heart-warming glow of a camp-fire and the timely scratch of thorns telling me to stop rushing and move with a more careful rhythm.

Too often we think of ourselves as separate from nature, forgetting that we are just a part of it. This book sets out to show how you can discover – or rediscover – a closer relationship with the things that, in my view, matter most.

This is, however, mainly a practical book. I don't spend much time waxing lyrical abut my experiences of nature, because you must have your own. Instead, I set out to explain how to utilise and enjoy the natural resources that surround us without damaging them. I am confident that if you go out and practise for yourself the skills and activities described here, you will find them as deeply satisfying as I do. In the process you will discover a new perspective on the world; for you will be learning to see through the eyes of an indigenous native – a person truly in tune with their environment. The more you understand of the ways of nature, the more you will value them.

There is something to be learned everywhere in the natural world. Yet how far removed from this most of us are in our everyday lives!

Sometimes in a town or city I am struck by the way we wear padded shoes to avoid bruising our feet on the concrete, how we have to crook and crane our necks to find the horizon and rush about to avoid being knocked over by the crowds. No wonder the sycamore trees pushing down the walls of derelict gardens, and the overflying geese, heron, kestrel and owl, all go unnoticed. With so many of us today inhabiting this modern urban environment, I can understand why the term 'wilderness' now conveys a sense of chaos and threat rather than describing a place devoid of human settlement and cultivation. To me, however, the urban landscape is far more threatening and chaotic.

The view from my yew tree stretches eastwards along a range of downland hills along which our first direct ancestors made their way inland. Ten or more thousand years ago, smoke would have risen from their fires as they made camp. They were venturing into vast empty tracts of land where no human footprint had been left since before the last Ice Age. As they travelled, they had to adapt to the conditions they encountered, without the machines and gadgets we consider essential today. Yet these people were fully equipped. In their heads was the accumulated knowledge of our species, in their hands the skill of translating thought into action with great refinement. Their most powerful tool was the ability to reason, for our early ancestors laid the foundations of what we now call science.

As you read in this book about the uses of the trees and plants which surround us, try to imagine a time when these benefits had not yet been discovered. Take string, for example. The idea of string was perhaps born when people observed the frayed bark of a lime sapling where a deer had been rubbing the velvet from its antlers. By experimentation they discovered the process for making strong twine and rope. Or think of hunting. Did early hunters learn to stalk their prey by watching the carnivores, just as we today can learn from the fox? Even now, you need only watch the poise and stance of a native spear-fisherman in Africa or Asia to realise that it was the heron that first showed humankind this skill.

Whatever the teacher, the method of learning from nature remains the same: observation. You can discover which leaves are the warmest insulators by observing the hibernating animals in the autumn. Or learn to create a waterproof shelter roof by observing the construction methods of the wood ant. And so on.

Few of us can today say in truth that we could survive with only what nature provides. We have become too dependent upon our gadgets to keep us alive. My aim in the book is to show a path back to the old ways, so that you too can sit under a tree and know that you can provide for yourself as long as the natural resources remain to make this possible. And here lies the real learning, for along the way you will encounter the raw truth of our total dependence upon the natural world.

Before venturing forth on your journey of rediscovery, however, spare a moment to adjust your way of thinking. When lecturing about plants and their uses, I notice that a lot of people are never really happy that they have learned about a plant or tree until they have a name to file it away by. To my way of thinking, the name is the least important piece of information I have to impart about that plant. Far more important are its uses, where it grows and why it grows there. I may have a need for a medicine, food or fibre that this plant can supply; if I know that it will supply it, I must then know where to search for it. The name rarely gives this information.

Among indigenous peoples, it was and is different. There is, for example, a very useful tree that the Sioux people had three names for: 'white wood', 'weapon wood' or 'wood that smells old when carved'. All these ways of calling the tree describe it accurately by its nature. If you are a woodworker you probably recognise it as ash. Of course, there are sometimes exceptions, when our names also describe a plant's value, a classic case being the lime tree. 'Lime' is a corruption of the tree's original name of 'line' from the Saxon *lin* which means 'thread'. This 'thread tree' was once the principal source of lines and ropes.

The moral here is simple. As we explore the values of the things which surround us, we need to keep an open and inquisitive mind.

In time, as your eyesight becomes better acclimatised to the natural world, you will see that you are surrounded by allies and resources. The grass becomes your carpet and the sky your ceiling. But you will also find that nature can be the harshest and most unsentimental force. Natural selection is the law; the slow and infirm fall victim, while the strong and intelligent survive. This is the way things must be if balance is to be maintained. Learn to recognise and appreciate nature's way and to live within it. Keep yourself in good shape – exercise for strength and stamina. In particular, make certain your can swim. You may need to go searching near to large bodies of water both inland and on the coast, and there is always the risk of falling in.

Just as I sat there on the hill this morning and watched the sun come up, take time to look about for the tiny, seemingly insignificant changes that occur every day. An infinite number of small details, such as an individual leaf falling in autumn, contribute to the make-up of a whole season. Our ancestors were bound up far more closely with seasonal influences than we are today. Doing our hunting and gathering in supermarkets, we need never taste the changes in the seasons, but they had to be acutely aware of small signals that heralded the new ripening or availability of foods. For this reason I have divided the book by seasons, so that you can go out at any time in the year and learn about the availability of resources. Of course, there are not always hard-and-fast rules. Nature moves to her own tune, and seasons start and finish in different locations at different times. Crossing from one side of a hill to the other can often bring dramatic change in the materials that can be used. You will have to look to your own location for the indicators.

Within the seasonal sections I have arranged the information to follow a logical progression which assumes that you begin your study in the early spring and increase in skill and ability through the course of the year. This is the best way to learn, for each season has its own character and will add its own special influence. If you have to start during the winter, bear in mind that you may need to refer back to earlier seasons in the book for the more basic aspects of the skills.

I have offered some advice on equipping yourself for the outdoors in case you have never been camping before. If you are in this position, and you are wondering whether to launch in with the rest of us, let me extend a welcome. We'd love to have you along. Don't pay any mind to those outdoors folk who seem to spend most of their time talking about gear and 'gizmos'. If you can only afford a tin can as a cook-pot and a blanket for your sleeping-bag, that's fine. Carrying gear like that, as long as you don't let on, you're well disguised as the expert who shuns flashiness and believes in simplicity!

Space doesn't allow me to teach you how to make flint tools to cut with. Instead, I am assuming you have access to a steel knife. Your knife will be all-important. On courses I have had people turn up with all manner of cutting tools, from kitchen knives to street-fighting weapons. A woodcraft knife is a special tool. On p. 21 you will see the Woodlore knife which I designed for my own use and have made available by popular demand through a custom knife-maker. If you cannot afford this, you will find that several of the suppliers under 'Useful addresses' at the end of the book (p. 230) stock a perfectly adequate cheaper knife. Remember: outdoors, your knife is your most important tool.

Almost from the start you will see that we shall be making demands on our environment for materials. With so many of our natural resources now threatened by human activities, we have the utmost responsibility to garner without damaging or destroying our surroundings. This is the way of the native North Americans (the 'Indians'), who look after the land with great reverence so that it will provide for their grandchildren. With care and understanding we can meet all of our needs without denuding the contryside (in fact, we can even do some good). Primitive skills make for lighter demands on nature than those made by the technology required to keep even the most environmentally friendly hike-stove operational. In the wild, I always go to great lengths to avoid leaving any trace of my presence on the land – even if that involves extra effort, which it usually does. Follow the maxim of taking only memories and leaving only footprints, and then try to make those as light as moccasin prints.

To learn the skills presented in this book you will have to get out and about. You may wish to link up with one of the youth organisations that already have a strong outdoors-pursuit interest, or to go on one of the many good courses being run. The skills featured here are chosen to give you a foundation in outdoors living that will take you safely into some of the remotest places; since they are carried inside of you, they cannot be lost. Most of the methods of preparing materials are universal. If you are venturing outside the temperate environment, into really cold or hot regions, you will find that by combining this knowledge with careful observation of the local resources and a few experiments you will soon be at home. The real thrill of these techniques is using them, but I don't advise you to throw yourself in at the deep end. All too often we seek artificial adventure to spice our over-secure lives. If you take the time to master these skills, the confidence you gain will entice you to places where there is plenty of adventure to be had without having to create it artificially.

Back there at my tree this morning, I tried to imagine you, the reader, and what I would say to you if we were to meet before you let yourself loose on the skills and activities in the book. It boils down to this. There will be exhilarating times when everything seems to go well – the 'up'-times. Enjoy them! But there will also be times when, no matter how hard you try, things go wrong; when you skin your knuckles and curse me as you struggle with something or other, most likely fire by friction. Remember at those times that all of us who have learned these skills have been there too. Struggle is part of the learning process. At no time do I claim that these skills are easy to master, but there lies the achievement.

Most of all, though, I hope that by interacting with nature, and feeling the sense of responsibility this brings, you will gain a deeper insight into the natural world and into our relationship with it. Just as, each day, small and seemingly insignificant events mark the change of the seasons, so your small and apparently unimportant deeds can contribute to a powerful force. Be caring towards the land and be seen to be so, and you will help to preserve the wilderness upon which we all ultimately depend and which we seem at present so bent upon destroying.

Clothing

Clothing for the outdoors must be practical. Choose carefully, and don't swallow sales-blurb too willingly. In my experience, once someone has settled on a favourite garment they use it for many years. No single garment will do all jobs – you need a versatile system of layers that can be arranged to suit all weathers. Your clothing will need to cope with hot dry conditions as well as cold, wind and wet.

If you are going to be involved with camp-fires, woodcraft or watching wild animals, tough natural fibres such as wool and cotton will be more useful than the synthetic alternatives. Whatever your primary interest, you will also need a good waterproof jacket, preferably of a breathable fabric such as Goretex which reduces condensation. Make sure that it is large enough to be worn over the top of your other layers and that it reaches to just above the knee.

Trousers take a battering, so don't spend a fortune on them. U.S. army lightweight trousers are cheap and comfortable; made from cotton, they dry quickly. Avoid ultra-lightweight synthetics.

Probably the most important item of clothing is your 'shell' (outermost) jacket. This needs to be windproof and to offer good waterproofness; it should be light and comfortable to wear, not too bulky. Several good pockets can also be an advantage. My choice is a Ventile jacket. This tight-weave cotton is comfortable, windproof, virtually waterproof and tough. It can be used in arid conditions as a shirt and in arctic conditions as a windproof shell. Refusing to become sweaty, it rarely needs more cleaning than hosing down.

Insulative layers can be adapted from pile jerseys; or use the traditional oiled guernsey. You will also need a woolly hat and mits for winter, many pairs of woollen socks and some waterproof Goretex socks.

Footwear is a matter of choice. In the mountains you will need good ankle support and grip in the sole. There are many models and makes of boots. A good starting place would be a comfortable Merrel boot. (Suppliers of clothing and equipment described throughout the book are listed under 'Useful addresses' on p. 230.)

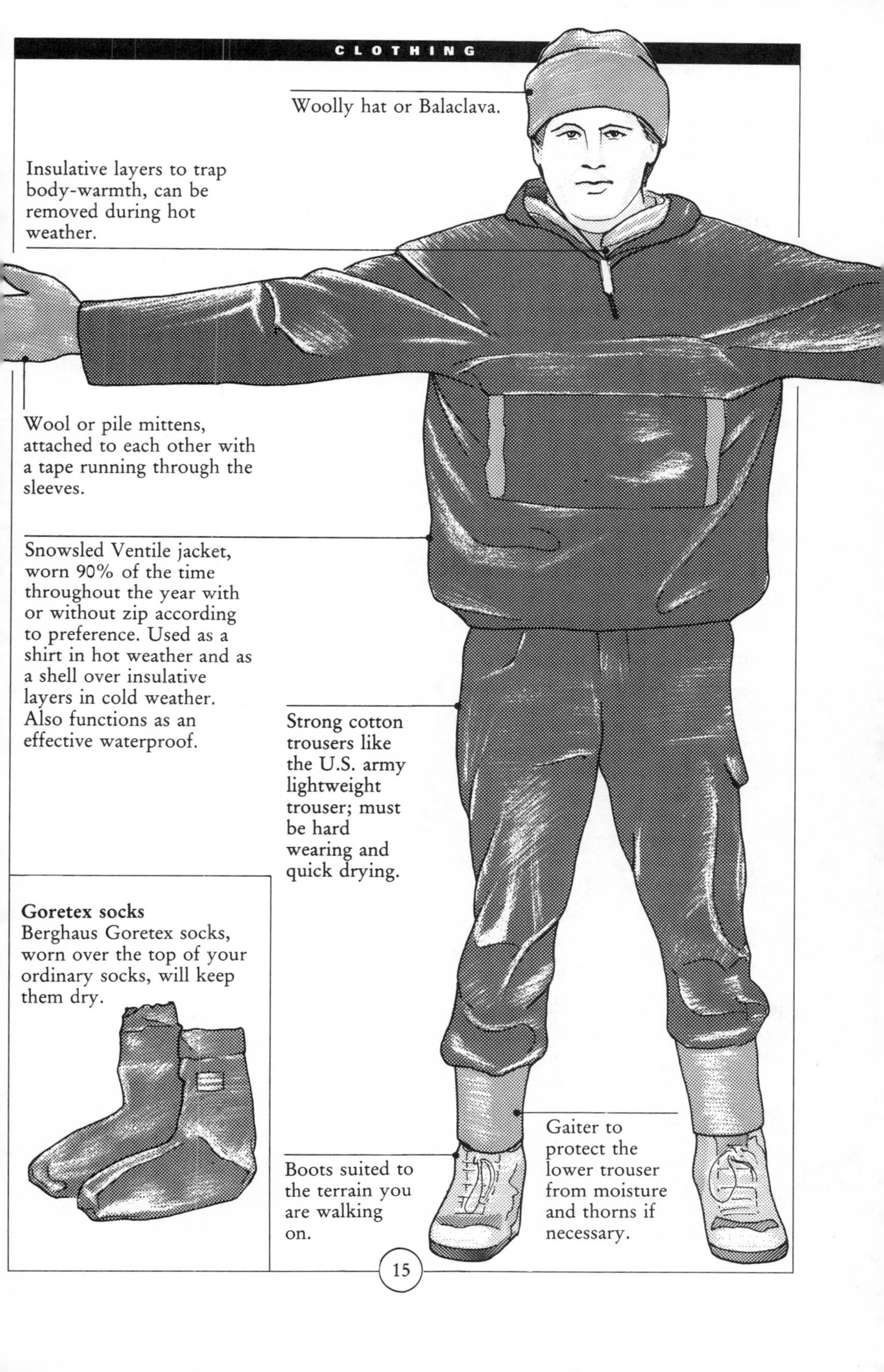

Goretex socks
Berghaus Goretex socks, worn over the top of your ordinary socks, will keep them dry.

Personal kit

To be comfortable when camping you will need to carry some basic items of equipment. In choosing what to include in your kit you should balance strength and versatility with compactness and lightness of weight. There is plenty of scope for choice. Personally, I work on the 'keep it simple' philosophy. So I avoid any equipment that involves fiddly little fittings that can be snapped off or easily lost on the trail.

Make sure that you carry only what you need, and not an item more. Over time assess what you have been carrying and discard things that you don't use – except of course emergency equipment such as whistle and first-aid kit. If you do get into trouble in the mountains or elsewhere, the internationally recognised emergency signal is six whistle blasts or torch flashes in quick succession, repeated after a minute interval. The reply is three blasts or flashes in quick succession, repeated after a minute interval.

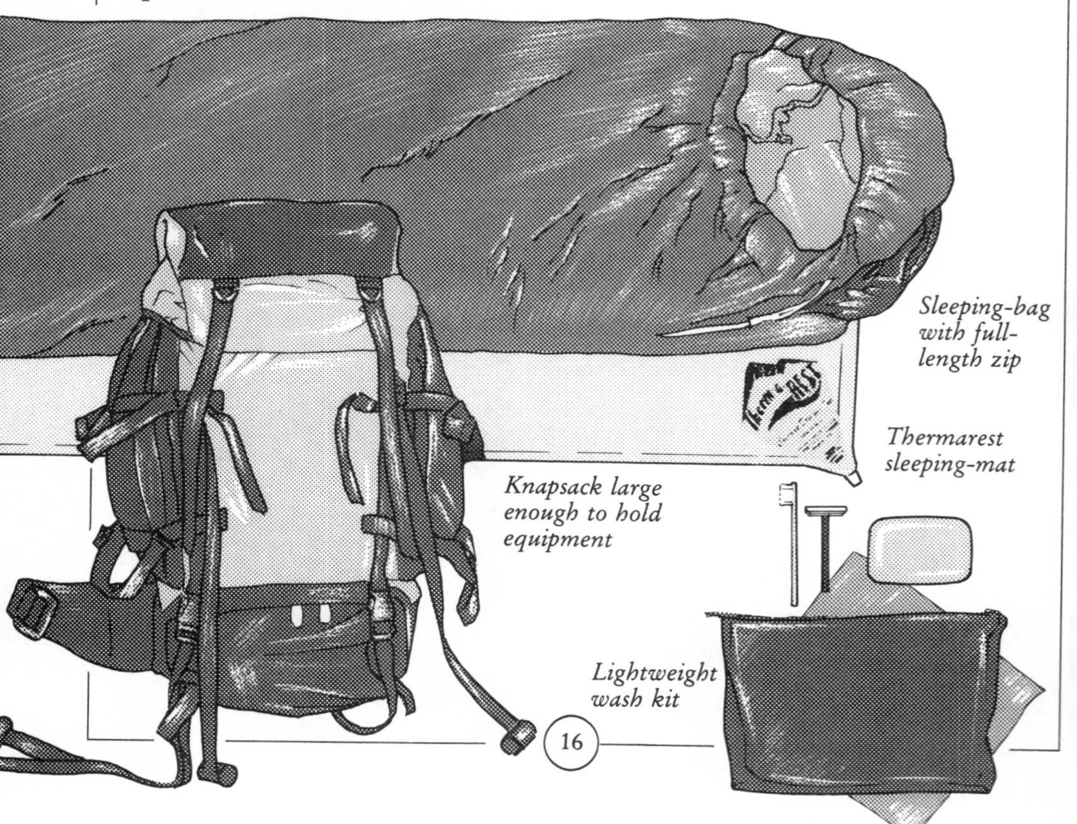

Sleeping-bag with full-length zip

Thermarest sleeping-mat

Knapsack large enough to hold equipment

Lightweight wash kit

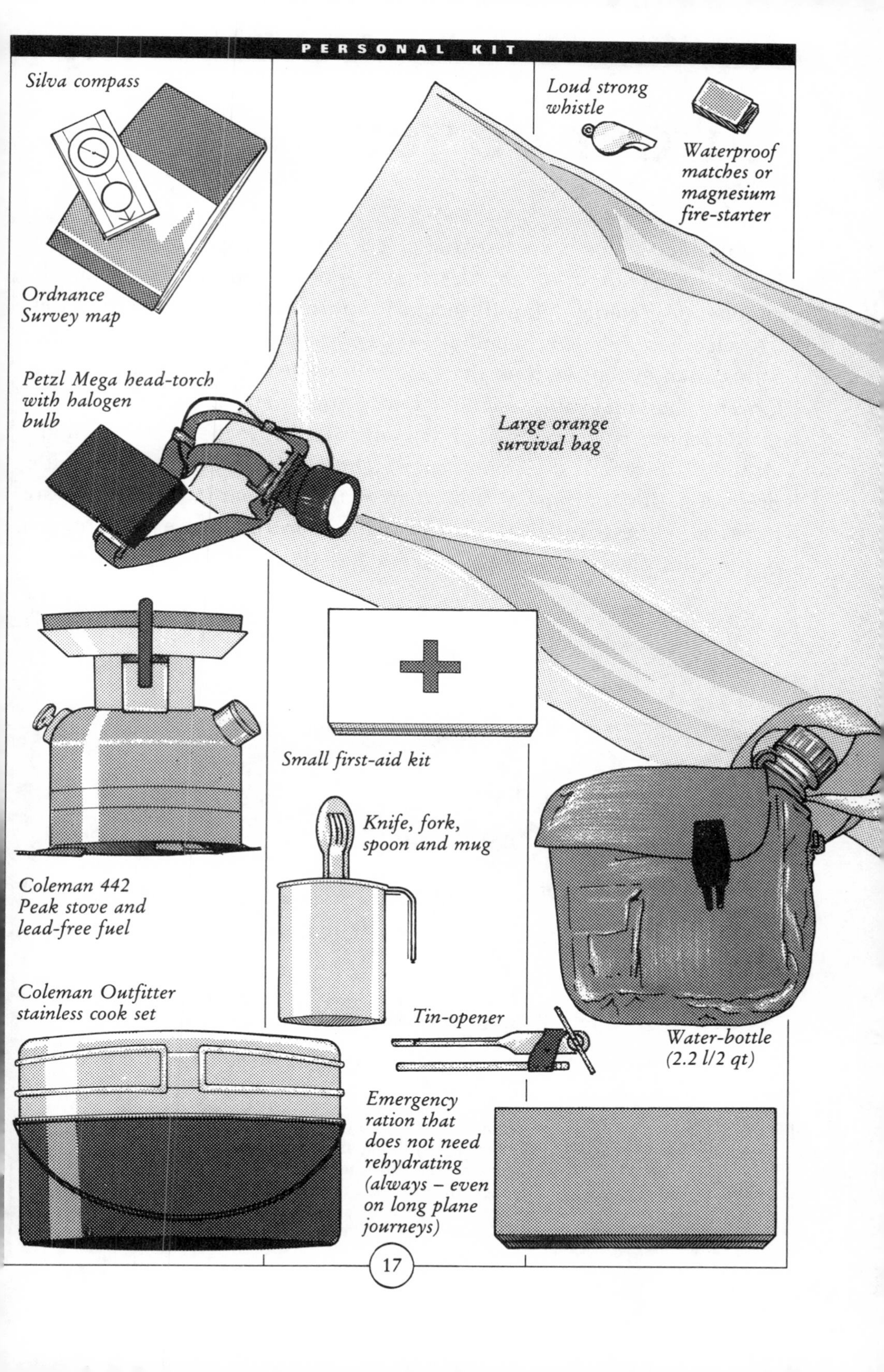
Silva compass
Ordnance Survey map
Loud strong whistle
Waterproof matches or magnesium fire-starter
Petzl Mega head-torch with halogen bulb
Large orange survival bag
Coleman 442 Peak stove and lead-free fuel
Small first-aid kit
Knife, fork, spoon and mug
Coleman Outfitter stainless cook set
Tin-opener
Water-bottle (2.2 l/2 qt)
Emergency ration that does not need rehydrating (always – even on long plane journeys)

Under cover

A portable shelter is an essential piece of outdoors equipment. There is a vast range of styles and designs to choose from, ranging from the simple but versatile nylon flysheet to sophisticated geodesic structures. To select your shelter, spend a few days carefully studying catalogues – this is an expensive item that you will use for a long time to come. Goretex has inevitably found its way into the fabrics used in tent manufacture, particularly in small bivouac tents and tents for high-altitude use where the saving in weight of a single-skin tent is at a premium. But for general use a tent with a fly and an inner is more practical. Unless weight is your primary concern, ensure the tent you opt for has plenty of internal space; geodesic designs offer plenty.

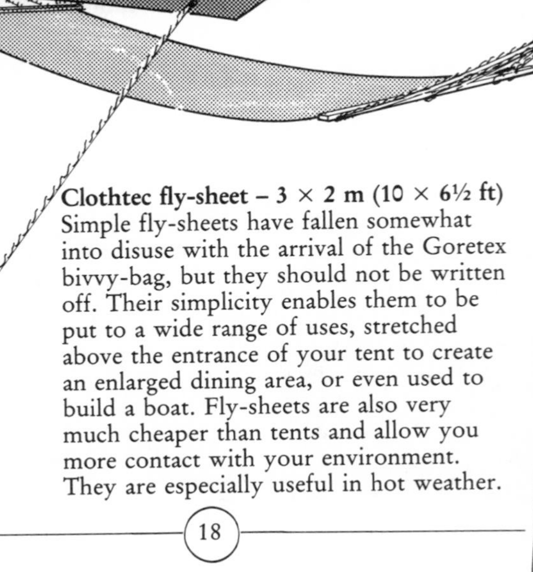

Clothtec fly-sheet – 3 × 2 m (10 × 6½ ft)
Simple fly-sheets have fallen somewhat into disuse with the arrival of the Goretex bivvy-bag, but they should not be written off. Their simplicity enables them to be put to a wide range of uses, stretched above the entrance of your tent to create an enlarged dining area, or even used to build a boat. Fly-sheets are also very much cheaper than tents and allow you more contact with your environment. They are especially useful in hot weather.

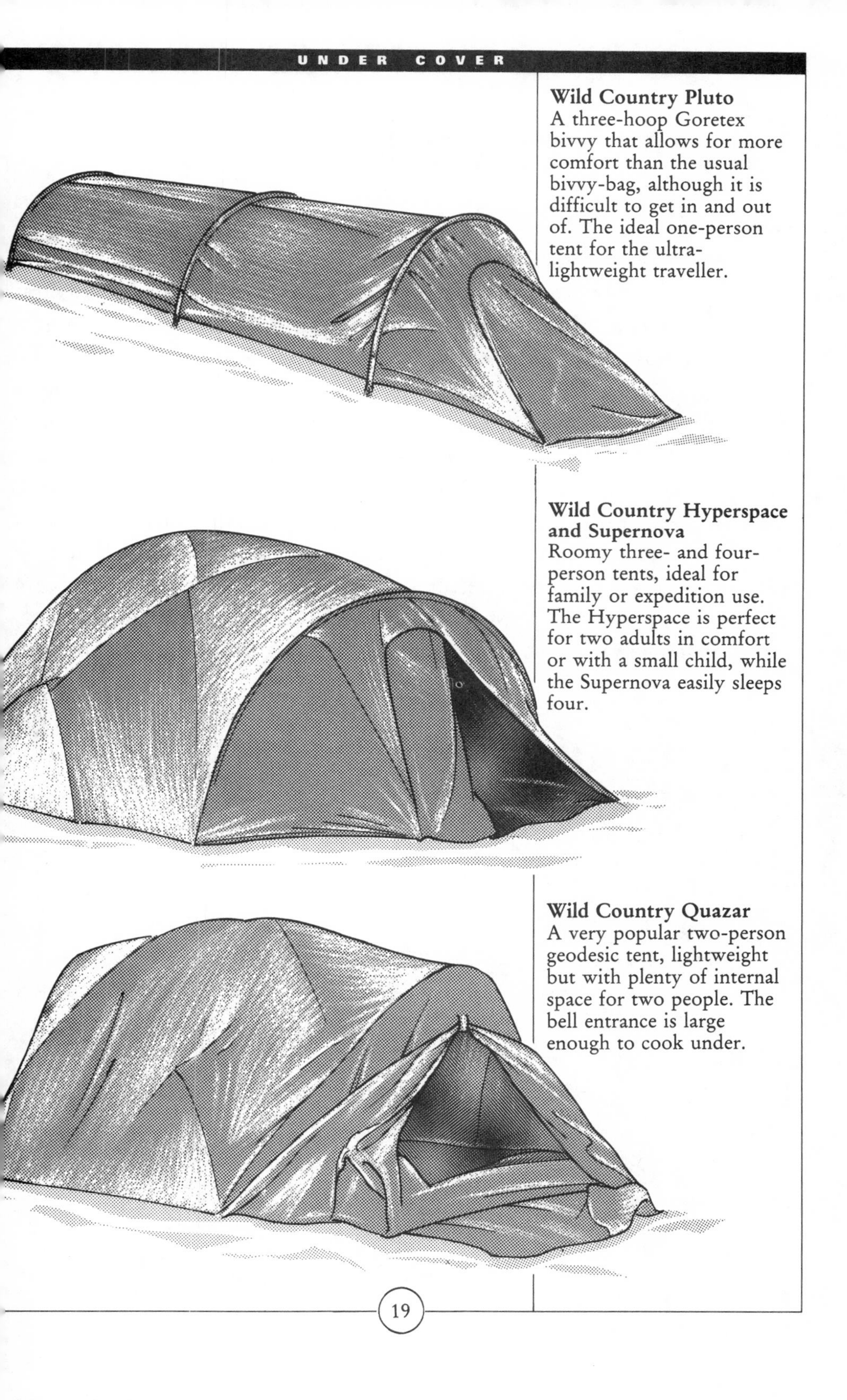

Wild Country Pluto
A three-hoop Goretex bivvy that allows for more comfort than the usual bivvy-bag, although it is difficult to get in and out of. The ideal one-person tent for the ultra-lightweight traveller.

Wild Country Hyperspace and Supernova
Roomy three- and four-person tents, ideal for family or expedition use. The Hyperspace is perfect for two adults in comfort or with a small child, while the Supernova easily sleeps four.

Wild Country Quazar
A very popular two-person geodesic tent, lightweight but with plenty of internal space for two people. The bell entrance is large enough to cook under.

Base camp kit

Sooner or later you will need a few less portable items of kit to make the campsite more comfortable, especially if working from a car. First on your list should be a camp lantern. You only have to arrive at a campsite once after dark for this beacon to become a firm fixture. The easiest to use are lead-free-fuel lanterns, as they require no priming.

Coleman makes an excellent range of camp equipment, especially lead-free-fuel stoves and lanterns which all have instructions for use firmly attached to them. Bear in mind that you may well be camping with people unfamiliar with their operation. Make sure you get a carrying case and some spare mantles to go with it. Second should be a double-burner unleaded-petrol stove; these fold up to the size of a briefcase and are perfect for group cooking. Add to these a small cool-box, a water jerrycan, some garden gloves and a pair of pliers, and you have all the basics.

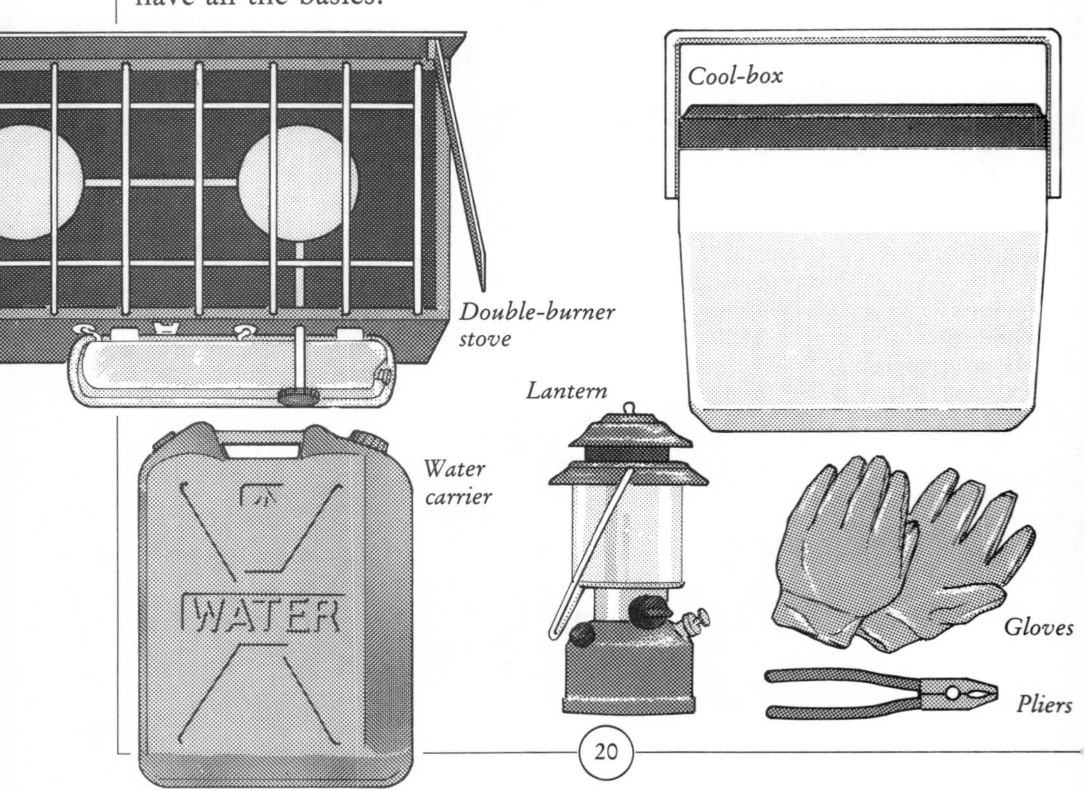

Cutting tools

Many campers are content to carry nothing more than a Swiss army knife or Leatherman tool with them. But if you are heading for more remote regions you are going to need a stronger cutting tool. My preference is for a small sheath-knife, backed up by a tomahawk and a folding saw – depending on where I am going, how light I wish to travel and what season it is.

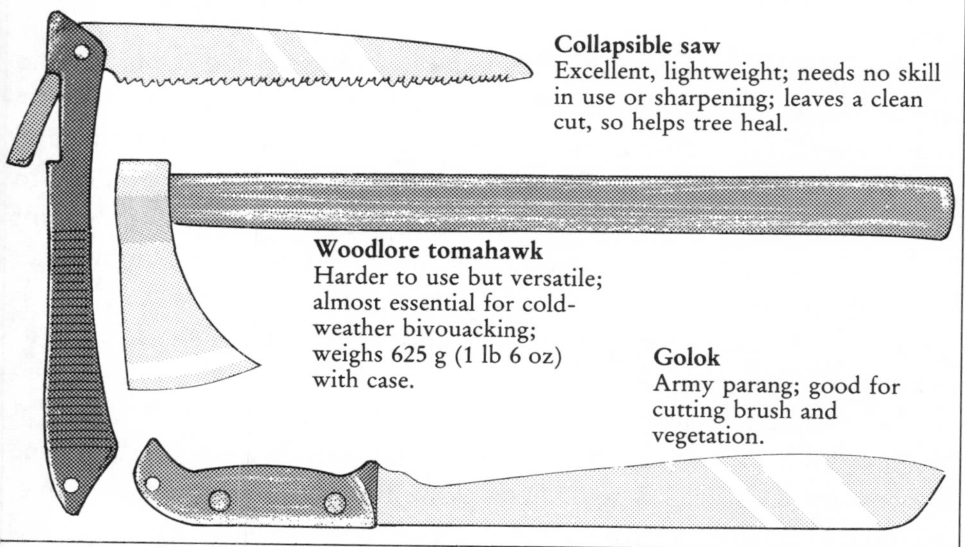

Collapsible saw
Excellent, lightweight; needs no skill in use or sharpening; leaves a clean cut, so helps tree heal.

Woodlore tomahawk
Harder to use but versatile; almost essential for cold-weather bivouacking; weighs 625 g (1 lb 6 oz) with case.

Golok
Army parang; good for cutting brush and vegetation.

The importance of your knife

A small knife is a necessity. A sheath-knife that cannot fold on to your finger is best. The knife should be compact, with a handle that is easily grasped. Above all, it must be strong and kept sharp.

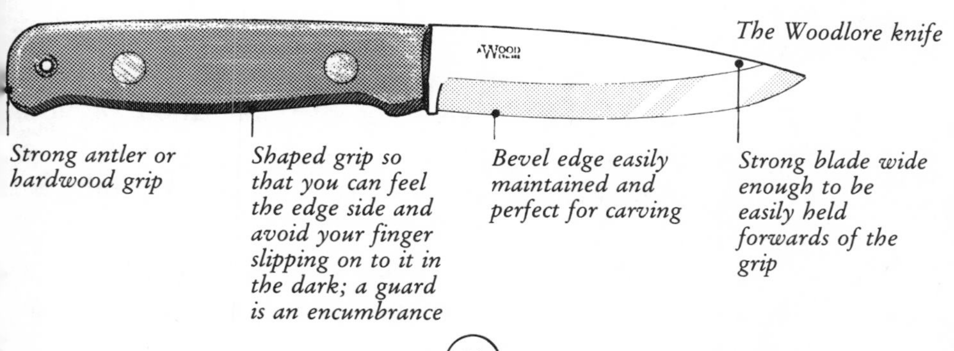

The Woodlore knife

Strong antler or hardwood grip

Shaped grip so that you can feel the edge side and avoid your finger slipping on to it in the dark; a guard is an encumbrance

Bevel edge easily maintained and perfect for carving

Strong blade wide enough to be easily held forwards of the grip

Navigation

The world we live in is, for the most part, very organised. The outdoors is far less organised. We may have a map and a compass to find our way about. But if we don't have them, we can learn to read signs that will give us at least a general indication of direction (see p. 28). Navigation is for the most part the application of good observation and common sense. It is an important skill for anyone venturing off the beaten track.

Navigation is more than just knowing how to use a map and a compass, however. The good navigator must be able to read a landscape, tell direction from any visible landmarks, look at a map and picture the way the land will appear in true life, look at the land and picture it shown as a map. In this way navigation from point *A* to point *B* is understood as a movement across the actual land surface, with all its ups and downs. Also, the navigator needs to understand which geographical features will be most readily identifiable and use them as a pointer to the intended destination.

For example, you may be moving cross-country, with the aim of making for a particular gateway in a stone wall. If your heading (line of movement) is straight for that gateway and you are a little off course, you may miss it. You then cannot be certain which side of the gateway you have arrived. The wise navigator foresees this problem. He or she deliberately aims off boldly to one side so as to know which direction to follow along the wall to find the gateway.

Triangulation points are fixed places of reference used in making maps

With practice, such thought processes become automatic. Within reason you should always know or be able to give a rough indication of your location, by reference either to the cardinal directions (north, south, east, west) or to prominent geographical features.

Don't be the kind of navigator who never looks up. Navigation is about looking around you – don't rely just on map and compass.

Your compass

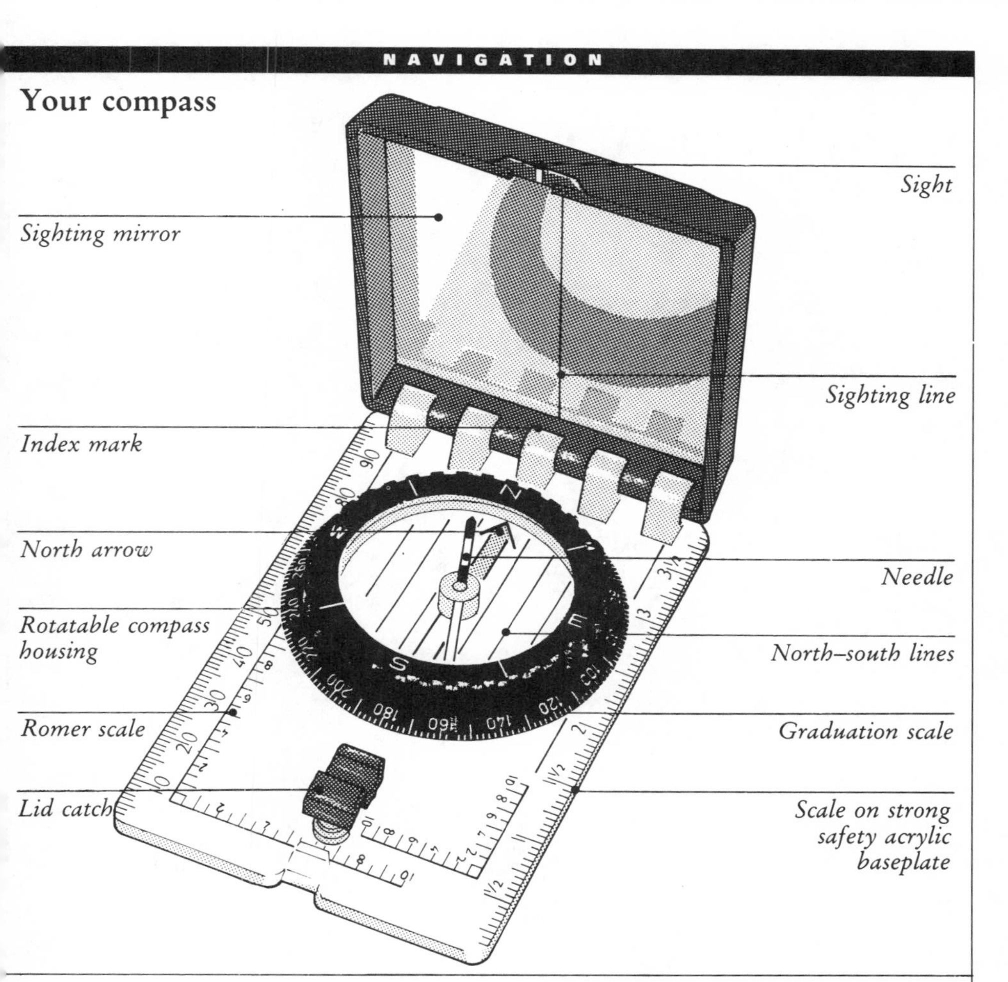

A compass always points north, doesn't it?

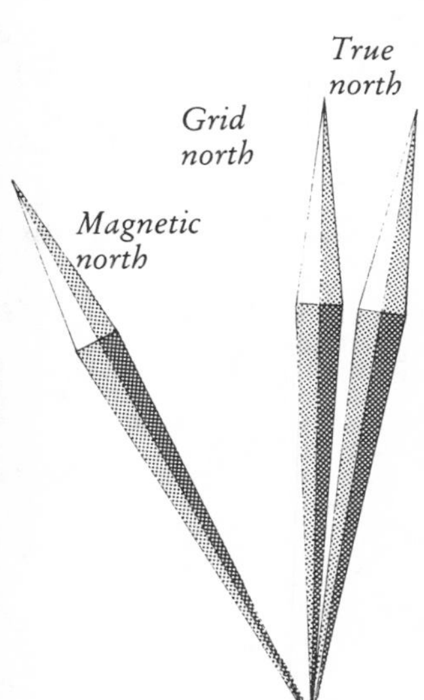

There are three norths. The one represented by the grid lines of your map may differ from the north from which you are gaining your physical orientation. In this case you will have to add or subtract the difference between them.

True north
The celestial north which is obtained from accurate sun readings or from the stars.

Grid north
The north of the map-maker which grid lines are in alignment with, and from which we take map bearings.

Magnetic north
The north to which your compass points; its position changes slowly over time. From this we take all our magnetic land bearings.

Using OS maps

Ordnance Survey maps are the ones you are most likely to use in the outdoors. You need to be able to find your way around the map. You should also be able to communicate a location to someone else with the same map who is at a remote distance. There is a standard way of doing this using the grid system.

Finding your way around an OS map

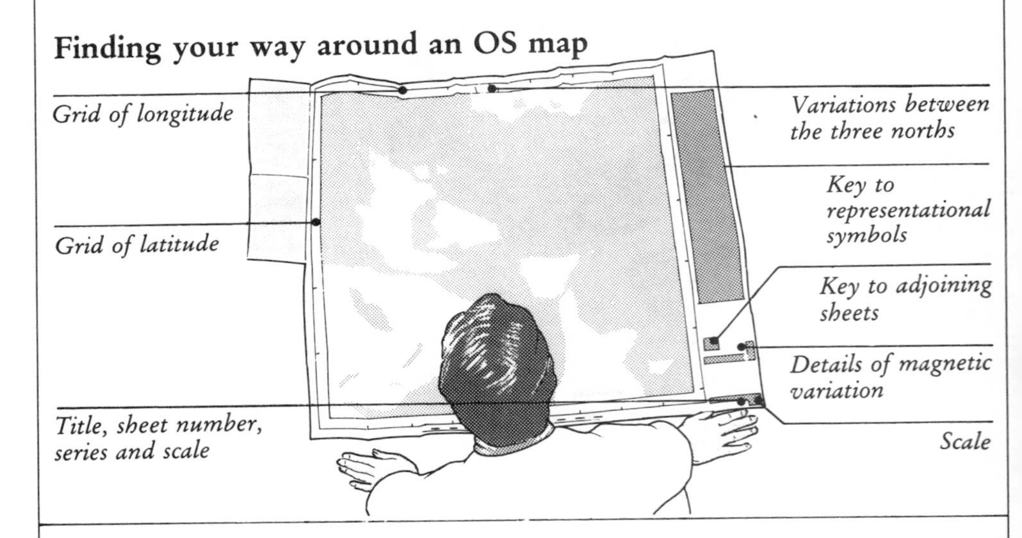

Each map in a U.S. Geological Survey series conforms to established specifications for size, scale, content, and symbolization. Except for maps which are formatted on a County or State basis, USGS quadrangle series maps cover areas bounded by parallels of latitude and meridians of longitude.

The use of color helps to distinguish kinds of features:

Black—cultural features such as roads and buildings.
Blue—hydrographic features such as lakes and rivers.
Brown—hypsographic features shown by contour lines.
Green—woodland cover, scrub, orchards, and vineyards.
Red—important roads and public land survey system.
Purple—features added from aerial photographs during map revision.
The changes are not field checked.

Contours

Features on a landscape are relatively easily shown on the map by the use of symbols. But the undulations and irregularities of the land surface are harder to represent. To translate a three-dimensional feature into two dimensions, the land surface is represented in imaginary slices at vertical intervals of 10 metres (about 33 feet). By studying the closeness of these lines you can build a mental picture of the land surface, complete with convex and concave surfaces, depressions and hillocks.

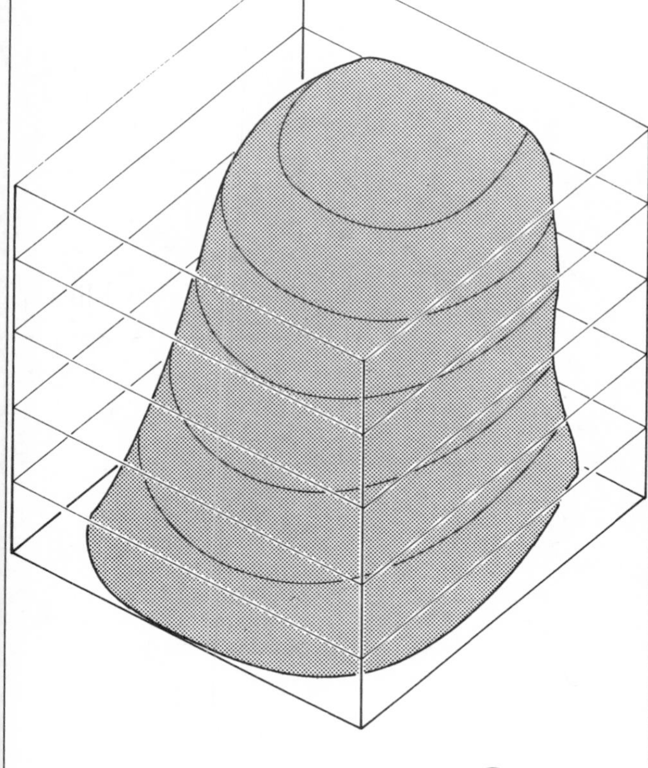

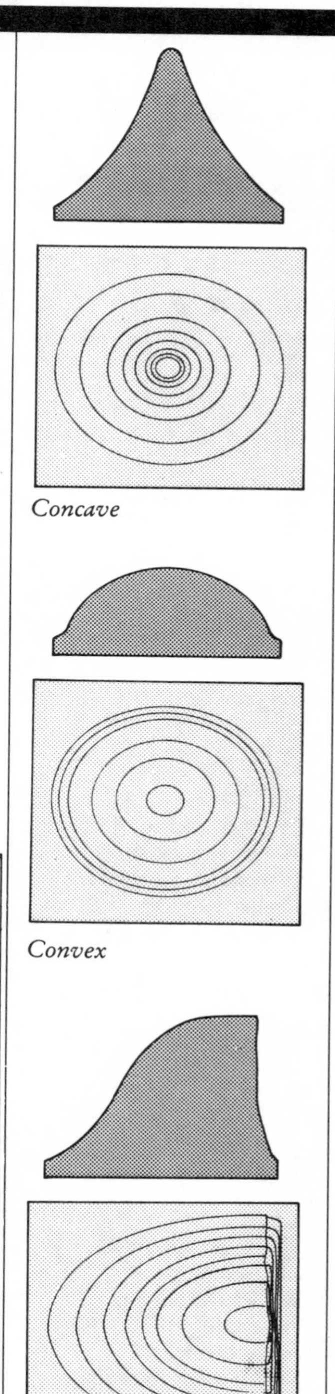

Concave

Convex

Cliff face

Using a Silva compass

To take a bearing to walk from point *A* to point *B*

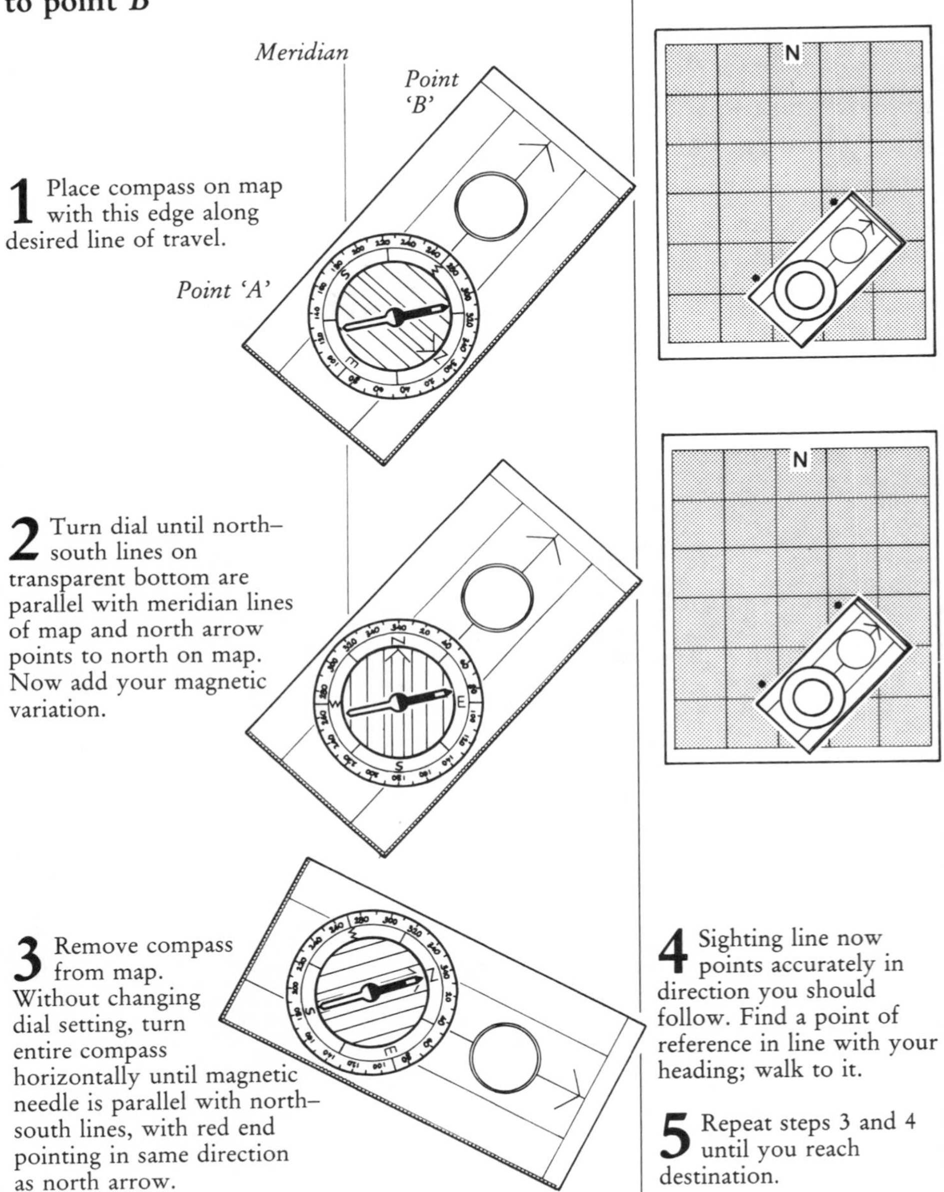

1 Place compass on map with this edge along desired line of travel.

2 Turn dial until north–south lines on transparent bottom are parallel with meridian lines of map and north arrow points to north on map. Now add your magnetic variation.

3 Remove compass from map. Without changing dial setting, turn entire compass horizontally until magnetic needle is parallel with north–south lines, with red end pointing in same direction as north arrow.

4 Sighting line now points accurately in direction you should follow. Find a point of reference in line with your heading; walk to it.

5 Repeat steps 3 and 4 until you reach destination.

To find out where you are by resection

1 Point sighting line of compass at an identifiable land feature. Turn dial until north–south lines are parallel to magnetic needle, with red end pointing in same direction as north arrow. Now subtract magnetic variation.

2 Place compass on map with edge of base plate on symbol for identifiable feature. Without adjusting dial, turn whole compass horizontally about this point until north–south lines are parallel to meridian, with north arrow pointing to map north. Your location is somewhere along line represented by edge of compass.

3 Take a second bearing from a different land feature and repeat steps 1 and 2.

4 Your position lies at point where two bearing lines intersect.

Natural indicators of direction

All around us our world is shaped by natural forces – wind, sun, rain and a host of other influences. Many of these are regular or constant forces, operating in a predictable way; for example, the sun is always south of us in the U.S. We can use signs of these influences in the growing things around us for an indication of direction. To use these signs with confidence takes a practised eye, but it is surprising just how useful they can be.

Trees and plants

Trees standing on their own, or the top of the highest woodland trees standing above the rest, are affected by both wind and sun. Winds blowing from the south-west (make sure you check your area's most frequent winds, taking account of local topography) will sweep the branches towards the north-east.

The sun, however, encourages greater growth on the southern side of the tree. This is shown by the more horizontal branches being found on the southern side and the more vertical branches on the northern side.

Trees also reflect their life history. The topmost branches are always the best guide; lower down, the tree may have been affected by growing in coppice or scrub, with less effects of wind and sun.

Reeds, especially in established beds, usually have their flowering heads on the lee side, i.e. away from the prevailing winds.

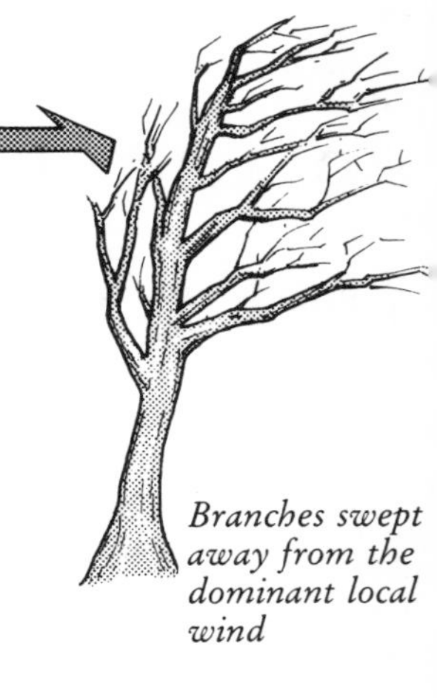

Branches swept away from the dominant local wind

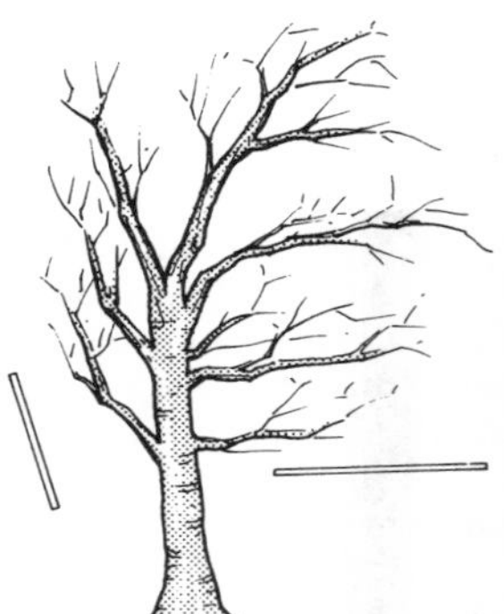

Horizontal growth to sunny south

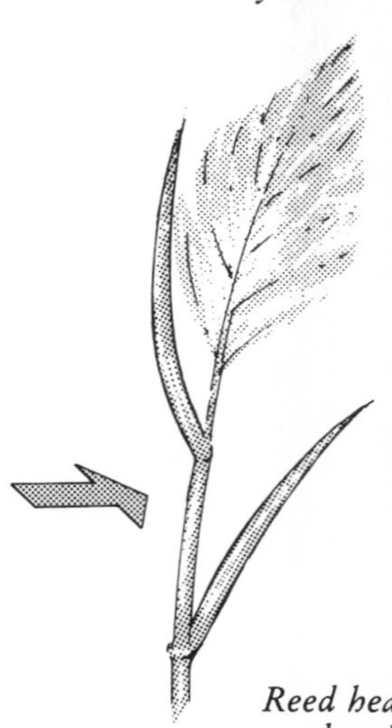

Reed heads on lee side (away from wind)

Sun and shadow

The sun can be an accurate indicator of true north. Without specialised equipment we can only obtain a rough estimate, but this is still good enough for our purposes.

Place a stick in the ground and mark the shadow end with a stone.

Allow enough time to pass for the shadow to move several inches. Mark the shadow again with a second stone.

The two stones lie on the west–east line, and the shadow moves from west to east.

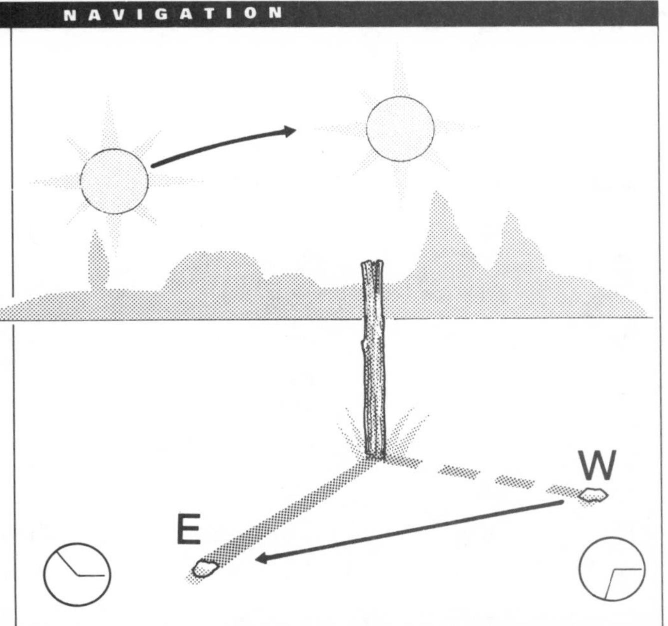

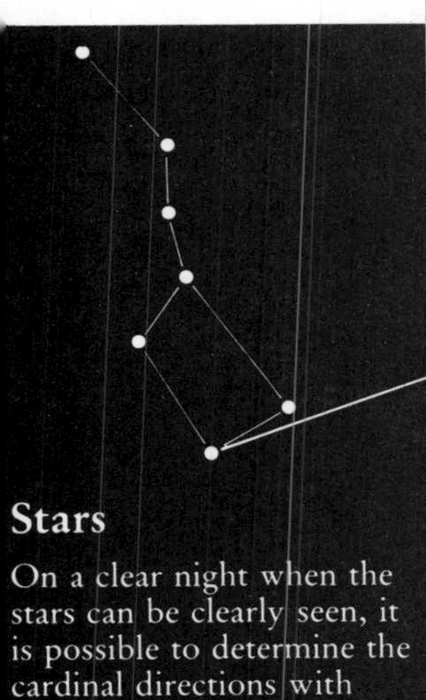

Stars

On a clear night when the stars can be clearly seen, it is possible to determine the cardinal directions with great accuracy.

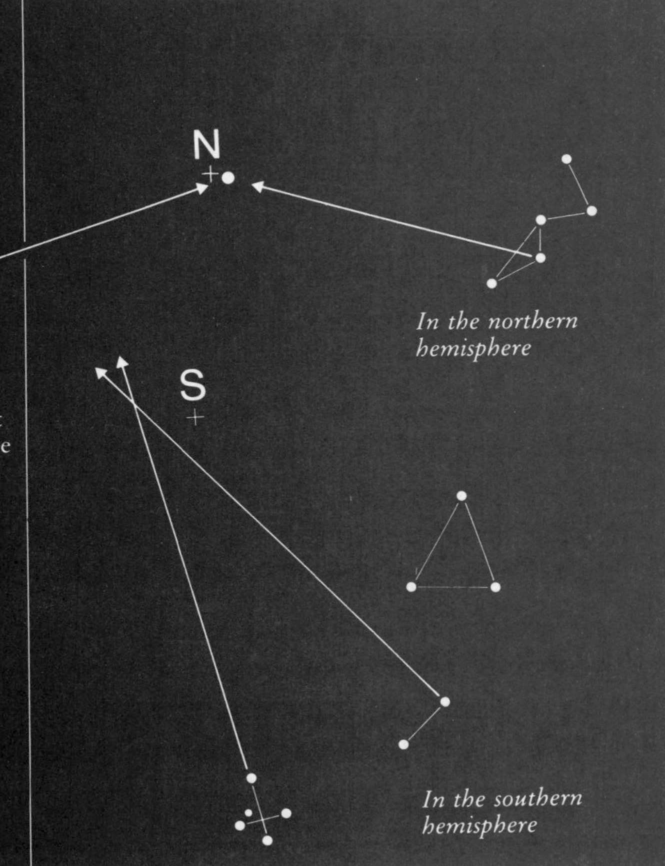

In the northern hemisphere

In the southern hemisphere

SPRING

If you look into the southern sky (northern hemisphere) during March, you will see Orion the hunter leave his winter vigil and fade into the western horizon. Now is the time for Leo to emerge from hiding and watch over us, a change that symbolizes the nature of the coming season with its shift in emphasis from hunting to gathering.

A time of new life for both plant and animal communities, spring is heralded by the dawn song of blackbirds willing the sun into the sky. The countryside stretches, yawns and slowly begins to unfurl. How great it is to be awake! The spring flowers burst open in celebratory colours – yellow, white and blue. Bright new emerald leaves begin to straighten as they receive the season's rains. With the first days of warm sunshine, heady scents fill the air, bewitching all true lovers of the outdoors. But those with experience are not fooled by this narcosis; they know that spring is a trickster apt to follow sun with rain, thunder or snow. Despite days of strong sunshine we are wise to carry plenty of warm clothing in our rucksacks.

Blackthorn blossom bursts forth in brilliant white starball clusters, a sure sign that spring has arrived

As explorers cocooned in cagoules and overtrousers, it is easy for us to become remote from nature, confident that we can for the most part ignore its influences. But if we are to be truly competent we must strip away our synthetic shells and learn to be an integral part of our surroundings, moving in tune with the spirit of the season. For our guidance we can draw from the accumulated learning of our aboriginal ancestors, who, recognising their dependence upon the earth, lived in sympathy with it.

For those living in such a way, spring starts harshly. For, with the winter food stores nearing exhaustion and the game animals vanishing to have their young, the paucity of available foods means lean eating. But as the season blossoms, more foods become available. The warmth of the lengthening days accelerates the mechanisms of life. As if in response to the thirsty cries of the plants, mountain snows melt and the skies darken with clouds hurrying rain from the oceans. Every day now the growing leaf-canopy of the trees casts more shade, and the sense of renewal, anticipation and rejoicing grows quickly.

Leo the lion seen in the southern sky (northern hemisphere), reminding the hunter to allow four-legged and winged creatures time to raise their young in peace

Come alive again, the forest's store of resources is newly available. To those who know about them, there is a glut of materials to make life easier. Learning where and how to find them is a large part of outdoors understanding and essential knowledge for those who would discover greater self-reliance and freedom. All of nature's gifts are given freely to those who show proper care and respect. The iron-clad rule we all must obey is to gather in a sustainable way, utilising without destroying the resources we depend upon.

If you are new to this approach to the outdoors, spring is the most fitting time to begin an exploration of the fundamental skills. With a fair but still challenging mix of changeable weather to encourage us, and the still virtually naked woodland affording minimal protection from wind and rain, we shall be forced to learn our lessons well. Used in a constructive way while we are learning, adversity can only serve to sharpen our skills.

Animal kingdoms

Native peoples in many parts of the world consider plants and animals to be brothers and sisters with whom they share the world. This attitude instils a respect that enriches our experience of the outdoors. Today, with ever decreasing wild areas and increasing numbers of people visiting them, the pressures upon many habitats and wild creatures are reaching crisis point. Even just letting a dog loose at the wrong time of year can cause damage and harm.

As we move through the outdoors, an understanding of what is happening in the lives of the wild creatures enables us to give them the space and respect they deserve. Take for instance the curlew, nesting in the low moorland heather during spring. If you approach too near to its nest it will circle you and feign injury in an attempt to draw you away. Naturally you should move off.

Learning to read these signs requires exactly the same ability that the native hunter possessed. Hunting for food and family, not sport, demands a detailed naturalist's knowledge. Only with this knowledge can the hunter reliably bring home food without jeopardising the success of future hunts.

There is no substitute for observation. Be inquisitive. Don't just accept the shadow of a bird passing overhead; look to see what bird it is so that you can recognise it next time by the shadow of its flight pattern. Some birds have become confident that we do not look upwards – the jay especially has the cheek to dash past us straight overhead. Similarly with animals on the ground; mice will scuttle across straight under your nose.

With the sun now bathing the spring soil for lengthening periods, our brothers and sisters emerge from hibernation for

Emerging frogs, early sign of spring

the mating season. So long as you tread softly, now is one of the most exciting times of year to be watching wildlife. First comes the emergence of the frogs, as their spawn floating at the pond-side testifies. Now these nimble amphibians must be fleet to avoid the attentions of the pike, wolf of the freshwaters, hungry after the exertions of spawning. Toads emerge in March to prepare for their migration to the mating ground.

On more solid ground the vixen has disappeared to give birth in a snug earth. The respite from her nightly screeches will soon give way to the sound of mischievous cubs play-hunting. As if taking advantage of their neighbours' silence, the badgers mate. After conception, gestation for badgers takes up to ten months to begin. The young from last year's mating can be recognised by their incongruously large heads on still juvenile bodies.

Fox cubs quickly become hunters, capable of the high-springing pounce that many a small mammal fears

Related to the badger, the weasel is one of the most interesting creatures. Weasel young are born early in the summer months. Once on the scent of their prey, these small but fearsome predators are invariably successful. Tradition holds that they can kill prey more than their equal in size. Often confused with stoats, weasels are distinguished by their short tail, which lacks a black tip.

Deep in the thickets the roe deer doe, heavy with young, begins her cautious retreat to give birth. To the less observant her discretion seems to be an amazing vanishing act. If you encounter her you must freeze and let her pass undisturbed. Born without an obvious scent to attract predators, her offspring will sleep for hours in the warm May sun, curled nose to tail, squeaking to call their mother if disturbed.

As the sounds of springtime activity grow, the robin brutalises all intruders to his territory, whether competitors or not, breaking only to court his mate with a juicy worm. In the tree-tops, squirrels are mobbed as they try to steal magpie eggs. Cuckoos stalk through the branches seeking an unattended nest for their egg.

Much animal activity takes place at night. With the ground softened by the spring showers, we have the opportunity to learn the tell-tale footprints of the animals around us.

Tracks – large mammals

Dog

Broad oval track shape, four toes with claws present. Wide variety of shapes and sizes. Difficult to distinguish between the front and rear toes.

variable

How you find them

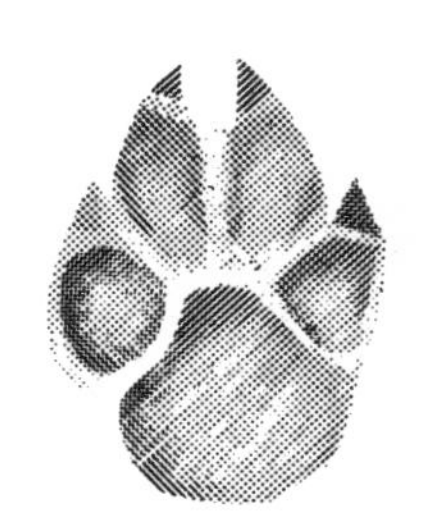

Fox

Narrow tear-shaped track, four toes with sharp claws present, front claws usually close together. Hairs between toes frequently show.

4 cm (1½ in)

How you find them

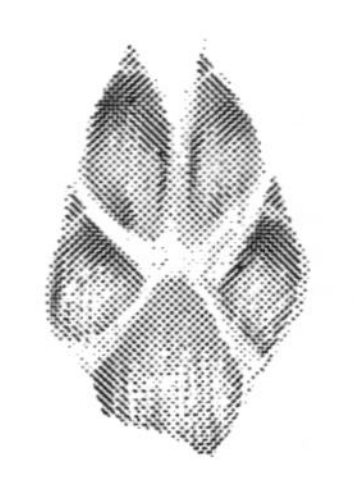

Cat

Very round track, four toes, claws very seldom present, strongly defined rear pad.

3 cm (1⅕ in)

How you find them

How you find them

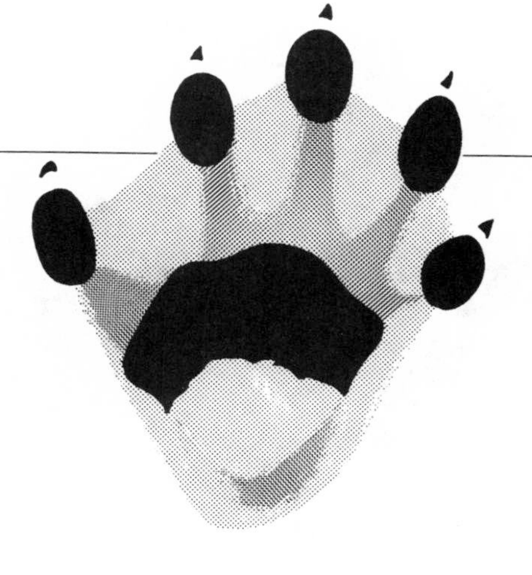

6.5 cm (2½ in)

Otter

Webbed feet with five toes and claws present.

How you find them

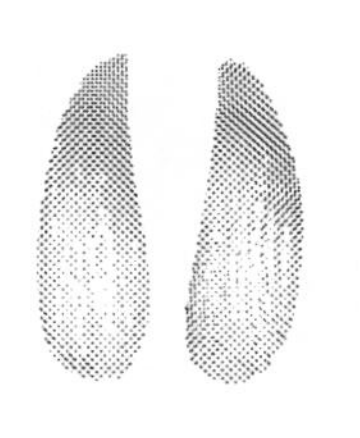

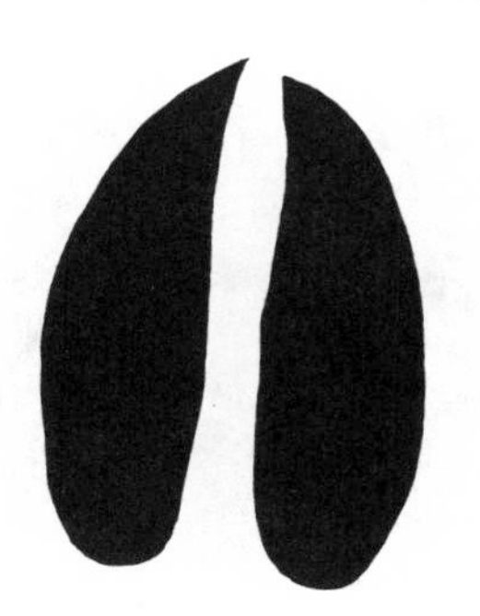

3 cm (1⅕ in)

Deer

Cloven hoofed. Size and other signs, i.e. droppings, differentiate between species.

How you find them

4 cm (1½ in)

Badger

Very broad track with five toes present although fifth does not always easily show. Claws are long and present for each toe, longer on front paws.

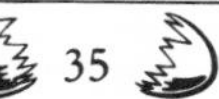

Tracks – common small mammals and birds

Rabbit and hare

Usually only the overall outline or only claw marks show. Four toes are present front and rear but are not well defined.

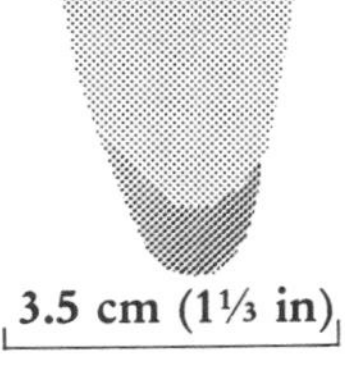

3 cm ($1\frac{1}{5}$ in) 3.5 cm ($1\frac{1}{3}$ in)

How you find them

Squirrels

Four toes show for the front feet, five for the rear. Claws are present for all. In the larger rear feet the middle three toes are almost in line.

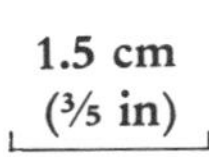

1.5 cm ($\frac{3}{5}$ in) 2 cm ($\frac{4}{5}$ in)

How you find them

Rats and mice

As for squirrels, five rear toes and four front toes, all with claws, but the rear feet are much more widely spread star-fashion.

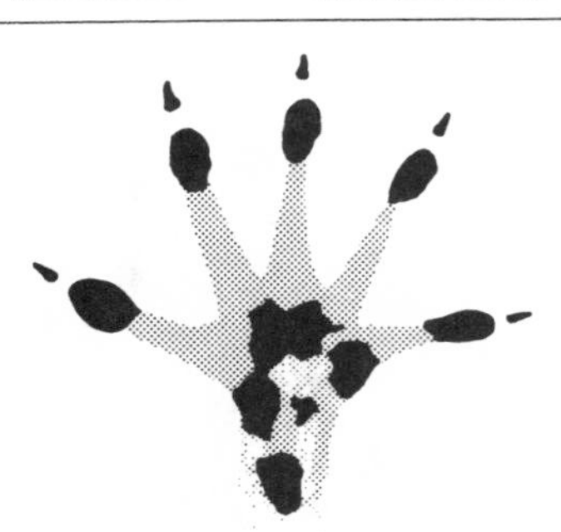

1 cm ($\frac{2}{5}$ in)

How you find them

How you find them

1–1.5 cm (2/5–3/5 in)

Weasels

Weasels are related to badgers and like them have five toes present front and rear, all with claws. Small creatures – you will only find their traces in exceptional circumstances.

How you find them

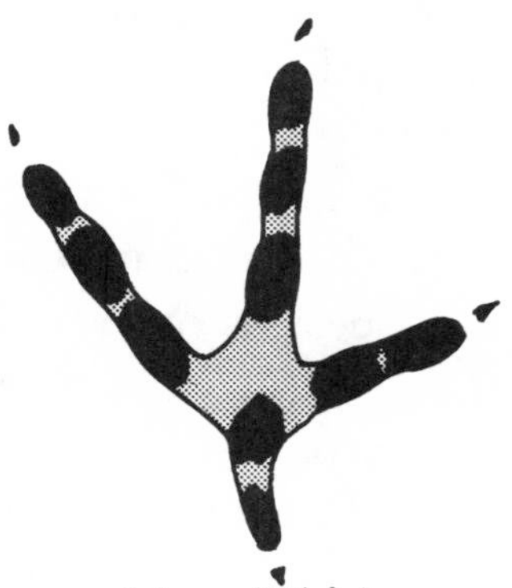

6.5 cm (2½ in)

Pheasants

Ground-dwelling birds whose tracks are bold and strong, generally showing three pads on the two major toes and two on the minor toe.

How you find them

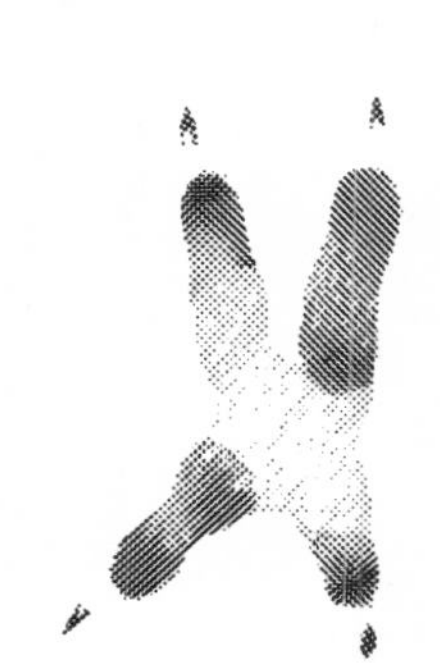

3 cm (1⅕ in)

Tawny owl

A characteristic H-shaped track which speaks of the way the talons function to grasp prey, two above two below.

Shelter

A well-constructed shelter soon becomes a sanctuary and a home. With well-insulated walls that trap your warmth and deaden the sound of the wind, natural shelters can often offer a better night's sleep than the most sophisticated hike tent.

The native peoples of the world inhabited what we today describe as wilderness. In and around their shelters they played out their lives from infancy to old age. Social organisation determined how this precious space was allocated, influencing the interactions of all who lived within. Compared to our buildings these simple constructions seem hopelessly inadequate, but they were not. All of the necessary space and protection from the elements were provided; the shelters were easy to build from locally available materials and could be adapted to the needs of the inhabitants almost daily.

A few years ago I was involved with the building of a large domed shelter, thatched with reed matting, following the designs of the Kickapoo native Americans. Large enough to accommodate a small car with plenty of headroom, the shelter was built by eighteen novices in one weekend. Had we been more experienced, I dare say we would have finished it more quickly and to a tidier finish. Only when completed did the magic of this shelter strike home. With light filtering through the reed matting, the structure emanated a womb-like sense of security. The shelter is still standing, having withstood rain, sun, snow and tempest. A little repair work is needed, as is only to be expected for any shelter not in full-time occupation. The one thing missing from this shelter is people and the sound of human voices – children playing, women poking fun at the hunters. Shelters and people go together; they take care of each other.

Knowing how to construct far simpler trail shelters is a fundamental skill of outdoors living. If you can put a roof over your head you are another step towards being at home in the wilderness and towards the confidence that comes with it. Such shelters are also highly rewarding; few things beat the experience of waking up under a fragrant roof of leaves and sticks. The spring weather can present almost any combination of conditions: from the wind and sleet of March to the warmer winds and rain of late spring. Such permutations pose challenging conditions for any shelter.

Versatility, always an essential quality, is especially necessary for locating a shelter. It may be that you can find some natural protection from the elements – perhaps a cliff overhang or a large sheltering tree. You will need to employ some common sense to determine the suitability of such a place. Is the ground wet? Will the wind blow through all night?

More often than not you will be better off building a shelter from scratch. This allows you to tailor the construction precisely to your needs. Start by searching for a good location, a place that will provide all the materials you need as close to hand as possible. For the shelter site itself, the ground should be as flat as you can find – building on gradients is a complication best avoided. The ground you choose should be well drained and not subject to soaking with rain runoff. People without experience often build a roof over an existing natural depression; in most cases such hollows fill with rain. Avoid building your shelter on a major animal run and keep away from any obvious sources of insects, such as stagnant pools. Especially in woodland, beware the overhanging dead branch. This is often overlooked by those camping in tents. A strong breeze may be all that is needed to bring a large limb down on top of you. Finally, if you are likely to be staying in your location for several days, it would be wise to be reasonably close to a reliable source of water.

Before you begin construction make certain that you are building a shelter that will shield you from the prevailing conditions. Most important of all, make a mental note to build the shelter right the first time.

Making a simple shelter

There are many different types of shelter, but for speed and efficiency few can equal these simple bivouacs. In a good location they can be built without a knife or any cordage from dead materials lying around. They are small and well insulated to help retain your body-heat, and they will keep out even the worst weather. If well built they are a stronger and cosier refuge than the most modern hike tent. They block out the sound of the noisiest gale, letting you sleep.

Remember to keep the bivouac's size as small as comfort will allow. Check your measure inside the shelter as you build it.

Given a good location, an average person working steadily in bad light can build the solo 'kennel' in about two hours. Two people can build the two-person kennel in half that time – as apart from an extra ridge-pole, the shelter contains the same amount of roofing material.

What you will need

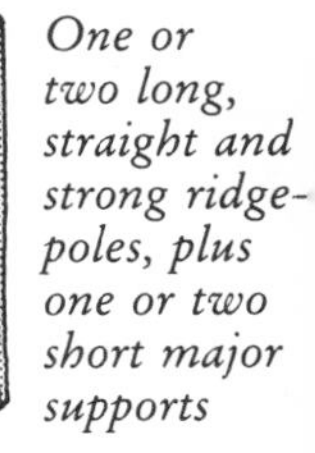

One or two long, straight and strong ridge-poles, plus one or two short major supports

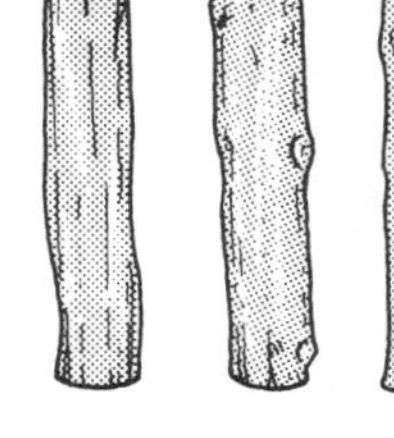

Many slim pieces of dead wood for the walls

Dead leaves, humus or turfs for thatching, plus light brushwood

Two-person kennel

Solo kennel

One-person kennel

1 Construct a strong tripod framework. Forked supports for the two short legs will save a need for cordage.

2 Measure up the height and width of the shelter with your body. It should provide just enough room to turn over with all of your bedding.

3 Using the dead branches, wall the sides of the shelter. These rafters should be as close together as possible, and the ends must not protrude more than 4 cm (1½ in) above the ridge-pole.

4 Thatch with an arm's depth of leaves or humus. Anchor down with a covering of light brushwood. Don't leave rafters protruding from the top of the shelter or rain will run inside.

Two-person kennel

1 Construct a tripod from two long poles and one short pole. Again try to avoid the need for cordage.

2 Wall as for the one-person kennel. Close off some of the gap between ridge-poles with cross-battens. Thatch and finish as before.

Fire

Woodsmoke! The very scent of it transports me down a trail of memories, to campsites alive with the fire's flickering shadows, and to friends sharing its warmth. When spirits are high, a fire's flames provide joyful light; and when spirits are low, the consoling warmth of the embers will thaw the frozen heart. For me, life is inconceivable without a camp-fire.

At the practical level, a fire is essential. It dries our clothes, warms us when we are cold, cooks our food, purifies our water, provides light at night, drives away biting insects and much more. Being able to start and look after a fire is a skill which must be mastered. It is not easy – I regularly see people fail to light a fire even when equipped with waterproof matches that won't blow out. Morale and fire-lighting are so closely linked that I advise people not to try to light a fire in bad weather unless they are certain they will succeed. It is one of those skills which you just have to practise and practise until, night or day, sun or snow, you can without any hesitation produce fire. In your outdoors equipment you should always carry some reliable means of lighting a fire. We shall learn the ways of our ancestors who managed without matches, because once you can light a fire by primitive means, using modern gadgets is a piece of cake.

Good in emergencies, lifeboat matches cannot be blown out in strong winds or damp weather

Starting and managing your fire

When starting a fire remember to search out the driest kindling and fuel available. This should preferably be dead wood snagged in the branches above ground. Dead wood found on the ground will burn but contains more moisture, making it more difficult to start the fire. In wet or windy weather make sure you have plenty of small fine kindling; this burns more readily and will give your fire a good hot centre.

Remember also that fire prefers to burn upwards. Flat fires smoulder; tall fires blaze. When lighting your fire, build upwards for a blaze.

But just lighting the fire is only the start. Your fire is a versatile tool which you can adapt and change to suit a wide variety of situations. Correctly managed, it will always be perfectly matched to the task you put it to, and in between it will burn slowly and efficiently, requiring the minimum of looking after. With a deft flick of the embers an experienced fire-tender makes fire management look easy; but in fact it usually takes people several years to learn to make the best use of this resource. Bear in mind that there is an inherent skill involved in tending a fire, and you will probably learn more quickly. Whether for light, warmth, cooking or company, there is a specifically related fire lay.

Strike-a-light: 200 years ago this was the principal way people lit their fires, by striking sparks from a steel with a gun flint

If you visit any national park or wilderness area, you will often come across an old fire site scorched into the turf beside a stream and usually filled with rusting tin cans. While the land will recover from this careless abuse, it shows a great lack of respect and spoils the sanctity of that stream-bank for all who come after. Use of a fire brings with it a responsibility to leave no traces behind. Always choose a location where the fire will do no obvious damage – preferably bare earth. Be constantly aware, too, of the danger of forest fires; camp-fires should be sited in an area of cleared underbrush at least 4 m (12 ft) across.

While surrounding a fire with stones fits the romantic image of camping, in reality it achieves little more than the scorching of the rocks, which remain a testament to your presence for many years to come. In some controlled wilderness areas fires are permitted when there is no fire risk. If you are forbidden to have a fire, it is better for every other fire user if you obey the regulations. Although they may sometimes benefit the natural ecology, promoting plant regeneration, forest fires are a serious threat to safety. With fire, safety considerations override all others.

How a fire burns

There are three vital ingredients to fire: fuel, oxygen and heat. For efficient burning there must be an unrestricted supply of each. The average wood fire consists of a fairly random lattice of fuel. This lattice must be open enough to allow oxygen in the form of air to pass freely into the fire, while at the same time being tight enough to allow the heat to travel from one piece of fuel to the next. If the fuel is damp or too large to catch light, the fire will smoulder or go out. Many a novice has suffered the smouldering fire, the fire with too little air supply or the one which started but then went out because the lattice was too loose for the flames to pass.

What you need to build a fire

Extra-fine kindling
Very dry twigs 30 cm (1 ft) long and matchstick-thin. Should catch light from a match alone. Keep these twigs at least two hand-spans long.

Fine kindling
Thicker than a match but thinner than a pencil. Brittle dry. Gather plenty.

Kindling
Brittle-dry wood of pencil thickness. This really gets the fire cracking. Again, gather plenty. Broken into pieces a hand-width long, this kindling is the best fuel to use when you need to control the heat of a cooking fire.

Small fuel
Thicker than a pencil but not thicker than your thumb, this fuel is the beginnings of the fire proper.

Main fuel
Sticks thicker than your thumb which you can break over your knee. For most trail fires this is the largest fuel needed. Anything larger counts as 'large fuel' and is more appropriate to fixed camp use or special fire lays.

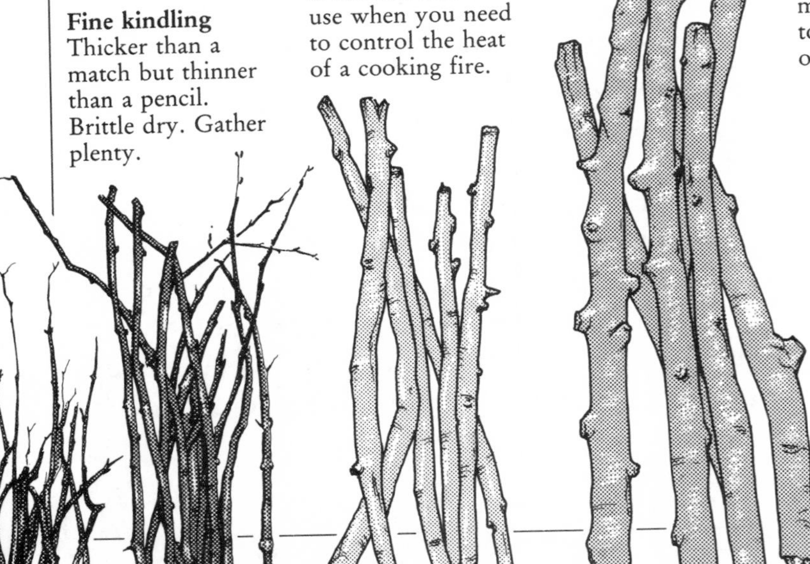

Building a fire

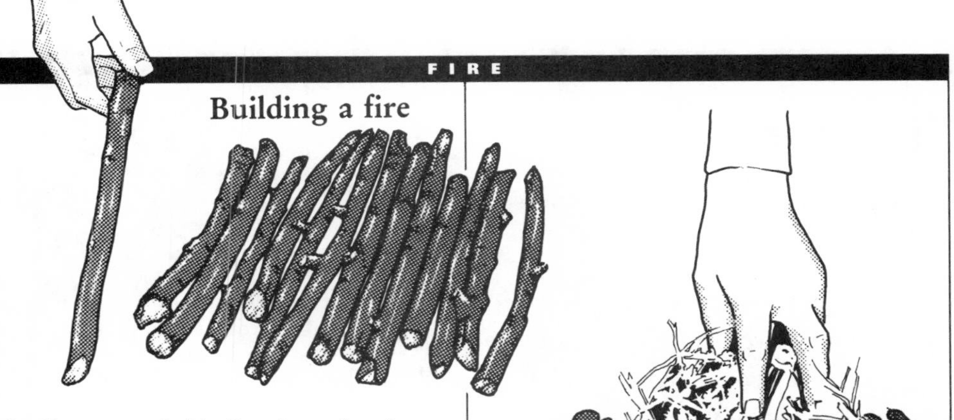

1 Choose a suitable fire site and gather all the necessary fuel. Use small fuel to build a platform about 30 cm (1 ft) square. This will protect your tinder from the damp ground and burn quickly at the fire's heart.

3 Take two full handfuls of extra-fine kindling and position them against the tinder with their tops overlapping directly above the tinder.

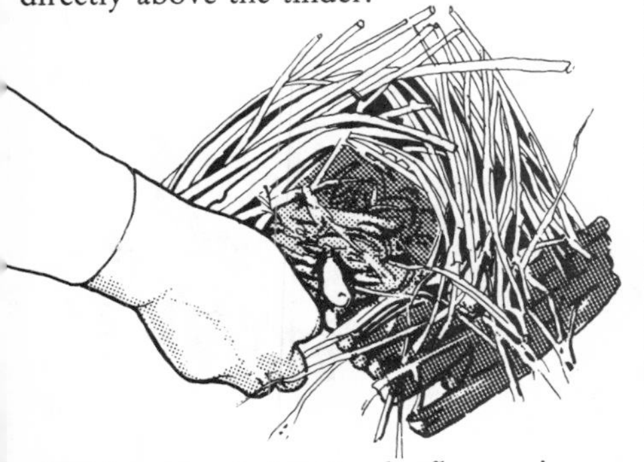

4 Light the tinder. As the flames rise, position the kindling in the flames from the tinder bundle. When flames burn through above the kindling, add the next size up, and continue this until you are burning main fuel.

2 Place a grapefruit-sized bundle of teased fibrous tinder on the platform (see pp. 46–7).

Birch bark spill

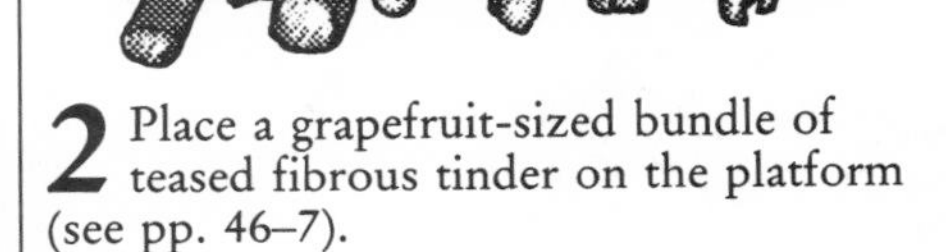

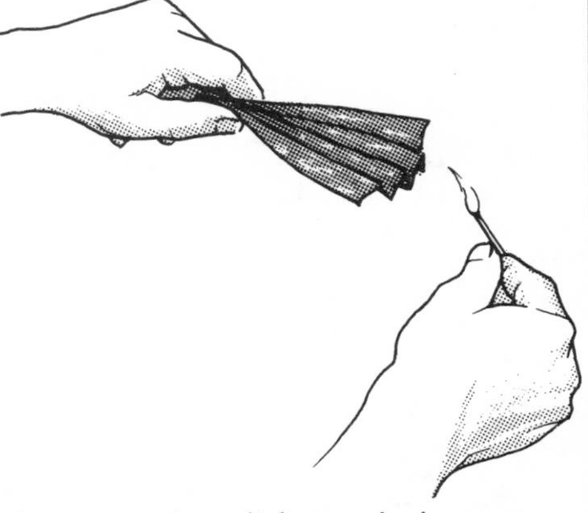

If you are using a lighter to ignite your fire it is sometimes difficult to pass the flame into the fire without burning yourself. An answer is to make a birch bark spill. Birch bark burns well because of the oils it contains, but it tends to curl up tight as it does so. To make a spill you will need to fold a small square sheet of the bark concertina fashion to prevent it curling up. Light this from your lighter.

Tinders

Tinders are in many ways the most important part of any fire, for they create the initial flame and enable it to grow. A large-sized tinder bundle, soccer-ball size, will start even damp kindling burning. A wide knowledge of what can be used for tinder and how to use it is an essential of successful fire-lighting. If you are wise you will fill your pockets with good tinder whenever you come across it.

Dead bracken
Excellent tinder, widely available. Readily dries out, especially in a dry breeze. Collect by stripping leaves from stems. Good for friction fire-lighting.

Birch and cherry bark
Burns long and hot. Bark peels naturally in small strips – gather and light with a match for a long-lasting hot centre for fire-lighting.

Clematis
The fire-lighter's friend. Provides a fluffy seed down giving a short burst of flame from sparks. The bark of its stems peels away and is easily buffed into a superior tinder.

Honeysuckle
Common in hazel copses. Naturally shedding silky bark can be collected and buffed into tinder for friction fire-lighting.

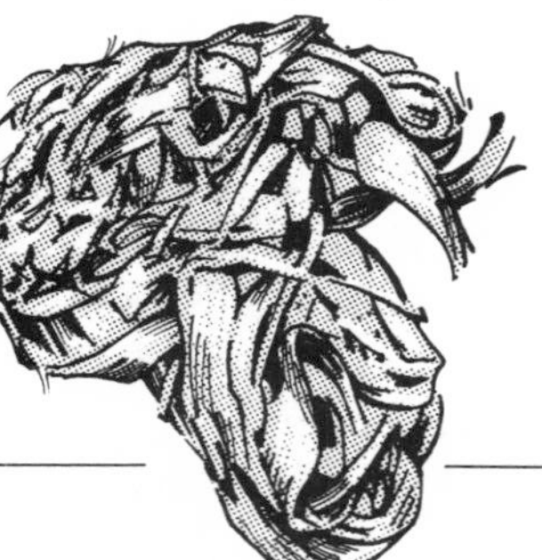

Cramp-balls
Hard black fungus, often on ash trees, excellent for fire-lighting by friction or with sparks. When dry, will take a spark and smoulder.

Bracket fungi
Various bracket fungi can be used to produce a tinder known as amadou. Good for use with a flint and steel.

Punk
The dried rotted remains of wood, reduced to almost a powder, can be used with sparks, especially if slightly charred.

Cedar bark
Fibrous and stringy, an excellent tinder to use with a magnifying glass. Buffed-up fibres make good friction tinder.

Rosebay willow herb
Seed-heads, collected into a tight cotton-wool-like mass, make good tinder for flint and steel. Improved by a slight charring.

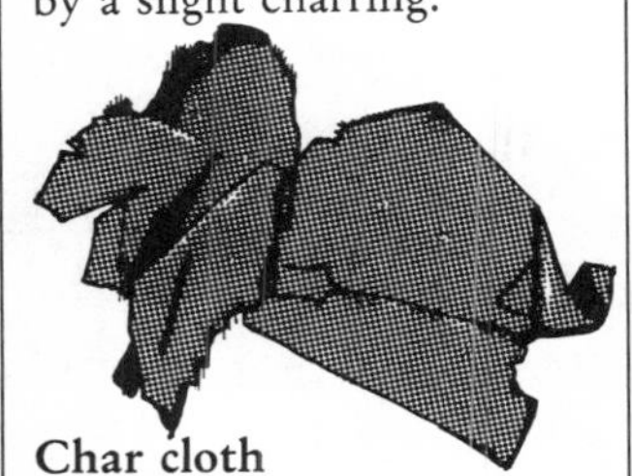

Char cloth
A 100% cotton or silk cloth, set alight and then stamped out when charred very dark brown, was once commonly used and takes a spark readily.

Cotton grass
Found in boggy ground during late spring and early summer. Collected together, this is another good spark tinder.

Dry grass
Humblest of all the tinders, dry grass can be easily buffed into a good tinder bundle for friction fire-lighting.

Preparing tinders

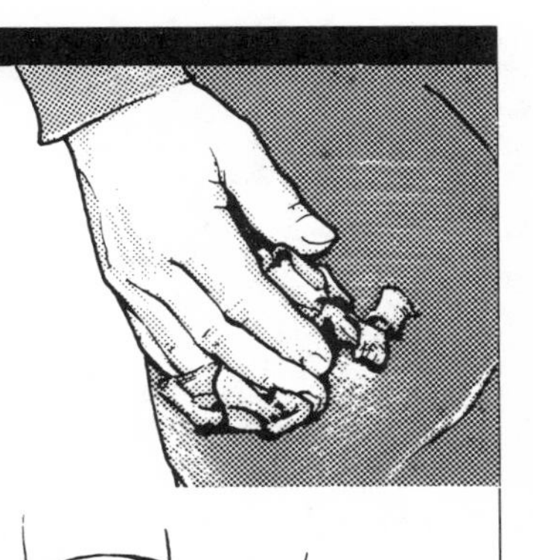

Body drying
If your best available tinder is damp or wet, it may be possible to dry it by rubbing on dry absorbent clothing, particularly the thigh of polycotton trouser legs. Placed in the pockets of such trousers, body warmth will dry out the tinder.

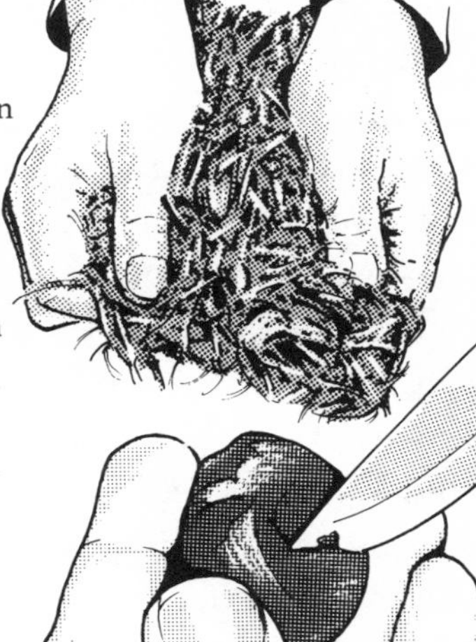

Buffing
The best tinder for friction fire-lighting is very fine and fluffy. Many fibrous tinders need to be improved in this respect. This can be achieved by vigorous rubbing between your hands or against a dry rock surface.

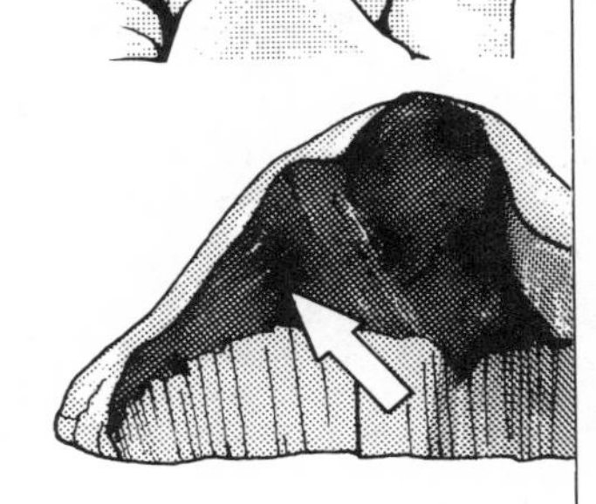

Nicheing
Using the point of your knife, make a small depression in the tinder into which to drop a glowing friction ember. This gives more surface area to catch and prevents ember cooling too fast.

Amadou
Break or cut open one of the bracket fungi to reveal the fluffy layer between pore tubes and cuticle. With the other areas cut away from it you have crude amadou for use with sparks.

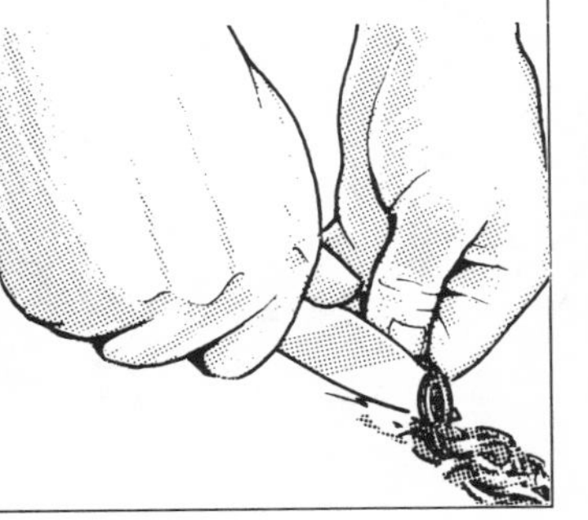

Tinder coils
Take one or two squares of paper-like birch bark about 22 cm (9 in) square. Roll into tight cigars and slice off finely to produce many tiny coils for your friction tinder bundle. Slightly difficult to ignite, but burn hot and long.

Fire from sparks

In the history of fire-lighting, self-igniting friction matches are only a recent invention. Until their introduction in the late seventeenth century, the most commonly employed fire-lighting method used in Europe was the flint and steel. In civilised circumstances the tinder box contained all that was necessary: the flint, the steel, the tinder and usually sulphur matches and a candle. The process was to strike the steel with the flint, showering sparks on to the tinder, which would begin to glow. Then a sulphur match – a simple spill dipped into molten sulphur which would not light by friction – was touched to the glowing tinder until it caught with a blue flame. Thus the candle could be lit. Quite a palaver if you had to rise quickly in the night. On the trail, however, sulphur matches were hard to come by. Instead, the glowing tinder was placed in some more fibrous tinder and blown to flame.

The use of sparks to light fires is today still a valid technique. Sparks can be produced from lighters which have run out of fuel, from synthetic flint and steels and from the ancient steel strike-a-light or the

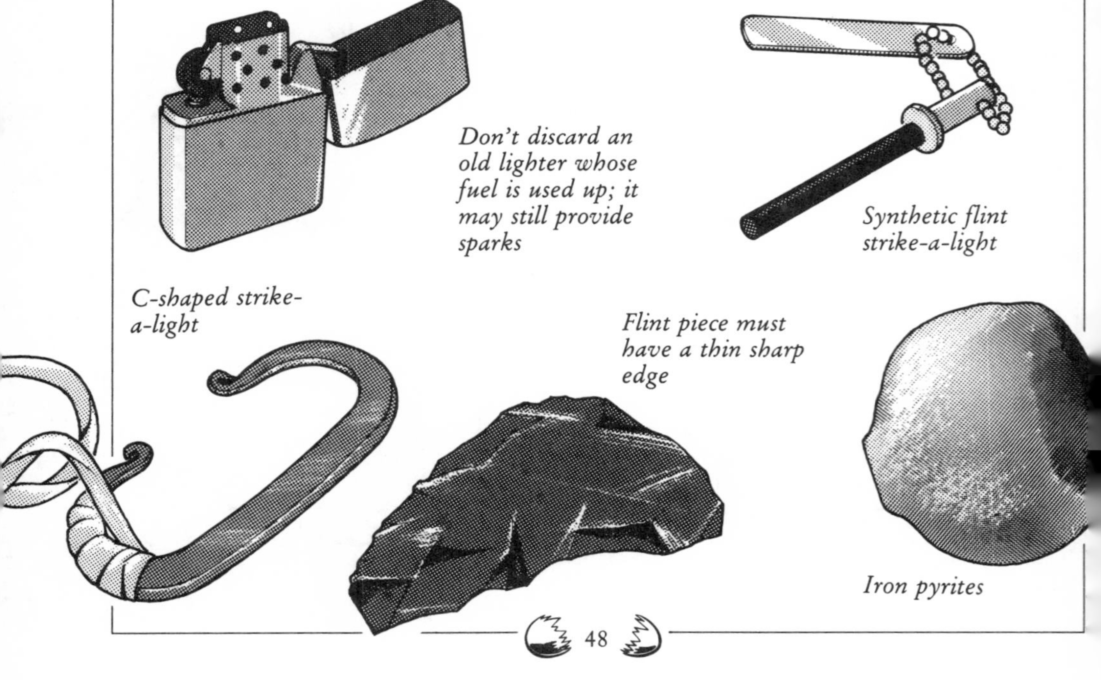

Don't discard an old lighter whose fuel is used up; it may still provide sparks

Synthetic flint strike-a-light

C-shaped strike-a-light

Flint piece must have a thin sharp edge

Iron pyrites

back of a carbon-steel knife. If you have access to iron pyrites, two pieces struck together, or one piece struck with flint, gives dull red sparks.

The best spark-producer of all these is the modern synthetic flint bar, which frequently comes attached to a block of magnesium. Scrape this bar with the back of your knife with a sort of wrist-flick to produce a bright shower of sparks which will ingite a wide range of tinders or even light trail stoves. So good is this shower of sparks that even the woody remains of umbellifer flowers can be drawn together and ignited. The magnesium block can be scraped to produce a small pile of shavings that will easily ignite from the sparks. Place the magnesium on a pile of tinder that will take light when ignited. An excellent tinder is the skeleton from a decomposing holly leaf. Sandwich the magnesium between two such leaves and set it alight by showering the sparks to fall through the leaf ribs. The leaves act as both tinder and a basket to prevent the magnesium blowing away.

Steel strike-a-light
The most practically shaped steel was C-shaped. The tinder was held on top of the flint, which was held steady while the steel was struck against it. This caused the sparks, tiny curls of red-hot steel, to be thrown upwards on to the tinder. Held in this way, the tinder was protected from the elements.

Knife strike-a-light
To strike sparks from a knife, hold the knife still above the tinder and strike it with the flint in a shaving action. The sparks will fall downwards on to the tinder. Strike only the back of your knife, not the blade edge.

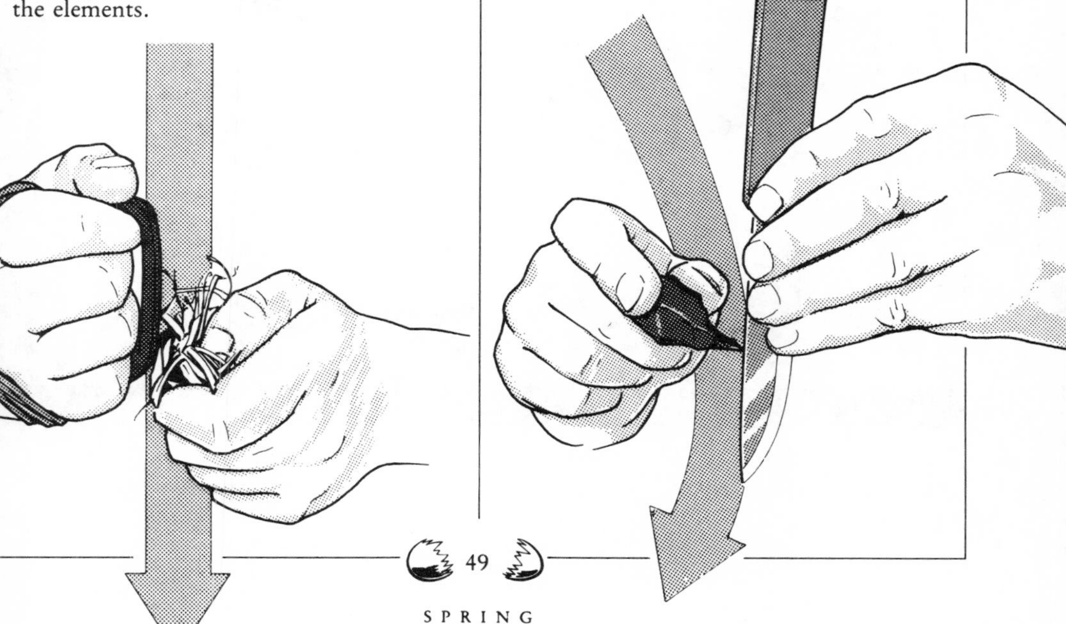

Fire by friction

The truly primitive way to light fires is by friction. This undervalued method is useful, because you are nearly always able to find the necessary materials. Once the equipment has been made it takes only a few seconds to produce fire. Friction fire-lighting does, however, take some time to learn, and you have to provide the initial energy! Mastery of this technique builds confidence and a sense of freedom.

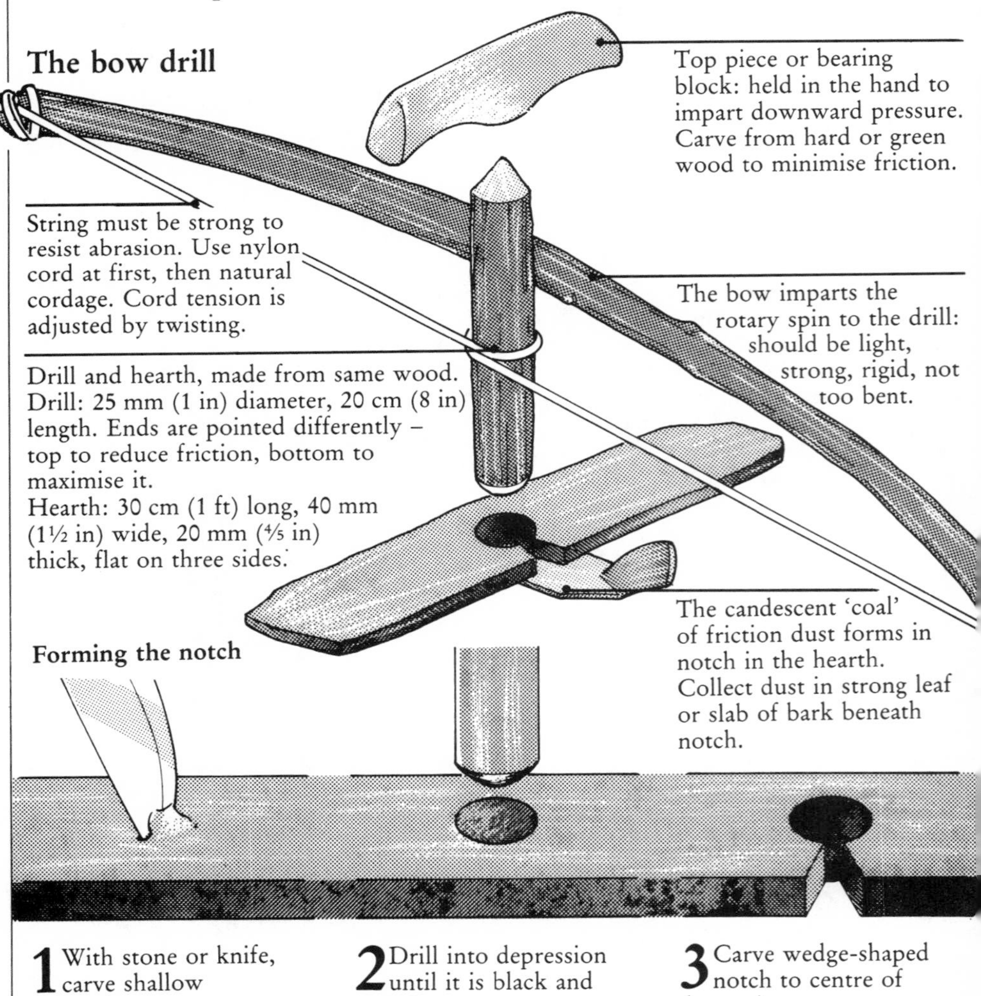

1 With stone or knife, carve shallow depression.

2 Drill into depression until it is black and round.

3 Carve wedge-shaped notch to centre of depression.

Operation

Knee positioned so as not to impede the free swing of your drilling arm

Bearing hand held firmly braced against the left shin, to prevent wobble

Drill twisted on outside of string held vertically; foot clamping the hearth to the ground

1 Drill smoothly, maintaining even pressure until smoke rises from hearth. If string slips, tighten it. Avoid squeaking due to insufficient pressure or dampness. As smoke rises, increase speed and pressure. Smoke should increase in volume, and notch will begin to fill with fine dark brown powder.

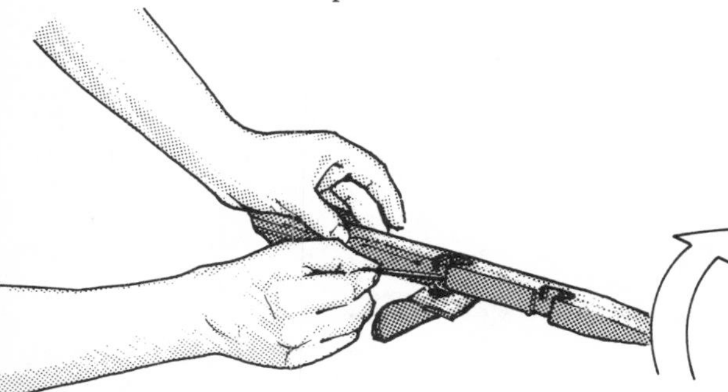

2 With notch full of powder and smoke sustaining itself, stop drilling and roll hearth away while gently holding powder with tiny stick or pine needle. Fan smoking heap of dust with your hand until it darkens and glows red.

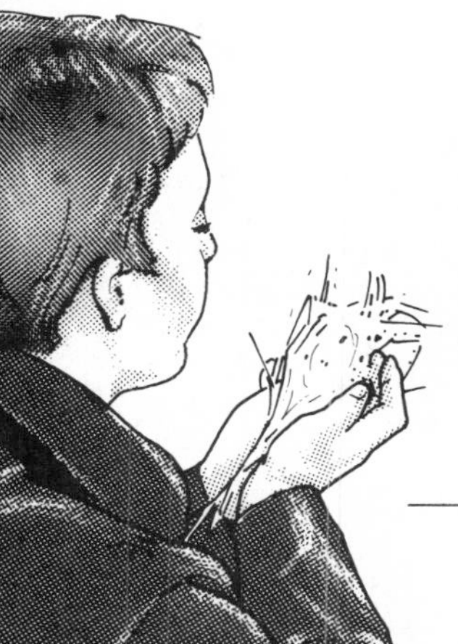

3 Transfer the 'coal' now formed to a waiting tinder bundle of the finely teased fibres. With your breath, blow the bundle to life, watching carefully to judge how hard to blow. People are more often too gentle than too harsh.

Suitable woods

Using the correct wood for the drill and hearth is vitally important. This wood must be in the correct condition – dead, dry standing wood, light but still strong, and not punky (pinch soft). Many species can be used; the following are six good woods commonly found.

Lime (basswood)

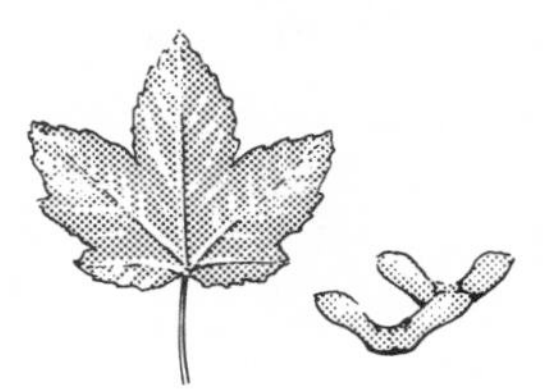

Sycamore

Willow

Birch

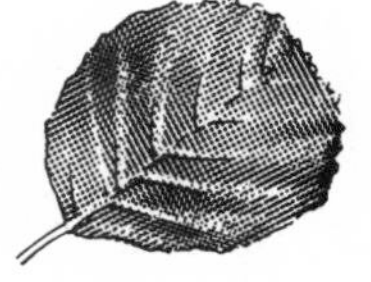

Alder

Hazel

Organising your fire

Experience in using fires shows itself most obviously in the way a fire is managed. If your fire goes cold midway through cooking or persistently smoulders, you are not managing it correctly. Looked after properly, a fire is the most versatile provider of light, warmth and cooking heat. Good fire control should become second nature with practice, requiring minimal thought, as you adapt the fire's arrangement – its lay – to your changing needs.

Tepee fire – quick to get going and to burn
This is a fire lay for bad weather or poor fuel, and one of the most popular ways to start a campfire. Arranged in this way the fuel burns quickly along its whole length, giving light and, after an initial burst, very little smoke, which rises straight upwards. The shape acts like a chimney, drawing in good quantities of air from its base and so enabling a fast burn to produce a deep bed of embers. The tepee does, however, lack stability; hence its most common application as the starter for one of the other lays.

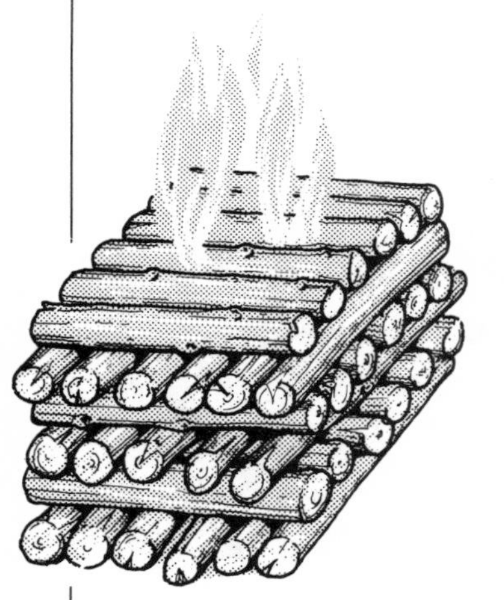

Criss-cross fire – for cooking
Not quite as fast burning as the tepee fire, it does still burn quickly, providing a deep and even bed of embers. It can be constructed before ignition or more usually is simply the method by which fuel is arranged prior to cooking. It also makes a stable 'council' fire – a social camp-fire where ideas are passed around and celebrations take place.

Indian's fire – for the trail
In between meals we need to keep our fire burning efficiently, with a minimum of fuel gathering. On the trail this is best achieved with the Indian's fire. Fuelwood is gradually fed into the centre, long pieces simply burned in half. If you are camping in the same place for a number of days, you can improve the fire by scraping out a shallow bowl-shaped ember pit underneath it. This helps the embers to retain their heat for long periods.

Star fire – permanent camp

The natural extension of the Indian's fire is the star fire. The difference between the two is the size of fuel. This fire is built with logs at least as thick as your thigh and often up to 7 m (20 ft) or more in length. The classic star fire is the ceremonial fire of the Cherokee; central to village life and tradition, it comprises four logs pointing north, south, east and west. This lay is an excellent way of maintaining a fire in a permanent camp.

Putting out your fire and leaving no trace

No sight so affronts the eyes outdoors than an old fire site filled with rusting cans and broken glass. When you leave your campsite you have two overriding responsibilities: to extinguish your fire and to leave the site in good order.

Putting out the fire is not difficult, but it must be done thoroughly. The first step is to spread the embers to allow them to cool. If you have already allowed the fire to die down, this is relatively easy. Now extinguish the fire by pouring water on it. To ensure that no underground roots are left smouldering unnoticed, allow the water to soak well into the fire site; probing with a pointed stick helps. Once the dead embers and ashes are cool, pick them up with your hands and scatter them widely. Brush over the site with a branch and camouflage it to show as little sign of occupation as possible. Take all your rubbish away in your rucksack. If you have been using a ready-made stone fireplace, as commonly found in many backcountry areas, tidy it as mentioned and pile any spare fuel in a dry spot for those who come after you. Make it obvious that you have done your clearing up carefully. Take only memories; leave only footprints.

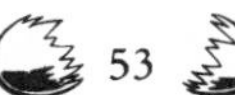

Water

We cannot live without water. The oceans, rivers, springs and brooks all speak the same language: the language of life. Native peoples the world over revere water. Aboriginal children are taught to memorise the location of water holes in their tribal territory. The Cherokee listen to the sound of tumbling water as a voice carrying a message. If you climb to a snow-capped mountain early in spring you can hear this voice begin as a whisper – the trickle of dripping snowmelt. Follow the snowmelt downhill and the voice grows stronger as the trickles become first rivulets and streams and then the river itself. At every major waterfall, tumbling into a spray mist, the river's crashing voice shouts its potency, a reminder of our mortal frailty.

Water is an elemental force, a neutral but powerful influence which can bring both life and destruction. Like all elemental forces it must be understood, and we must move in tune with it. As anyone who has travelled on foot through arid desert lands will tell you, water can dictate the course of your journey.

Within our bodies water is responsible for a host of vital functions: removing waste, supplying energy, the regulation of body temperature and mental acuteness. To be healthy and fully functional we need to have access to sufficient pure water each day. During spring there is usually no shortage of water, so we shall concentrate here on how to make it pure. While there are still springs of pure water to be found, it is best to suspect all water as being contaminated. Stagnant, smelly puddles are unimpressive sources of water, yet they can be made potable when necessary. On the other hand, clear, cool, fast-running, oxygen-rich streams that are apparently safe to drink without purification may well be home to a host of potent tummy-bugs. Put simply, treat all water for contamination, rather than run any risks.

A host of modern water-purifying systems are available for the traveller to remote places. Widely used by trekkers in regions where fuel for boiling is scarce, these are a convenient and easy way to clean your water. The important thing to remember with these systems is to follow the instructions for use precisely. Here, however, we shall assume that we do not have access to such devices.

There are basically three operations involved in gathering water safely. First, always search for the purest available water source, the freshest and healthiest looking water with no obvious traces of contamination. Generally, the further water travels from its source the greater the level of contamination. Having collected the purest water you can find, you need to remove any suspended matter by straining the water through a bandanna, some other item of tightly woven clothing or a millbank bag (see below). When this has been done, you must boil the water thoroughly. The majority of waterborne problems are destroyed below boiling point; but for safety you should always boil water furiously for at least five minutes. Increase the boiling time at higher altitudes, where water boils at a lower temperature.

Particularly in arid areas, boiling water can become an unpleasant chore, which in turn can lead to a sloppy camp routine and resulting upset stomachs. A disciplined routine with your water supply is the sign of good outdoors skill. Always take advantage of reliable sources of water.

Before going to sleep, boil sufficient water for the following day; bottle it and set it in the open to cool. This is one of those occasions when a large billycan with a lid is really valuable.

The millbank bag

A simple filter bag used by the British Army for decades, the millbank bag remains an effective way to remove suspended matter from your water. First soak the bag in the water, then fill it to the brim. Suspend the bag from a branch and allow the first few inches of the water content to pass through the filter before collecting the filtrate. If necessary, filter the water again. Sterilise the water chemically or by boiling before consumption.

The bag can be flushed out, dried and re-used. You can also use it as a filter bag for brewing wild coffee drinks.

When the sap flows

So far we have dealt with the simple things of outdoors craft, the basic skills and know-how. But there is another level of knowledge you can attain, which to the uninitiated is often a source of wonder. I speak of course of the intimate secrets of the land – the hiding places of important resources and the seasonal gluts.

Early in spring the trees wake from their winter slumber and the sap within them begins to move again. For us this is a significant event, signalling several beneficial changes. The most dramatic change comes when hazel leaves are no larger than a squirrel's toe; for birch trees can now be tapped for their sap. Between 4 and 5 litres (1 gallon) per tree per day is not an unreasonable expectation of yield; but this free flow ends abruptly after only two to three weeks.

What is the value of birch sap? It can be used as a pure source of water in an emergency, although it is unwise to drink large quantities due to its sugar content. It is especially good in place of water for wild tea infusions. The sap can also be boiled down to a sugary syrup, although this requires a very large quantity of sap and much laborious boiling. It can be used to make wine, vinegar and also beer.

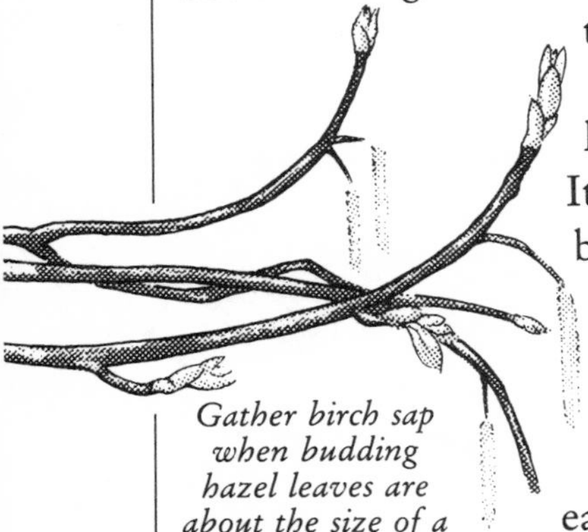

Gather birch sap when budding hazel leaves are about the size of a squirrel's toe

There are several ways of tapping the tree for its sap. These range from the native Y-shaped slashes to the modern method using plastic tubing and a bored hole. However, the easiest and least damaging method of all is a simple deep axe-chop made at an upward slant. Hammer a short gutter into this slant; this can be improvised from a piece of split elder with the pith removed. The sap should flow down this channel and drip into your waiting receptacle. Once you have finished tapping the tree, remove the gutter and push back the slightly raised flap of bark to help the birch to heal.

Other trees can also be tapped for their sap: beech, sycamore, hickory and, most notably, the maple, which provides sap for longer than the birch and with a higher sugar content. Natives and settlers in Canada traditionally gathered maple sap at the springtime sugar camp. The sap was evaporated in a heated vessel and the resulting maple syrup was preserved.

Sugar cones

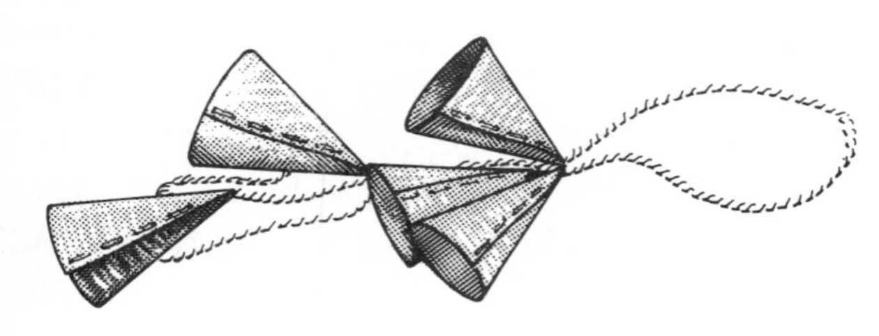

Among the native Americans of the northern woods the annual sugar-making camp was a popular event greatly anticipated, especially by the sweet-toothed youngsters. At the camp, people tapped the sugar maple and boiled its sap into a variety of products, taking advantage of the changing nature of the sap as the season progressed. Careful overnight boiling reduced the sap to a syrup; sometimes deer tallow was added to help the sugar remain soft. Sap taken early in the season was best suited for granulating, while that taken later was set in moulds to form sugar cakes. Often cleverly carved wooden moulds were used to form interestingly shaped sugar cakes. One of the most popular ways to use the sugar was to fill small cones, fashioned from birch bark – a sort of a backcountry lolly.

One or two taps can be placed in the tree to provide sap – they are best placed low down on mature trees; trees in damp or boggy ground usually give greater quantities; the wooden spile (peg) guides the sap into a waiting container

Cordage

Cordage is a perennial need in the outdoors and a resource that takes time to produce. This is so much the case that the experienced become expert at avoiding the use of string or rope wherever possible. But sooner or later the inevitable has to be faced and cordage needs to be made. Once you start, however, like most people you will probably find it hard to stop; for the act of making cordage is highly enjoyable.

Spring provides the ideal circumstances to gather inner bark fibres. The flowing sap helps to loosen the bark from the wood, which enables you to remove long strips with ease. Fibres for making natural cordage fall into two categories by their usage: fibres best used dry and fibres best used wet; only in a few cases does a fibre fall into both categories.

To list all of the available bark fibres would fill volumes, so we shall investigate here two of the best. Lime bark is best used dry but can be used wet. Willow bark is mostly used wet but can be used dry. In each case it is the inner bark, sometimes called the bast, that we use.

With all cordage materials the gathering and preparation of the fibres take longer than the actual manufacture. For everything but the most quickly made cordage it is best to think of the three stages of gathering, preparation and manufacture as independent activities.

Gathered and dried, bark can be coiled and stored ready for use

The best cordage is produced from fibres which have been allowed to dry and then are resoaked before manufacture. This is because the fibres shrink more when dried from green than when dried from a resoaked state, which means the weave of the cordage will be tighter due to the reduced shrinkage. With careful manufacture and weaving, you can produce long, even, strong lines ranging in size from fishing line to bridge-building hawsers.

Willow bark
For willow bark you need to find a fallen willow which has shoots rising vertically from its side, or a pollarded willow. You are searching for healthy looking wands about 130 cm (4 ft) long, of finger-to-thumb thickness and with as few side-shoots as possible. Thus found, cut the wand away cleanly at the base with a saw or sharp knife. A tree found for this purpose will often provide wands for many years if carefully managed.

Lime bark
The name 'lime' is a corruption of the Old English 'linden' or 'line' (meaning 'rope'). The tree is so called because of its reputation for providing valued cordage. Lime bark is easily gathered. The traditional method was to cut away a hand-wide strip from near the base of the tree and then, by pulling down and outwards, to strip off a piece up to 7 m (20 ft) long. However, a sounder method is perhaps to strip the bark from one of the sucker saplings emanating from the tree that lime is so prone to. The sucker can be cut away, leaving a neater scar.

Preparing bark for cordage

Most cordage materials can be pressed into rough service as soon as they are collected, but to make the best cordage you invariably need careful preparation. Always make sure you have prepared enough before you begin manufacture. To avoid getting into a tangle, it is best to organise your raw materials into manageable bundles.

Willow bark

1 Using the back of your knife, scrape away the thin green outer bark, being careful not to break the inner bark. The scrapings can be saved for making a dye (see p.63).

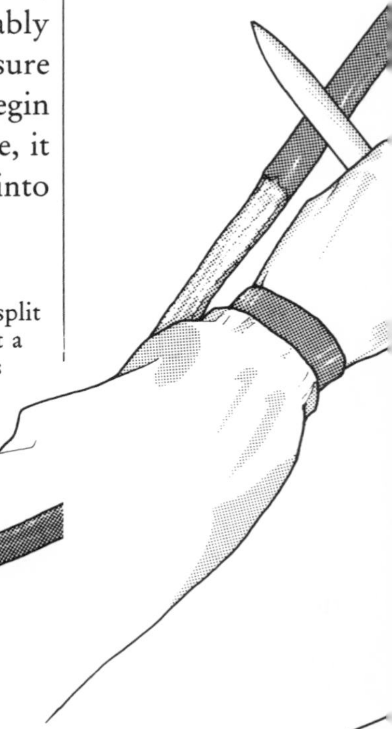

2 Run the point of your knife up the bark so as to split it open down one side. Try to maintain as straight a cut as possible, although you should follow the bark's natural grain.

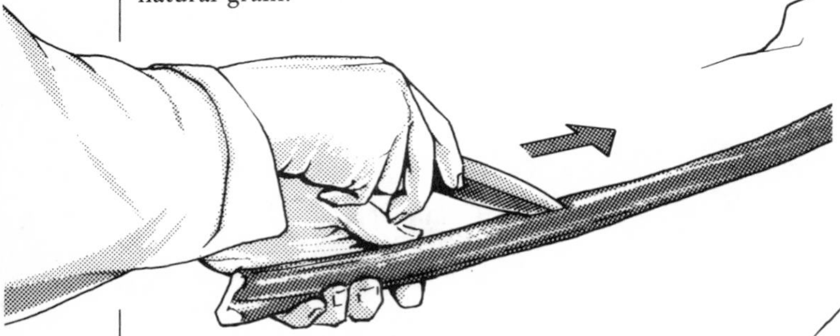

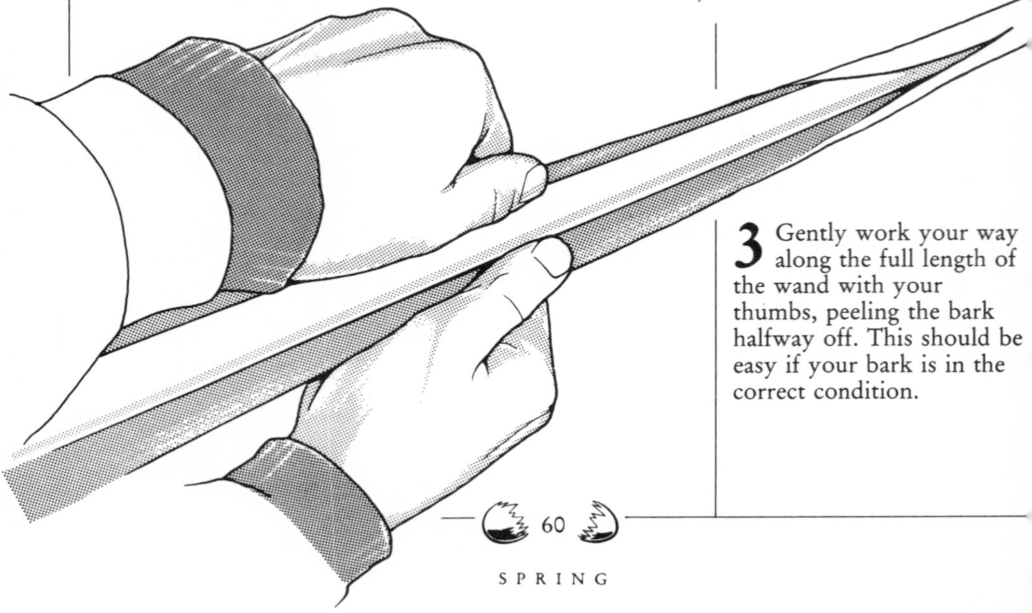

3 Gently work your way along the full length of the wand with your thumbs, peeling the bark halfway off. This should be easy if your bark is in the correct condition.

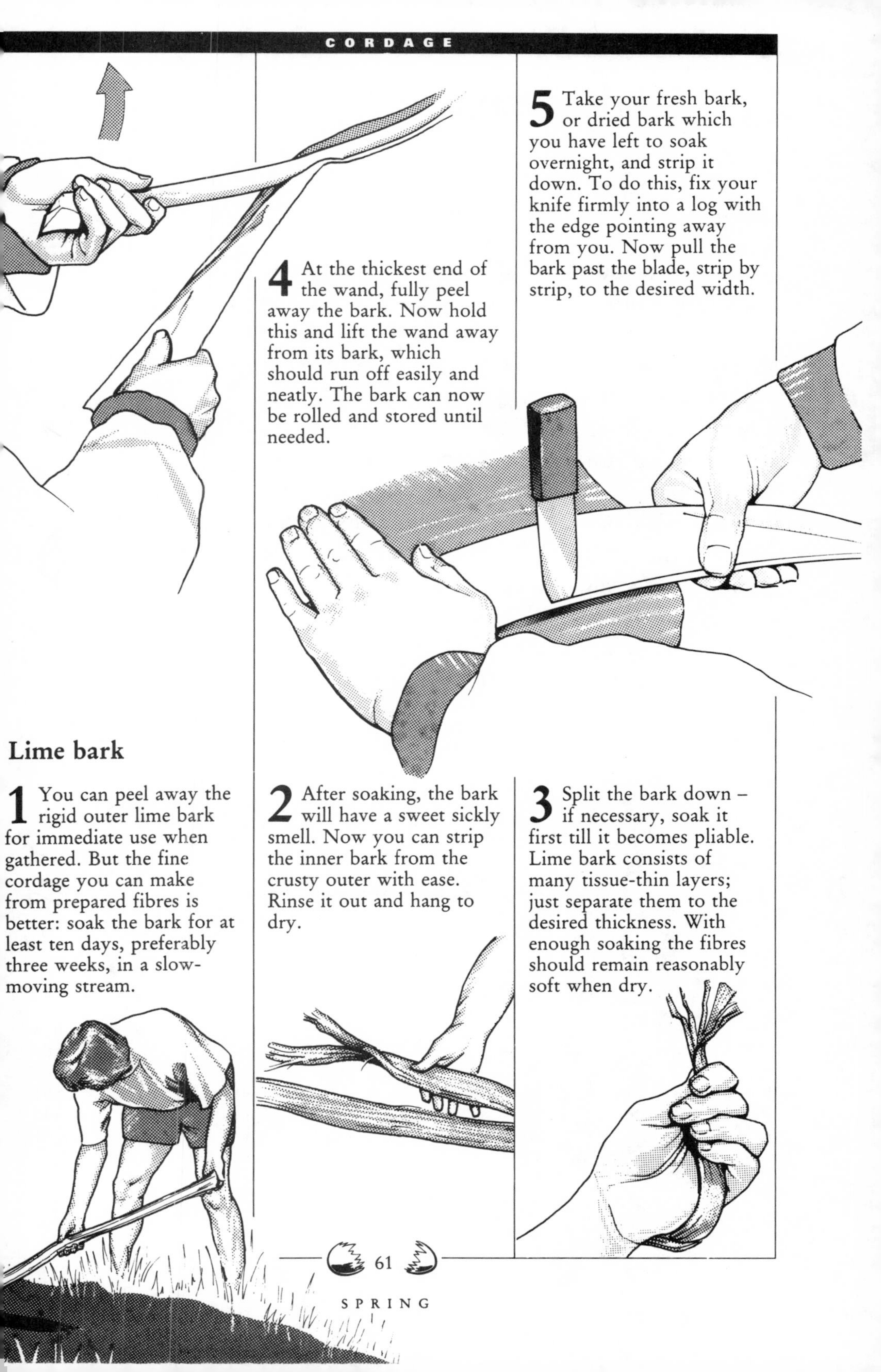

4 At the thickest end of the wand, fully peel away the bark. Now hold this and lift the wand away from its bark, which should run off easily and neatly. The bark can now be rolled and stored until needed.

5 Take your fresh bark, or dried bark which you have left to soak overnight, and strip it down. To do this, fix your knife firmly into a log with the edge pointing away from you. Now pull the bark past the blade, strip by strip, to the desired width.

Lime bark

1 You can peel away the rigid outer lime bark for immediate use when gathered. But the fine cordage you can make from prepared fibres is better: soak the bark for at least ten days, preferably three weeks, in a slow-moving stream.

2 After soaking, the bark will have a sweet sickly smell. Now you can strip the inner bark from the crusty outer with ease. Rinse it out and hang to dry.

3 Split the bark down – if necessary, soak it first till it becomes pliable. Lime bark consists of many tissue-thin layers; just separate them to the desired thickness. With enough soaking the fibres should remain reasonably soft when dry.

Plaited cordage

Plaits are quick and easy to make and, with different-coloured strands, highly decorative. Plaiting is often the best method of producing cordage from less flexible fibres. Make a simple clamping device from a piece of split stick and your task will become much easier, because both of your hands will be free to do the plaiting. Be sure to keep the plaits tight. With materials such as willow bark that are best worked damp, place a second clamp at the end of the workpiece to allow you to dry the strap under slight tension. Without this the strap will become loose as the fibres shrink. This tensioning is a principle to apply to all cordage materials made from damp fibres.

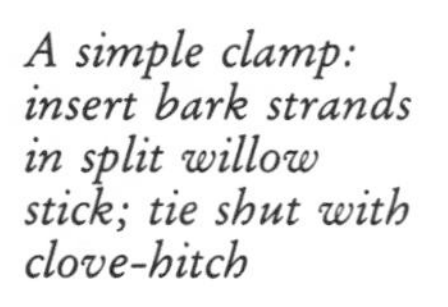

A simple clamp: insert bark strands in split willow stick; tie shut with clove-hitch

4-stranded round plait

1

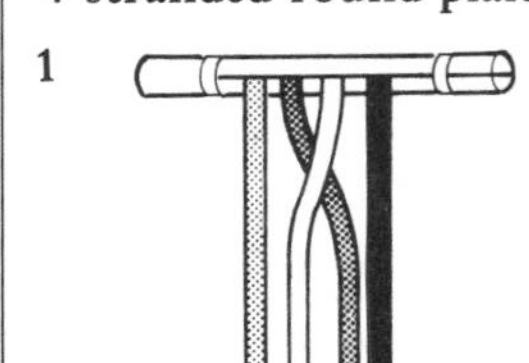

2

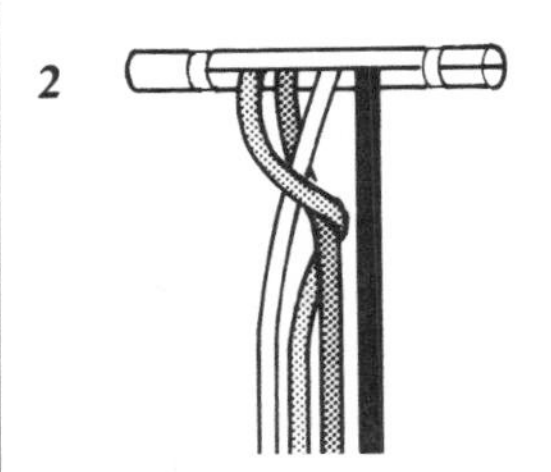

3

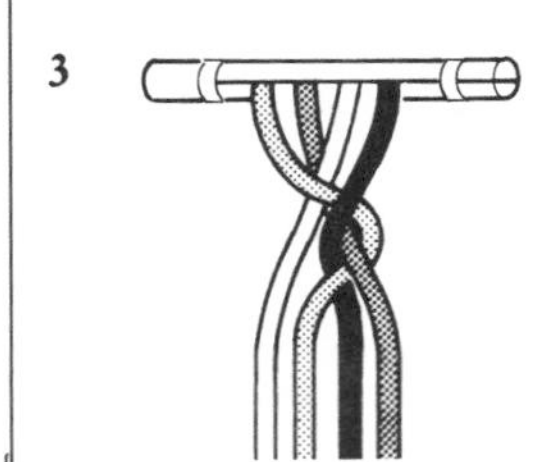

4

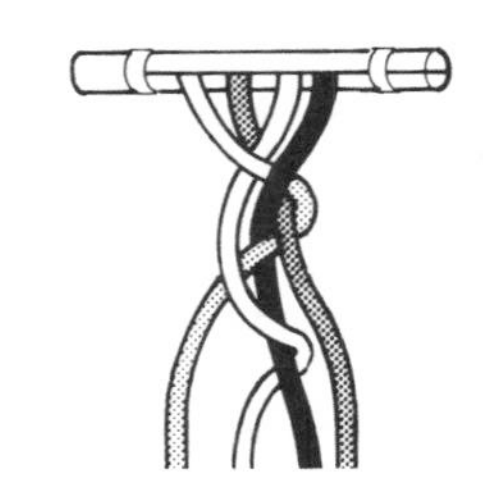

5

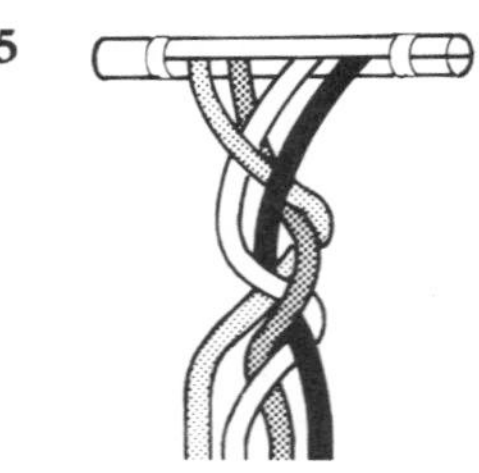

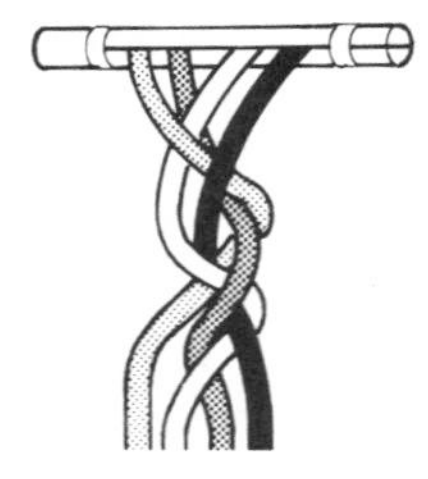

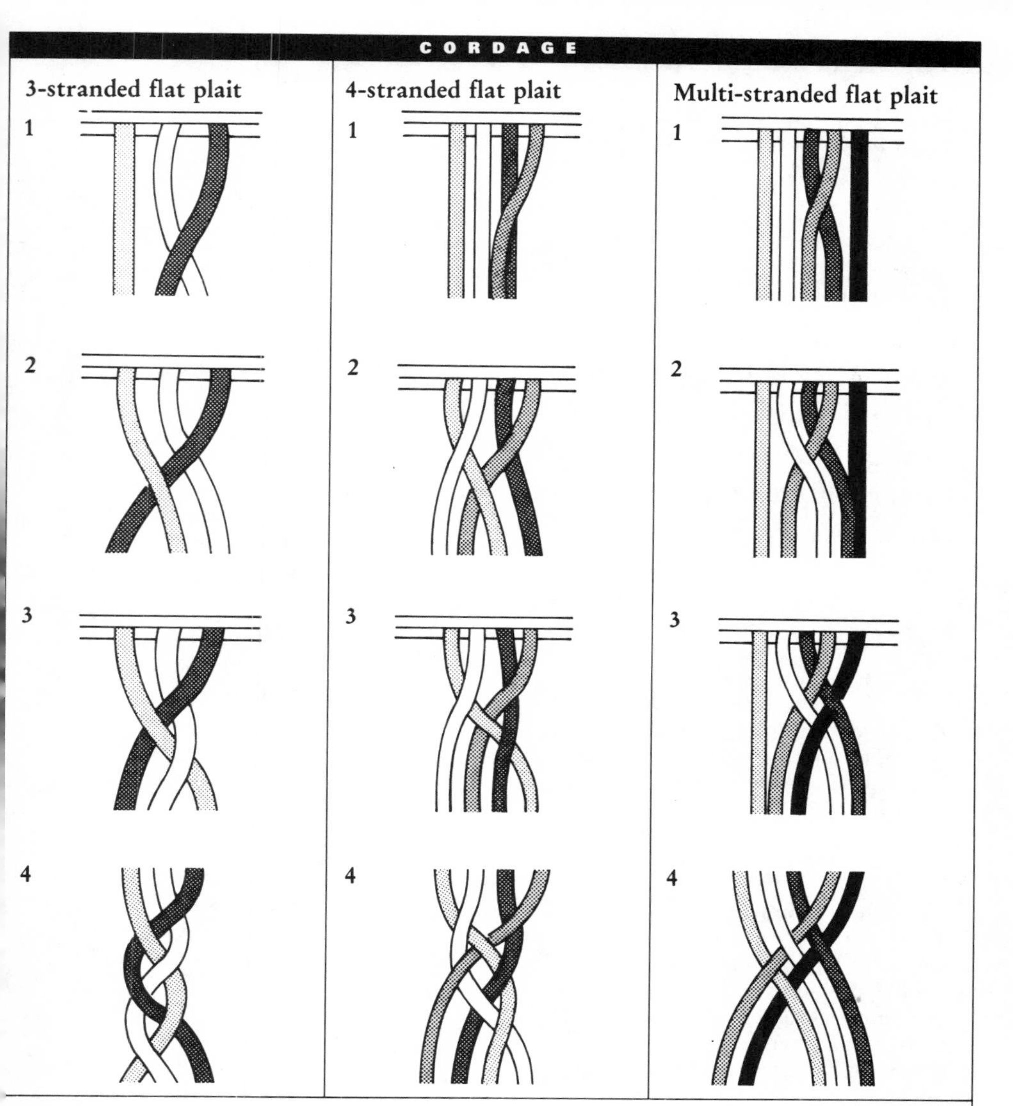

Dyeing cordage

Any plait is greatly improved by the addition of a touch of colour. If you have saved the scrapings of the outer willow bark you have the makings of a strong ruddy-brown dye. The procedure to follow is this. Take two good handfuls of ashes from your fire, place them in a billy and add water to a depth of 25 mm (1 in) above the ashes; boil this furiously to produce a concentrated solution. Drain off the ashes if you wish (not completely necessary) and add at least one good handful of bark scrapings. Boil this furiously for thirty minutes before adding the fibres to be dyed. Dying can take up to an hour depending on the strength of your dye. Rinse out the dyed strips and hang them up to dry.

Laid cordage

This is the most versatile way to make natural cordage. It is easy to do and relatively quick when mastered, and it gives a remarkably strong finished product. You can produce laid cordage as strong as you need it – from light fishing-lines to ropes strong enough to carry you across chasms.

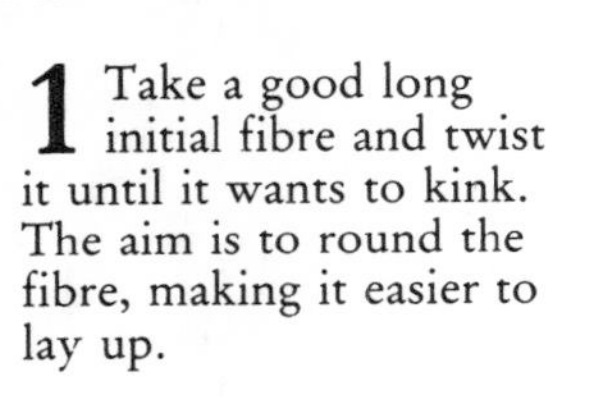

1 Take a good long initial fibre and twist it until it wants to kink. The aim is to round the fibre, making it easier to lay up.

2 Fold the fibre a third of the way along its length. If you fold it in the middle, any joins will be opposite each other – a weak arrangement compared to staggered joins.

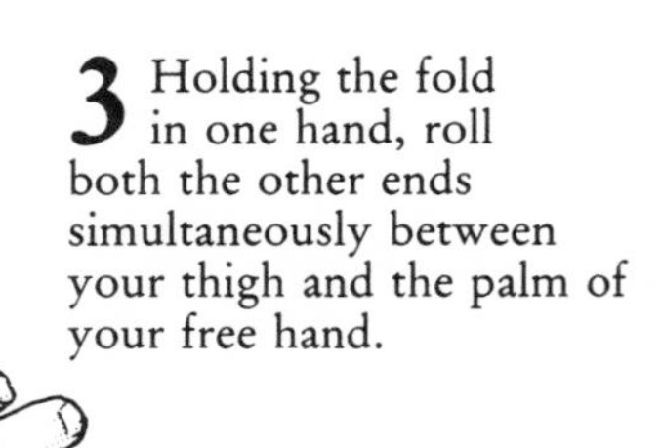

3 Holding the fold in one hand, roll both the other ends simultaneously between your thigh and the palm of your free hand.

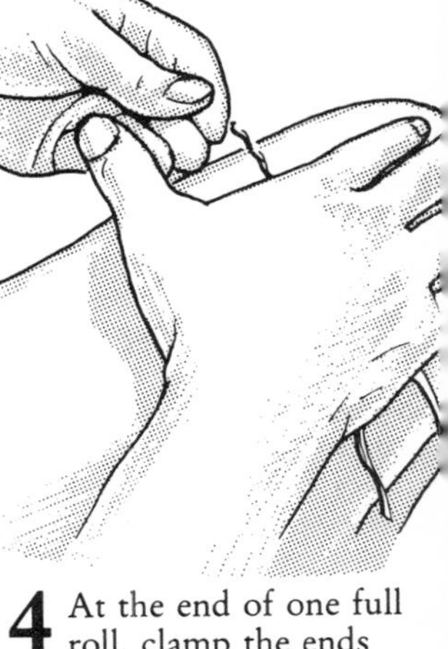

4 At the end of one full roll, clamp the ends against your thigh to prevent them untwisting and release the end you have been holding; it should begin to twist up. With control this can be persuaded to twist up in a very neat fashion.

5 Grasp the cord again where the twisting ends and repeat the process. With practice your co-ordination will improve and your speed increase. Keep repeating the process until you are within 5 cm (2 in) of the shortest end. Now you will need to join in a new fibre.

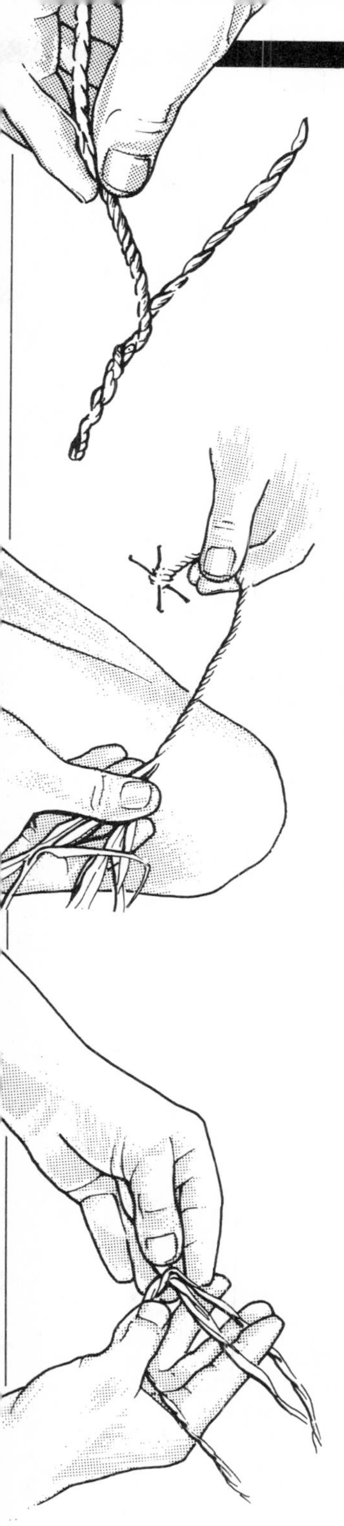

Additional techniques

Joining in
Joining in is not difficult. Just lay the end of a new fibre alongside the short end and twist it in, always twisting in the same direction as the thigh-rolling. Keep going. It helps to taper the fibres where they join so as to maintain an even twist.

Spooling
As the length of cord begins to grow, it must be able to revolve freely; if not, it will begin to unravel. The solution is to gather it up on to a free-hanging spool. Two crossed sticks will suffice.

Stronger cordage
Stronger cordage can be made by three methods: first, by using thicker bundles of fibres; second, by doubling up the existing cordage; and third, by laying in an extra strand.

To double up existing cordage, you must twist in the opposite direction to that in which it was originally laid. Cordage twisted originally to the right (Z-laid) must be twisted to the left when doubled (S-laid).

To produce cordage with that extra strand – three-ply cordage – simply add the extra strand or bundle of fibres at the start. With three strands it is a little more difficult and consequently slower to roll on your thigh.

Knots for natural cordage

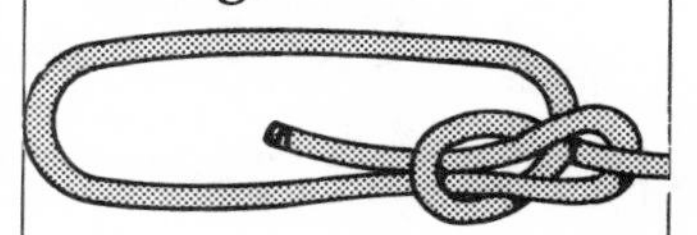

Bowline – a quick, secure, non-slipping loop at the end of a line.

Double sheep bend – used for joining lines of differing diameters.

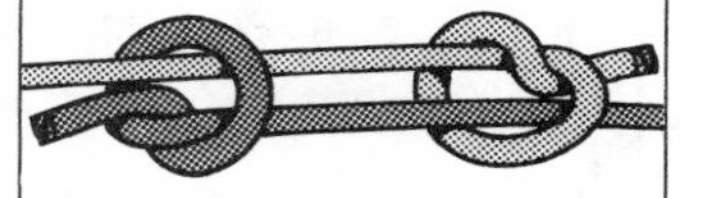

Single fisherman's – well suited to joining the more springy natural fibres.

Reef-knot – good for tying off ends, but not a safe knot.

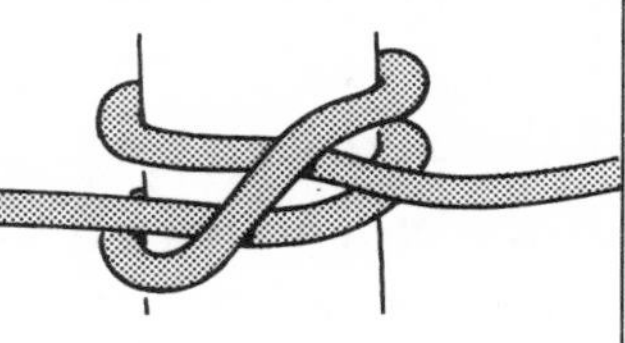

Clove-hitch – simple and versatile, well suited for starting lashings, easily adjusted.

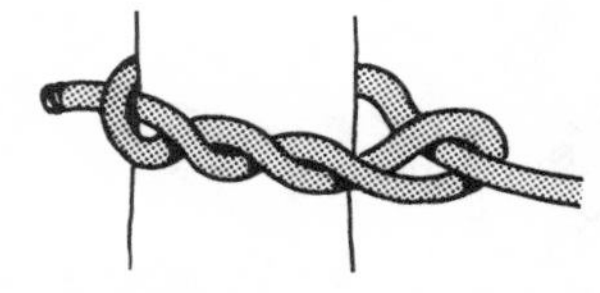

Timber-hitch – quick and efficient to attach to a post or peg.

Birch bark

For northern folk spring is the traditional time to gather birch bark, made easy now that the bark has loosened. The fresh bark available now has an enduring, leather-like quality. There are countless uses for this wonder material: for containers, roofing, torches, canoes, shoes, toys, knife handles, snow goggles and sleds.

If ever a tree was the ally of people it is the birch. Yet its very tenacity has earned it the label of weed among many modern foresters. Birch trees are prolific colonisers, growing fast and thickly even in poor conditions. There was an almost constant supply of birch bark and wood for the native peoples of the north.

In the north country where the birch grows in abundance, gathering bark from living trees is acceptable. In other places where the tree grows less abundantly we must be more frugal. Fallen birch trees are a common site, the bark far outlasting the wood. Although not as good as fresh bark, for most of our purposes this bark will suffice.

There are two basic techniques for removing birch bark – as a sheet or as a long spiral strip, depending on the bark's future use.

Baskets and shoes are made from strips of birch bark using a twined weave

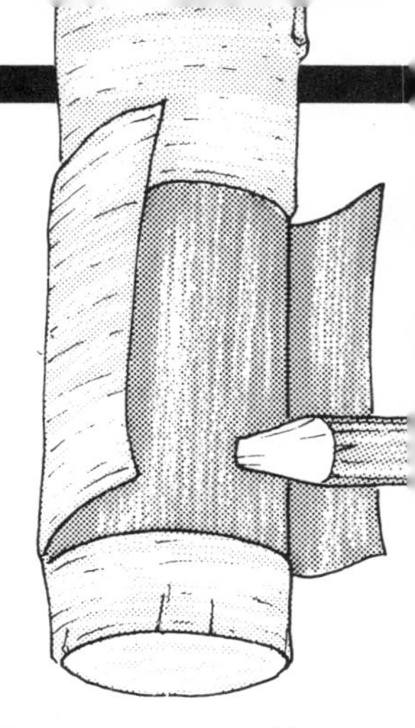

To remove sheet of bark, first cut border of piece to be removed. Then carve large chisel-shaped piece of wood and use to lever off bark. Work carefully. Gentle pounding on outside will help bark lift, as will dousing with warm water. Once freed, lay sheet of bark on ground and weight down flat.

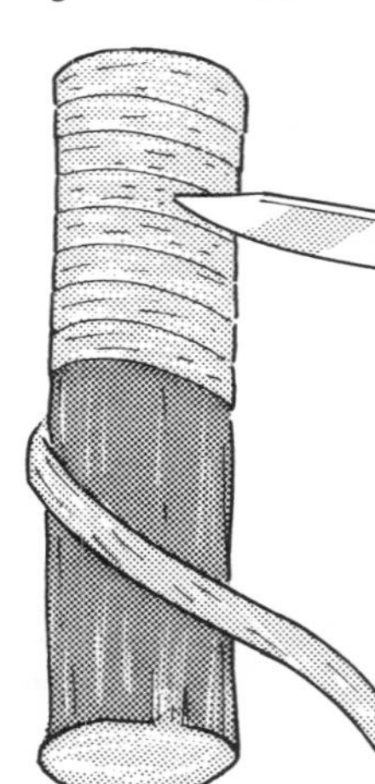

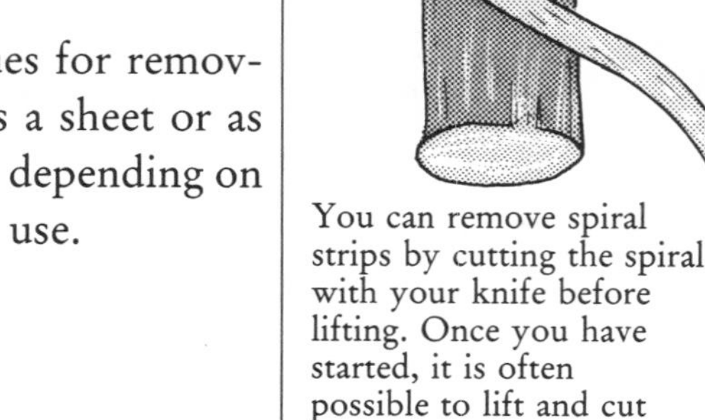

You can remove spiral strips by cutting the spiral with your knife before lifting. Once you have started, it is often possible to lift and cut simultaneously, so long as the knife cuts ahead of the lifting strip.

Working with birch bark

Birch bark is the easiest of all basketry materials to work with. It simply has to be folded to shape and pegged, pinned or sewn in place. The bark has an obvious grain along which it will split easily. To alleviate this and make the bark more pliable, douse with warm water. Or hold it in the warmth of your fire. For basket making, place the stronger brown side on the outside.

Tab-folding

1 Cut out the basic basket shape with tabs attached to help in construction.

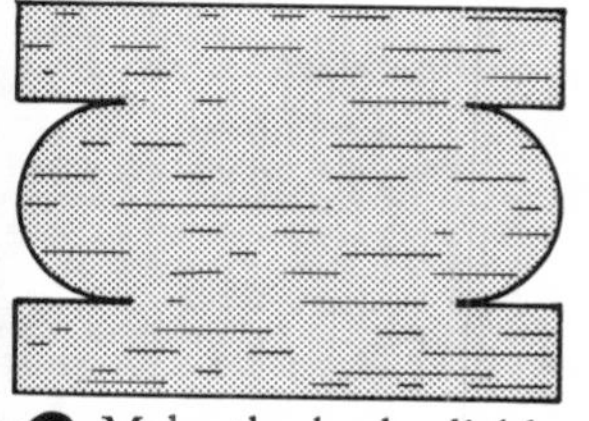

2 Make the bark pliable with heat, then carefully fold it into shape at one end.

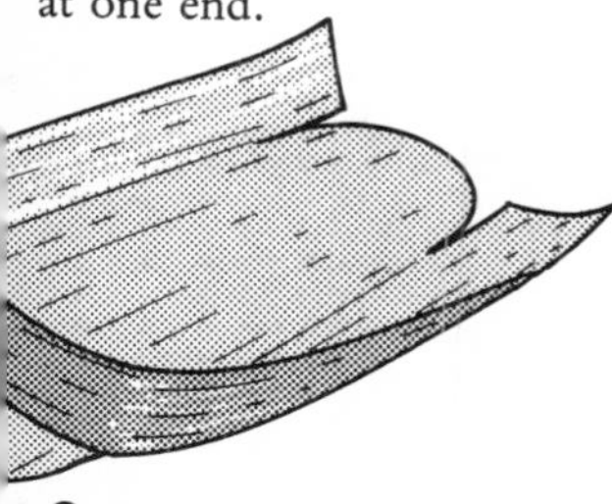

3 Now peg the end before folding and pegging the opposing end. Finally lace together.

Lacing designs

Lacing designs add extra beauty to your basket and can help prevent splitting

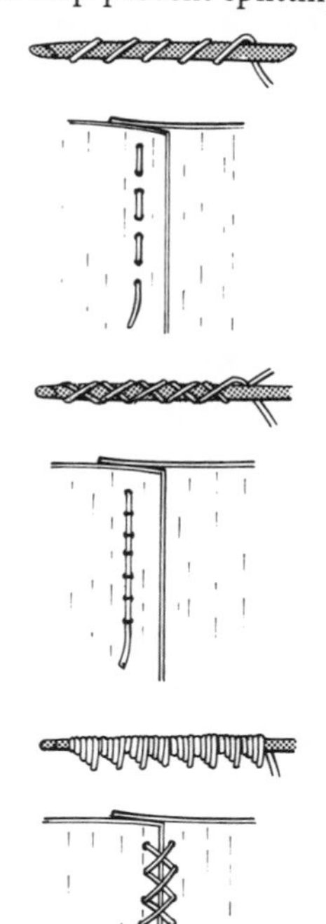

Crease-folding and pegging

1 Creases are best roughly formed and coerced into shape before folding. With perfect sheets of bark, folding will produce watertight emergency cooking pots.

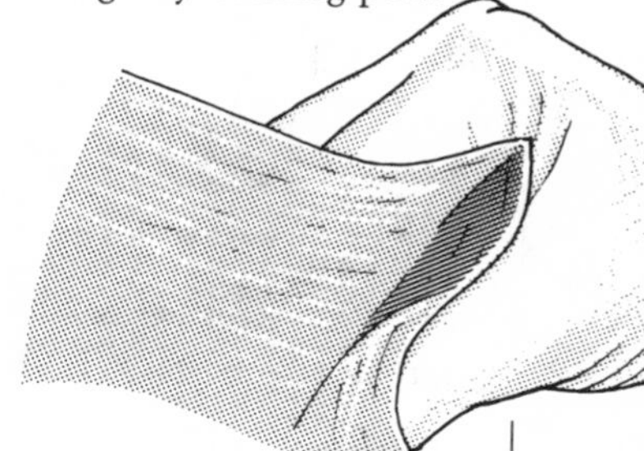

2 Having creased the bark, make the fold. A forced fold will result in splitting.

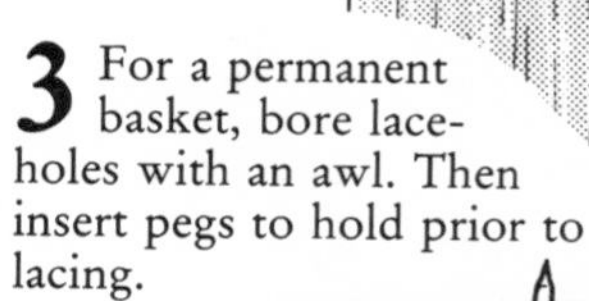

3 For a permanent basket, bore lace-holes with an awl. Then insert pegs to hold prior to lacing.

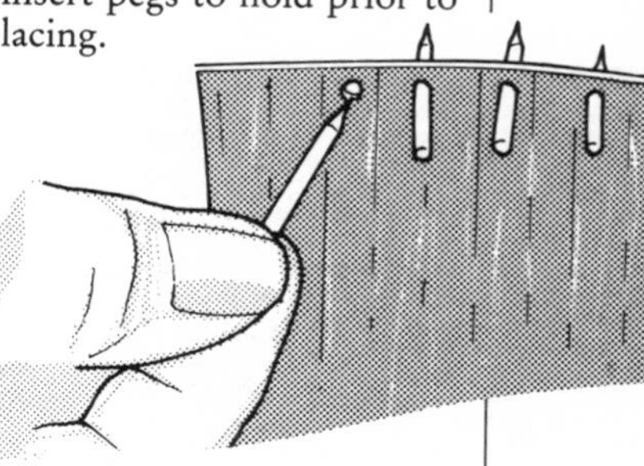

4 Take a pliable strip of willow or lime bark, remove peg and make stitch; then remove the next peg and make another stitch, etc.

Resin

Glue is a modern material we take for granted. The outdoors provides us with several types of glue; and the easiest to process and use is the resin which oozes from rents in the bark of evergreen trees. Pine resin has the added bonus of being waterproof, making it useful for caulking water-holding bark vessels.

It is a curious thing that the pine tree provides more resin to heal its wounds than is actually needed. We can take advantage of this gift, searching for and finding all the resin we need without having to slash a tree.

The resin you collect will inevitably be full of impurities – twigs, needles, even insects. These have to be removed if you are to produce fine glue.

To clean the resin, heat it till it melts. The native method was to place the resin in a coarsely woven bag which would allow the molten resin to seep out but keep the impurities in. This bag was placed in boiling water to melt the resin, which would then float to the surface, where it was skimmed off. Resin so treated remains clear.

Pure resin is brittle – too brittle for most purposes. To overcome this you need to add a tempering agent to plasticise and strengthen it. The most available such subtance is finely powdered charcoal; better still, if you have it, is beeswax.

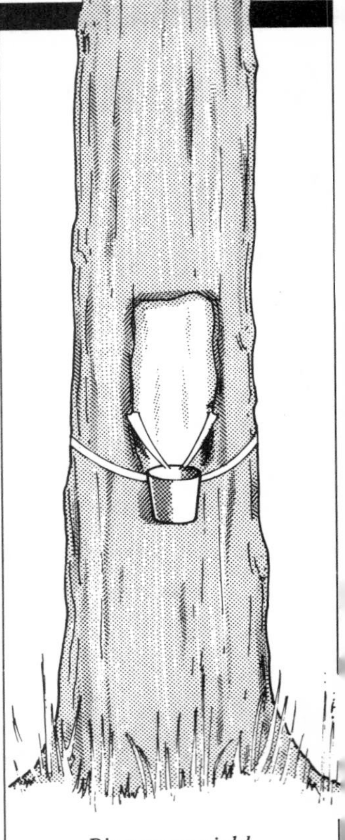

Pine trees yield plenty of resin when tapped

Using resin

Resin can be used as glue, waterproofing, medicine and chewing gum. For glueing and waterproofing, heat the resin gently and apply it with a spatula. Once this is done, two pieces can be brought together and gently heated with a close-held glowing ember to soften the resin and weld the pieces together. Such a joint will set hard when cooled. Caulk any leaks with the addition of more resin.

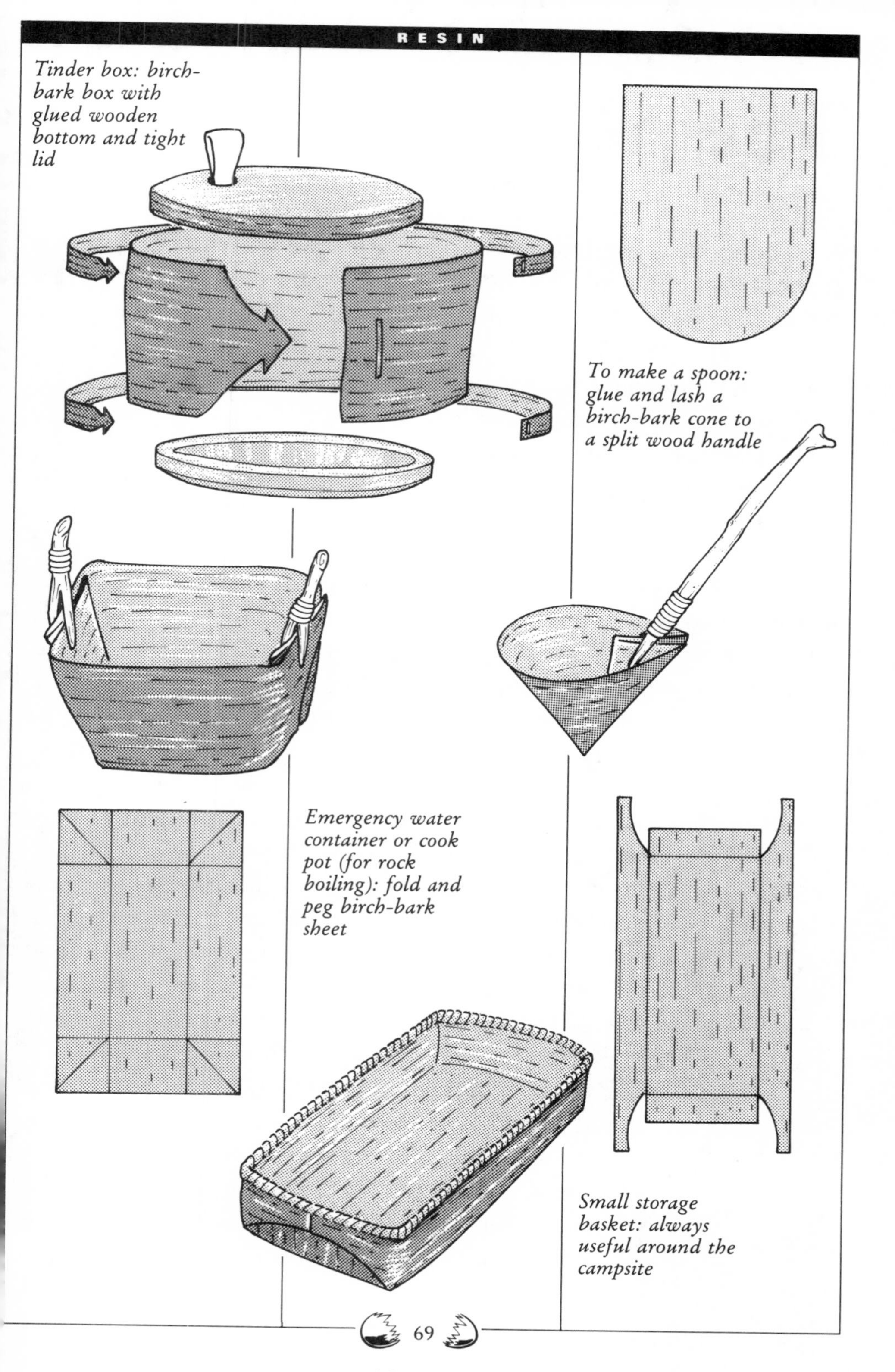
Tinder box: birch-bark box with glued wooden bottom and tight lid
To make a spoon: glue and lash a birch-bark cone to a split wood handle
Emergency water container or cook pot (for rock boiling): fold and peg birch-bark sheet
Small storage basket: always useful around the campsite

The pursuit of food

If there is one thing which sets us apart from our earliest ancestors it is the way we find our food. For them life and food-gathering were totally integrated. An essential social activity, food-gathering required an intimate understanding of what foods were needed and available at any given time. To live fully dependent upon nature's bounty is an eye-opening experience; you cannot let any opportunity of food, no matter how meagre, pass you by. You also quickly learn that for your long-term well-being you need to gather wisely to avoid starving in future seasons.

For our distant ancestors, for example, it may have been necessary to open clearings in the primeval forest to encourage the germination of wild herbs. To follow these naturally imposed laws can be a highly rewarding experience as your life moves in synchrony with nature, your diet following the changing tides of ripening wild foods.

Few people today ever live this way, and to do so demands a great deal of self-confidence and an adaptable palate (to say the least!). However, given a few ingredients from home, most wild foods become a pleasant culinary adventure to liven the cooking pot, a reason in their own right for making a hike. I like to think of these foods as colours in my paintbox of flavours; each season the colours change and with them the mood and appearance of the food. Food and morale are closely linked, so a knowledge of using those colours is a good skill to develop.

Close observation will show the right time for gathering

Spring is an interesting time for the keen gatherer. The season starts starvation poor, requiring a versatile approach. This early famine seems to serve as a reminder not to take the coming gluts for granted. First to break the famine are the green tops of the edible root plants. This root feast leads us into the heart of spring and the arrival of the early salad plants. Meat is scarce while the animals' young are born, for we have an obligation to let them raise their young. But by the end of spring there is a plethora of naïve young animals to fall easy prey to the smart predator. To our sensibilities softened by civilisation this may seem cruel and unfair, but in reality it is the way of nature. Only the intelligent, fast, strong and lucky will survive to raise their offspring. So long as we take only what we really need, and not more than a population of plants or animals can sustain, the balance of nature will will remain undisturbed. It is worth bearing in mind that, despite seeming to be removed from this process, we are ourselves part of the food chain and at death return to the earth.

Nature dictates that unwary young do not survive

The possibilities for finding food in the wild are much greater than most people imagine. The potential risk of eating something poisonous is not a serious threat if you take care to learn your recognition well. It is always advisable to get to know a local expert who can put the right plants in your hands for you to smell, touch, taste and see.

The golden rule of food-gathering is *only eat those things you have positively identified as edible*. Avoid advice that recommends field testing unknown plants – it is not worth the risk.

How you pursue your food is as important as what you pursue. Although wild foods are freely available, they are not for free. People have a responsibility to give back their care and assistance, a sort of halfway farming. Gather plants in a sustainable way; for instance, collect leaves in ones and twos and from many widely scattered plants, rather than from one individual plant, so as not to impair plant growth. When gathering roots, try to gather after the plant has gone to seed, and if this is not possible plant seeds for every plant you dig up.

The leading example of this sustainable use of the food supply is the Australian Aboriginal, who in some instances removes only half of a root, replacing the rest so that it will continue to grow.

The importance of roots

The spring famine was a serious proposition for our ancestors, as is testified by the fact that they learned to make use of the wild arum lords-and-ladies for food. One of the earliest roots available in early spring, all parts of this perennial plant are poisonous unless specially cooked.

At the end of each summer there are plants which have not flowered – the biennials. These die back to overwinter on a store of carbohydrate that they have been collecting in their roots all summer. With the penetration of the warmth of spring, they send up new leaves, ready for their flowering, dispersal of seeds and death later in the year. For those who know about them, biennials provide a store of energy. Look in spring for the emergent leaves of these plants and dig them up. Over winter the carbohydrate stored in the plant has begun to turn to sugar, and they taste sweeter now than at any other time. The real secret lies in being able to identify the plant correctly by its youngest leaves – not an easy task for a beginner, as most field guides show the plant only in flower. My suggestion is to dig up the plant carefully later in the year when identification is more certain; examine the root by cutting it in half lengthways to learn its structure.

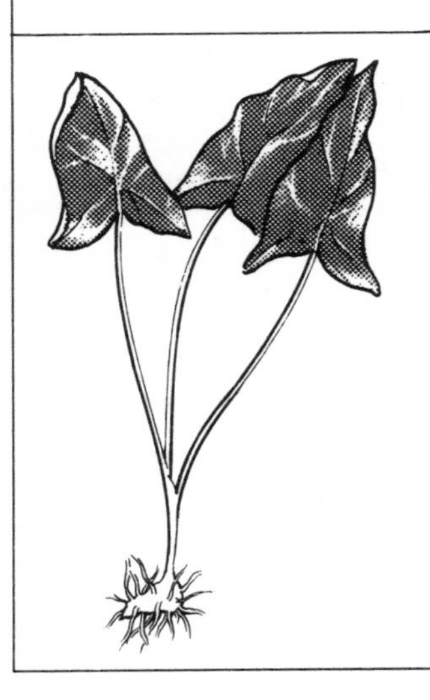

Warning

Although the arum was once used as a food source, it required specialised preparation and cooking to neutralise the poisonous substances it contains. It was thoroughly roasted or dried and baked; but even so, it is doubtful whether this rendered it completely harmless. From records of explorers and travellers in contact with native peoples who still used the arum, it seems that poisoning through insufficient preparation was common, although rarely fatal. All parts of the plant are poisonous, causing severe burning irritation to the mouth if eaten. Even the juice of the roots will cause irritation to skin, especially to any cuts or sores. For this reason arum is best avoided entirely as a source of food.

The digging stick

Some wild roots are easily dug up, but the majority cling tenaciously to the soil to avoid being uprooted for food. By far the best method for their extraction is with the careful and patient use of a digging stick, one of humanity's oldest tools. If you try to use brute force the roots will simply break off, leaving you tired and hungry. Remember that to make a positive identification it is preferable to extract the roots still attached to the leaves.

The stick is easy to carve from hard wood. The point or digging tip should be fire-hardened – heat it to just below scorching to drive out any moisture and harden off the fibres. A stick works very effectively, especially for the extraction of long tap-roots. In many instances it is more versatile than modern digging implements; it also leaves a very small hole.

Making the digging stick

A digging stick needs a bevelled chisel end, sharp but strong. It helps if the end is fire-hardened – heat it close to the embers of your fire until just before scorching.

Using the stick

1 With a casual, relaxed action, excavate a deep hole alongside the root. If possible follow the root down, making sure you reach down to its tip.

2 Work patiently – you will discover that many of the best wild roots cling tenaciously to the soil. Weaken the soil thoroughly on either side of the root so that it can be eased sideways into the hole you have dug. Carefully fill in the hole again after extraction.

Salads and greens

With the re-emergence of the plants our diet can again become more balanced, with a healthy complement of vitamin-rich greens. Wild plants are more strongly flavoured than the green plants present in our normal diet, and a taste for them can take some acquiring. The best way to familiarise yourself with them is to include them in your usual meals where they benefit from the addition of seasonings and condiments.

Beech leaves (*Fagus sylvatica*)
The earliest soft tender leaves are an excellent sandwich filler and can be lightly cooked in butter or by steaming to make a fine dish.

Nettles (*Urtica dioica*)
Nettles are one of the most all-round-useful plants and make an excellent cooked green. Select the fresh and tender tops and cook them in just enough water to cover them. Drain and serve piping hot with butter. Cooking destroys the stinging properties.

Mallow (*Malva sylvestris*)
A wonderful plant. Too glutinous ever to be a really good cooked green, mallow makes an excellent thickener for soups and stews. It can form the basis of an amazing soup needing only some wild roots and some stock or a bouillon cube.

Lady's smock (*Cardamine pratensis*)
My personal favourite salad ingredient, very high in vitamin C, with a pungent peppery flavour. A real treat, greatly undervalued. Include in wild stews.

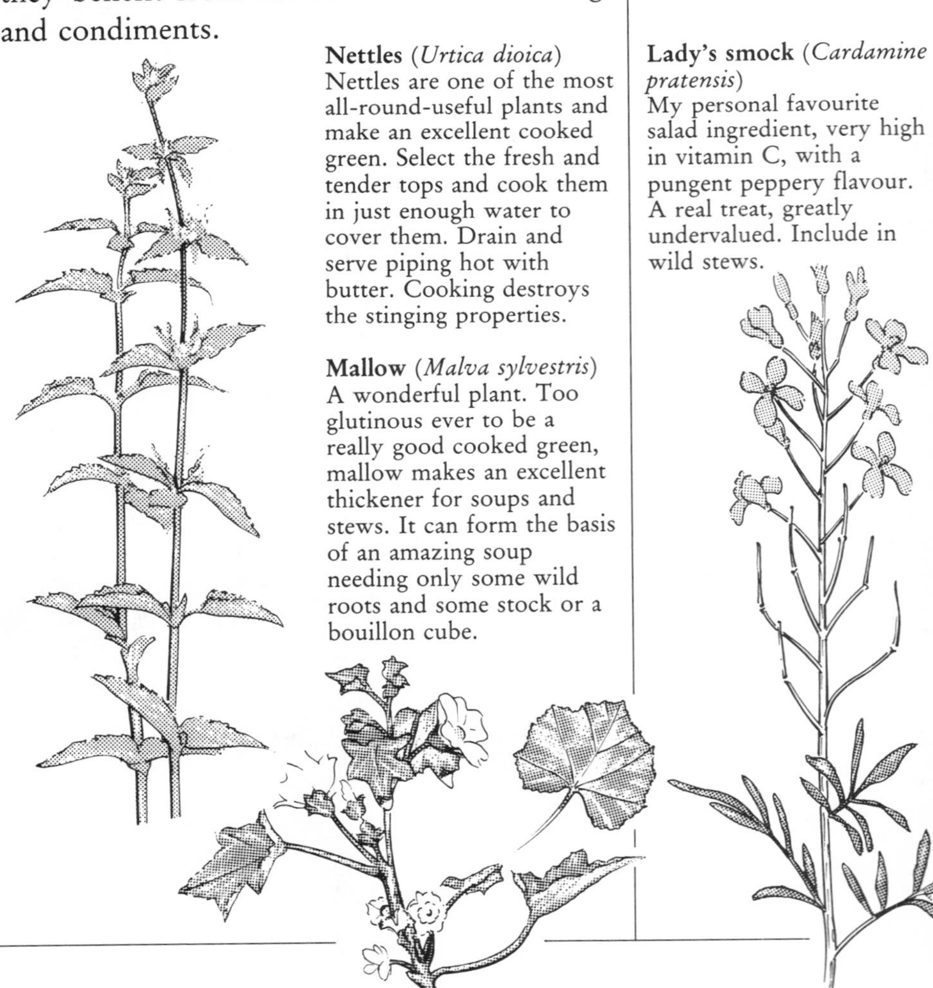

Rosebay willow-herb (*Chaemerion/Epilobium augustifolium*)
Use only the youngest shoots and leaves. Cook shoots like asparagus by steaming or boiling in the least amount of water possible. Cook leaves the same way as nettles. Use dried mature leaves as a wild tea.

Sheep sorrel (*Rumex acetosella*)
Boil for a few minutes and serve with butter. Better still, make it into a purée and serve with fish. Don't eat large quantities – sheep sorrel contains oxalic acid.

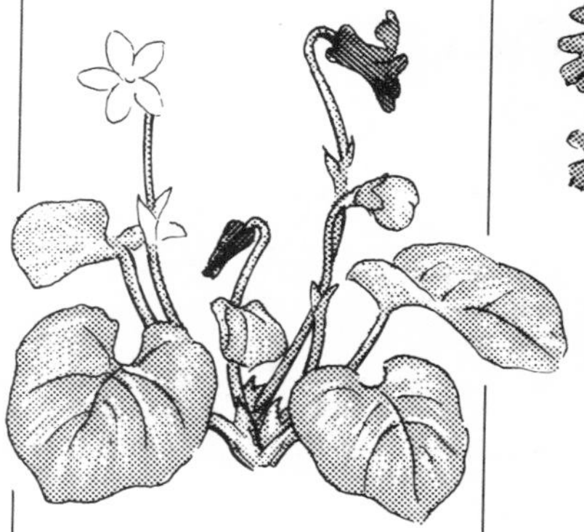

Violets (*Viola odorata*)
Violet leaves are a good addition to any salad and can be used as a thickener for stews and soups.

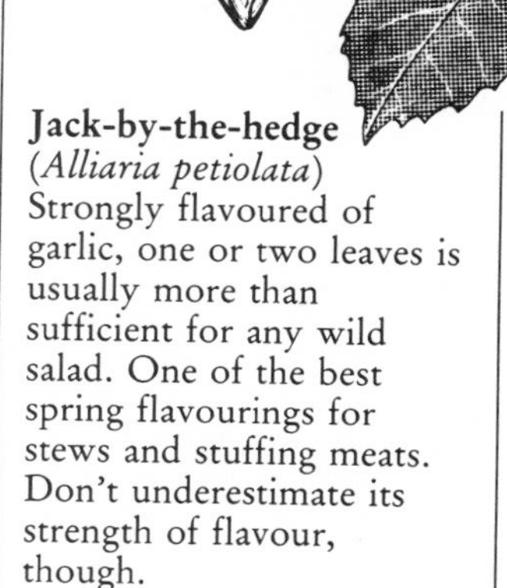

Jack-by-the-hedge (*Alliaria petiolata*)
Strongly flavoured of garlic, one or two leaves is usually more than sufficient for any wild salad. One of the best spring flavourings for stews and stuffing meats. Don't underestimate its strength of flavour, though.

Hawthorn (*Crataegus monogyna*)
Tender young leaves have a distinct yet subtle flavour. An invaluable ingredient for salads.

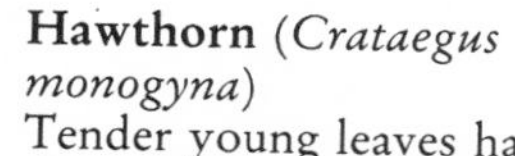

Lady's thumb or redshank (*Polygonum persicaria*)
Can be added raw to salads but better used similarly to nettles as a spinach substitute. Also a good addition to any stew.

Sweet roots

Wild roots are generally smaller and more fibrous and earthy tasting than the cultivated varieties we are used to today. But they are tasty and filling when you are hungry.

Arrowhead (*Sagittaria sagittifolia*)
You can use the tubers of this aquatic plant like potatoes. Tasty, filling and energy-rich – an important plant to know.

Wild onion or ramsons (*Allium ursinum*)
So strongly flavoured you can usually smell them before you see them, ramsons can be used to flavour salads and stews. The bulb resembles a spring onion and can be gently cooked on a bed of embers or braised in soup stocks or stews. Use dried for year-round flavouring.

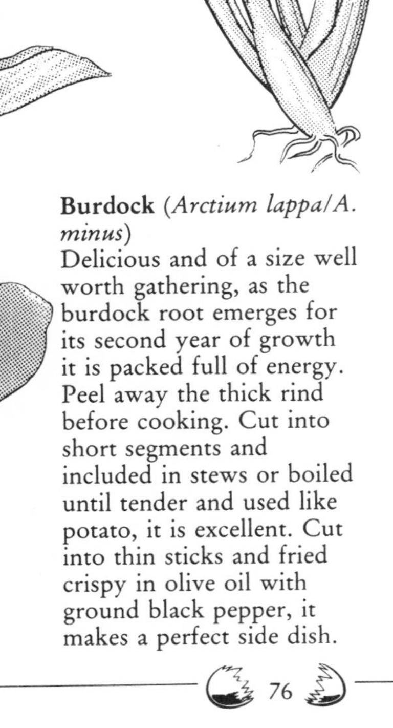

Burdock (*Arctium lappa/A. minus*)
Delicious and of a size well worth gathering, as the burdock root emerges for its second year of growth it is packed full of energy. Peel away the thick rind before cooking. Cut into short segments and included in stews or boiled until tender and used like potato, it is excellent. Cut into thin sticks and fried crispy in olive oil with ground black pepper, it makes a perfect side dish.

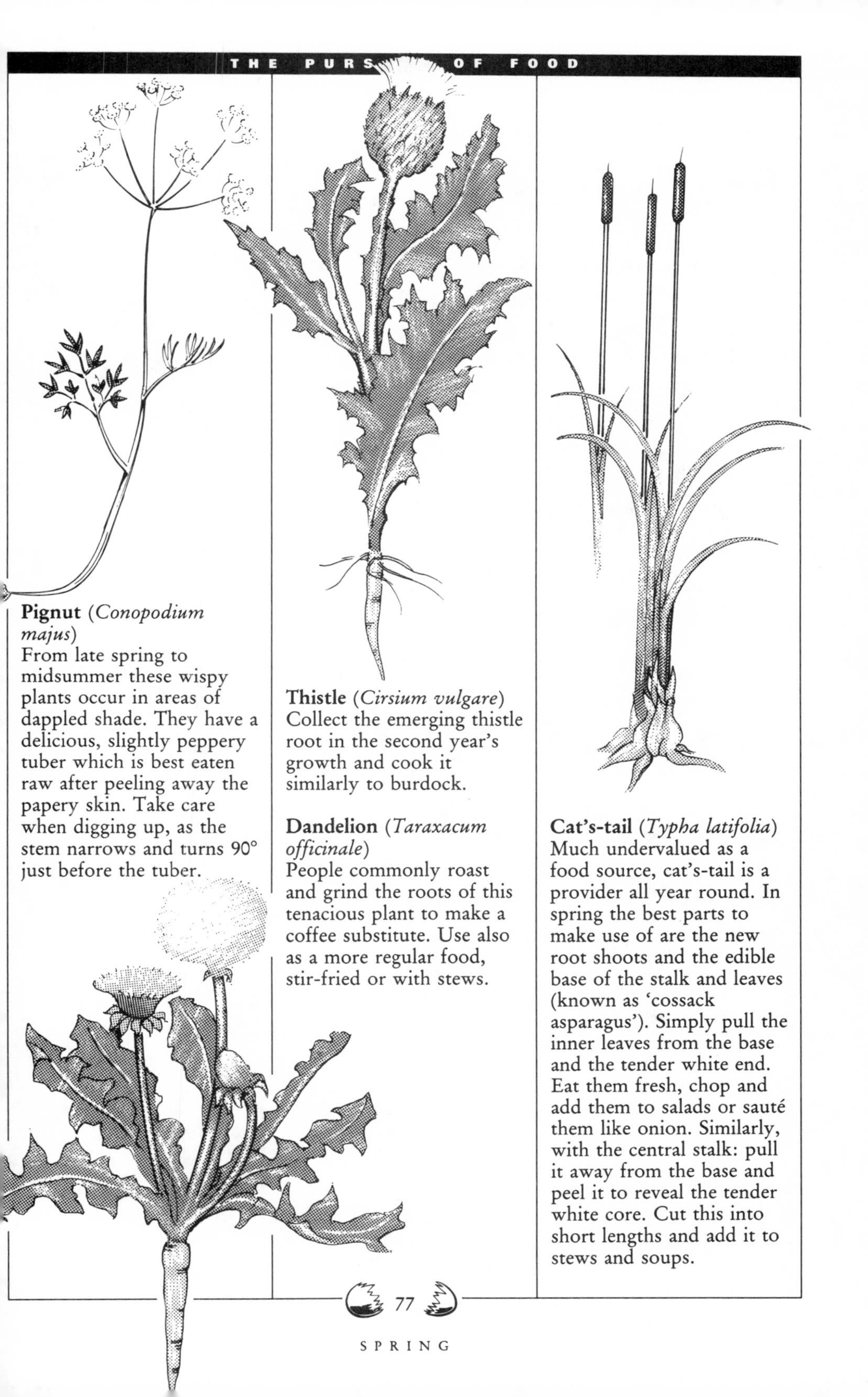

Pignut (*Conopodium majus*)
From late spring to midsummer these wispy plants occur in areas of dappled shade. They have a delicious, slightly peppery tuber which is best eaten raw after peeling away the papery skin. Take care when digging up, as the stem narrows and turns 90° just before the tuber.

Thistle (*Cirsium vulgare*)
Collect the emerging thistle root in the second year's growth and cook it similarly to burdock.

Dandelion (*Taraxacum officinale*)
People commonly roast and grind the roots of this tenacious plant to make a coffee substitute. Use also as a more regular food, stir-fried or with stews.

Cat's-tail (*Typha latifolia*)
Much undervalued as a food source, cat's-tail is a provider all year round. In spring the best parts to make use of are the new root shoots and the edible base of the stalk and leaves (known as 'cossack asparagus'). Simply pull the inner leaves from the base and the tender white end. Eat them fresh, chop and add them to salads or sauté them like onion. Similarly, with the central stalk: pull it away from the base and peel it to reveal the tender white core. Cut this into short lengths and add it to stews and soups.

Drinks and flavourings

Few things are more uplifting at the trail's end than a tasty and nourishing drink. Nature provides a surprising diversity of pleasant drink flavourings which are easily found and prepared.

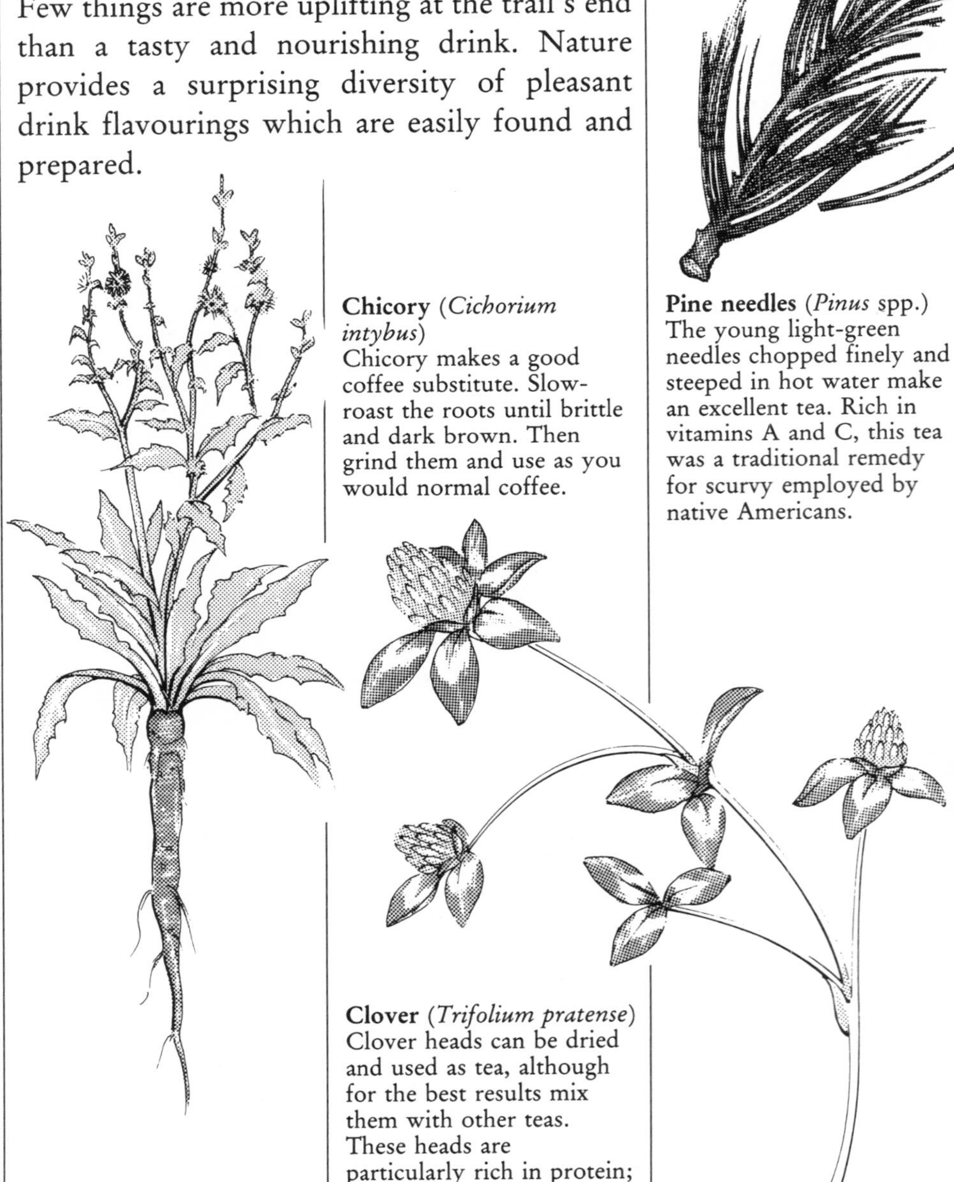

Chicory (*Cichorium intybus*)
Chicory makes a good coffee substitute. Slow-roast the roots until brittle and dark brown. Then grind them and use as you would normal coffee.

Pine needles (*Pinus* spp.)
The young light-green needles chopped finely and steeped in hot water make an excellent tea. Rich in vitamins A and C, this tea was a traditional remedy for scurvy employed by native Americans.

Clover (*Trifolium pratense*)
Clover heads can be dried and used as tea, although for the best results mix them with other teas. These heads are particularly rich in protein; to make them more digestible, boil briefly.

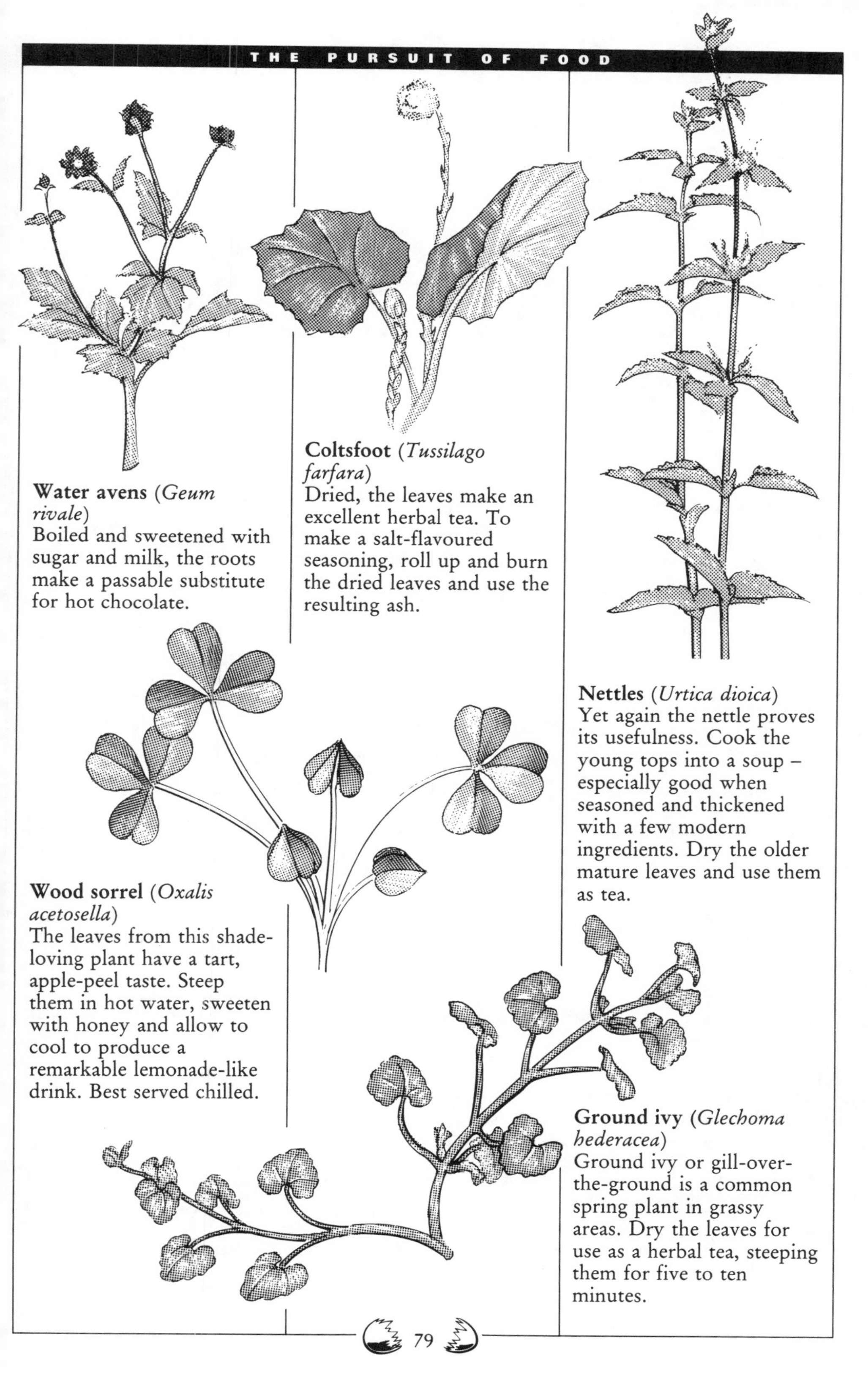

Water avens (*Geum rivale*)
Boiled and sweetened with sugar and milk, the roots make a passable substitute for hot chocolate.

Coltsfoot (*Tussilago farfara*)
Dried, the leaves make an excellent herbal tea. To make a salt-flavoured seasoning, roll up and burn the dried leaves and use the resulting ash.

Nettles (*Urtica dioica*)
Yet again the nettle proves its usefulness. Cook the young tops into a soup – especially good when seasoned and thickened with a few modern ingredients. Dry the older mature leaves and use them as tea.

Wood sorrel (*Oxalis acetosella*)
The leaves from this shade-loving plant have a tart, apple-peel taste. Steep them in hot water, sweeten with honey and allow to cool to produce a remarkable lemonade-like drink. Best served chilled.

Ground ivy (*Glechoma hederacea*)
Ground ivy or gill-over-the-ground is a common spring plant in grassy areas. Dry the leaves for use as a herbal tea, steeping them for five to ten minutes.

SUMMER

Summer is the season of growth, a time of discovery and learning. With the sun at its strongest, the pace of life changes; the division between the cool of morning and evening and the sultry heat of midday becomes more marked than at any other time. This is most perceptible in the activity of the birds. Their song grows almost silent as the stifling midday heat forces them to seek shade and stillness – the silence broken occasionally by the joy of a starling splashing in a cool puddle.

Even in the city, summer reaches through the air-conditioning and seasonless exteriors of office buildings. It draws people out into parks and other open spaces, to relax, meet friends, play football or enjoy an impromptu picnic. This season is an easy time to feel enthusiastic about the outdoors.

On the backcountry trails every season has its advantages, but summer is unique in the opportunities it brings for the outdoors way of life. It is a time to remove the burden of insulative clothing and let your skin make contact with grass, bark and earth, the warmth of sunlight and the cooling waters of streams. A season of long days, warm nights and lots to see, summer is the ideal time to introduce youngsters to the trail. No sight is more natural than that of a family enjoying the countryside.

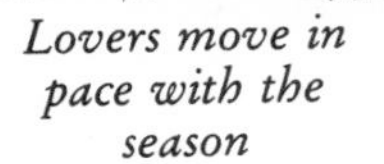

Lovers move in pace with the season

For people who do not usually subsist upon

natural resources, it is a forgivable mistake to think of summer as a time to relax. But this is simply not the case. Summer's glut of warmth and light influences every one of us. Watch the competitive struggle between plants reaching out of the shade into the light to gather energy from the sun, and consider that we are also connected to this struggle through the inescapable bonds of the food chain.

As the season begins to fade, yet just before nights begin to draw in too obviously, the wild fruits and seeds can be gathered. This reminds us to begin preparations for the coming of autumn. Our ancestors did not waste these last days of favourable weather: besides harvesting natural resources they used the time to make preparations for the colder months ahead, fashioning containers for storage and preserving meats and grains.

Of course, summer has its own problems – thorns, stinging plants and biting insects, small inconveniences which we have to cope with. As we get older, these discomforts fade quickly in the light of happier trail recollections. The magic of the season is that irresistible force that draws us outside; and when you feel the same magnetism during the other seasons, you will know you are addicted to the outdoors.

For me, summer is never long enough. Almost as soon as it has started, it seems to be rushing to its end. Try to be aware of the rapid growth cycle – from soft, moist, lucious plants competing for sunlight to the spent, dry and withering vegetation at the end of the season. This process of irreversible change is the spur we need to make the most of the summer days.

Taught to children by their grandparents, daisy chains link the generations

Summer is the most forgiving of seasons. You can usually travel lightly, and the ground is firm underfoot. Take the opportunity to explore new places; go walk-about; share in the vitality which surrounds you. Walk the mountain valleys with a field guide to plants in your haversack. Go and listen to the waves on the seashore. With the sun beginning to set behind your tent, and your meal cooking on the stove, you'll feel in tune with the cheerful song of the blackbird, which proclaims 'how good it is to be alive'!

Animal kingdoms

The sound of summer is the background hum of a billion insect wings beating in the warm air. Insects are usually considered to be a nuisance – pests interfering with the balance of nature – but this could not be further from the truth. They are an essential part of the natural order, and what they lack in size they make up for in numbers. Chomping away incessantly, insect mandibles devour the natural greenery, acting as a control on growth. And these feeders themselves serve as an essential food for larger creatures such as birds. In fact, some bird species rely upon them so much that they time their broods to coincide with the emergence of specific insects.

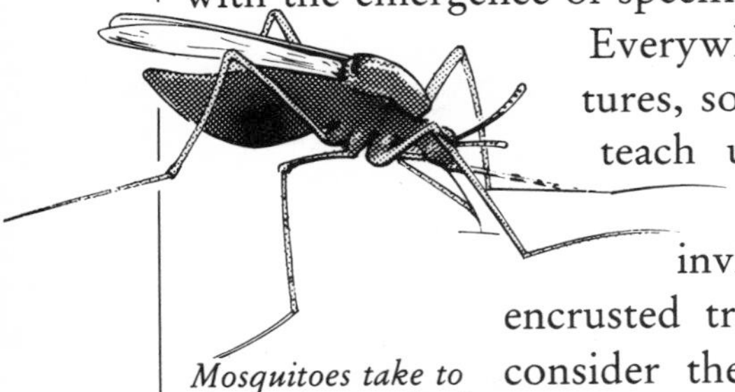

Everywhere we look now there are wild creatures, some obvious and others less so; each can teach us something. Take, for example, the peppered moth, which blends almost invisibly when resting upon a lichen-encrusted tree, a perfect lesson in camouflage. Or consider the kestrel hovering over a meadow, an example of supreme patience as it waits poised to make the kill.

Mosquitoes take to the air in search of unguarded flesh

The litters of spring mammals have now grown to boisterous young, endlessly inquisitive to explore. Fox cubs play hunting games outside of the earth – any unsuspecting cub can become the rabbit of another's pounce. These young foxes are already capable of catching voles. In the early evening, if you are stealthy, you may be able to approach closely to an earth or clearing and observe the young foxes' comic antics, before they set off on their nightly patrol.

The late summer evenings are also a perfect opportunity to watch badgers at close quarters. These short-sighted mammals rely heavily upon their senses of smell and hearing. With care you can often

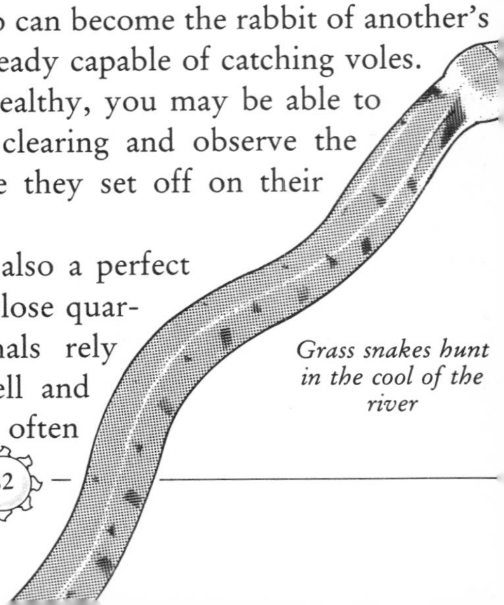

Grass snakes hunt in the cool of the river

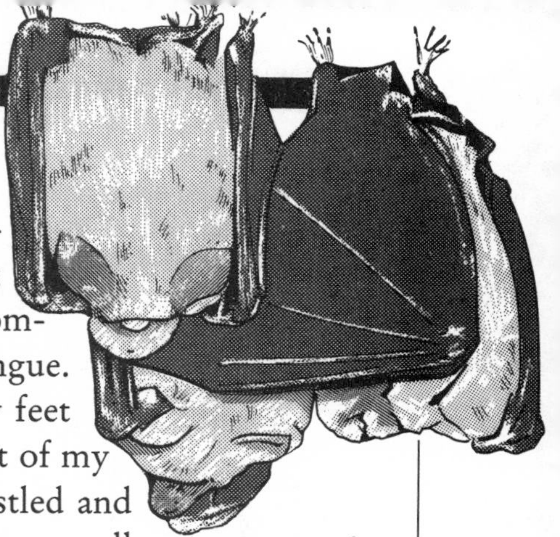

approach to within a few feet of a family at play.

In such circumstances one summer evening I had an adult badger run into me; surprised, he dashed into some brambles, complaining in the strange grunting badger tongue. Shortly after this, as I crept to within a few feet of the set, a young badger caught a faint hint of my scent. He moved cautiously towards me, jostled and crowded by four of his brothers and sisters, all curious to investigate. Probing ahead with their noses till they were only a few inches from my feet, they suddenly recognised the odour. They recoiled as if struck by lightning and disappeared into the night, making a noise rather like the sound of children giggling at some mischievous adventure.

Bats emerge after dark to hunt moths

Perhaps it is the lethargic warmth or the abundance of food, but wild creatures seem to be less on their guard in the summer months. If you are sharp eyed there is every chance you will see mice, voles and even the elusive roe deer at close range. But you have to use all of your senses, for the thick greenery offers much cover to conceal them.

Snakes can be found near water as their mating season begins. One of my favourite sights is that of a grass snake swimming, a ribbon of menace moving sleekly through the water. Snakes have rather a bad press in the West; but, highly sensitive to vibrations, your footfall is usually enough to send them into hiding, for they are more afraid of us than we are of them.

All creatures have their place in the natural order. We need to temper our reactions to those which seem to threaten us with an understanding of the role they play. While we may sometimes need to defend ourselves, more snakes are killed out of panic than is necessary. In Britain all snakes are now protected by law.

Snakes serve as a reminder to us to search for understanding rather than fearing in ignorance. For all of our great skills and abilities we must bear in mind that there remain places on the earth where we are not the top of the ladder, places where other creatures are better adapted than us, where we ourselves may be considered the prey. Visiting these places is a humbling and educating experience.

Droppings

Wherever you go in the countryside you will come across animal droppings. While the thought of examining them may seem repugnant, they can be of great value as packages of intelligence. Droppings can tell you the species of the creature which left them, its size or age, its condition, what it has been eating, how long ago it passed and sometimes even which direction it was travelling in.

To start with, learn to recognise the characteristic dropping shapes of the major species you are interested in. You need not handle the droppings; but if you feel you must, wear a pair of disposable surgical gloves and be hygienic, because droppings can contain harmful organisms.

Pellets

Pellets are not droppings but the indigestible food remains regurgitated by birds, often containing small mammals' bone matter and fur. The pellets of larger birds of prey resemble fox droppings but lack the musty odour and are compressed.

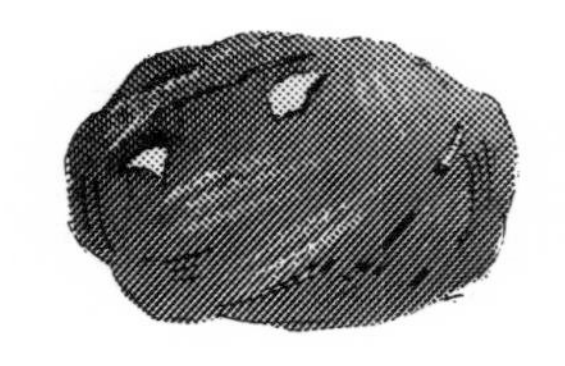

Barn owl
Pellets very rounded at the ends, cylindrical, like a slightly elongated ping-pong ball.

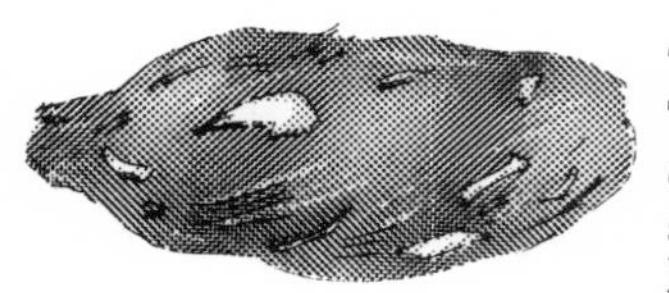

Tawny owl
Typically tapered at one end, about the size and shape of a cocktail sausage, lighter coloured than the barn owl's pellet.

Spherical

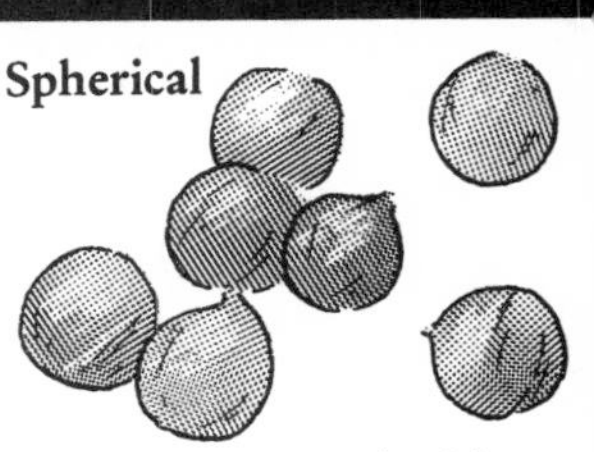

Usually associated with herbivores. Size, content, colour (dark brown to light straw), consistency and location help distinguish species:

Hare 15–20 mm (over ½ in) diam., fibrous grass remains.

Rabbit 8–10 mm (under ½ in) diam., fibrous grass remains, often in large quantity and on mounds.

Squirrel 5–8 mm (¼ in) diam., rare, more moist and finely digested than rabbit.

Cylindrical

With rounded ends, usually droppings of rodents. Species vary mainly in dropping size and habitat location:

Rat 5×15 mm (⅕×½ in)

Water vole 4×9 mm (⅙×⅓ in).

Field vole 2×6 mm (⅒×¼ in).

Wood mouse 2×4 mm (⅒×⅙ in).

Elongated

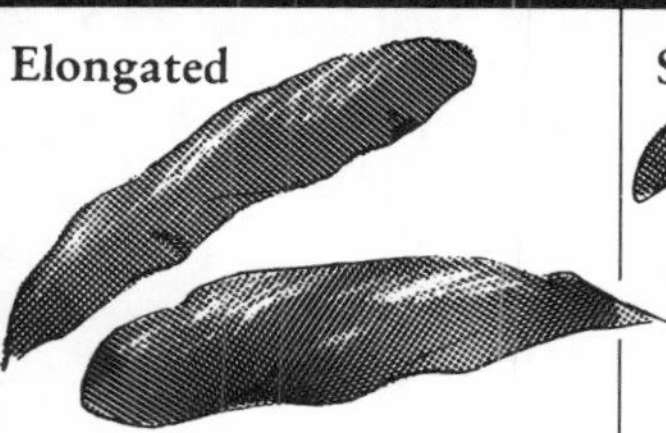

Usually associated with omnivores, great diversity in size:

Shrews 1×2 mm (1/20×1/10 in).

Hedgehog 1×4 cm (½×1½ in), one end pointed, often black and shiny.

Bear 4 cm (1½ in) thick, large quantities.

Squiggles

Like squeezed-out toothpaste, associated with weasel family. Musty scent, often moist, containing remnants of prey. Generally ten times longer than diameter, with tail:

Weasel 2 mm (1/12 in) diam.

Stoat 8 mm (⅓ in) diam.

Pine marten 1 cm (½ in) diam., very smelly.

Badger 15–20 mm (over ½ in) diam. × 8 cm (over 3 in), found in 20 cm^2 (8 in^2) square pits.

With tail

Usually droppings of carnivore. Colour lightens to grey or white when diet comprised largely of bones:

Fox 15–20 mm diam. × 8–10 cm (over ½×3–4 in), twisted tail, often on tussocks.

Bottle shape

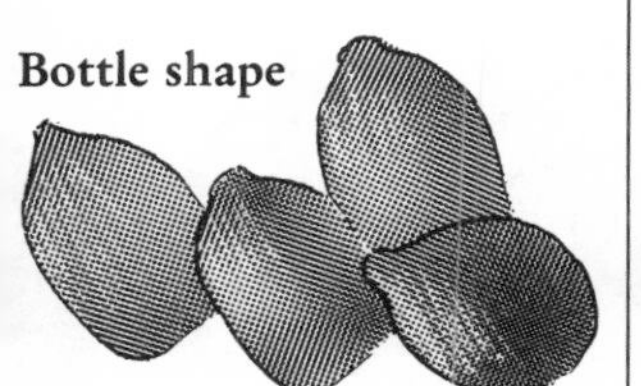

Most deer droppings: slightly bottle shaped, tapering at one end and broadly indented at other, usually dark, moist, plasticine-like:

Red deer 15 mm diam. × 25 mm (⅗×1 in), very bottle shaped.

Fallow deer 12 mm diam. × 15 mm (½×⅗ in).

Rugby ball shaped

Roe deer, particularly young deer, leave rugby-ball-shaped droppings, 10 mm diam. × 15 mm long (⅖×⅗ in), often as fewmets (bunched together in a mass).

Spraints

Otters' droppings: unusual black oily splatter with fishy scent, found especially on raised ground and tussocks, often contains fish remains.

Shelter

Shelter is less of a problem during summer than at other times of the year. Especially under the canopy of the broad-leaved trees, there is less need for thick thatching. In the worst conditions you can always use the shelters you built in the spring, and in the best circumstances you can sleep under the stars by the camp-fire. To be woken by the first rays of daylight beside the ash of last night's fire is a wonderful, timeless experience.

You may be able to make a temporary home in the lee of a large tree or some other natural shelter, such as a dry cave or overhang. Keep a look-out for the available possibilities.

Holly bush
In really heavy downpours I have often retreated to the shelter of a large holly. These often provide a natural hollow, usually also supplying enough dry kindling to fuel a small brew fire.

Arbour

When the sun is very hot and intense, you need shade. Where there is little or no natural shade, the answer is to build a simple arbour. Even the dappled shade cast by the poorest roof makes life much more comfortable.

Wickiup

In arid regions you need a warm shelter from the cold of night. The Paiute native Americans would build a simple structure from the available brushwood, packed tightly to exclude drafts. With a fire burning at the entrance, even the smallest wickiup becomes a cheery home.

Water

The fierce heat of the summer sun scorches the land below, and trails become hard as the surface moisture evaporates. With the disappearance of the last puddles, competition among trees and plants for water intensifies. Long periods of drought, particularly in summer, can cause problems for humans as well as for animals and for ripening fruit and grain.

To cross an arid stretch of wild country, you need to be cunning and resourceful with regard to water. It is essential to prevent unnecessary moisture loss – it is amazing how many tragic cases of fatal dehydration are attributable to wrong decision-making in this respect. The basic principle is to avoid moving about when the sun is at its hottest.

Water can be found in tree hollows after rain

If you can, travel in the early morning and late afternoon. In the middle of the day, find shade and have a siesta. If you have to move in the middle of the day, move slowly in the heat, as economically as possible. If you have no water, don't eat; if you have some water in your bottle, drink it – it is better inside you than carried on your back. Most importantly, recognise that exposed skin keeps you cool through the evaporation of your sweat: keep as much of your skin covered as possible to reduce this loss of moisture. Also keep your mouth closed to avoid exhaling more moisture than is necessary – sucking a stone helps.

Having taken these steps, you can now think about searching for water. Water prefers to take the route of least resistance downhill. So you need to look for places along its route where it becomes trapped: hollows in rocks or trees, depressions in clay, boggy areas, shaded gullies and canyons or fissures in rock where water can only trickle through.

Look for water-loving plants

To help your search there are a few indicators to look out for. Grain-eating birds need water and subsequently are never far from it. The presence of many large mammals is also an indicator of likely water availability.

But most important of all as a sign of water are the water-loving plants, such as hart's-tongue fern, horsetails and mosses.

Good places to search for water are at the base of cliffs or among natural declivities on gently sloping hillsides. On the coastline you can find water trickling from sea cliffs; or dig for it behind sand dunes above the tide line. Narrow shady canyons and rock clefts are also good areas to search.

Failing these methods you can squeeze the moisture from damp mud using your bandanna. If you are on a long trip and expect to have difficulty finding plentiful supplies of water during the day, choose a shady camp site. In the morning, make the effort to rise early so that you can mop up dew with your bandanna and squeeze it out into a receptacle.

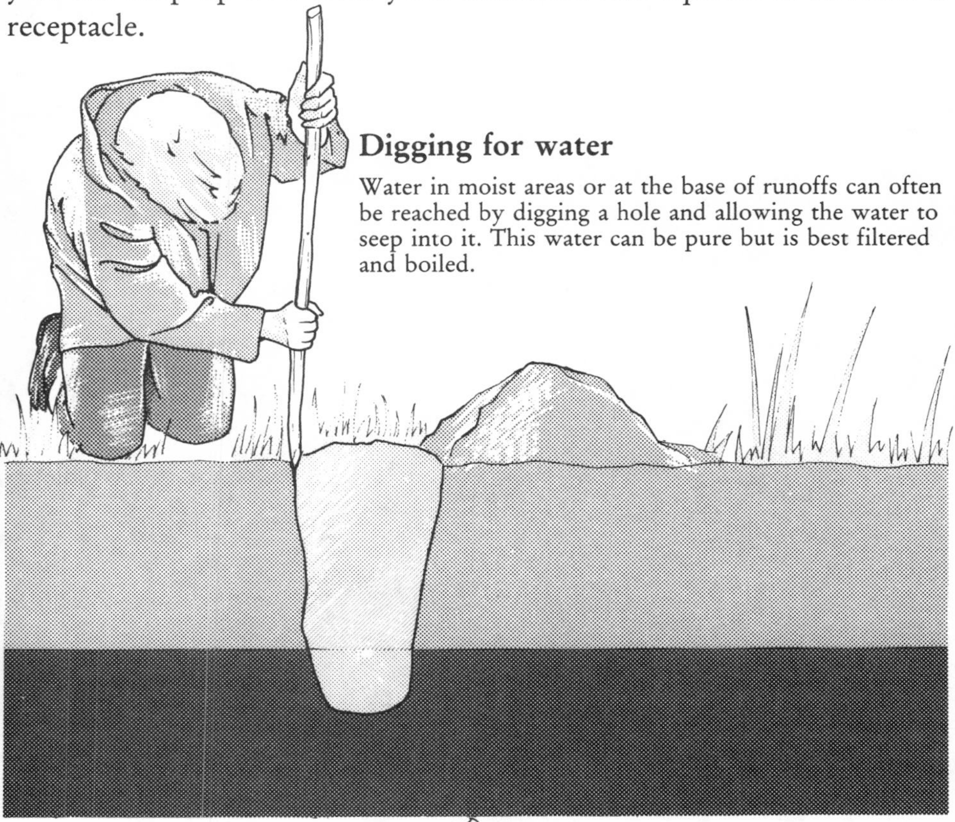

Digging for water

Water in moist areas or at the base of runoffs can often be reached by digging a hole and allowing the water to seep into it. This water can be pure but is best filtered and boiled.

Fire

With the drier weather you can use the simplest friction fire-lighting technique: the hand drill. The advantage of this method is ease of portability and the fact that it does not require cordage. It does, however, require fitness and a good technique. The drill should be about 1 cm (up to ½ in) in diameter and 60 cm (2 ft) long. The hearth should be about 30 cm (1 ft) long, wide enough to accommodate the drill and about the same thickness as the drill diameter. The principle is the same as for the bow drill (see p. 50): drill a depression into the hearth to collect hot friction dust.

1 With the notch cut and a piece of bark ready to collect the dust, spin the drill between your palms, applying a steady downward pressure. Hold the hearth beneath your foot.

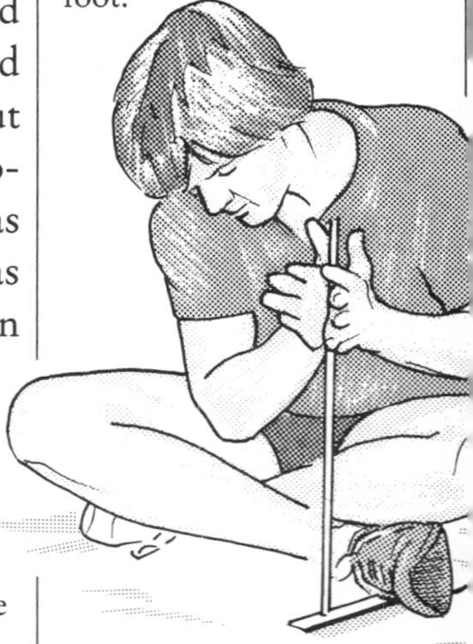

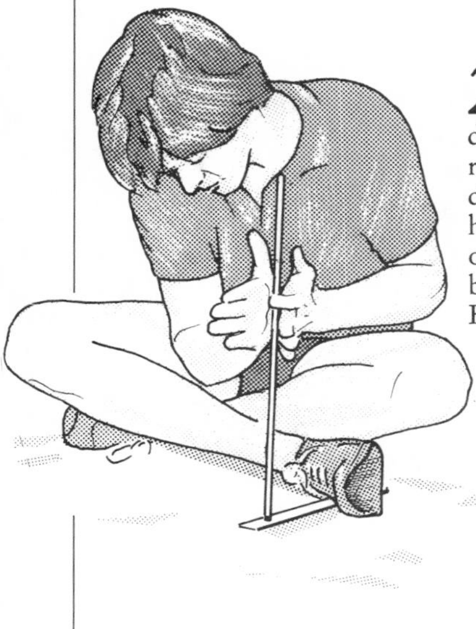

2 As you drill, your hands will move downwards. When they reach the bottom, hold the drill in place with one hand, quickly move the other back to the top, then bring the other hand up. Resume drilling.

3 Gradually build a coal. Watch the friction dust; you may need to drill faster or modify downward pressure. Once the coal is formed, treat it as for a bow drill (p. 50).

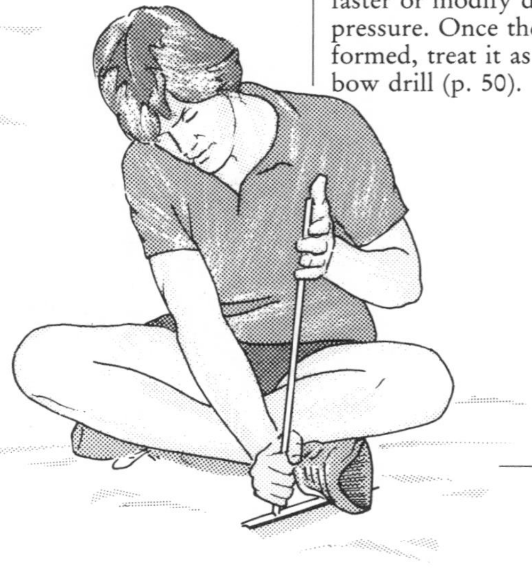

The two-piece drill

It may be that you cannot find a piece of suitable drill wood long and straight enough. A solution frequently used by native peoples was to lash a short piece of suitable wood to a long, straight non-suitable piece: for example, a willow drill-bit lashed into a straight shaft of green elder.

1 Cut the non-drilling end of the bit (overall length 8–15 cm, 3–6 in), to a fine square-sectioned taper.

2 Bind the end of a straight green piece of elder of the same diameter. Smooth the wood for blister-free drilling.

3 Push drill bit into pithy centre of shaft; hammer firmly into place. If shaft splits slightly, binding will contain split.

Suitable woods for drill and hearth

The wood for a hand drill set must be perfectly dry. It was usual for native people to gather and season their fire sets deliberately. The following make excellent drills:

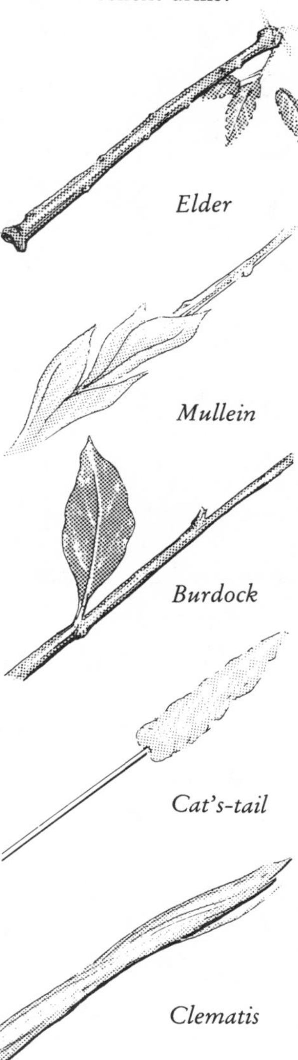

Hearths can be formed from any of the bow drill woods but clematis is also especially good.

Hygiene

Hygiene is an important consideration at the campsite throughout the year but becomes especially so during summer when insects and bacteria thrive. Good organisation helps alleviate the problems – for example, siting a latrine at a slight distance from the camp, although not so far as to be inconvenient – 30–40 m (90–120 ft) is ideal. The easiest latrine to construct is a simple earth hole with a perch bar for a seat. After using the latrine, cover over fresh droppings with some of the excavated soil. Make the latrine deep and long enough to meet the needs of the camp, and site a shovel on the excavated soil to facilitate cover-up.

Unscented soap is your best defence against disease

Camp hygiene depends upon individuals following the routines; so precautions need to become habitual: clean hands prior to preparing food, keeping food covered, washing food in purified water, cleaning out billies (cook pots) and drying them over stove or fire, washing hands after using the latrine. This is all very basic but it works and keeps the tummy bugs away.

To clean the grease from your cook pots, improvise a scourer from a small clump of grass roots. Shake off most but not all of the soil from the roots; this will act as an abrasive. With a little water, scour away all traces of food remnants. You will be astonished just how effective this scourer is. Once scoured clean, rinse away the grime and dry the billy over your fire so that any moisture left is boiled to kill any remaining bugs.

A chewed hazel twig makes a good toothbrush

Plastic eating utensils are popular in camp because of their indestructible nature, but I would not recommend them. Plastic mugs and plates hold on to grease tenaciously, requiring hot washing water and detergent to make them clean. Scouring only makes matters worse by roughening their surface, which allows the grease to collect. It is also difficult under bush conditions to sterilise plastic utensils. Stick with simple stainless-steel cooking sets and eating utensils.

Stay clean – your best ally is soap! Wash regularly and pay special attention to those sweaty areas that rarely see the light of day and to your feet. Don't wash in a stream but wash instead on land so that the soap suds are greatly dispersed before entering the stream and thereby have less environmental impact.

Soap can be made from wood ash, animal fat and salt, but this is a lengthy process better carried out at home than in the field. You can find more convenient substitutes for soap in the plant world – see below.

Regular hair-combing keeps away infestations

Brush your teeth every day. If you have no toothpaste or toothbrush you can improvise by chewing the end of a hazel twig until it frays to a brush and then use wood ash for toothpaste. To prevent infestation of your scalp, follow the Victorian advice and thoroughly brush your hair daily. If you don't have a comb you can easily carve one from bone antler or wood or even use a bunch of strong-stemmed grasses.

Soap plants

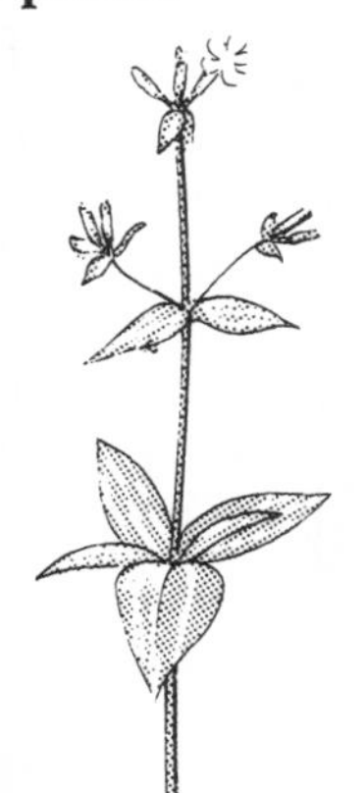

Soapwort
Best of the soap plants, prized for cleaning delicate fabrics. Crush it in warm water or boil for liquid soap.

Horse chestnut
Not as good as soapwort but more common, mildly antiseptic. Crush the leaves in warm water.

Chickweed
Like horse chestnut, contains saponin and can be used as soap but is inferior to the other two.

The sweat lodge

The sauna is not just the preserve of the sports and fitness centre. It is a means of bathing that stretches back through time to our ancient history. As far as can be discovered the sauna first came to Britain with the Saxons, although it may have been here earlier than that.

The simplest sauna for our purposes is the sweat lodge of the native American. More than just a place of bathing, the sweat lodge was a place of spiritual rebirth, a necessary preparation in the ritual of tribal ceremony.

It is easy to build and use a sweat lodge, and it provides an excellent means of bathing in wilderness areas where the water contains dangerous parasites which prevent bathing and swimming. As with any sauna you should be fit and healthy; claustrophobia, asthma and heart conditions do not mix with a sweat lodge. Drink plenty of water before you enter!

Inside the lodge one person should direct proceedings, guiding people in and out safely. Water is gently poured on to the rocks, producing copious amounts of hot steam. In no time you will be clean.

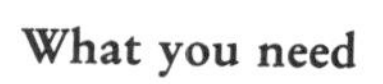

What you need

Twelve saplings about 2.5 cm (1 in) thick and 2.5–3 m (8–10 ft) long, plus steam-proof covering: tent fly-sheets, blankets, towels, polythene bags, etc.

Rocks: say, ten, at least grapefruit size (capable of withstanding heating). Volcanic rock and sandstones are good. Avoid damp rocks, flint and concrete – they may explode when heated

Two or three large containers or buckets: fill one with cold water in case of accidents; use the other two to pour heated water on the rocks

A ladle or dipper to pour the water

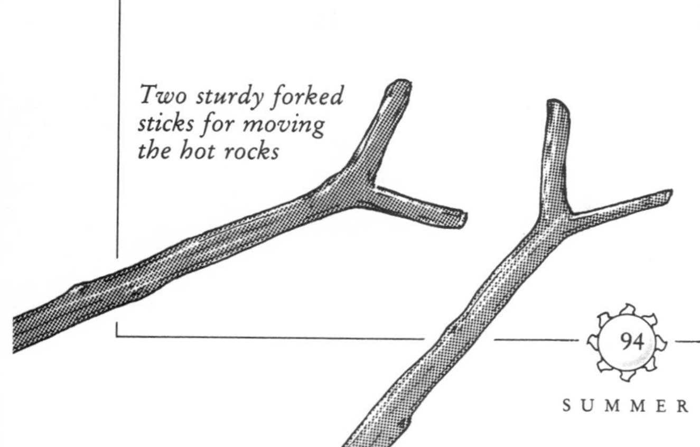

Two sturdy forked sticks for moving the hot rocks

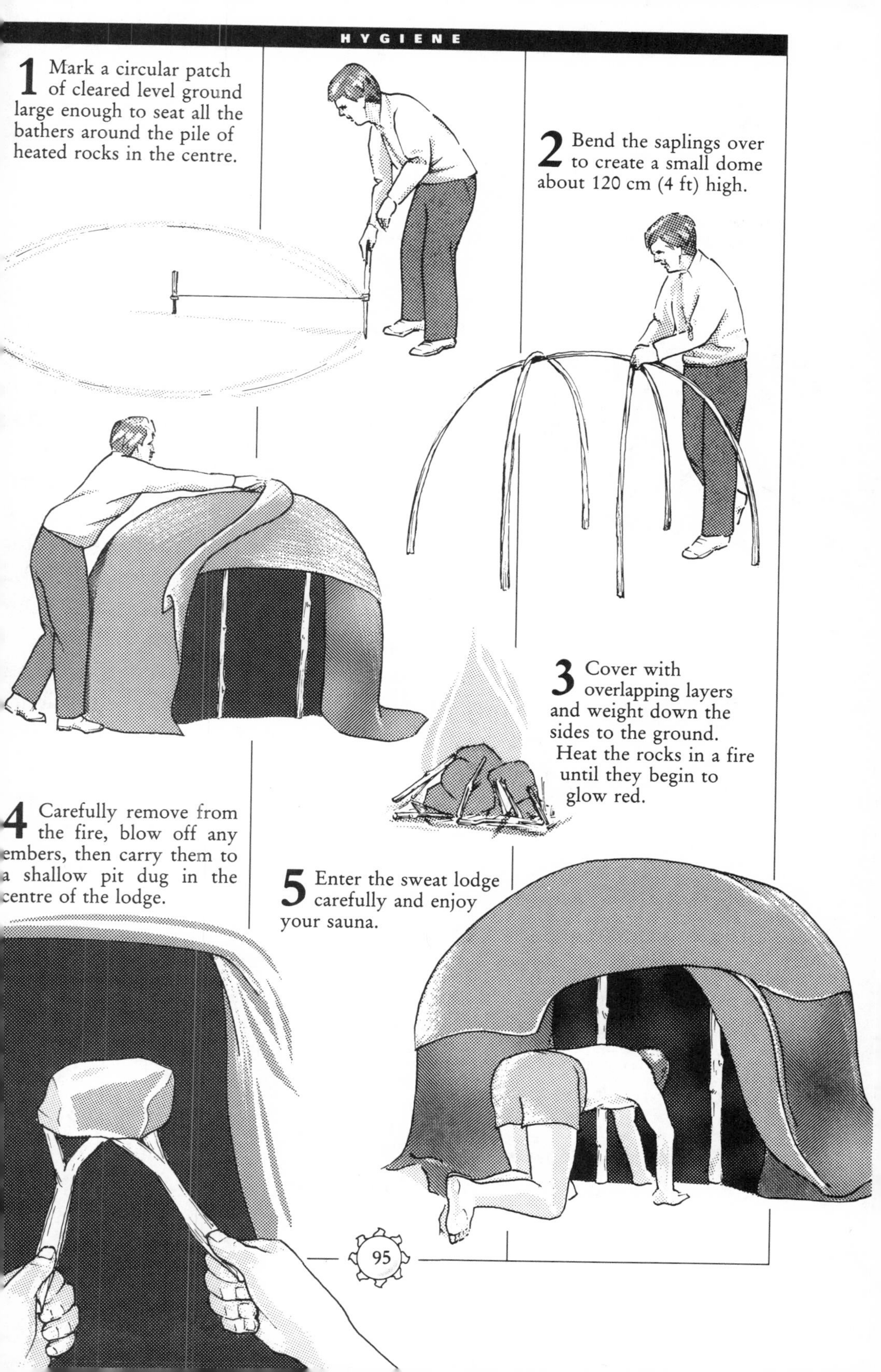

1 Mark a circular patch of cleared level ground large enough to seat all the bathers around the pile of heated rocks in the centre.

2 Bend the saplings over to create a small dome about 120 cm (4 ft) high.

3 Cover with overlapping layers and weight down the sides to the ground. Heat the rocks in a fire until they begin to glow red.

4 Carefully remove from the fire, blow off any embers, then carry them to a shallow pit dug in the centre of the lodge.

5 Enter the sweat lodge carefully and enjoy your sauna.

Senses

We human beings are gifted with excellent sensory abilities, which for the most part we take for granted or deride in comparison to the sharper faculties of other animals. True, we may not have the nose of a bloodhound, but we make up for that in other ways – notably in our ability to reason. But human rationality would be useless if we could not gather enough information to reason with. Today, while our bodies are still well adapted for life in the bush, our senses have become blunted by modern life. Our hearing is bombarded with the noise of traffic, jackhammers, and telephones. Our sight is dazzled with TV screens and neon advertisements in bold primary colours. Our taste buds are numbed with preservatives and artificial flavourings, our sense of smell stifled with deodorants and exhaust fumes. This is a far cry from the subtleties of outdoors sensitivity where the gentle sound of a branch brushing against fur or the halftone of a woodland colour gives away the presence of a forest creature, where the taste of a plant betrays its potential and the scent of a fungus helps you identify it.

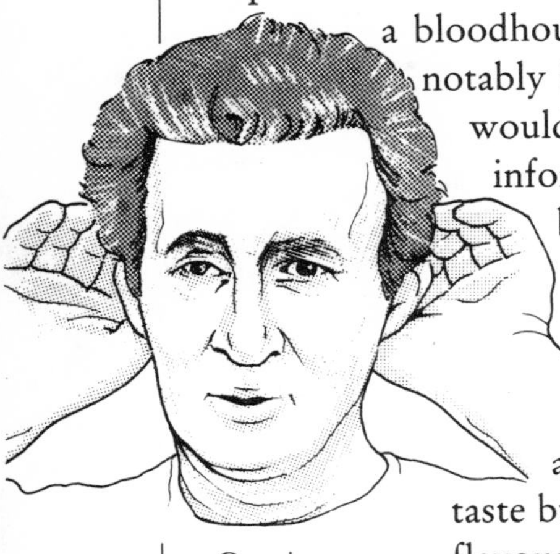

Cupping your hands behind your ears greatly amplifies your hearing

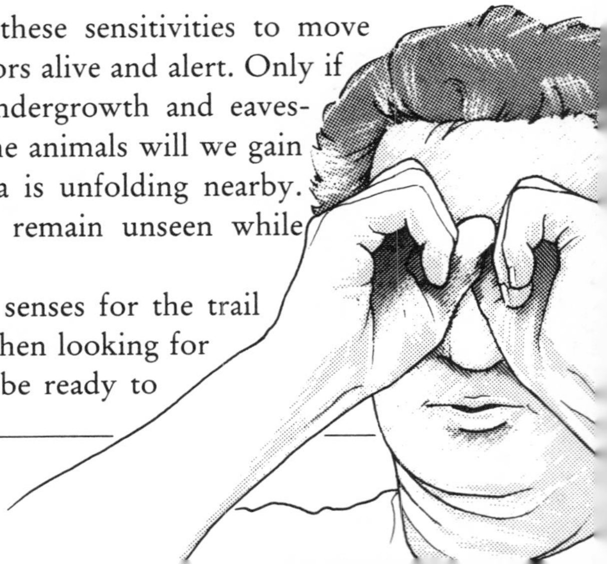

Looking through your hands in poor light helps to reduce image contrast

We need to rehone these sensitivities to move again through the outdoors alive and alert. Only if we can peer through undergrowth and eaves-drop on the chatter of the animals will we gain a clue as to what drama is unfolding nearby. And we must learn to remain unseen while seeing.

Our most important senses for the trail are hearing and sight. When looking for wild creatures we must be ready to act upon any information which presents itself. With most wild creatures expertly camouflaged and highly alert, we are unlikely to spot them unless they are moving. If we master the art of a silent approach we may be lucky enough to spot them in the open, but it is far more likely that we shall hear them first. In fact, a good habit is from time to time to stop, be absolutely silent and scan ahead with your hearing. You can greatly amplify your power of hearing by cupping your hands behind your ears like radar dishes. This will also help you determine accurately the direction and distance of the sounds you detect. Once you have detected a sound, then try to spot the movement.

Your sense of smell is important for identifying fungi and plants

Another good habit is to emulate the wary deer or rabbit by using your peripheral vision. This means using all-round sight, focusing on the whole of your field of vision rather than any one part of it. In this way you can more readily detect movement near or far – and then focus in on it.

Your sense of taste protects you from eating bad or poisonous foods

In poor light it helps to look slightly to one side of the object to make better use of the eye cells used for gathering light in poor conditions. Also, you can make your hands into tubes to look through; unlikely as it may seem, this reduces overall contrast, enabling you to concentrate your attention on the subject more effectively.

There are a variety of other tricks of awareness, but the real secret is to constantly practise being more alert. This way, it will in time become second nature to you – a natural alertness that requires no extra concentration. Learning to track animals and searching for wild mushrooms are the two best ways I know of practising awareness skills.

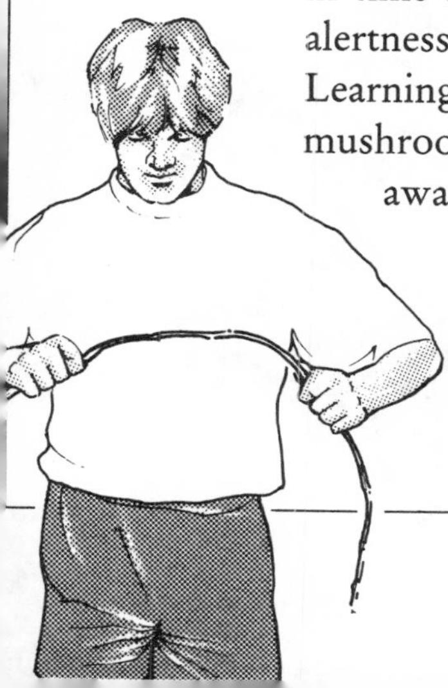

You can judge the potential of a piece of wood by feeling the strength of the fibres

Seeing more

You can greatly improve your understanding of wild creatures by using a pair of binoculars. These enable you to watch from a discreet distance as animals go about their lives totally unaware of your presence. It's an experience not to be missed, but you will need a pair of binoculars well matched to this type of activity.

The parts of a binocular

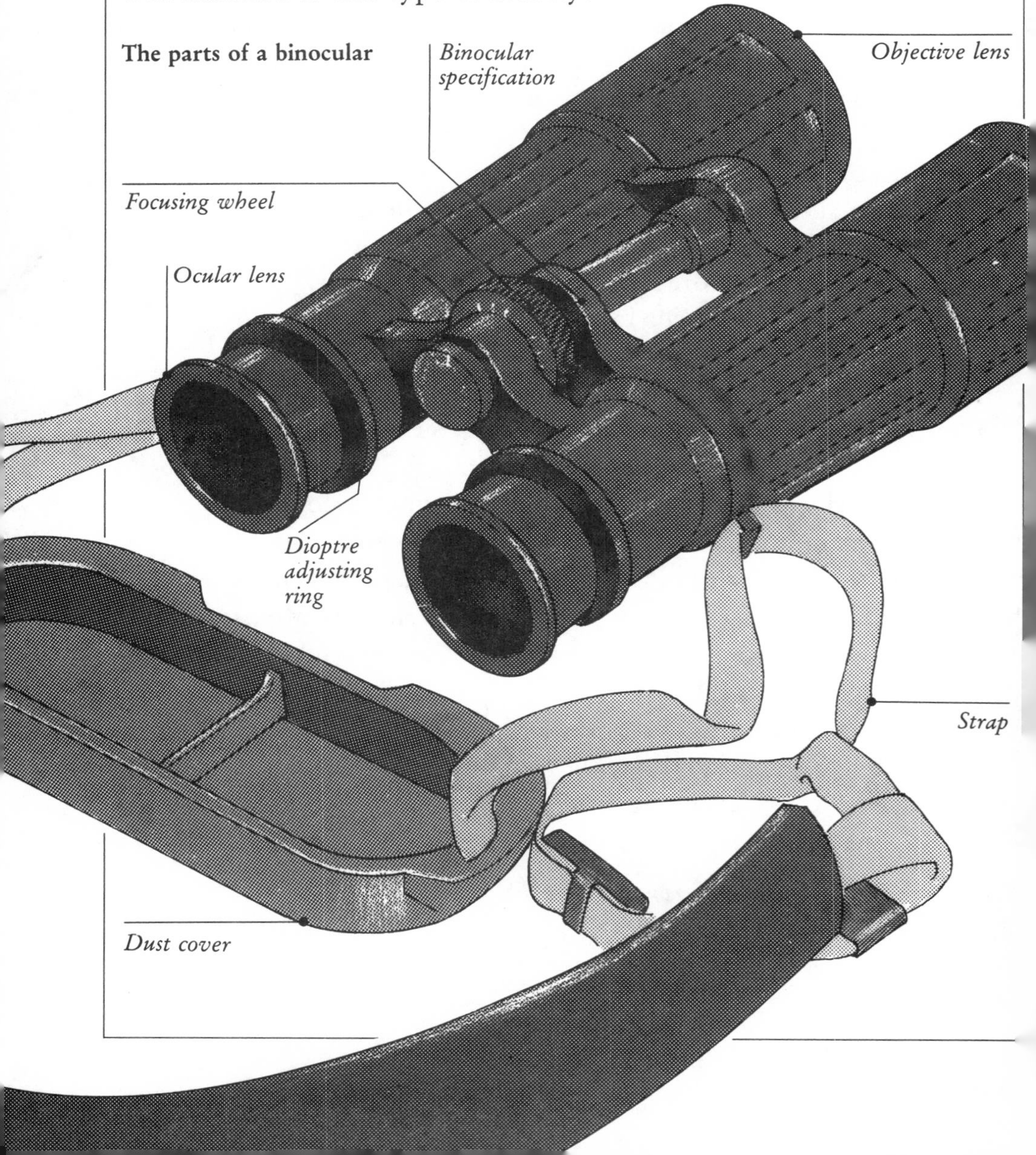

Choosing your binoculars

Light

The best opportunities for observing mammals occur at dawn or after sunset, so binoculars with good poor-light characteristics are best. This means a pair with an exit pupil of between 5–7 mm (1/5–1/4 in), which will closely match the human pupil in poor light.

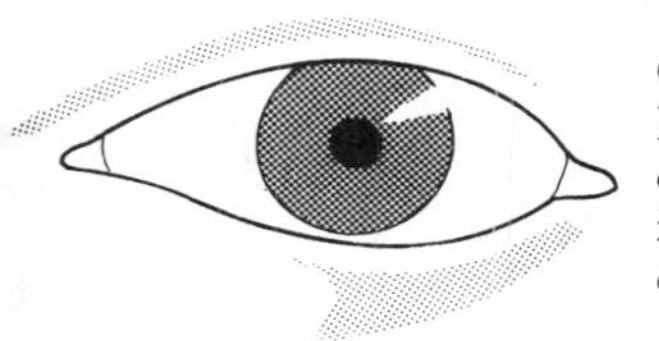

Good light
In good light the pupil contracts, focusing the image upon the eye's rod cells.

Poor light
In poor light the pupil dilates, allowing the image to be focused upon the cone cells.

Exit pupil
Exit pupil = size (diameter) of image as it leaves the ocular lens. Calculated by dividing objective lens size by magnification.

Magnification

With greater magnification, depth of field is shorter and it's harder to hold the binoculars steady. For hand-held field use, magnification should be no greater than ten times.

Size and cost

Small size and low weight will ensure you have the binoculars with you when you most need them. Top-quality binoculars are expensive because of the coatings used on the lenses, but a cheaper pair are better than nothing.

Comparing models

Carl Zeiss make an excellent range of popular natural-history binoculars:

8 × 56
Optically, probably the best binoculars for watching wildlife. Good magnification for bird-watching and best night performance. Size and bulk make this model cumbersome, best suitable to static observations from hides.

7 × 42
Ideally compact, with superb night performance, a wide field of view and close focusing – perfect for watching animals on the move, in bad light or in remote places. Again the magnification is slightly less than ideal for bird-watching although it remains popular with ornithologists as you can pick out birds on the wing more quickly.

10 × 40
Bird-watchers' favourite; compact, with good magnification, especially useful for identification by body markings. Small exit pupil means poorer night performance, and 10 × magnification makes holding steady difficult.

8 × 30
Pocket binoculars – excellent when space and weight are at a premium. Good magnification for navigation and climbing. Small exit pupil means not suitable for poor light.

Setting up

To get the most out of your binoculars, they need to be correctly adjusted to the width between your eyes and to your eyesight itself. All good binoculars allow you to make suitable adjustments.

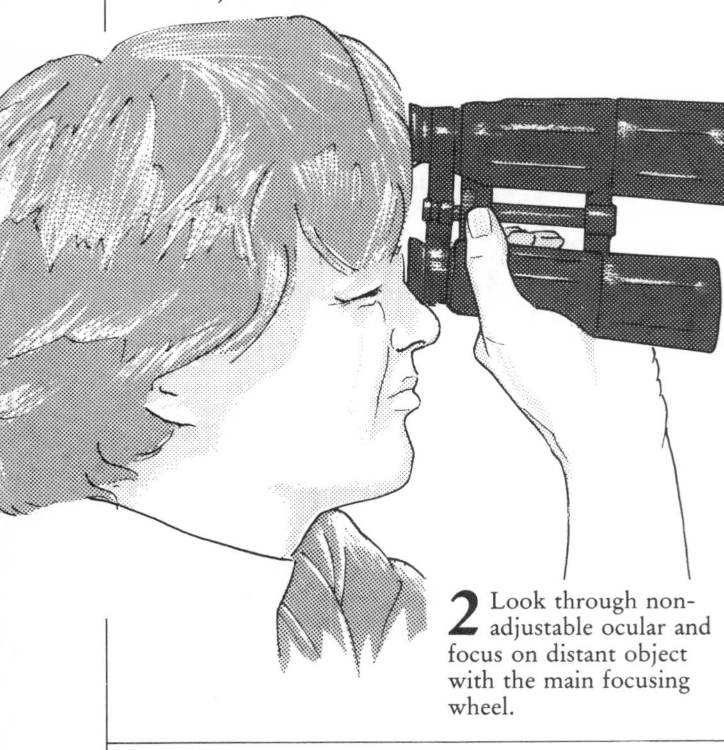

2 Look through non-adjustable ocular and focus on distant object with the main focusing wheel.

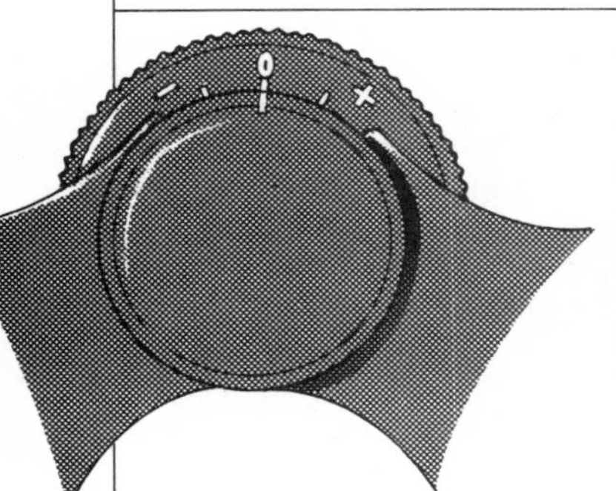

Night viewing

You will discover your binoculars' optimum point of focus – more or less the infinity setting. Set them permanently to this point at night when focusing becomes difficult.

1 Open or close binoculars on hinge until ocular lenses are perfectly aligned with your eyes.

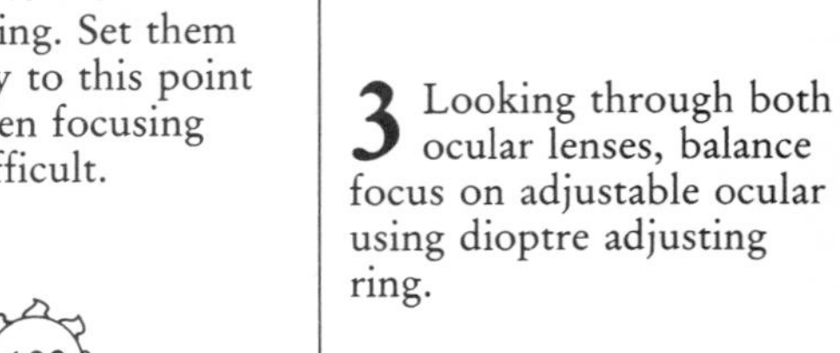

3 Looking through both ocular lenses, balance focus on adjustable ocular using dioptre adjusting ring.

Using your binoculars

Practise focusing so that you can adjust correctly if your subject moves towards or away from you. Practise finding quickly with the binoculars what you were looking at with your eyes; use a reference point to guide you to the subject.

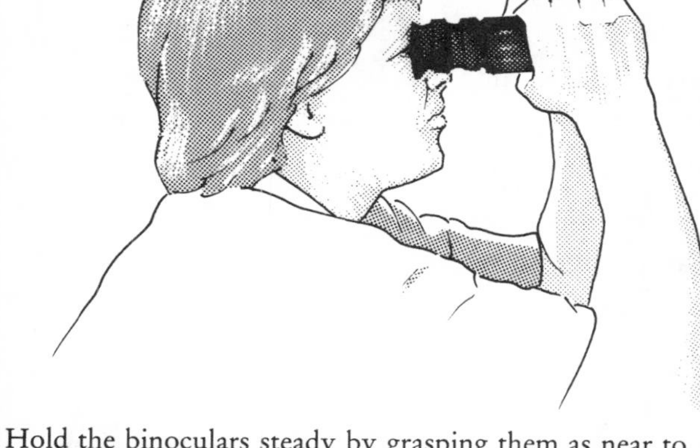

Hold the binoculars steady by grasping them as near to the objective lens as possible.

When sitting, steady your hands by resting your elbows on your knees, triangulating your posture.

Whenever possible, steady yourself by leaning against a tree or similar steady object. Hold the binoculars against this firm support for maximum steadiness.

Finding wild animals

We have learned the skills of observation; we have equipped ourselves to see more. Now where do we look and when?

Whenever you walk in the outdoors you can be certain of one thing: you are being watched. Voles along the trail-side watch in stillness as your silhouette passes by. Pigeons in the tree-tops will flee at the first sign of your movement below, while wrens and great tits will challenge your right to be in their territory. To find wild creatures you need first to reduce the commotion caused by your presence. If you watch a fox hunting you will see that at some times of day he does not pay any attention to the mobbing attacks and alarm calls of the other animals; but everything changes as he starts to hunt, slipping silently into the local cover, purposeful, alert and stealthy.

The best time to observe most animals, especially the larger mammals, is during the early morning and early evening, the main feeding times. This is a good reason for choosing binoculars with good poor-light performance.

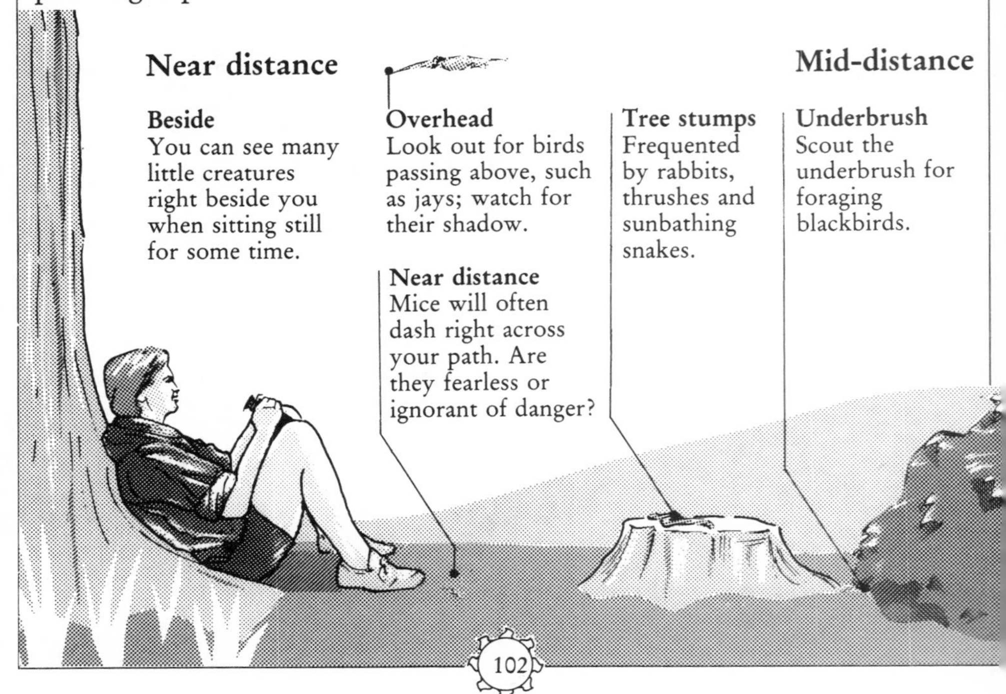

To prepare for successful animal watching, first of all wear drab colours – not necessarily camouflage, just drab mute colours that will blend in with the surrounds. Second, reduce your body scent as much as possible; don't wear antiperspirants or other smelly products. Old country poachers would have their special outing jacket hanging in an outbuilding away from cooking smells so that it picked up only the countryside scents.

Before you start, be relaxed. I usually sit down for a few minutes and just absorb the tempo of natural sounds before moving into the area I have chosen for my observation. Now, moving slowly and quietly alert as a hunting fox, you can slip through the cover in search of a siting. Many of the best observations come from sitting and watching, but you should not rule out moving observations, approaching to very close quarter.

You need especially to concentrate on where to look. In the modern environment we are conditioned to look in certain directions, for example for road information signs, and we know that a wall cannot be looked through so we do not bother with it. In the outdoors things are very different; learn to scan different places and to look through the wall of vegetation as if it were a lace curtain. Constantly vary your focus from near to far distance.

Basketry

The first basket carried in the hands of our hunter-gatherer ancestors was perhaps a bird's nest full of eggs (who knows?). But basketry was certainly an important skill of nearly all native peoples – a craft which allowed for a multitude of functions and designs and allowed endless self-expression. Today we may buy a basket as a place to collect dirty laundry in the corner of our bathroom, but we hardly notice the great endurance of these containers; and only children feel the thrill of the satisfying creaking sound they make! Yet to anyone who has made a basket that sound is a voice, and the basket's warp and weft tell the story of its manufacture; from the pruning of the wands from the pollard, and their debarking, to the strong, sensitive hands of the weaver bending nature to his or her will to complete the basket for use.

Basketry is a skill you should not pass by. It will enable you to manufacture all manner of useful items; some may be only quickly and crudely made, others may be works of art to be cherished for years to come. Basketry also teaches patience and gives new value to the natural materials surrounding us.

Water carrier used by desert peoples

Simple basket container

Uses for baskets are many and varied, limited only by our creativity

Basketry rain-hat

Gathering basketry materials

Divide your labour between gathering and basket-making as two separate tasks. (Leave the actual basket-weaving for rainy days or for evening entertainment.) As you gather your materials, you may make interesting new discoveries as the search for fibres draws you off the beaten paths. When gathering, try to take the most plentiful local materials, not the rare or sparser resources.

Pick a lazy summer day. Take your knife, a bandanna full of sandwiches and a refreshing canteen of water, and go foraging for your basketry materials. Take your time! There is almost no limit to what you can select; anything fibrous and flexible, from grasses to twigs and wands, will do. Gather always by pruning – that is, cut so that the providing plant can regrow. As always, gather widely; never denude just one area. As your pile of accumulated materials grows, spread it out in the sunlight to dry.

When you have gathered what you will need, bundle it up. Lots of small bundles are better than one large bundle; they dry better, reducing the risk of the material becoming mouldy, and can be more conveniently handled when you start to make the basket. As a rule, basketry materials need to be thoroughly dried before use. If you weave with green materials the basket will become loose through shrinkage when the materials dry. Green basketry materials are best dried on trays or slatted shelves in an atmosphere that is free from damp. Airing cupboards, dry cellars and outhouses are good places. In general, fibres collected in summertime will be ready for use by the late autumn. Don't be tempted to accelerate the drying process artificially, or your materials will become too brittle. If the fibres are stiff when you come to work with them, soak them briefly in a basin of water to moisten them again for flexibility in manufacture. This will reduce the risk of shrinkage.

Basketry materials, once gathered, can be surprisingly heavy

Coiling

Coiling is the first basketry technique to learn – simple to carry out, less fiddly than other methods and just as useful. It is particularly good for producing strong basketry from weaker materials such as grasses and rushes and can be woven so tightly as to be virtually watertight. Coiled baskets are ideal for containing food materials such as seeds and flours and can be woven to almost any size. As with all the basketry techniques featured, there are many alternative techniques to the basic ones portrayed here.

What you will need

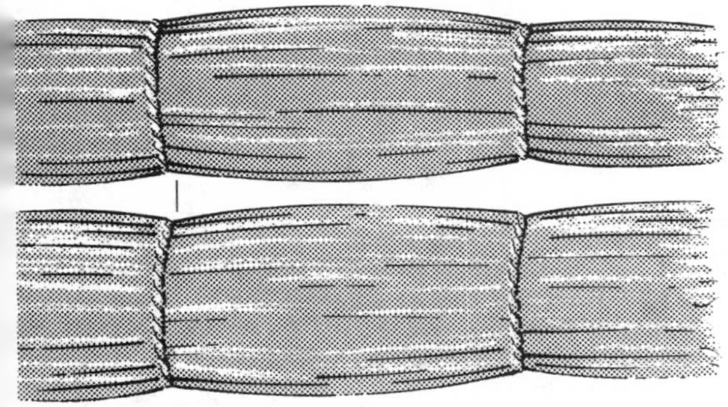

A strip of, say, willow or lime bark, made flexible by dampening, for the weft

Dried grasses for use as the warp

An awl, easily improvised from a bone

Your knife

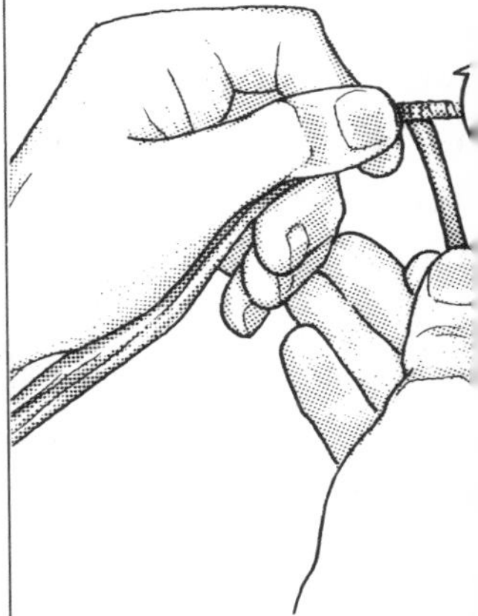

1 Hold a small bundle of warp fibres so they gradually taper to a point. Starting at the point, wrap with the weft strip for about 8 cm (3 in).

2 Start to coil up the tapered warp. Occasionally tuck the weft through the previous turn to hold the coils together as shown – the basic principle of coiled basketry.

Frequency and tightness of the weft will determine the properties of the finished basket.

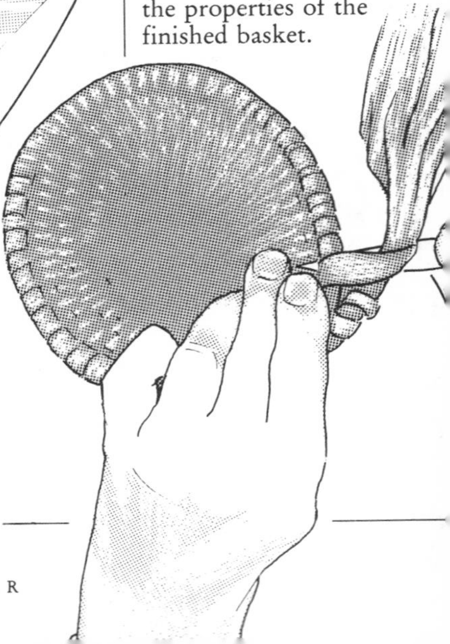

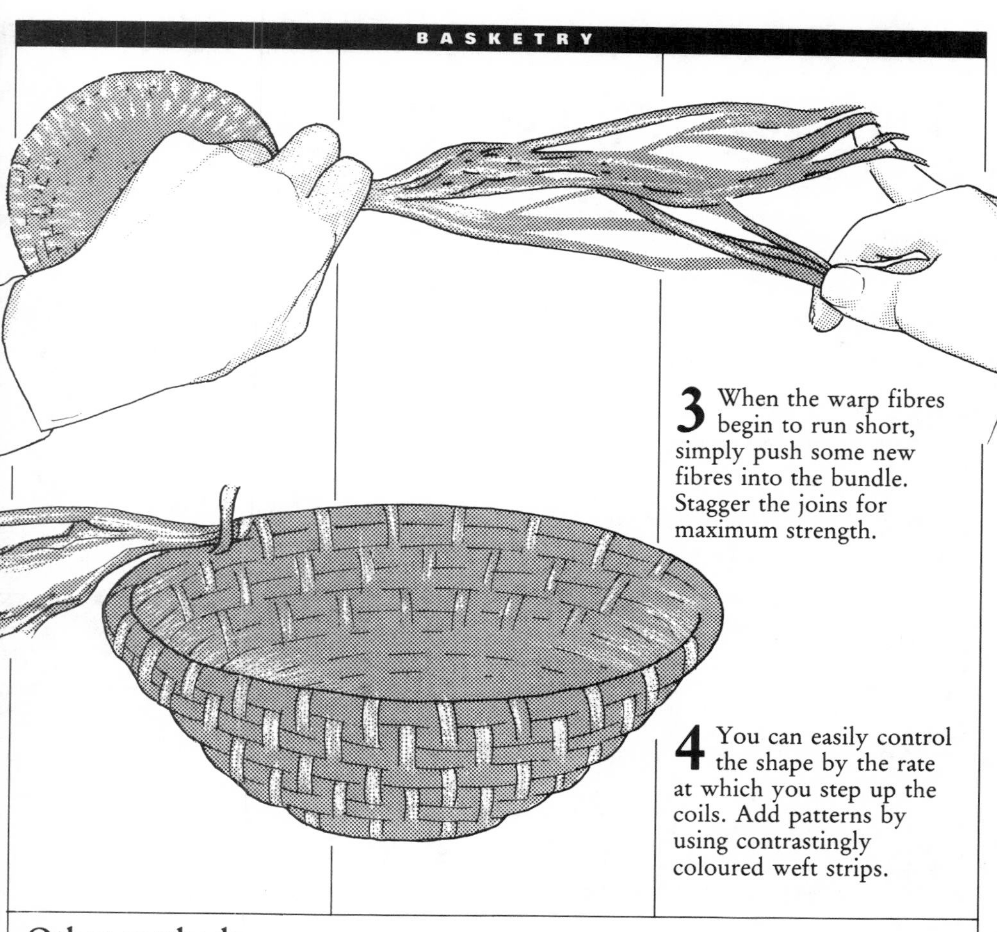

3 When the warp fibres begin to run short, simply push some new fibres into the bundle. Stagger the joins for maximum strength.

4 You can easily control the shape by the rate at which you step up the coils. Add patterns by using contrastingly coloured weft strips.

Other methods

The way the weft stitches are made and the coils are laid together will determine the quality of the finished product. Try some experiments using these alternative methods.

Stitching

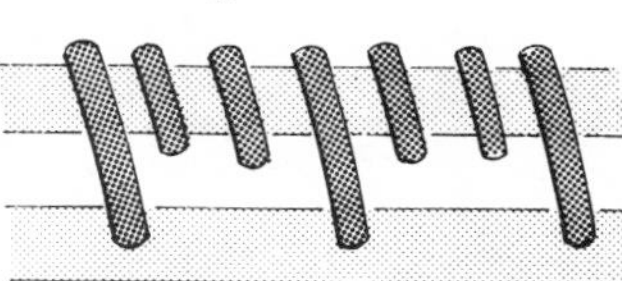

Quick stitch strong enough for general use

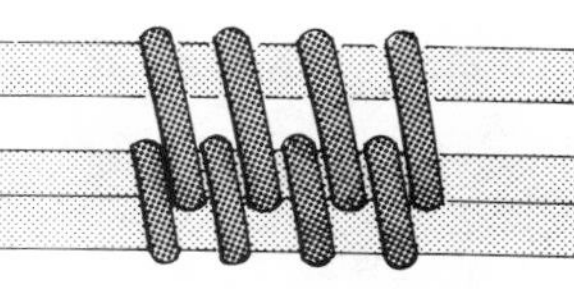

Slower (needs more stitches), but tighter, stronger and longer lasting

Coil construction

Some ways to make the stitch around the warp bundles

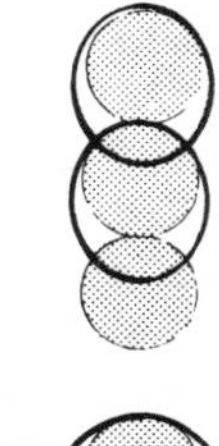

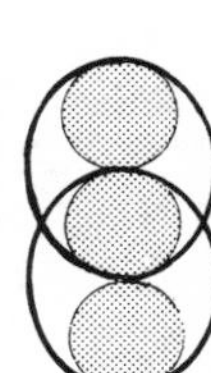

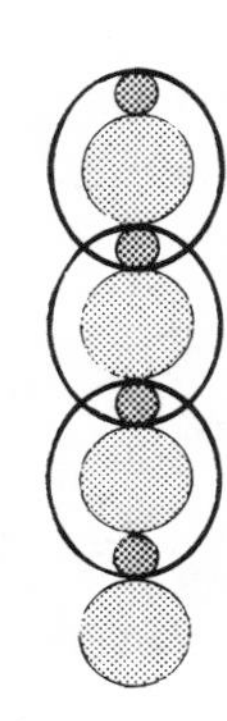

Plaiting and twining

Plaited basketry is the simplest weave that can be employed, where the weft follows a simple under-and-over route through the warps. Twined baskets are generally stronger and more tightly woven. They are slightly more complicated in that they employ two wefts which pass either side of the warps, twisting to exchange sides between each warp. Both techniques are versatile, allowing for many variations.

Plaiting

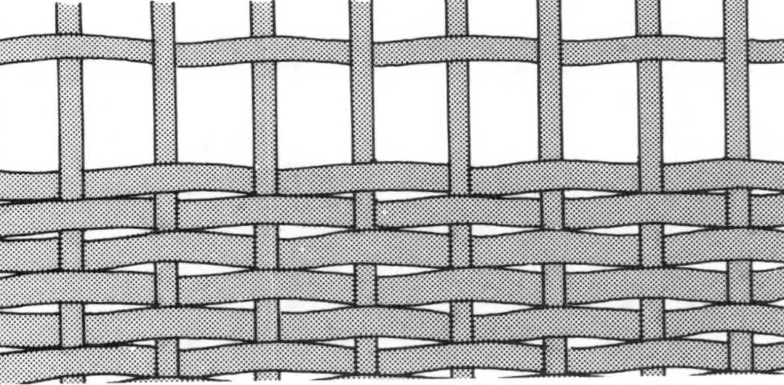

Simple under-and-over weave can be difficult to keep tight but gives a smooth finish

Twining

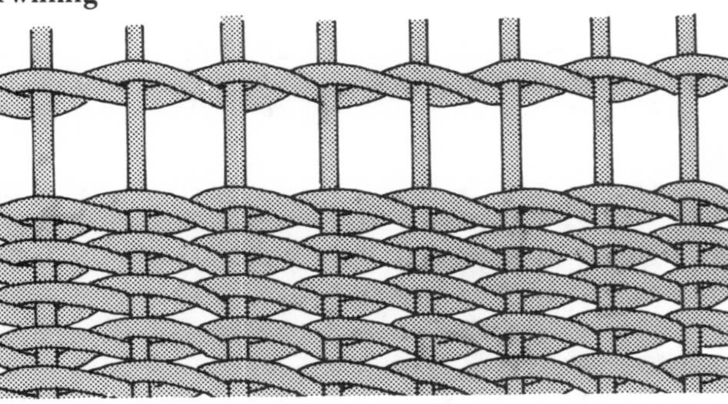

Wefts pass either side of the warps and cross between them, ensuring a tight strong weave

Starting

There are many different ways to start twining – here are two methods.

Method A

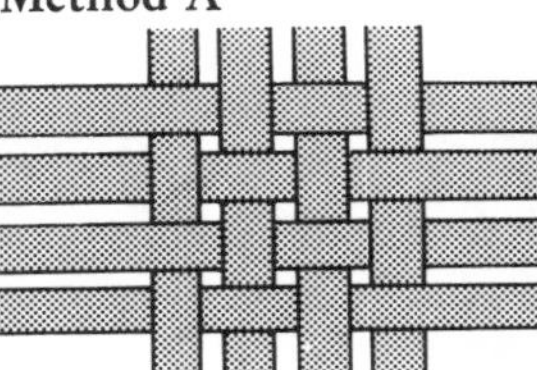

1 Plait warps where they cross, a good method with flat weaving materials.

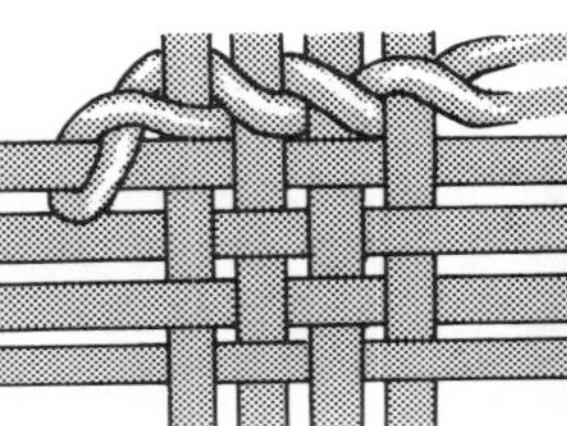

2 Start weft by folding in half; twine it between warps; warps will spread out as basket grows.

Method B

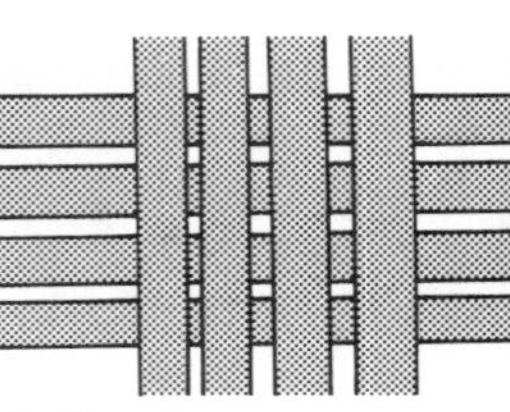

1 Simply cross warps across each other.

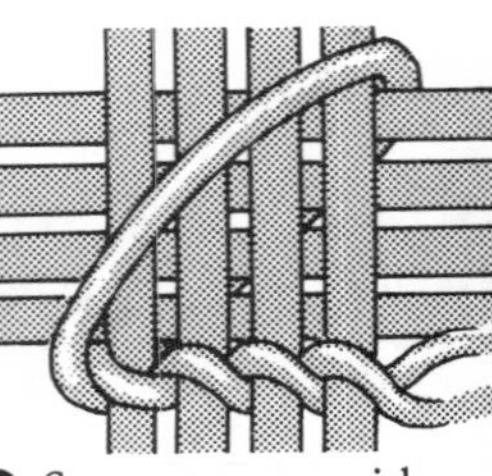

2 Secure warps with initial diagonal turn of weft, which once again is doubled.

Adding weft

1 As basket grows, weft will run short. Lay new length of weft alongside old while still long enough to effect a binding, join and keep going.

2 Join should vanish into weave. Stagger joins and maintain even diameter of weft.

Adding warps

As basket grows, warps tend to spread out, requiring wider weft stitches or new warps. Adding warps is easy: push them into the weave and carry on, incorporating them as you weave.

Finishing off

The simplest way to finish off is to bend warps over last weft and plait them into the weave; try to interconnect each warp with its neighbour.

Basketry projects

Once you start to get a feel for the warp and weft of basketry there will be no limit to the possibilities open to you. The following are basketry projects commonly employed by native peoples from different parts of the world. The water bottle was used by desert peoples in North America, tightly woven by coiling or twining and waterproofed with pine resin. Coming in a wide variety of sizes, these had to be strong and shaped for maximum water retention. The European mushroom basket is still commonly sold. The honey-gathering basket from Cameroon is quickly made and used for lowering honey from the trees. The dilly bag was the standard gathering basket of the Australian Aborigine.

Water bottle

Classic bottle shape: narrow neck prevents accidental spilling and reduces evaporation of contents. Two carrying handles incorporated in original weave.

Melted pine resin to waterproof the bottle is added every few inches during weaving.

Simple baskets
Simple baskets, made by whatever technique, are used extensively in the preparation of wild foods, particularly seeds and nuts.

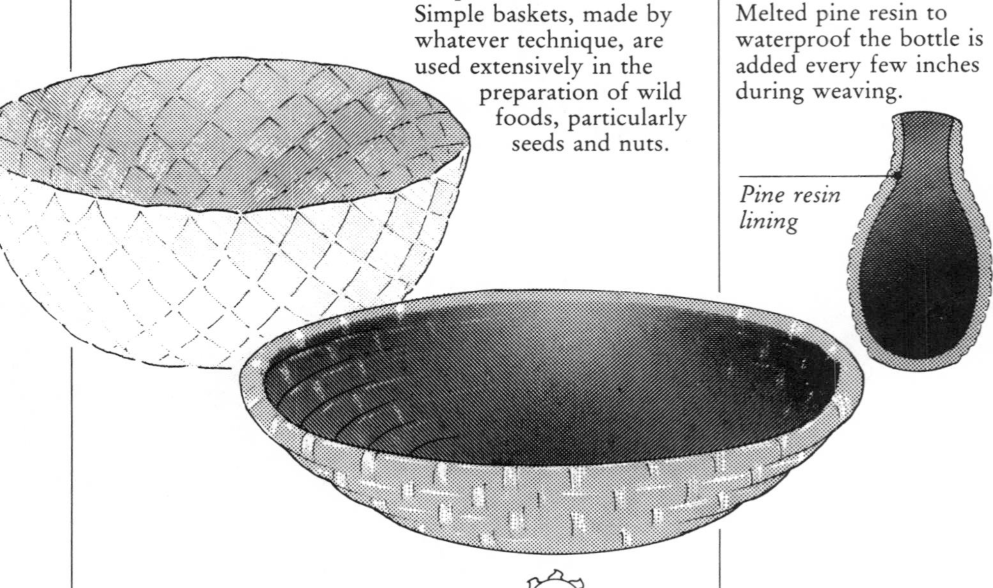

Honey-gathering basket
With a simple frame quickly lashed together and laced with natural cordage, the body of the basket is made of large leaves.

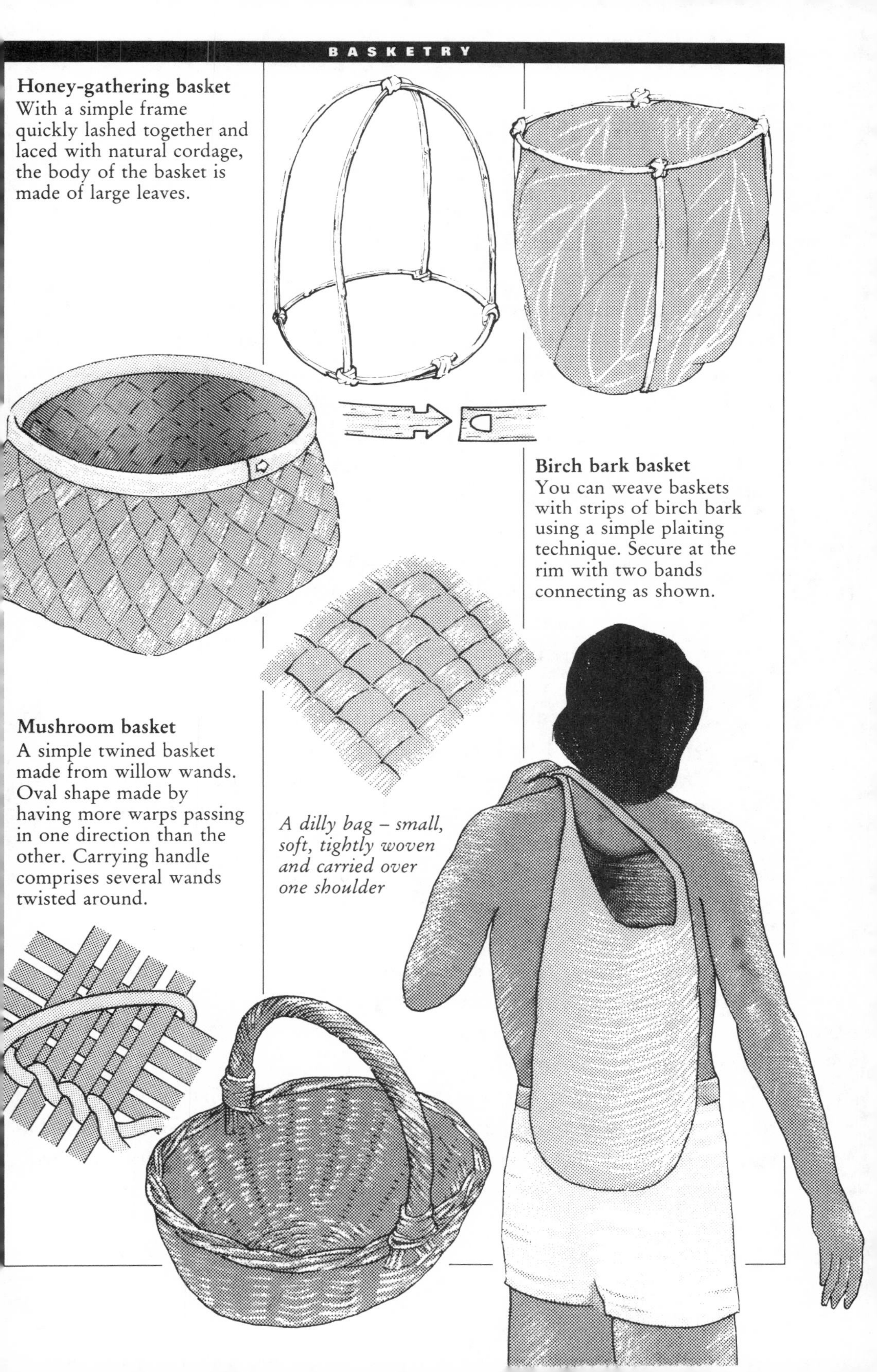

Birch bark basket
You can weave baskets with strips of birch bark using a simple plaiting technique. Secure at the rim with two bands connecting as shown.

Mushroom basket
A simple twined basket made from willow wands. Oval shape made by having more warps passing in one direction than the other. Carrying handle comprises several wands twisted around.

A dilly bag – small, soft, tightly woven and carried over one shoulder

Pottery

Reach into the ground, pull our some clay, shape it with your hands and water, then harden it with fire: an elemental experience! The process was perhaps discovered when someone noticed how hard the ground became beneath a ceremonial fire. We cannot say, but we know that today's superfine pottery descends directly from an ancient ancestry. Making pots in fun, therapeutic and a useful practical skill – the more so if you have gathered the clay from the ground yourself.

Take a stroll around your local museum and you will almost certainly come across exhibits of primitive pottery. This is probably your best starting place, for you will see many shapes and pot finishes as well as clay colours that will help build your confidence and understanding. You should also be able to discover the whereabouts of the best local clay.

Another avenue worth exploring is pottery evening classes. Here the clay you will be working with will be ideal – commercially prepared and a far cry from the clay you pull from the ground. It will educate your hands to the task and techniques of the potter's art.

Digging clay from the ground is an elemental activity

The hardest part of pottery under primitive conditions is the firing. Be prepared for disasters while you are learning, as it is not easy to learn how to control the firing conditions without a kiln. If possible, team up with some friends so that you can produce a quantity of pots for firing and can all share in the labour.

Finding and preparing clay

Clay is a very common material most easily found in the steep banks of streams of water-eroded ditches. You may find it in a variety of states, from wet and slurry-like, through perfect for pottery, to hard, dry and compacted. Whatever its state it can be made ready for use by simple processes.

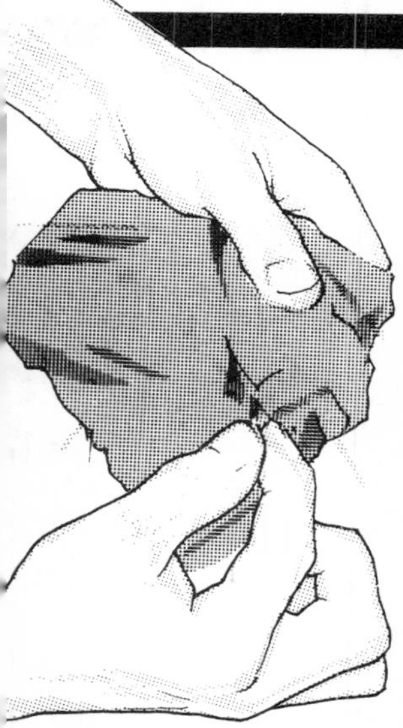

Cleansed of impurities, knead the clay until silky smooth

Wet clay should be dried in the sun. Dry clay needs to be finely crushed and then rehydrated; this is my favourite method, as the clay can be sifted or picked over to remove all impurities. Finely crushed clay is cool and talcum-like to touch; mix in only small quantities of water with plenty of kneading. It is important to remove impurities, which can ruin the workability of your clay and its firing.

Having removed these problems, knead the clay thoroughly, working it steadily until it attains a slightly moist, plastic consistency. To test for this, pinch the clay between your thumb and index finger – good clay will contort to the shape produced without cracking.

Having cleaned your clay, you need to add temper. Made from a wide range of materials, temper serves several purposes: it helps give body to the clay, preventing sagging during manufacture; it helps regulate the shrinkage and expansion of the clay, preventing cracking; and it increases the durability of pots that are to be heated for cooking.

The amount of temper you add depends upon your locally available materials: discover through experimentation. Add the temper directly to the clay and knead it well in. If you are making a pot for use on the fire, add a larger amount of temper. By now your clay should be just right: pliable, plastic and not too willing to crack. Try rolling out some coils and snaking them up; they should not crack.

When ready, the clay can be coiled without cracking

Making temper

You can make temper from sand, ground-up pottery shards ('grog'), burned seashells or many other materials. I use sandstone heated to glowing in a fire, allowed to cool and ground to a fine sandy powder, ranging widely in colours. Whatever temper material you use must not expand or contract greatly when the pot is fired, or cracks will result. So materials which have already been stabilised in fire are best.

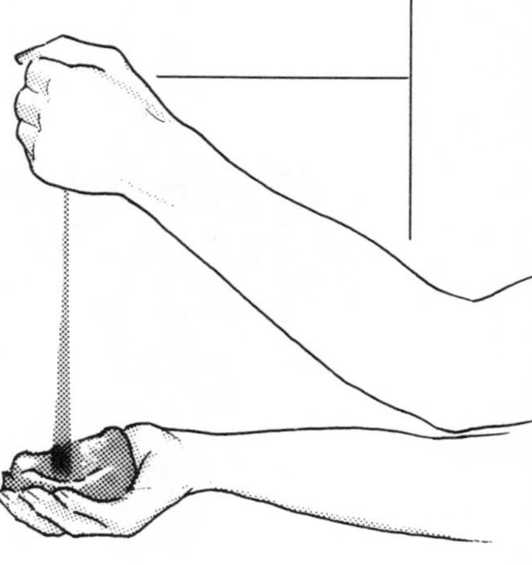

Making a pot

If there is one piece of advice it must be 'have patience', for pottery is a more demanding skill than its outward appearances would suggest. Pottery should not be rushed. Store your prepared clay for use wrapped in a damp cloth to prevent it drying out. Then pick a good day when there is not much else on your mind. There are many ways to make a pot; we shall concentrate upon a combination of the simplest methods of pinching and coiling. These techniques have been used since the dawn of pottery and can produce beautiful and elaborate pots – if the potter is skilled enough. As with any natural material, you need empathy to work with clay. Discover how it responds to your manipulation and how fast it dries out under a variety of conditions – neither can be learned overnight.

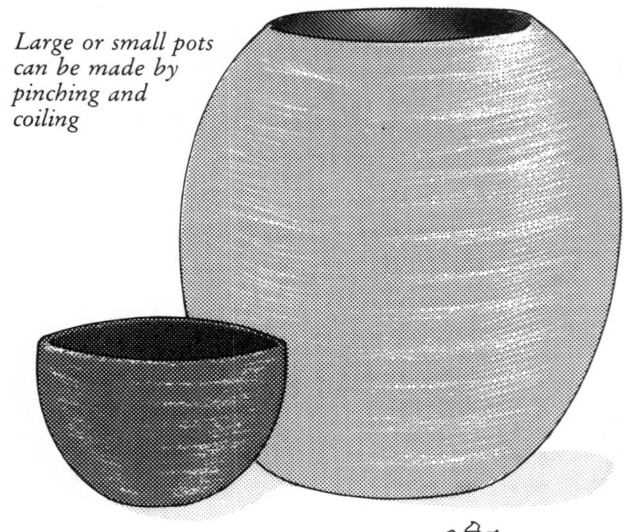

Large or small pots can be made by pinching and coiling

Pinching

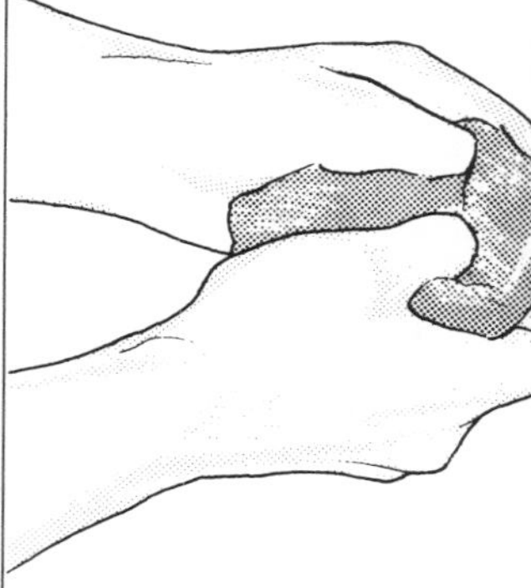

1 Simplest pottery technique: start pinching a depression into a lump of clay, feeling how it responds.

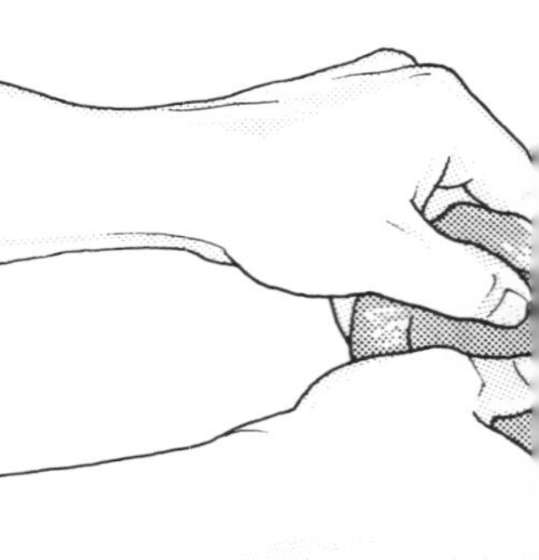

2 Deepen the depression and start drawing the walls upwards with subtle pressure.

3 Continue until you have a cup-shaped piece of clay for the pot base.

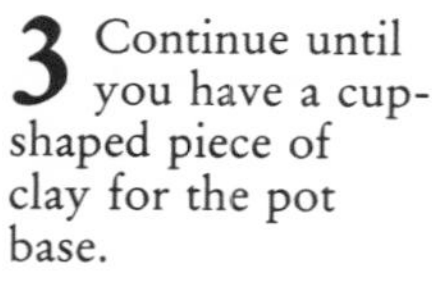

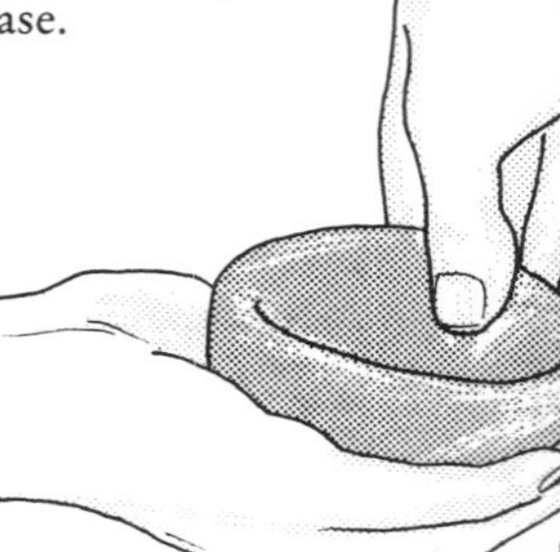

Coiling

4 Take more clay; roll out a coil of about finger thickness – either between your palms or, easier, on a flat surface.

5 Add the coil to the top of your pinched base, ensuring it is seated snugly.

6 Pinch and blend the coil into position – weld it in. Keep adding coils until the pot is the size you want.

Paddling

7 Gently beat the pot over its surface with a small paddle-shaped piece of wood to even it off.

Finishing and firing

Now comes the frustrating part of pottery, for no matter how skilled you are, there will be failures.

The finish you apply to your pot depends to some extent on its intended use. If you are making a cooking pot it is sensible from a hygiene point of view to polish the inside of the pot, and there is little point in ornamenting the exterior.

But for storage vessels pottery can be burnished smooth and designs etched on to the outside (geometric patterns work well). The secret lies in letting the clay dry to a leathery texture before employing the finishing techniques.

A visit to your local museum may provide ideas for designs you can incorporate, as well as many shapes of pot you could make. Once you have had a go at making a pot, you will certainly look more carefully at those crude and often neglected pots in the museum cases.

Native potters all over the world pride themselves on the finishes they achieve. The tools of their trade – polished burnishing stones and special recipes for clay and temper – are often handed down through the family in great secrecy. Such is the pride that they take in their craft.

Leave the finished pot in a shady place to dry out thoroughly before firing. If it dries too quickly, cracks will develop.

Finishing

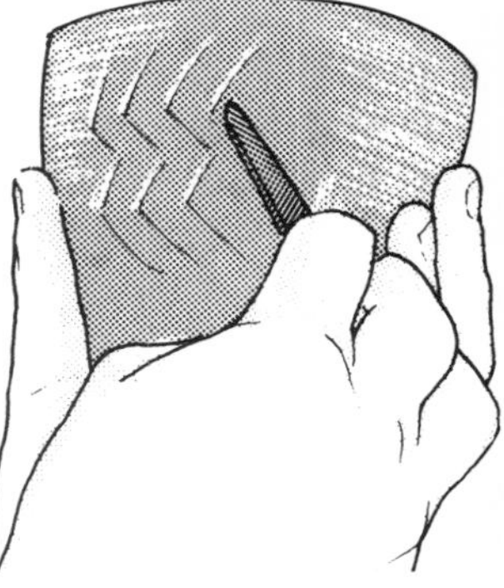

1 Having smoothed the outside of your pot, you can incise a pattern into its surface.

2 Achieve a polished inner surface by burnishing with a glassy smooth pebble.

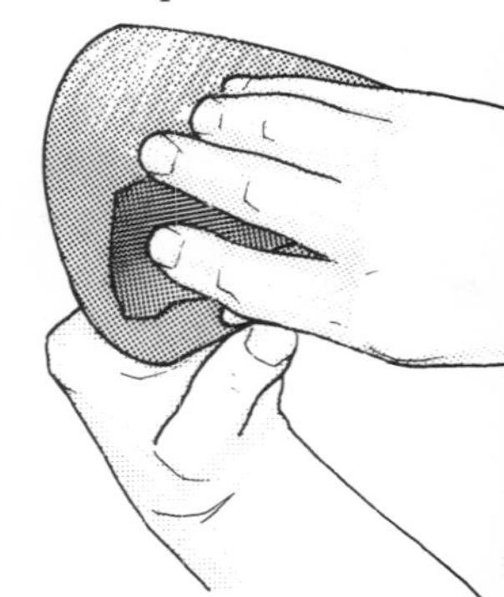

3 You can also burnish the outside of a cooking pot to a polish.

Firing

1 Build a small fire and surround it with the dried pots – warming them through will dispel trapped moisture.

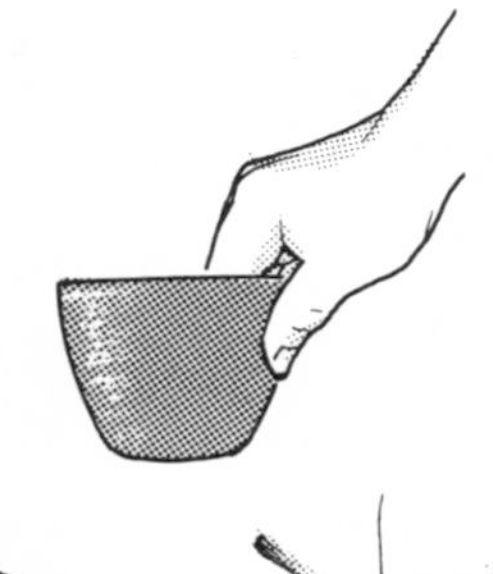

2 With the pots hot but still touchable, scrape the fire into a circle; place pots in the centre to heat to firing stage.

3 Gradually build the fire inwards to cover the pots; build high – don't overburden pots with timber.

4 Let the fire cool naturally at its own pace to reveal the fired pots.

Using a pot

For a pot to be used over fire you need a high temper-to-clay ratio. Burnish the inside smooth. Support round-bottomed pots over a fire on three rocks. Never put a hot pot into cold water or fill it with cold water, or it will crack – that's all there is to it! A well-made pot will last for several seasons if carefully stored.

The pursuit of food

For our ancestors foraging from the land for their food, summer wa: a time of changes. As the season starts off there is a lull between sprin; foods and summer foods without any great delicacies to look forwar(to. But, with standby plants such as nettles and an abundance of game there is no real shortage. As the sun does its work on leaves an(flowers, the ripening comes fast; and evening thunder-storms hel; swell the succulent fruits. Our need for food eases, and soon the ful harvest will be upon us!

The magic of summer food-gathering is its social aspect. This is season for sharing and celebration – a season especially for children t(search out the hedgerow fruits. At this time of year I often recall m; own childhood and cannot help wondering whether or not natur intentionally places the juiciest berries just out of arm's reach as a incentive for children to grow taller. Where better to start a child' interest in natural history than at the bramble patch in summer?

Summer is for me a season of aesthetics, time to unpack the picni hamper – listen to it creak with anticipation of an outing Plastic cool-boxes and paper cups have far less appeal tha the traditional picnic hamper. Every family should b equipped with one – nothing less than a willow basket wit leather straps will do. You might even consider making you own, adapting the basketry techniques described elsewher in the book.

There is a necessary ritual with the picnic basket First, the eating utensils should be packed: n(plastic here, but glass and silverware and crisp white linen tablecloth. For wine ther really is only one choice: a good English win bursting with the flavour of summer fruits, o perhaps a home-made wine. Real lemonade fo refreshment. Now for the sandwiches and salad. Her is where you can use the seasonal delicacies themselves, salad plant

Spearing fish was once probably a common sight on our river-banks

and flavourings cunningly added to the dishes.

The very nature of summer weather also lends itself to sitting by the brook fishing and to preserving our catch by drying or smoking. If we were relying upon the wild land to feed us we would have to use the daylight well in setting aside stores of the harvest goodies in preparation for the coming lean times.

If you listen carefully to the sounds in the wild during the later part of the summer, you can sense the bustle and excitement everywhere, especially among the birds. Families of magpies pick the grass for grubs; and the hobby swoops to within inches of the oaks' canopy to pick a moth out of the sky and eat it on the wing.

Solo travel is relatively easy at this time of year, because the long summer evenings allow plenty of time to search for food at the day's end. The summer flowers will help you identify edible plants from field guides (learn to recognise their characteristics without the flowers too).

You forage best when you know the territory well – regular walking reinforces the memory of where edible plants are located and when they will be ready for harvesting. Over the course of several seasons in one area, you will learn the effects of your simple 'management' practices as you scatter seeds to replace the roots you gather. Bear in mind, however, that you share your food resources with other creatures; it is better for them if you gather lightly and widely rather than heavily in a confined area.

Families still gather berries today as they always have

Fishing

Sadly our rivers today are dirty, poisoned and barren, not a patch on the fountains of life they once were. Over the last century, the steady rise in industry has been paralleled by a dramatic decline in many forms of river life.

Many of our rivers and other waterways are now too polluted by industrial effluents to support the number and variety of fish that once made their homes there. Increasingly, both sea and river fish are reared in the aquatic equivalent of factory farms and every year sees a reduction in the number of wild fish in our streams, lakes, rivers and oceans.

Town and city dwellers are distanced from their local rivers; on the fishmonger's marble slab and at the supermarket counter they can buy different varieties of fish that have been imported from all over the world. But nothing can beat the taste of a 'dead fresh' herring, cooked within hours of being caught, or the summertime flavour of that king of fish, the salmon.

We no longer celebrate the return of the salmon now that our rivers flow with waste being flushed away. Yet every year these masters of the wet world are driven to meet their destiny, guided by senses of direction we can only marvel at.

Simple thorns were the earliest fish-hooks

These fine fish are able to navigate back from the wide expanses of ocean to the shallow gravel-bottomed brooks whence they hatched, exhausting themselves utterly in the drive to fulfil their purpose. Today some have to swim home via the polluted effluence that was once a noble river.

From late summer, salmon return to their spawning grounds

Our ancestors waited expectantly for these silver swimmers and caught them with net, line and spear, taking only sufficient for their needs but enough food to see them through the winter.

Fishing remains one of the few ancient pastimes still carried out both for food and for sport.

But the elaborate equipment of today's fishermen would have surprised the first anglers; they had no acid-sharpened hooks, intricate flies, sophisticated rods or polyester-fibre line. They had their eyes to watch the fish, the knowledge of where to find cordage and the ingenuity to improvise hooks from thorns.

Even experienced anglers jest that these traditional methods do not work, but they are wrong; for these methods were the foundation of fishing itself, although requiring even more skill than does an angler of today.

Many (although not all) of the techniques employed by our ancestors are outlawed. They require infinite patience, ingenuity and skill. Only poachers dare to use them, for they are unsporting: in other words, deadly effective and efficient.

Tickling fish

Tickling is still carried out on the Falkland Islands as a principal method for catching fish, but it is outlawed more or less everywhere else. It is probably the most primitive of all fishing methods: when you see fish in the water it is only natural to try to pick them out. The secret is to enter the water and ease both of your hands very slowly and gently under the fish; in open water this is very difficult. An easier way is to chase the fish into a convenient eddy pool which can be dammed off, and then you can stalk the fish at your leisure. Gently reach through the water with your hands so as to be able to grasp the fish with a lightning action that prevents its wriggling away.

1 Ease your hands very slowly under the fish with your thumbs upwards.

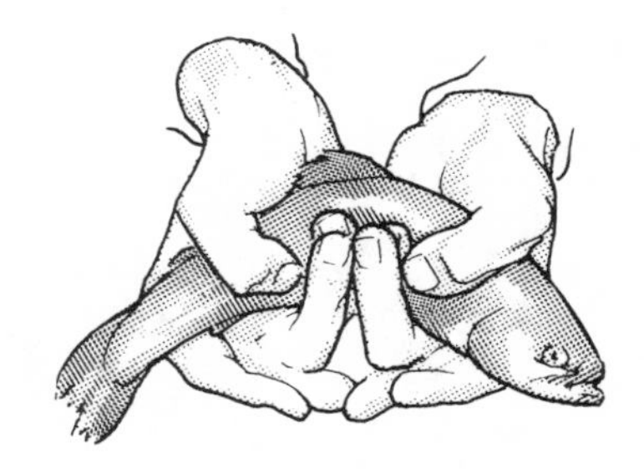

2 In position, grasp and bend the fish, draw it to the pit of your stomach and cast it ashore high on the bank where it cannot wriggle back to the water.

Fishing hooks

Think of fishing and you almost instinctively think of hook and line. Hooks and line are today sophisticated materials maximising strength for size. Improvised hooks – the precursors to modern gear – were made in many different ways from a variety of natural materials, from slivers of bone to thorns. Below are just a few varieties which can be used, fishing usually from a static line.

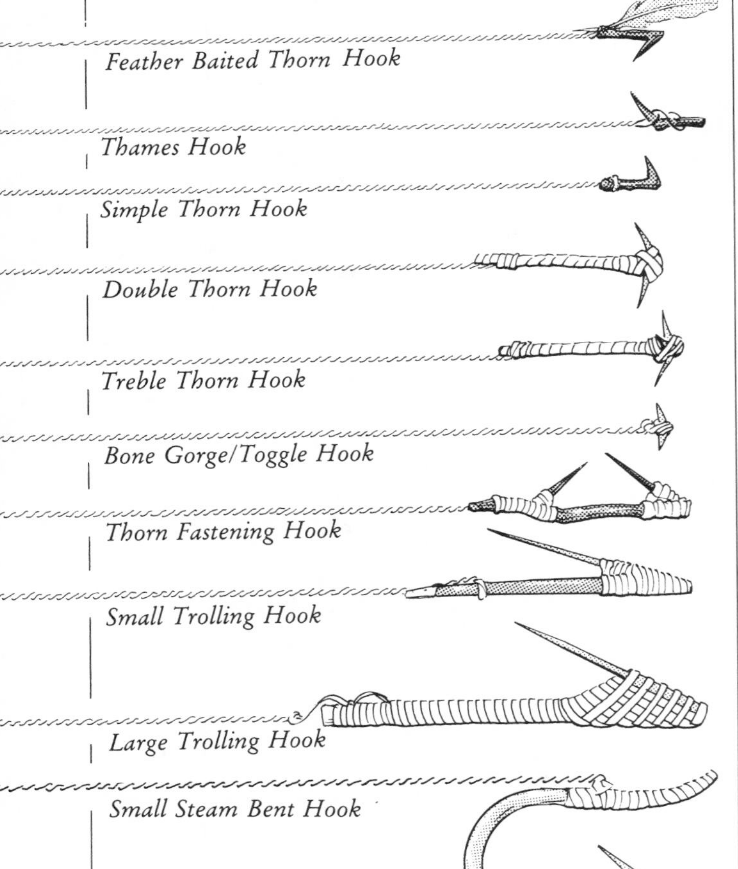

Making a three-barbed hook

What you will need

Strong bramble thorns still attached to the bramble

Fine cordage fibres: dried nettle strands (see p. 156)

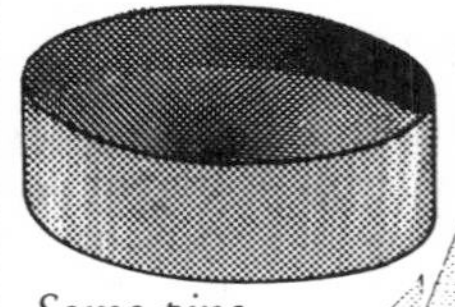

Some pine resin

A feather

1 Strip off the feather's blades and retain the stem.

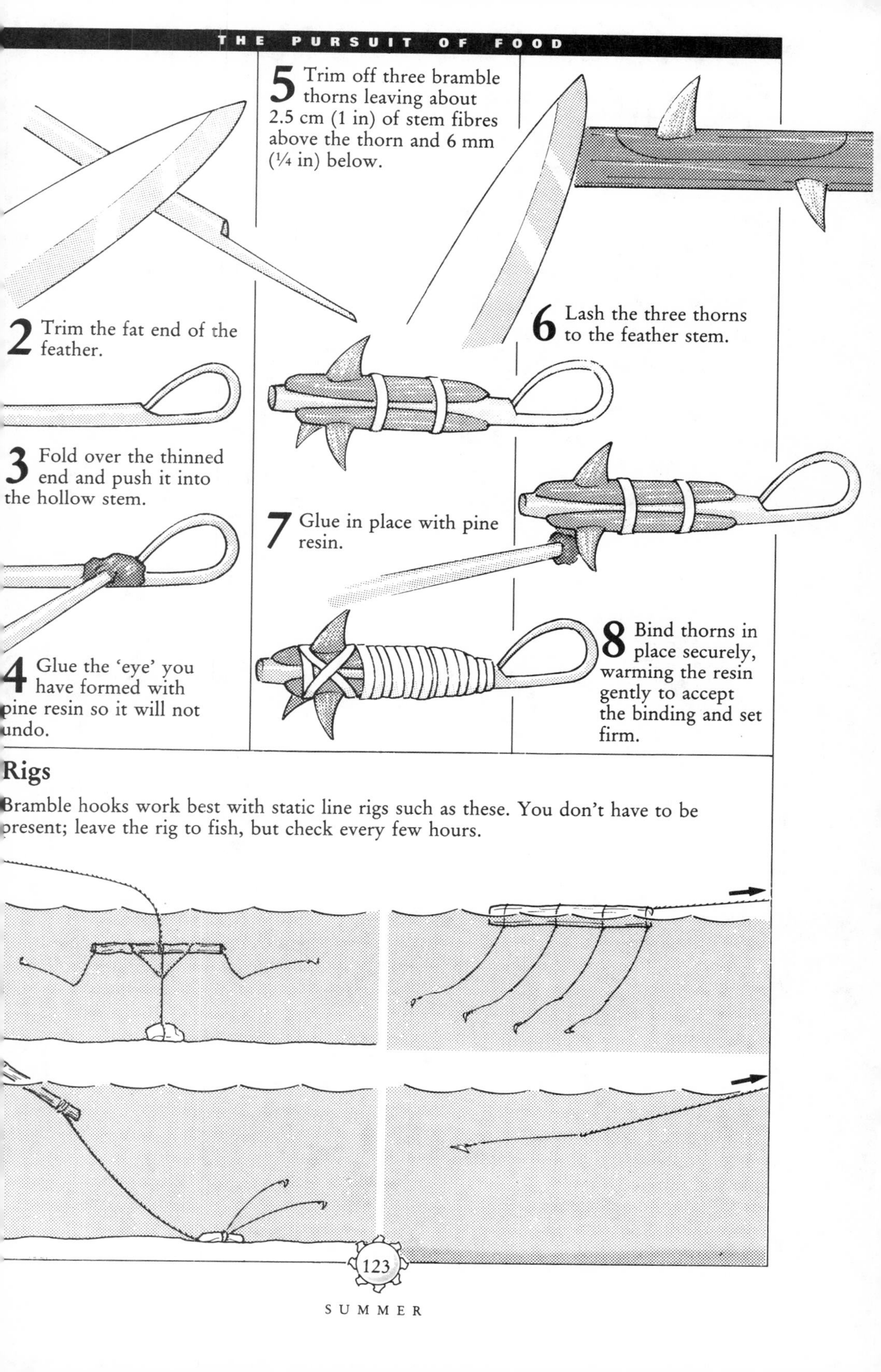

5 Trim off three bramble thorns leaving about 2.5 cm (1 in) of stem fibres above the thorn and 6 mm (¼ in) below.

2 Trim the fat end of the feather.

6 Lash the three thorns to the feather stem.

3 Fold over the thinned end and push it into the hollow stem.

7 Glue in place with pine resin.

4 Glue the 'eye' you have formed with pine resin so it will not undo.

8 Bind thorns in place securely, warming the resin gently to accept the binding and set firm.

Rigs

Bramble hooks work best with static line rigs such as these. You don't have to be present; leave the rig to fish, but check every few hours.

Filleting a fish

Having caught your fish, kill it with a firm blow to the back of its head with a pebble or hard stick. Use plenty of force for a swift, clean job. Assuming you have caught a trout, here is a way to fillet it. After gutting, leave the fish for 6 to 12 hours to allow the nerve endings to die; then it butchers most easily.

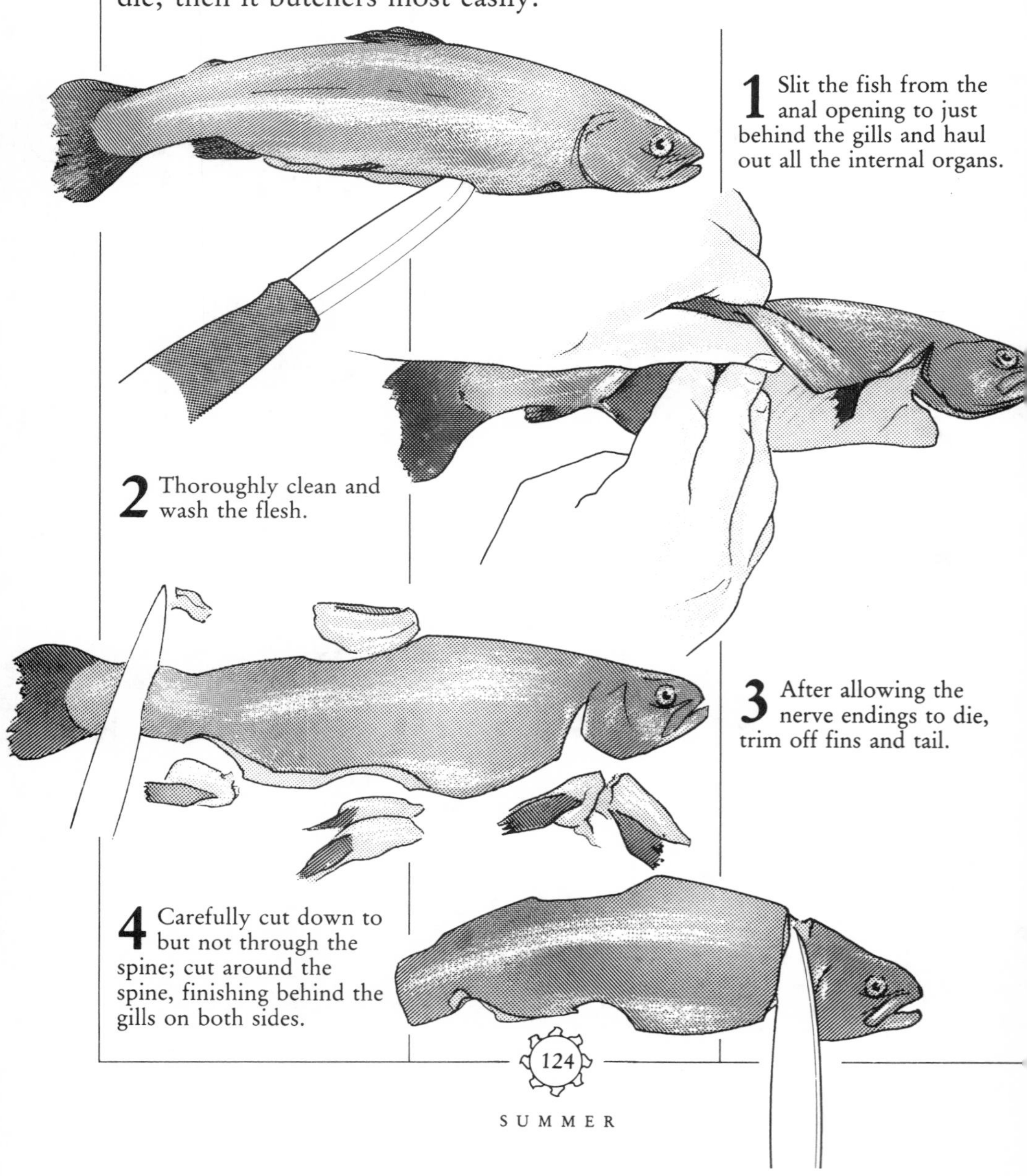

1 Slit the fish from the anal opening to just behind the gills and haul out all the internal organs.

2 Thoroughly clean and wash the flesh.

3 After allowing the nerve endings to die, trim off fins and tail.

4 Carefully cut down to but not through the spine; cut around the spine, finishing behind the gills on both sides.

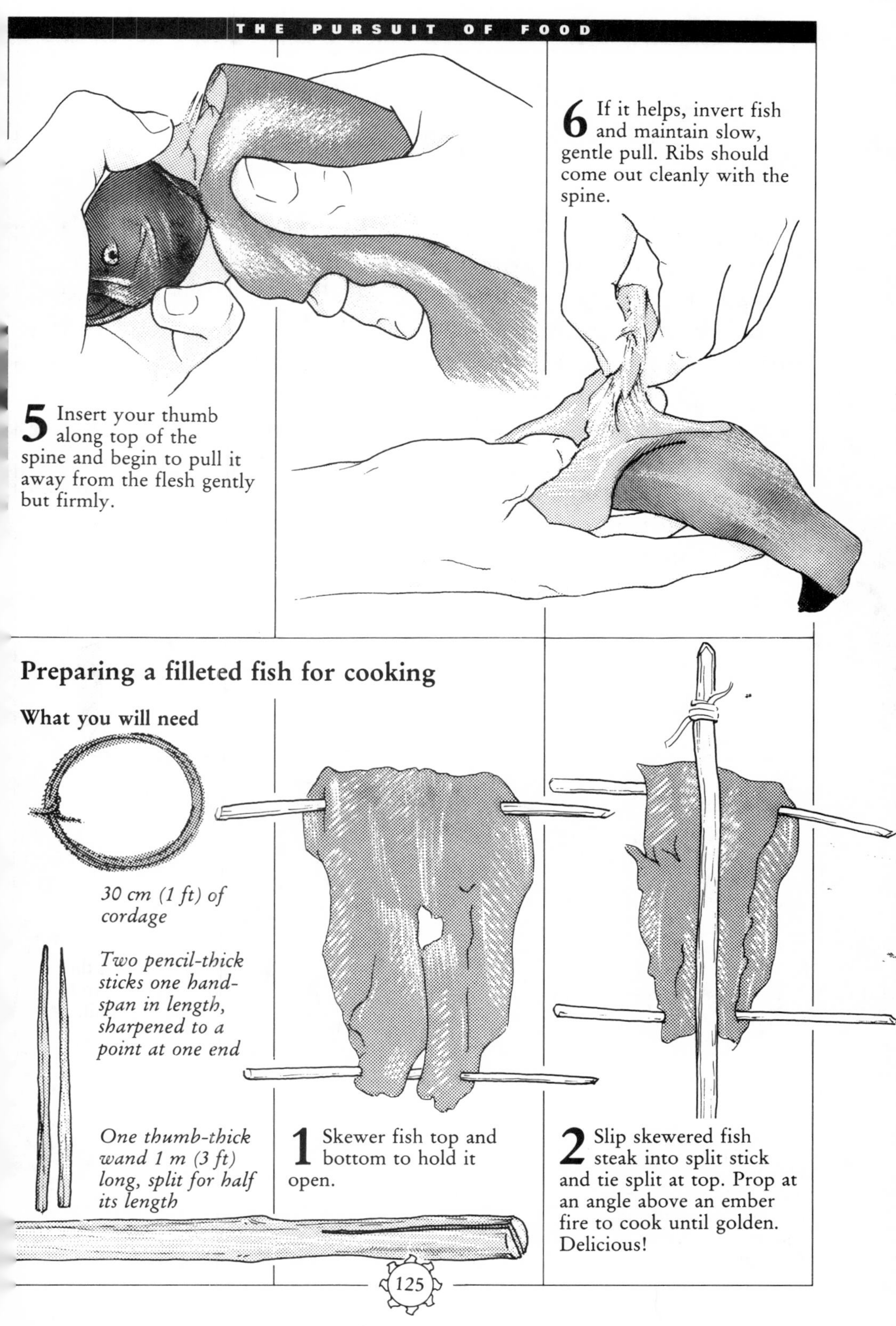

5 Insert your thumb along top of the spine and begin to pull it away from the flesh gently but firmly.

6 If it helps, invert fish and maintain slow, gentle pull. Ribs should come out cleanly with the spine.

Preparing a filleted fish for cooking

What you will need

30 cm (1 ft) of cordage

Two pencil-thick sticks one hand-span in length, sharpened to a point at one end

One thumb-thick wand 1 m (3 ft) long, split for half its length

1 Skewer fish top and bottom to hold it open.

2 Slip skewered fish steak into split stick and tie split at top. Prop at an angle above an ember fire to cook until golden. Delicious!

Drying meat and fish

If you have caught plenty of meat and fish it can be stored for use in later seasons. There are two principal techniques used to dry meat: sun drying and smoke drying. Undried, the surface of any exposed flesh is an ideal breeding ground for bacteria and fly larvae, but once dry these problems are greatly reduced. In hot sunny conditions all you need do is skewer the meat open and suspend it on racks to dry. Site the rack away from camp out of reach of scavengers and preferably where a slight breeze will keep away flies. Dried meat stores well over long periods if its dryness is maintained. It can also be ground and pounded up to make a highly nutritious survival food ideal for adding to wild soups and stews.

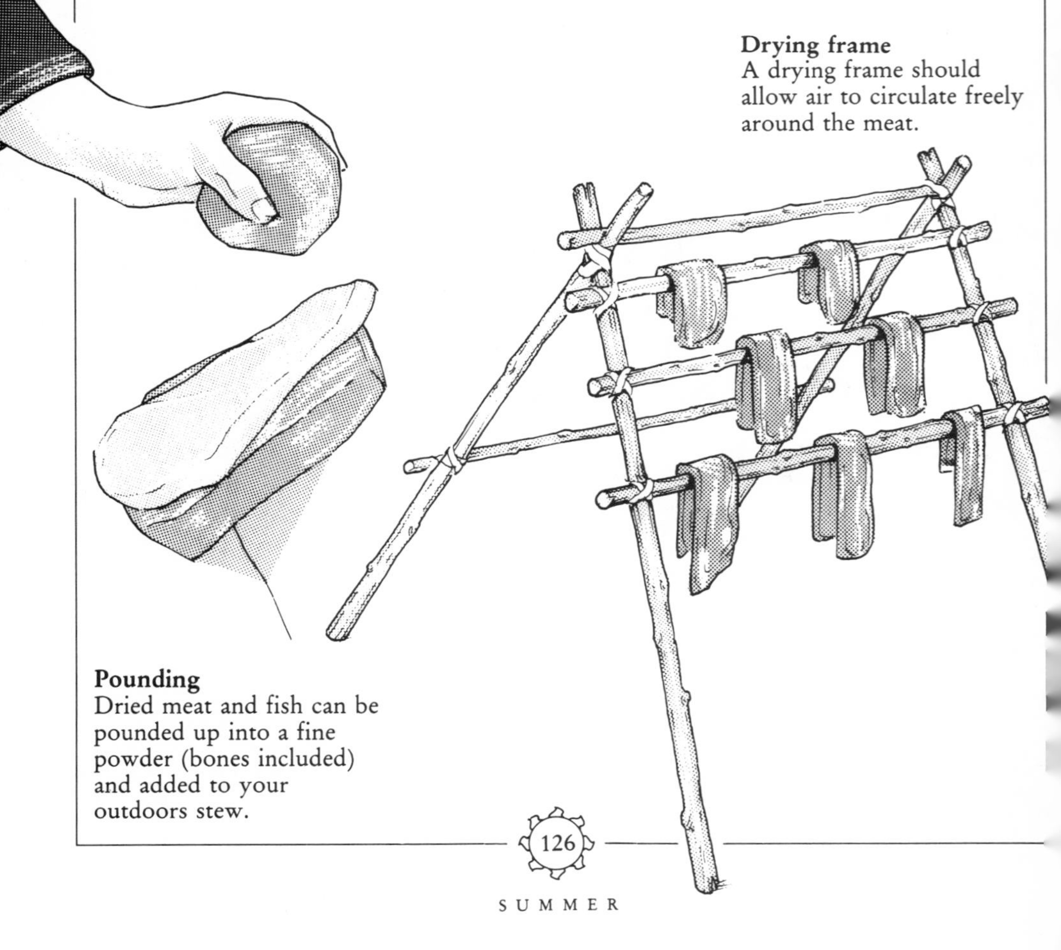

Drying frame
A drying frame should allow air to circulate freely around the meat.

Pounding
Dried meat and fish can be pounded up into a fine powder (bones included) and added to your outdoors stew.

Smoking meat and fish

If you are likely to have problems keeping pests away during the drying process, dry your meat in a smoke house. The principle is simple. Suspend the meat in an enclosed space with cool smoke passing around it to speed up the drying and prevent pests settling on it. If the smoke is too thick (it should be a hazy light blue) or too hot, the meat will be ruined. Build the 'smudge' fire in a trench some feet from the smoke house and channel the smoke in through an enclosed trench.

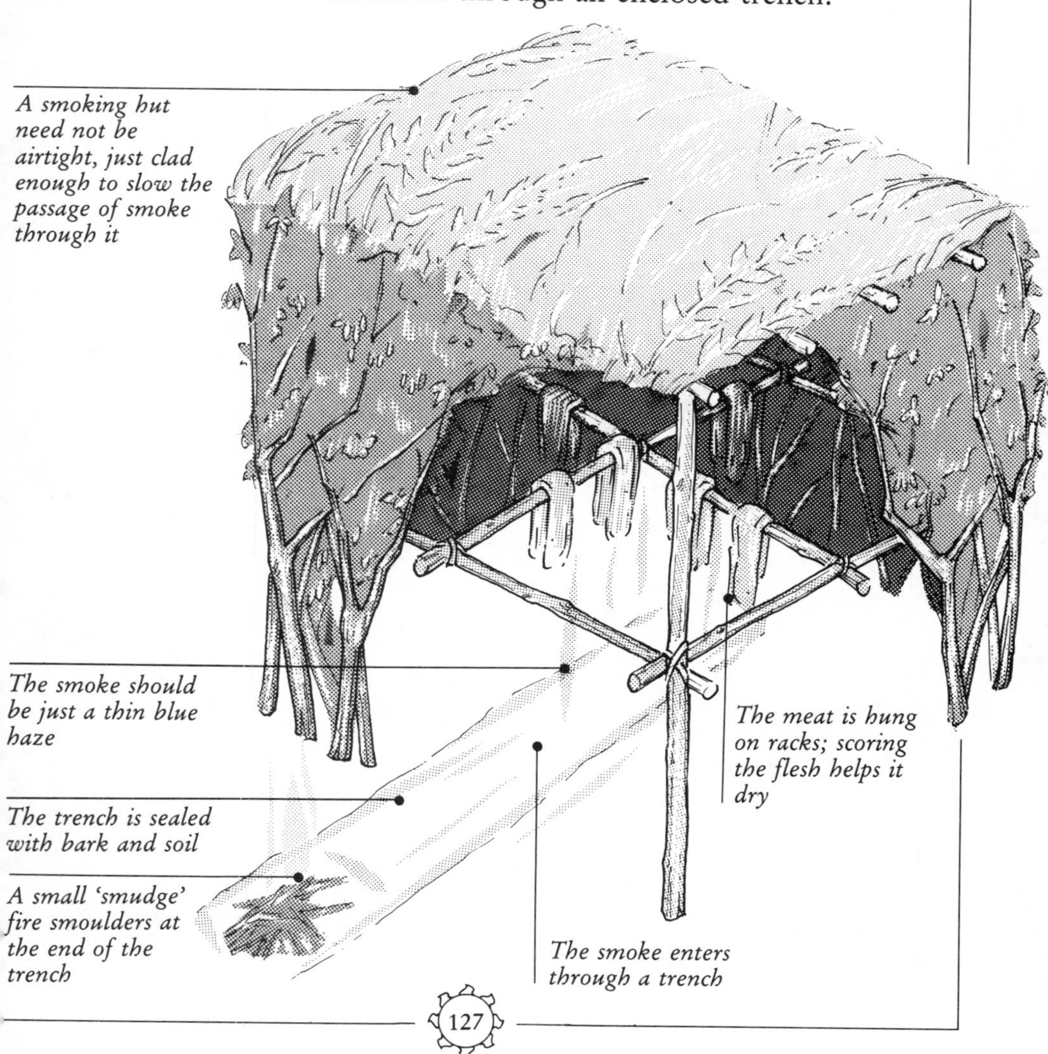

Cooked greens

Rich in vitamins and minerals, cooked greens are a health-giving addition to any summer feast. As always, pick fresh young tender leaves just as you would at a market and wash them before cooking. Overcooking destroys much of the goodness of these plants, so cook them very lightly in as little water as possible. By far the best method for cooking these greens is steaming.

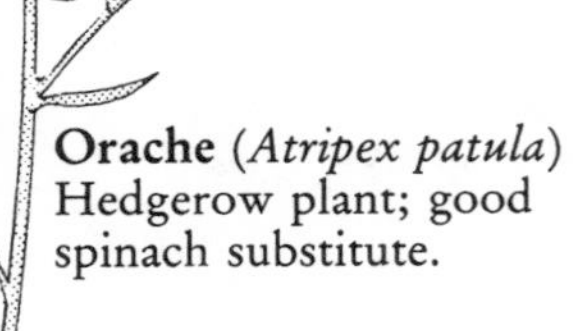

Orache (*Atripex patula*)
Hedgerow plant; good spinach substitute.

Ground elder
(*Aegopodium podagraria*)
Brought to Britain by the Romans; excellent eating – don't confuse with dog's mercury.

Shepherd's purse (*Capsella bursa-pastoris*)
Prefers waste ground; can be used like spinach or salads; use seeds as pepper substitute.

Marsh samphire
(*Salicornia europaea*)
Grows in salt marshes and tidal mud-flats; boil lightly in a little water or steam; suck flesh clean of stem.

Cleavers (*Galium aparine*)
Little green seeds stick to clothing; looses hairiness when cooked; goes with any wild meal.

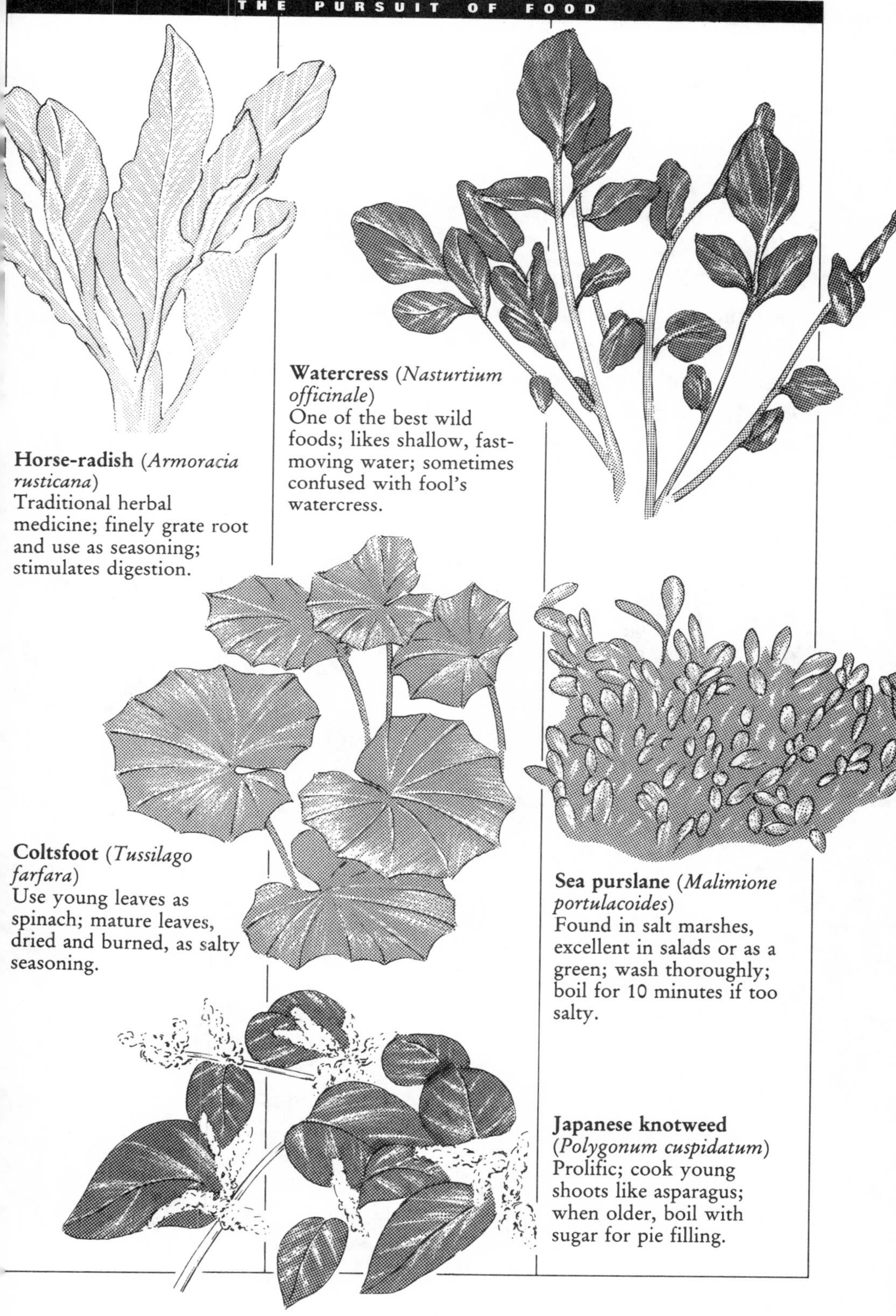

Horse-radish (*Armoracia rusticana*)
Traditional herbal medicine; finely grate root and use as seasoning; stimulates digestion.

Watercress (*Nasturtium officinale*)
One of the best wild foods; likes shallow, fast-moving water; sometimes confused with fool's watercress.

Coltsfoot (*Tussilago farfara*)
Use young leaves as spinach; mature leaves, dried and burned, as salty seasoning.

Sea purslane (*Malimione portulacoides*)
Found in salt marshes, excellent in salads or as a green; wash thoroughly; boil for 10 minutes if too salty.

Japanese knotweed (*Polygonum cuspidatum*)
Prolific; cook young shoots like asparagus; when older, boil with sugar for pie filling.

Fruits

Late summer never really comes fast enough! Succulent fruits dangle tantalisingly by the trailside. Nibbled straight from the bush, they are simple and tasty; but oh how they sing when made into pies and flans or incorporated in breads and shortbreads! No part of the wild harvest is as popular as this.

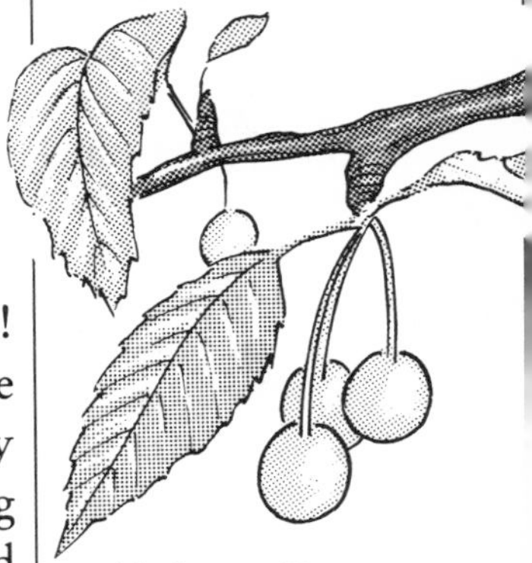

Wild cherry (*Prunus avium*)
Pits (stones) contain cyanide so should be discarded: tart berry meat can be dried and incorporated into scones.

Blackberry (*Rubus fruticosus*)
Humble but versatile; avoid gathering along busy roads – pollution taints goodness and flavour.

Wild strawberry (*Fragaria vesca*)
Smaller and fewer than when domesticated, but oh the flavour

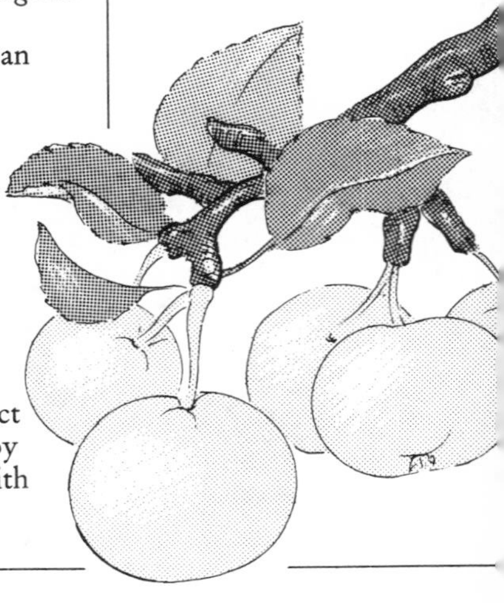

Crab apple (*Malus sylvestris*)
Too neglected: collect by shaking tree; a joy in pies, especially with blackberries.

Elderberry (*Sambucus nigra*)
Wine-makers' favourite; can be gathered quickly; dry and add to baked goodies.

Bullace (*Prunus domestica*)
Wild damson, often mistaken for sloe berry; plum-shaped and deliciously sweet.

Bilberry (*Vaccinium myrtillus*)
Found in acid soil areas; add to summer pudding, cook in pie or dry for use like raisins in cakes.

Raspberry (*Rubus idaeus*)
Wonderful, tempting berries; leaves make fine herbal tea.

Flour

Flour is an important source of energy. It is easy to store and available from a wide variety of sources, from plants to seeds, bark and roots. Obtaining flour is labour-intensive but well worth the effort. In an emergency or primitive situation the wild flour can be used as is, but the best results are obtained by mixing it fifty-fifty with ordinary wheat-flour.

The following methods show how to produce wild flour from a variety of sources. Store it dry, preferably in an airtight container.

What you will need

The raw material: cat's-tail pollen, roots or plants in seed

A pestle and mortar or 'mano' and 'metate'

A gathering bag or basket and a bucket

Cat's-tail root flour

1 Crush up cleaned root and root stock in a bucket of water. Wash starch from fibres into suspension in the water; repeat with more roots.

2 Once starch has settled, pour off water and save starch. Repeat with more roots until you have a good quantity of starch.

3 Pour the starch on to a tray to dry to flour.

Cat's-tail pollen

When the cat's-tail spike is rich in pollen it is easily gathered. Bend the cat's-tail head over into a bag and give it a tap – the pollen falls off easily. Add to other flours to give a golden-baked finish.

Cat's-tail sweet corn

Before the cat's-tail seed-heads open they are sheathed in leaves. Cook them just like corn on the cob – boil lightly and eat from the stalk, especially with a little butter.

Wild seeds

1 Best collected with a gathering bag: bend seed-heads over into bag and beat with a stick to shake seeds loose.

2 Winnow seeds to remove chaff. Being lighter than seeds, chaff blows away in a breeze as you toss seeds in a basket.

Plants for flour

Cat's-tail

Clover

Hazelnut

Bulrush

Reed

Lamb's-quarter

Pine bark can be dried and ground into emergency flour

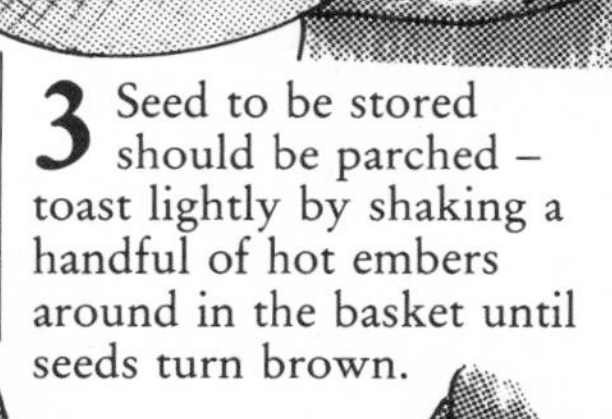

3 Seed to be stored should be parched – toast lightly by shaking a handful of hot embers around in the basket until seeds turn brown.

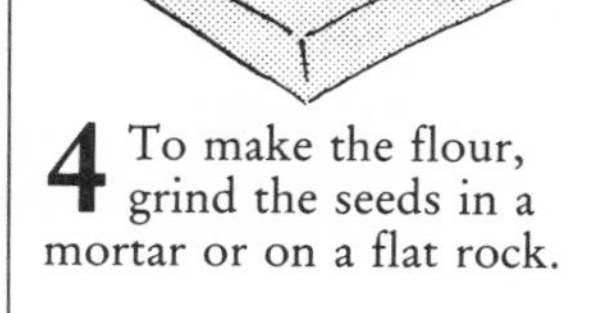

4 To make the flour, grind the seeds in a mortar or on a flat rock.

Cooking

Cooking is a skill of great importance, for food and morale are inextricably linked. There are methods of cooking other than the usual boiling or frying. With flat rocks available to us we can grill our food; with mud and grass we can steam small packages of food under our fire while we are busy doing other things. Or if we are a large group we can steam our meal underground or build an oven – the possibilities are endless. We should follow the example of the Australian Aborigines, who cook their food in its skin straight on the fire. This may look dusty but it is really hygienic, for the food is well cooked with the minimum of handling.

The recipe for a successful outdoors meal is fresh and healthy ingredients, the chef's creativity and well-presented and filling portions. Cooking should be fun, not a chore, so be adventurous. Even mundane trail foods can be enlivened with a wild greens garnish or spicy sauces. Never hit the trail without having made some preparations for mealtime, even if only as simple as slipping some chilli sauce and a couple of bouillon cubes into your knapsack.

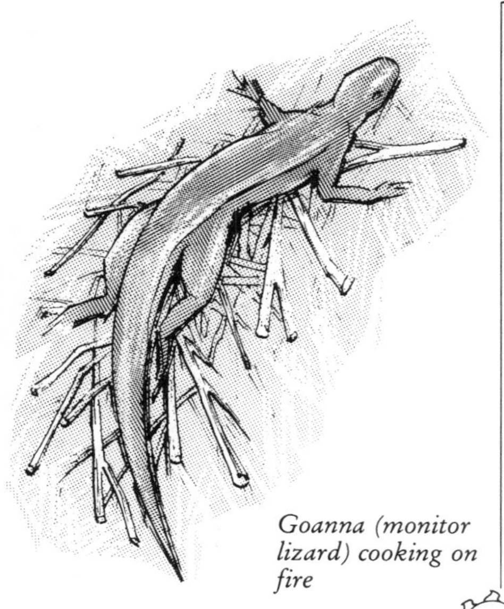

Goanna (monitor lizard) cooking on fire

Dampers

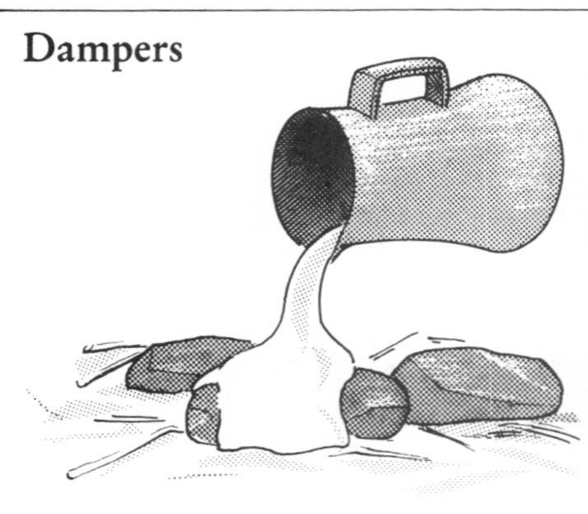

If you grind up seeds or other wild flours into a paste and pour it on to a bed of hot embers and ashes or a hot stone, this will cook into a crude unleavened bread called a damper.

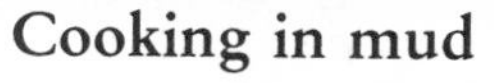

Cooking with hot rocks

1 Lay down a griddle of large flat stones fitted closely together.

2 Build a fire over the top and let it burn for 30 minutes or more. Prepare your food.

3 Brush away fire and embers with an improvised brush.

4 Cook food directly on the hot rocks.

Cooking in mud

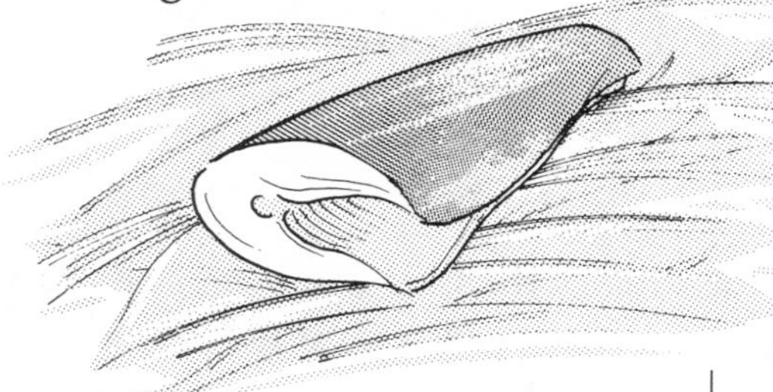

1 Wrap your meat in grass.

2 Bind the grass bundle neatly with natural cordage, completely covering the food.

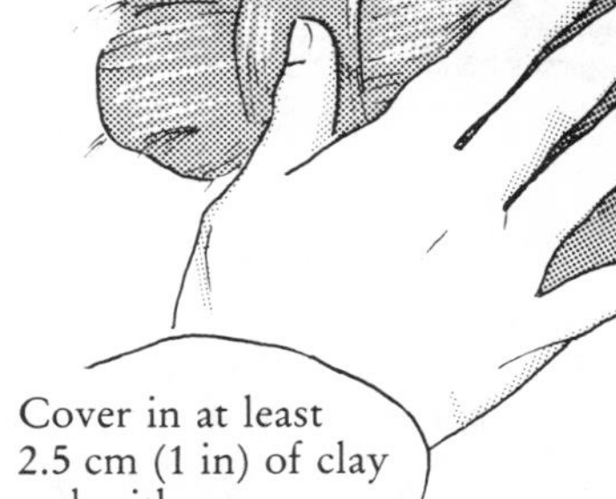

3 Cover in at least 2.5 cm (1 in) of clay or mud with no grass showing through.

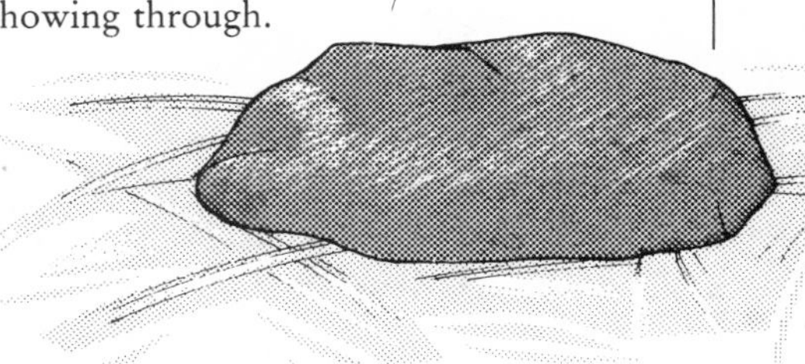

4 Place on a deep bed of embers and build the fire over the top. A trout takes about an hour to cook, a rabbit four hours.

The steam pit

One of the best ways to cook food is steaming, which seals in the food's goodness. A steam pit is also useful if you are cooking for several people – once prepared, it can be left without any further looking after (it's difficult to overcook with this method).

1 Dig a pit large enough to accept the food you want to cook.

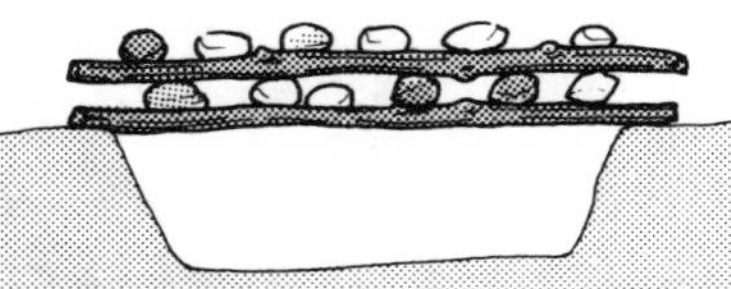

2 Build a fire over top of pit laced with rocks suitable for heating (see 'The sweat lodge', p. 94), about the size of apples, no larger.

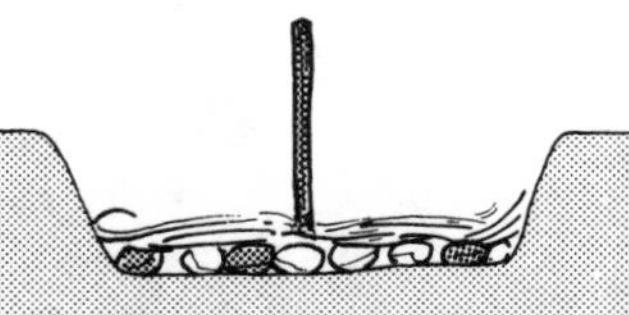

3 Once fire has burned down into pit and rocks are hot, brush away all but hot rocks and embers. Insert a stick in centre of pit and line with green grasses.

4 Put in layers of food wrapped neatly in leaves; cover with more grasses.

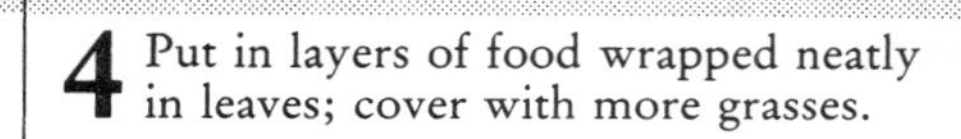

5 Cover pit with a woven mat and soil to make airtight seal.

6 Pull out stick and pour in a little water to create the steam. Seal off and leave for four hours or longer.

The mud oven

The smell of freshly baking bread wafting across a campsite has no equal. An oven is easily improvised or you can buy collapsible ovens to fit petrol stoves for use in regions where fires are prohibited.

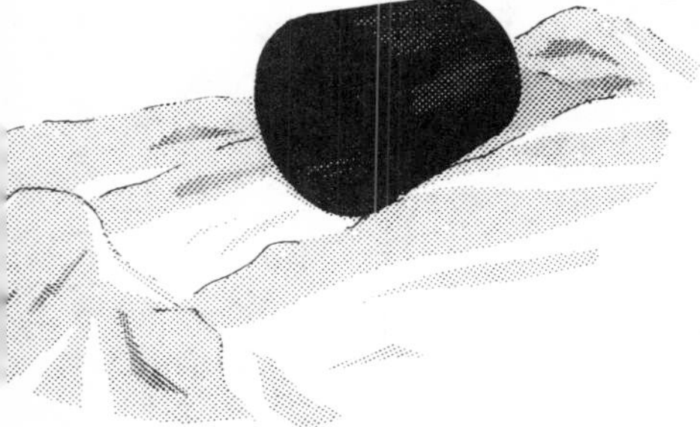

1 Dig a narrow trench and sit a large cooking pot over it as shown. (You could use rocks or clay instead of a pot, but this takes longer.)

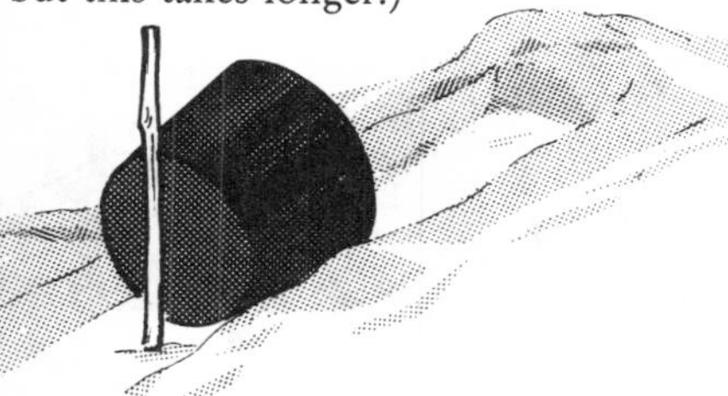

2 Push a 5 cm (2 in) diameter stick into the trench behind the oven.

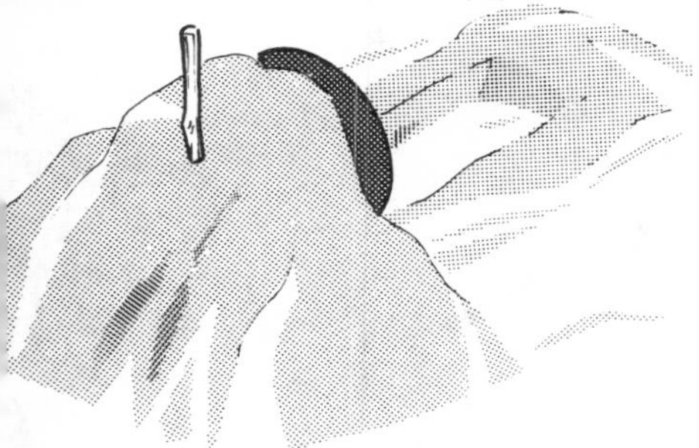

3 Cover the whole with clay and remove the stick, which leaves the chimney hole.

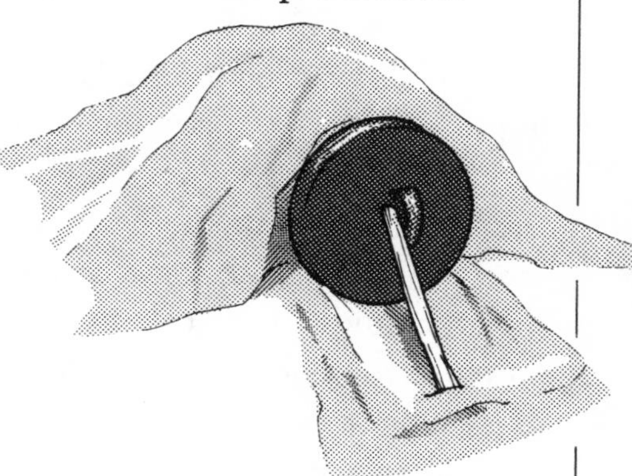

4 Fit the lid as a door, propped closed with a stick. Light a small fire in the trench; when the clay is dry, just keep the fire going to heat the oven.

Portable oven

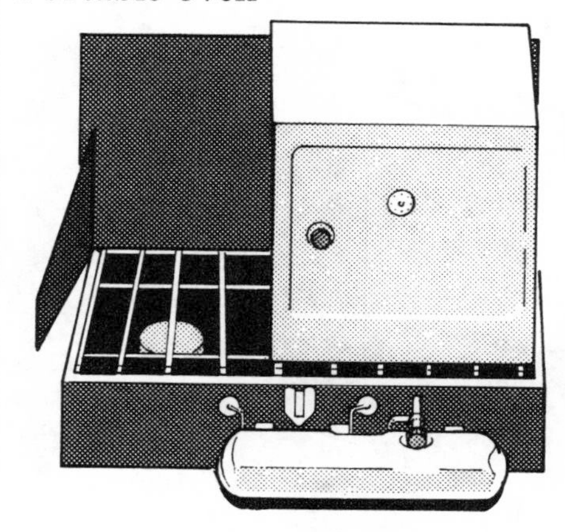

You can buy collapsible oven boxes that fit on the top of camp stoves. These are convenient and ideally suited for baking in regions where fires are banned.

The harvest feast

Starting early, armed with digging sticks, knives and baskets, small parties scour the surrounding countryside for wild delicacies. Along the way there will be many opportunities to see wild creatures. By midday the sound of the returned foraging parties rises above the camp as they show their finds. With some basic ingredients brought from home, the aim is to produce a feast fit for a king.

Hard work though it may be, the atmosphere around a wildwood feast is unique; but there remains much work to do. The children are shown how to bake bread and set to kneading dough with an adult to tend the mud oven for them. There is a great deal of preparation before the wild foods can be cooked. Each recipe on the growing menu has its own team employing a variety of cooking techniques. With our oven we can cook breads, pies and shortbreads; under our fire we can cook

Woodsman's pie – venison with arrowhead root topping

Crab-apple and blackberry pie

Cat's-tail pollen-drop scones piled high

herb-filled rabbits; soups simmer alongside stews and a stock for a very special pie. The little clearing becomes a field kitchen as gastronomic scents rise to the sky.

Eventually, with all the food cooking and the time for the feast agreed, a mat is woven for the display; for all wild foods should be well presented, adorned with the flowers from the forest. Strangers have become friends; families have unwound. Women sit comfortably by their fire with the infants drinking in the new sights and sounds, while men stand and stare into the flames (this is exactly what happens!). Everyone is captivated by the blend of woodsmoke and stew scent. All that remains is the clearing of the ground, the laying down of mats for a table – and the eating.

Gatherings of this sort were once a seasonal event for extended families and tribes. Lasting several days or more, they were an opportunity to celebrate long-standing friendships, to gossip and to trade stories, ideas and craft goods. At such times we broaden our outlook on the world.

Salad of wild greens with mint-steamed rabbit

Wild strawberry and cob- (hazel-) nut bread

Rabbit and burdock root stew with dumplings

Recipes

Bread

Ingredients: 1.3 kg (3 lb) of flour – half white and half wholemeal – plus 5 teaspoons of salt, 15 g (½ oz) of dried yeast, 1 teaspoon of sugar and 0.8 litre (1½ pints) of room-temperature water.

Mix the sugar with the water and sprinkle the dried yeast on top. Wait for about ten minutes and stir well. Meanwhile mix the flour and salt together and place in a large billy can (cook pot). Make a well in the centre of the flour. Pour in the yeast liquid and sprinkle the top with flour. Cover with a cloth and leave until the surface of the mixture is covered with bubbles.

Now mix the liquid with the flour; you may need to add some more water. If the consistency is correct you should have an elastic dough. Turn this out on to a floured log and knead it until it is smooth. Put it back into the billy can (cook pot) and cover again to enable it to rise until double in size. Turn it out and knead it again. Form it into three loaves and allow to rise for another twenty minutes beside your oven. Bake in a good hot oven until it sounds hollow when knocked underneath.

Try adding wild strawberries or other fruits and nuts to the bread mix.

Pastry

Ingredients: 225 g (8 oz) of plain flour, a pinch of salt, 112 g (4 oz) of fat, cold water.

Sieve the flour and salt together and mix in the finely cut fat with your fingers until the mixture resembles breadcrumbs. Add water until the mixture binds together. Form into a ball, place on to a floured tree-stump and roll out. Handle pastry ingredients with delicacy and try to keep the mixture cool.

Greens

Wild greens tend to be very bitter and sometimes have to be boiled in several changes of water. Unfortunately this greatly reduces the goodness of the plant. With the most bitter plants it is wise to add them to other strong-flavoured dishes such as soups and stews, where the sharpness is sufficiently disguised. Other, more pallatable greens should be steamed or cooked briefly with the barest minimum of water.

Roots

Many roots can be treated just like potatoes – boiled, baked, boiled and mashed, boiled-mashed-and-fried, boiled and then caramelised in honey or maple syrup, or even turned into french fries. Preparation in this way can make the roots more presentable to the less adventurous wild food devotee. Try cooking a woodsman's pie, exactly like a cottage pie except using venison for the meat and arrowhead tubers for the potato.

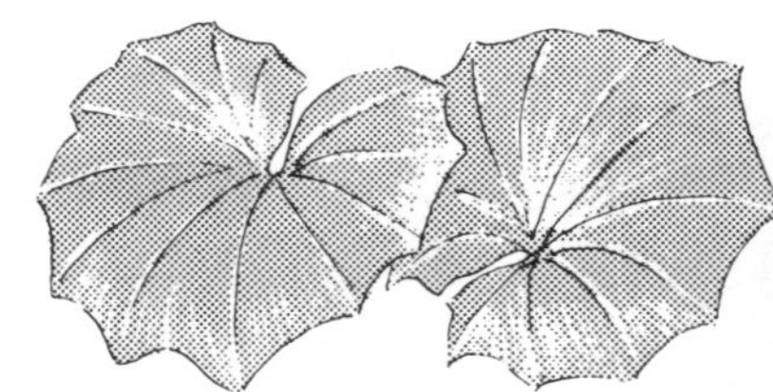

Cat's-tail pollen drop scones

Cat's-tail pollen can be added to flour to produce a more golden bake. Try adding 55 g (2 oz) of pollen to 55 g (2 oz) of flour, a pinch of salt, an egg, a little fat and enough milk to make a syrupy batter. Drop spoonfuls of this batter on to a lightly greased hot stone to produce a pollen-drop scone – simply delicous!

Stews

Backcountry stews are easy to cook, tasty and very popular at the end of a day's activities. The long, slow cooking serves to tenderise the toughest meats. Start by intensifying the flavour of your meat, by passing it through the flames of your fire or by braising. Then place it in a large billy with cold water or better still stock, enough to cover the meat, and begin to simmer it. If you have some fat, add it at this point. Now prepare your other ingredients: coarsely chopped roots, greens, fungi, etc. As the cooking progresses, add these ingredients at intervals – those which need the most cooking first and those needing the least last. As you become more familiar with the various ingredients you use you will be able to judge this easily.

A tasty and satisfying embellishment to any stew is the addition of some dumplings. Mix 112 g (4 oz) of plain flour, a teaspoon of baking powder, a pinch of salt, pepper, dry mustard and 66 g (2 oz) of suet and water to bind the dumpling together. Form the mix into six round balls. Bring the stew to the boil and add the dumplings. Cook at this heat for about 5 minutes and reduce to a simmer for a further 25 minutes.

Steamed meat

Steaming under your fire is an excellent way to cook. Small mammals such as rabbits are especially delicious cooked this way. Additionally you can season them by stuffing them with herbs such as marjoram, sweet cicely or, best of all, wild mints. Personally I like to carve the meat from the carcass after cooking and use it cold in wild salads.

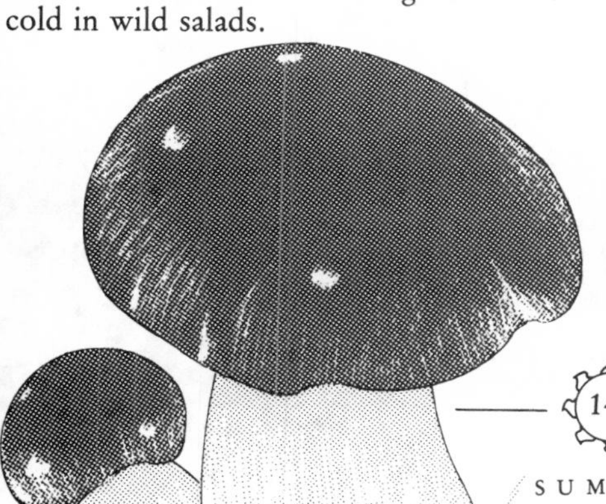

Broiled meat

Meat cooked on a stick over the fire is probably the first bush cooking skill children aquire. Simple and effective, it can be used with great results in creative outdoors cooking. Try making kebabs with meat and wild roots and cooking them over different types of hardwood coals; alder wood is especially good.

Soups

The key ingredient for a good soup is a good stock. You can make stock from the carcass of a game meal, from the skins and bones of fish or from shellfish shells. To make a stock, place the flavouring ingredients in a large billy can (cook pot) with enough cold water to cover them. Bring to the boil and simmer. Meat stocks need to be simmered for up to three hours, whereas fish stocks should be simmered for no more than one hour. Strained off, the stock can also be added to stews and pies, but is difficult to store.

Soups made outdoors are better made from a stock beginning. Improvising a vegetarian alternative is difficult, bearing in mind the limited resource of flavourings. However, if you don't mind a watery soup many wild greens can be used. Add seeds and starchy roots or mallow leaves to help thicken the liquid.

You can add meat, vegetables or whatever is available – even fruit – to your simmering stock. Any ingredients that cook slowly should be very finely chopped before adding to the stock. Taste the soup regularly during the cooking; continue simmering until the main constituents are tender.

AUTUMN

Autumn is the end of the growing season for the plant world. The broad-leaved trees put on a dazzling display of gold and russet that no artist's palette can ever fully capture. This pageant is the trees' song of farewell, like our 'Auld Lang Syne', and it signals to the animal world to prepare for the coming of winter. As the leaves fall and carpet the ground, the young foxes born earlier in the year play mischievously, rummaging through this springy, noisy carpet. But this will be the last autumn that the old vixen witnesses – for her teeth are now failing, and winter will be hard.

Autumn is a time to remember the season past and drink in the last of the warm sunlight. Soon dark, cold winds will blow through woodland bereft of sheltering leaves.

The fallen leaves lying on the forest floor still have a vital contribution to make. They must return to the earth to complete the circle of life, their nutrients being absorbed by the soil through the late autumn and winter months so as to provide nourishment for trees and plants. In the woods and fields, autumn is also the time of the mushroom harvest. Rapidly bursting out from under the carpet of leaves, fungi stretch into the air to disperse their spores. Fungi are often trampled down by those who do not understand them; but they are an important part of the ecosystem and grace the

Mice are keen to put on weight to help them through the winter

woodland with their diverse colours and forms.

This is a good time to be out of doors. Drink in the clean autumnal air; watch children chasing falling leaves and kicking up mounds of the leaf carpet; feel the spirit of the season! There are invigorating autumn activities, too – go into the forests with a basket in search of edible fungi, or hike a ridge-trail and blow away your cobwebs in the biting wind.

As the nights draw in, the camp-fire becomes an important source of comfort and cheer once again. We appreciate its warmth as we cook, eat and sip warm drinks, laugh and enjoy the last of the year's fair weather.

Autumn is also the time to prepare your winter equipment. Check your torch, change the bulbs and charge it with fresh batteries. You will soon need your waterproofs, winter boots, warm gloves, woolly jumpers and hats again. Before long, all these clothes will carry the sweet, damp, fragrant scent of autumn woodsmoke.

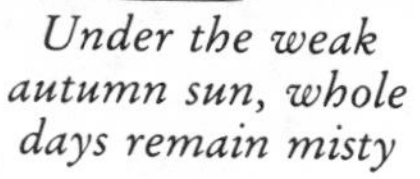

Under the weak autumn sun, whole days remain misty

If you started to learn the outdoors skills described in this book in spring, then autumn is your first test. With the cold and damp to cope with, your skills will be thoroughly challenged. Now is the time to learn rudimentary winter skills and generally sharpen up your performance.

Silence falls on the woodland as the autumn takes its course. The summer visitors have all departed now; and the stark outlines of the oaks, limes, elms and beeches hover, melancholy in the fog. From above the bare boughs of these slumbering giants, the greyness of the sky seems to reach down into every hollow, bringing with it an enveloping chill. Barring the unseasonal appearance of an over-enthusiastic violet and the subtle shades of fungi, this is the end of the year's colours. The call of a pheasant rises from across a clearing as though in defiance, but is swallowed in the thick, breathless November air.

Strong winds herald the approach of winter. Next will come the frosts and then the snows. The time for last-minute preparations passes quickly. Don't be caught out!

Animal kingdoms

For the animal world, autumn is a time of great change. The year's harvest at the end of summer and in early autumn brings a glut of berries and nuts which must not be wasted. Competition for these foods is fierce. Overcome by the instinct to store food all around its territory, the squirrel stashes away nuts, seeds and even fungi. Working away busily, the squirrel pauses only to sound the long-drawn-out squeak that demarcates its territory.

Squirrels like fungi as much as people do

Along with the early-autumn glut of nuts come large numbers of mosquitoes hatched in the rain puddles. But as the sun's path slips further down towards the horizon, and the temperature falls, these insects die off. Late-emerged butterflies survive, however, by finding sanctuary and sleeping through the winter; they will be the first of their kind that we see in the spring.

With the loss of the insects, the food supply for larger animals is greatly reduced. Now the skies are empty of swallows and swifts. Even the reptiles slip away into hibernation – although if you are lucky, you might see a pair of grass snakes coiled intimately together, basking in the remaining sunshine, even as late as November.

In the cities, starlings that have opted to stay at home fly in from the surrounding countryside. They congregate in chosen trees, roosting together in the warmth given off by the metropolis. The shrill evening chatter of these birds is often just audible above the sounds of commuter traffic. Long autumn nights sap the energy of all wild birds, and their dawn song seems very subdued at this time of year.

Across the moorlands and large forests rises an eerie bellow. One of the most magnificent of nature's displays is about to begin. Stretching high its powerful neck with its tousled mane, a red deer stag proclaims its right to a harem of does. All year the stags have been building their strength and growing their crown of mighty antlers. On a king stag the antlers frequently weigh more than 28 kg (50 lb). Now motivated by the strong procreative instinct, they wallow in mud to prepare themselves for the hinds.

Then the stags battle furiously for control of a harem, and the clash of their antlers clatters across the countryside. By the end of the rut they will have utterly exhausted themselves – sometimes to the point of endangering their own survival during a cold winter. The sight of stags fighting symbolises more vividly than most spectacles the coming of the harsh season when all must struggle for another year of life or die.

In the mountain streams, salmon are now in full fury as they battle their way to the spawning ground. The fulfilment of their life's purpose stretches them to the limits of their endurance, and sometimes beyond. The white underbellies of those who lose the fight will soon gleam to the sky as the lifeless bodies drift in the river current – easy pickings for otter or osprey.

The instinctive drive to mate or to gather food dominates the lives of wild creatures during this season. For the good stalker this can make for close encounters. The animals behave in a predictable manner; and it also often seems that, blinded by their instincts, they throw all cautions to the wind.

Deer have frequently run through my campsite at this time of year, whereas usually they would never come so close. One deer actually approached so near to the camp-fire as to upset a billy set by it, even with four or five of us sitting around. Even the fox, which usually prefers to pass unspotted, can be seen going about its rounds in daylight with a swaggering autumn audacity.

Starlings roost as a group

Being out and about with the wild creatures in autumn is a special experience, and one made more intense if you are also relying upon the land to feed you. For you then share the sense of urgency that fills the air at this time and make the most of the opportunities the season offers.

Feeding signs

As you move about in the countryside during autumn, you inevitably come across the remains of the fruits and nuts eaten by animals. With common sense it is easy to ascertain what has been eating what by studying the signs. Nuts and fungi, for instance, often show clearly the tell-tale tooth marks of rodent incisors. The size of these marks gives an immediate clue to the size of the animal – and therefore the species – which left them. Like all tracking, identifying animals from feeding signs is a matter of applied common sense and deductive reasoning.

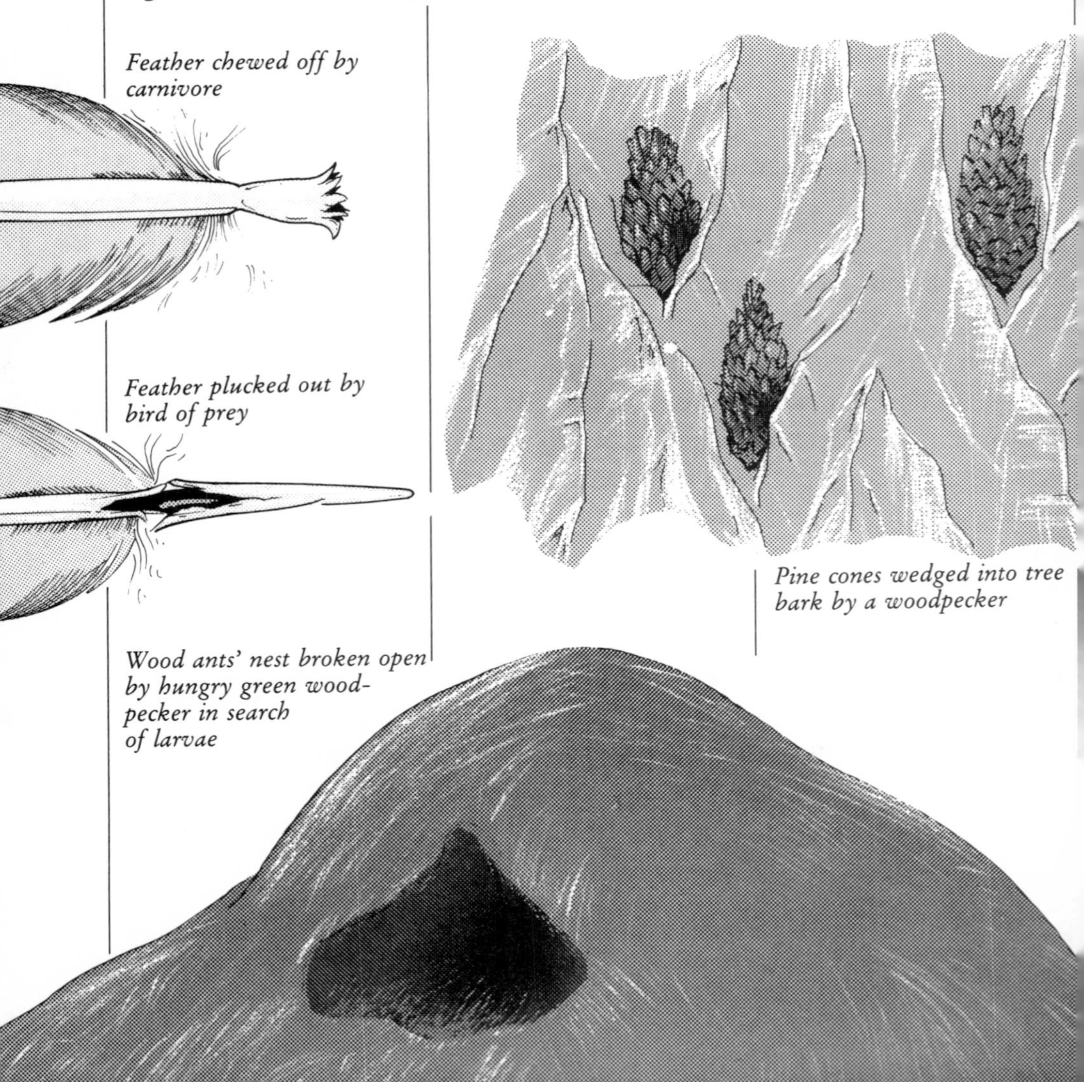

Feather chewed off by carnivore

Feather plucked out by bird of prey

Pine cones wedged into tree bark by a woodpecker

Wood ants' nest broken open by hungry green woodpecker in search of larvae

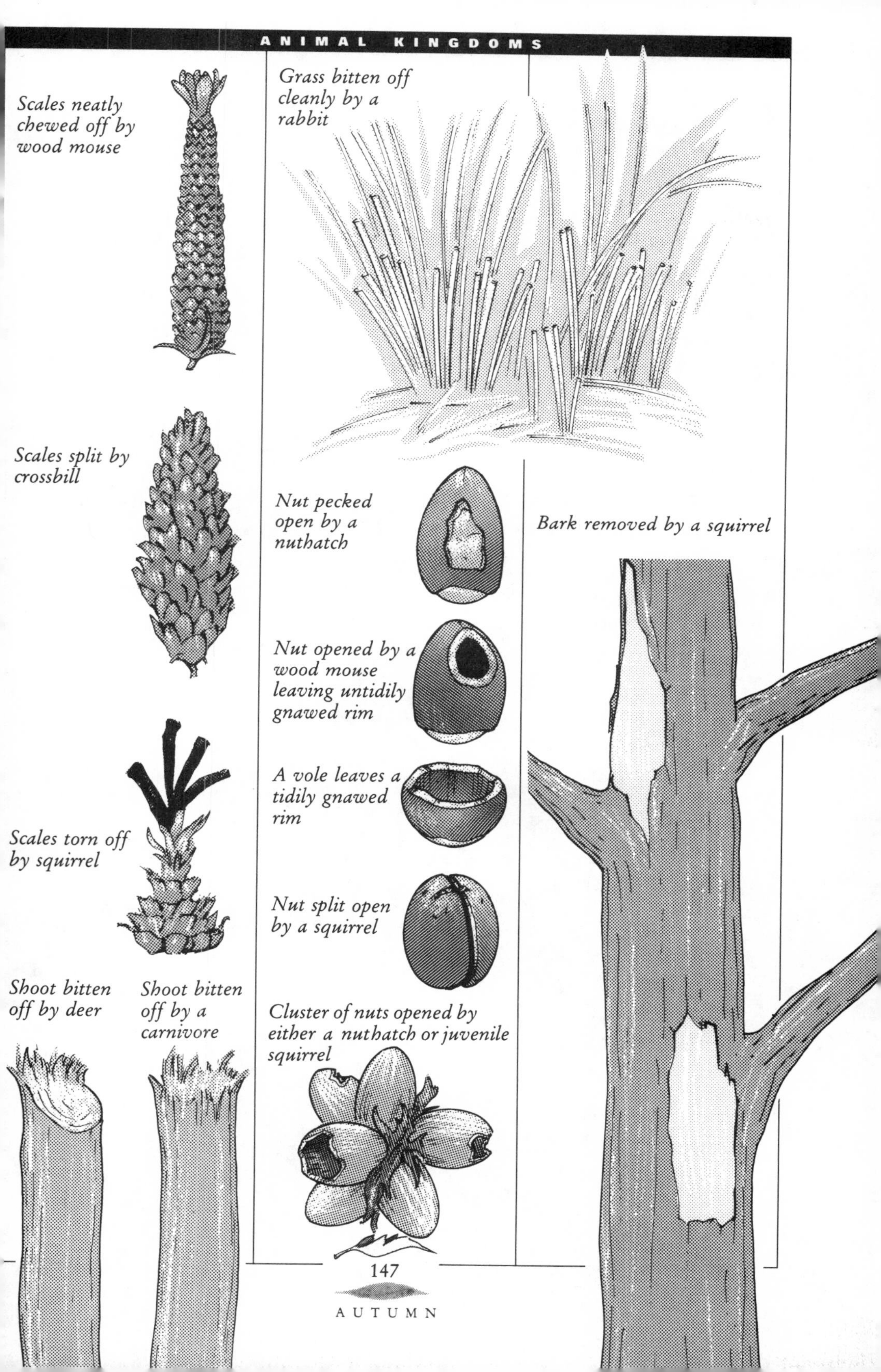
Scales neatly chewed off by wood mouse
Grass bitten off cleanly by a rabbit
Scales split by crossbill
Nut pecked open by a nuthatch
Bark removed by a squirrel
Nut opened by a wood mouse leaving untidily gnawed rim
A vole leaves a tidily gnawed rim
Scales torn off by squirrel
Nut split open by a squirrel
Shoot bitten off by deer
Shoot bitten off by a carnivore
Cluster of nuts opened by either a nuthatch or juvenile squirrel

Shelter

Once the cold weather of autumn really takes hold, you need to start thinking about using winter shelters, particularly those which incorporate a fire. The classic cold-weather shelter is the open-fronted lean-to, which relies on a fire to provide warmth. Open down one side, it is designed to allow the fire's heat to be reflected into the shelter and down on to you from the roof. The sloping roof is easy and quick to construct but must overhang you far enough to prevent rain or snow landing on your bed! To make the best use of this shelter, you need the correct type of fire and bed.

What you need

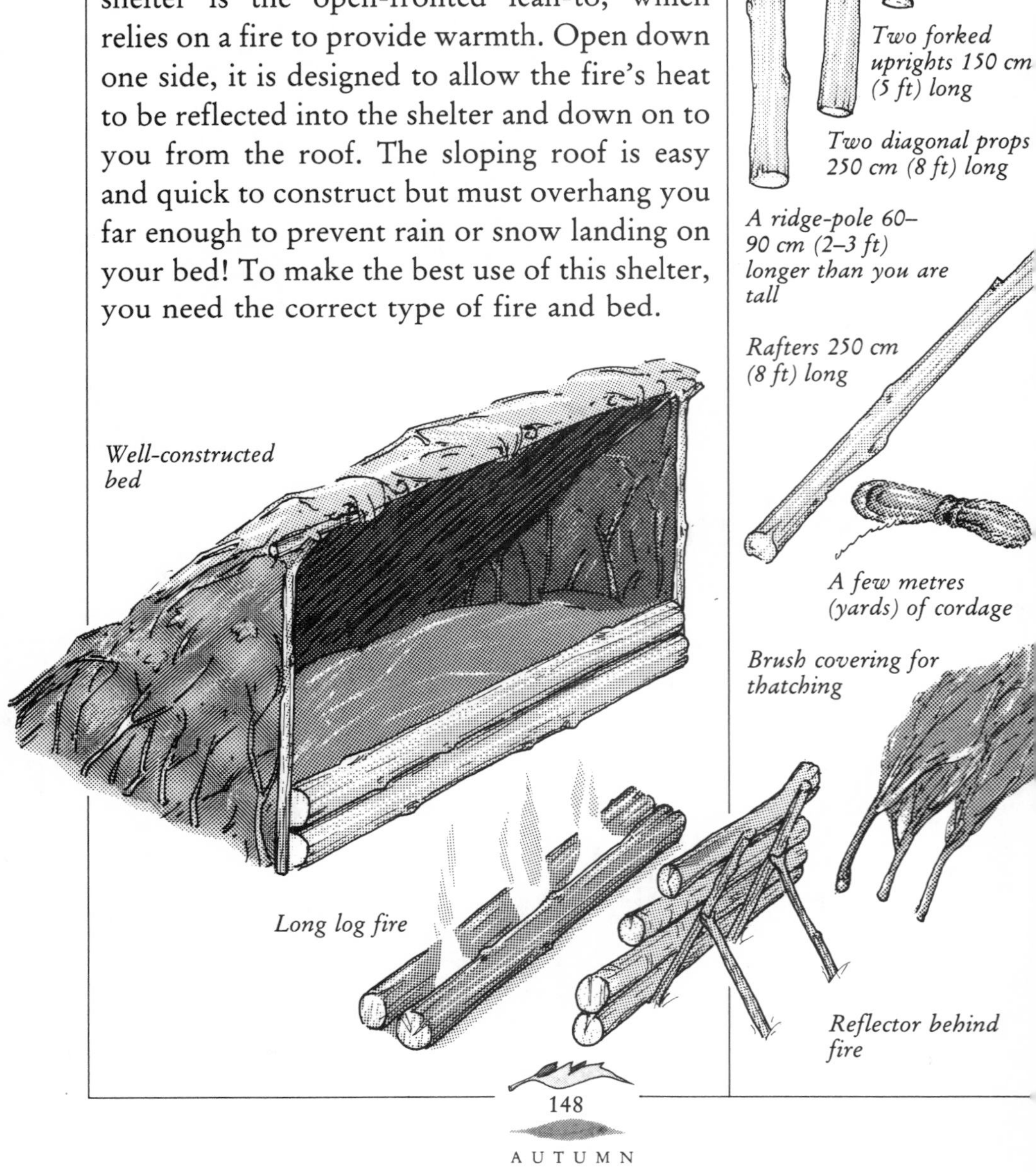

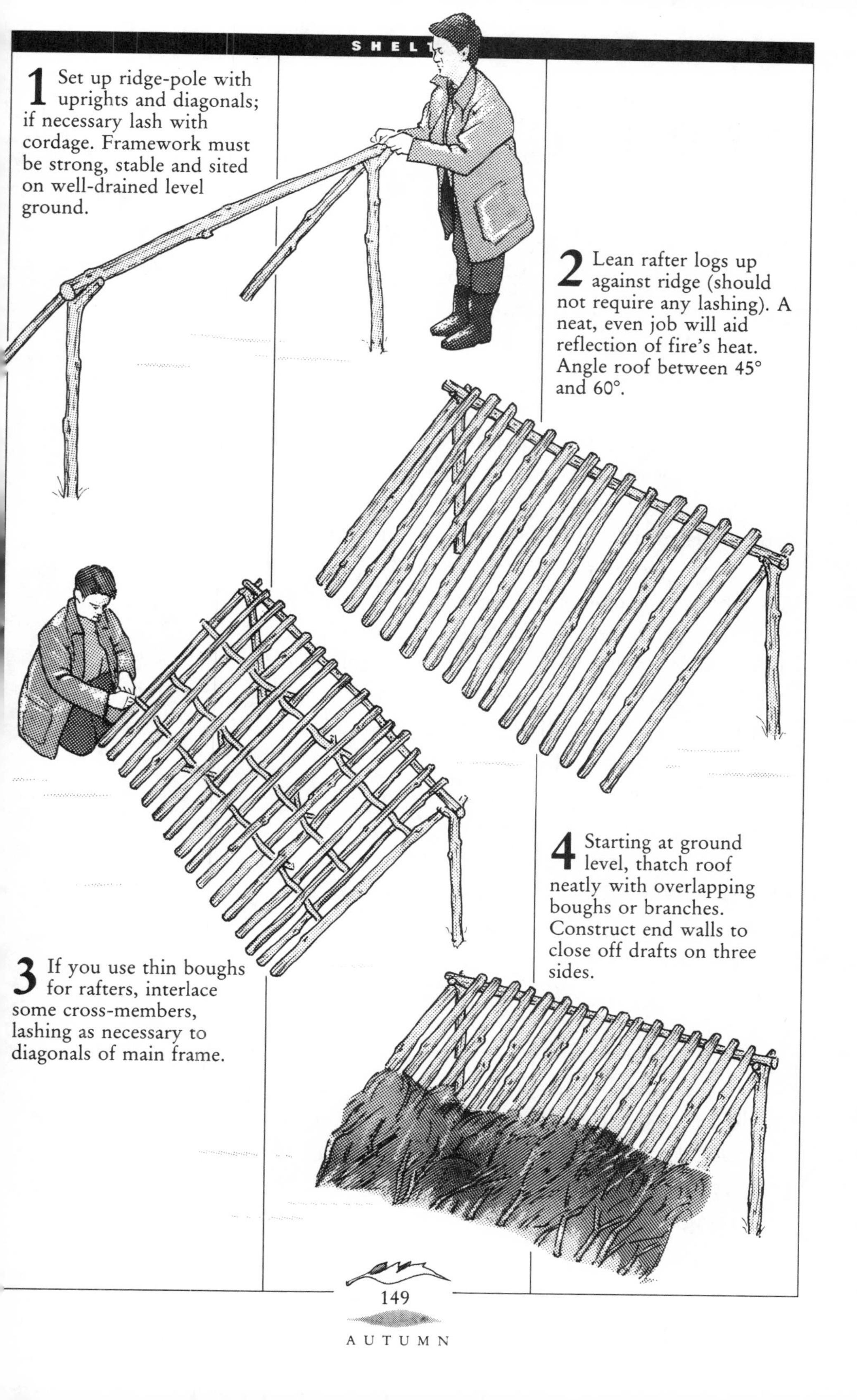

1 Set up ridge-pole with uprights and diagonals; if necessary lash with cordage. Framework must be strong, stable and sited on well-drained level ground.

2 Lean rafter logs up against ridge (should not require any lashing). A neat, even job will aid reflection of fire's heat. Angle roof between 45° and 60°.

3 If you use thin boughs for rafters, interlace some cross-members, lashing as necessary to diagonals of main frame.

4 Starting at ground level, thatch roof neatly with overlapping boughs or branches. Construct end walls to close off drafts on three sides.

Bedding

Few aspects of camping are as important to morale as a good night's sleep. This is easily provided by modern camping equipment; but if you are doing without this luxury you need to know the correct techniques. Many experienced campers are astounded by the comfort of their first night on an improvised bed – as good as any modern mattress, if not better!

Our main considerations are to raise ourselves above the heat-sapping ground, to be away from the damp and to provide comfort. You can build a good bed with one hour's work. That may not seem much now, but when you have constructed a shelter as well you may wonder whether it is worth the effort. It is. Weigh that hour against all the hours of sleep it will give you.

To help reduce the amount of bedding material needed, and to prevent it spreading, you need to enclose the bed by a frame, either specifically made or incorporated as part of your shelter. With the open-fronted lean-to, the rear wall will act as one part of the frame, and a simple opposing wall can be added on the fire side.

It is important to have sufficient bedding material: when you are on the bed, and the bedding has compressed under your weight, you need to be just at the level of the top of the retaining wall. This gives you the best advantage of the warmth of the fire.

Types of bed

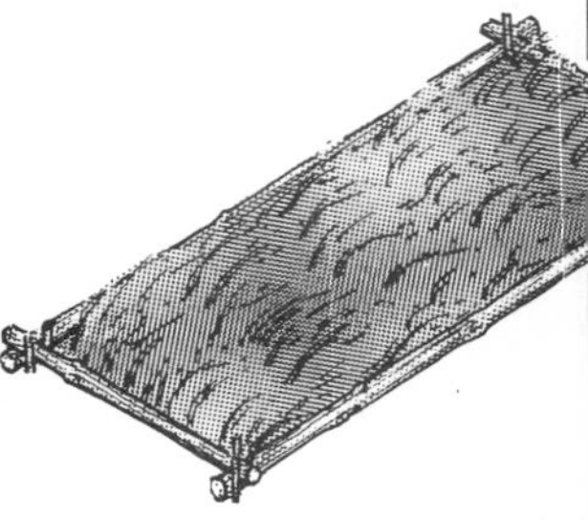

Bough bed
Traditional North-country bed, using bough tips of evergreens. Boughs are pushed into ground. Best contained by a frame.

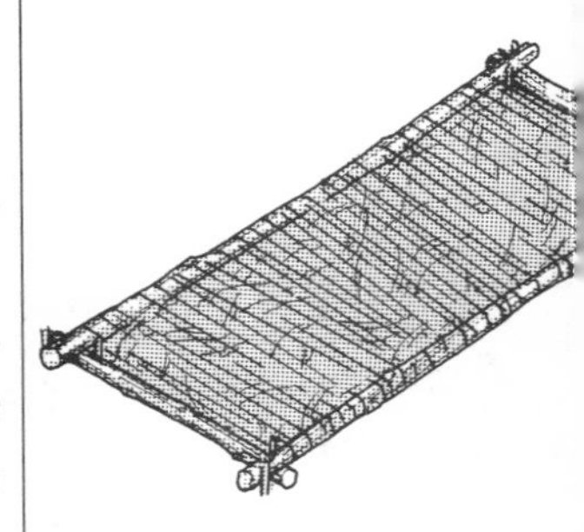

Withe bed
Frame with willow withes passed across it and lashed securely in place. Extra central lashing is advisable.

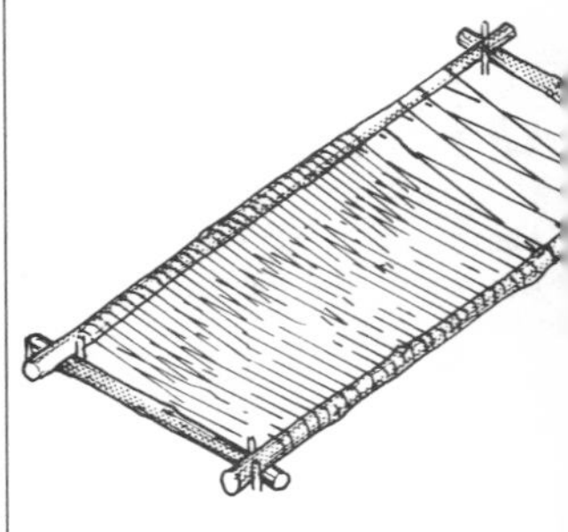

Rope bed
Improvised hammock-like from climbing rope or grass rope.

Making a simple bed

1 Lay crosswise moisture barrier of dead logs about 5 cm (2 in) in diameter, as wide as bed.

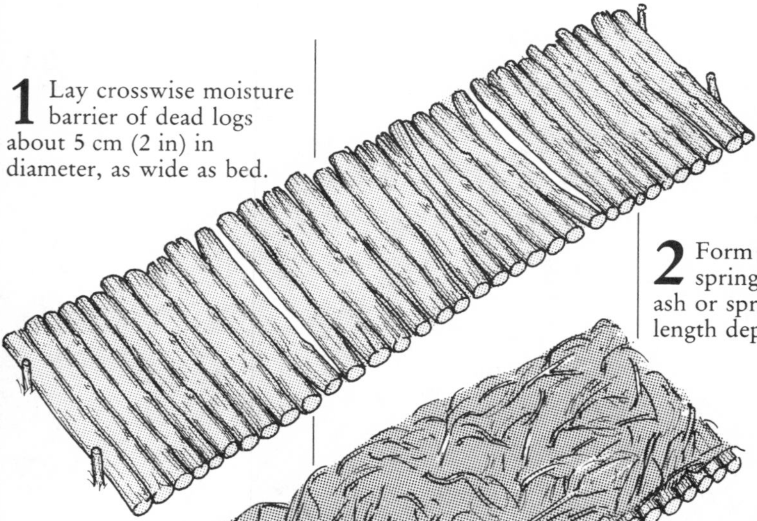

2 Form mattress from springy branches (e.g. ash or spruce) to arm's length depth.

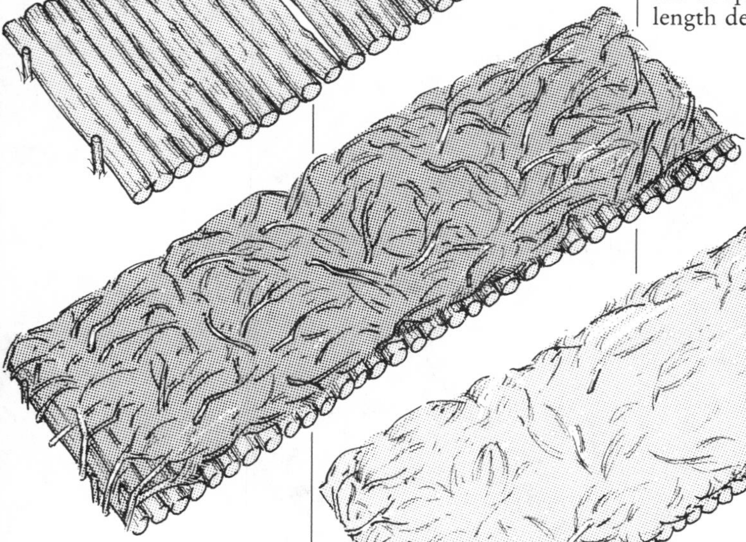

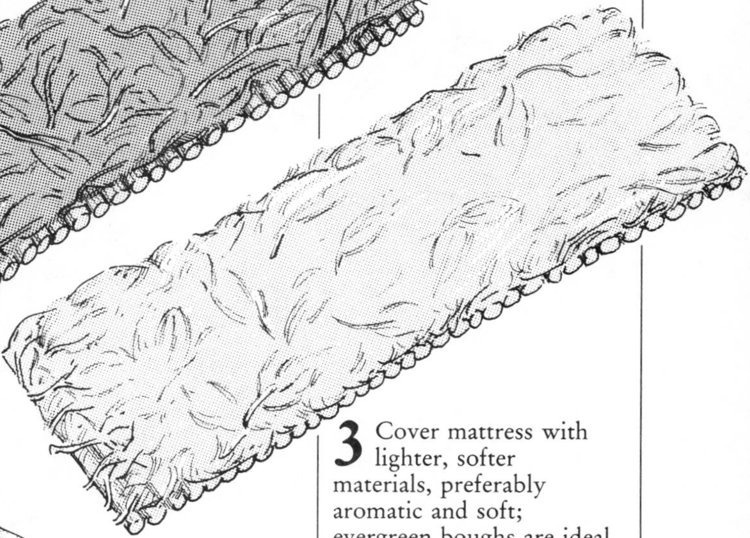

3 Cover mattress with lighter, softer materials, preferably aromatic and soft; evergreen boughs are ideal.

4 If bed is incorporated in an open-fronted lean-to, contain it with a low retaining wall.

Duvet

A shelter and a bed will keep you warm, but without a covering you are unlikely to sleep soundly. Making a blanket or duvet from natural materials is not as difficult as you may think. A host of dry materials such as grasses can be woven into a duvet that is both warm and practical. They can even be used to make roof covers and sleeping mats.

There are several ways to make a duvet – you can even build a makeshift loom. But I have found the best way is the simple hand method shown here; with this method you can fashion a very tightly woven and long-lasting duvet that may even shed rain.

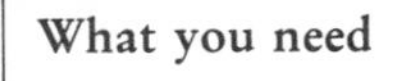

What you need

Plenty of cordage

Good dry thatching materials – dried grasses or other plants

Your bush duvet can double as a makeshift portable shelter

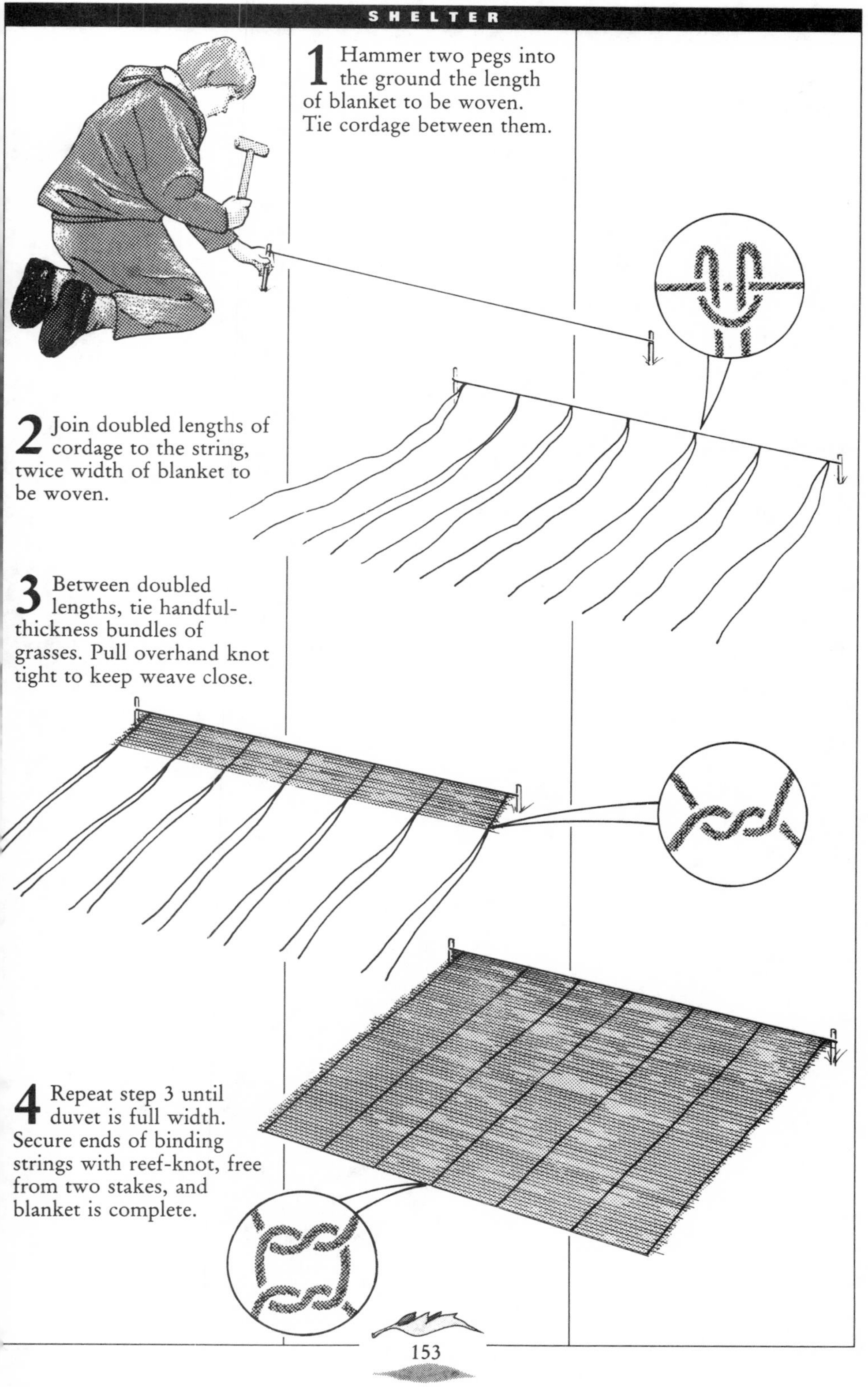

1 Hammer two pegs into the ground the length of blanket to be woven. Tie cordage between them.

2 Join doubled lengths of cordage to the string, twice width of blanket to be woven.

3 Between doubled lengths, tie handful-thickness bundles of grasses. Pull overhand knot tight to keep weave close.

4 Repeat step 3 until duvet is full width. Secure ends of binding strings with reef-knot, free from two stakes, and blanket is complete.

Fire

There is one fire lay that is ideally suited to combat the cold of autumn and winter: the long log fire. This fire burns logs along their whole length, enabling you to sleep alongside it and receive warmth along *your* full body length. Better still, the long log fire is also virtually self-regulating; few if any other fires need so little looking after. Once properly laid, this fire will burn steadily through the night, keeping you warm as you sleep. The effect on morale can be remarkable!

The long log fire is perfectly suited to use with an open-fronted lean-to. It can be further improved by building a reflector behind it to bounce into your shelter the heat otherwise lost to the wilds.

1 Start an Indian's fire (see p. 52), building a good bed of embers.

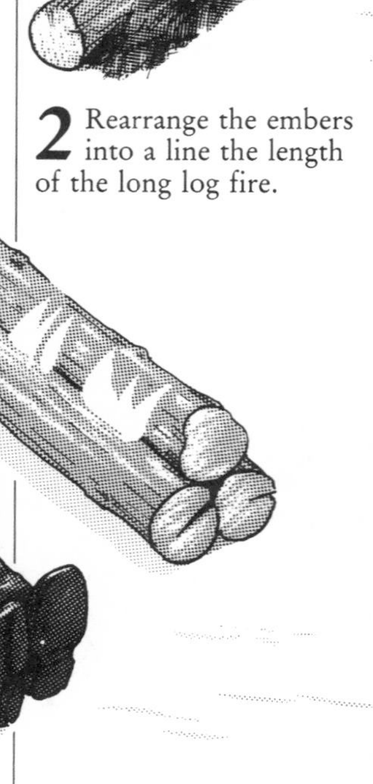

2 Rearrange the embers into a line the length of the long log fire.

3 Add two 15 cm (6 in) diameter logs either side of embers, filled between with light fuel to start blaze.

4 Add a third long log again 15 cm (6 in) in diameter.

Fire reflector

1 Hammer into ground two sturdy 90–120 cm (3–4 ft) long stakes angled 60° away from fire.

2 Arrange supporting prop for each stake.

3 Build up cabin-like wall of logs to form reflector.

Nettle cordage

The nettle is one of our most common plants and also one of the most useful. Available for making cordage from early summer, now that the plant has gone to seed we can gather the tall mature stems for making into one of the strongest natural cordages. This plant is blessed with very long fibres which have good strength when shock-loaded, making it ideal for fishing lines and duvet manufacture.

You can avoid the stings by wearing gloves or caking your hands in a layer of mud. With practice and confidence, however, you will find that you can process nettles with your bare hands without getting stung. If you do get stung, take a large fresh dockleaf, crush it up, roll it between your palms and then squeeze out its juice to apply to the stings.

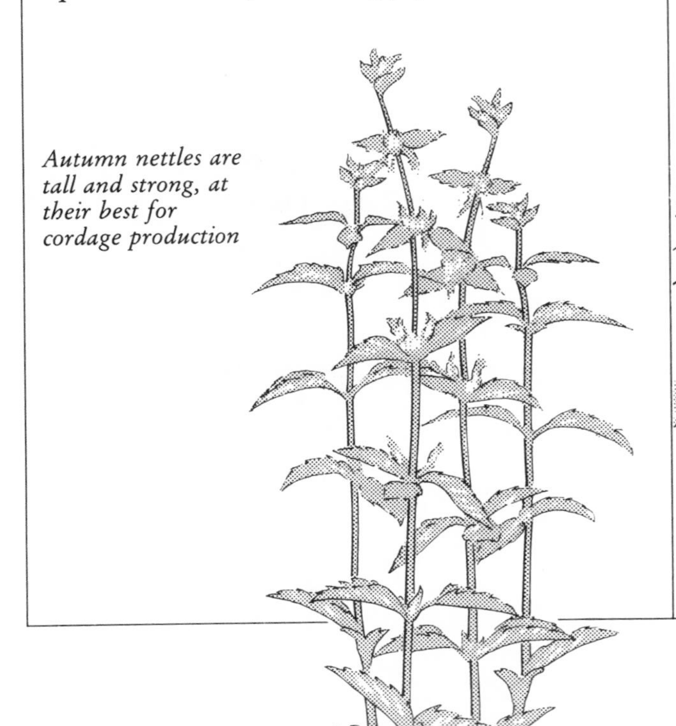

Autumn nettles are tall and strong, at their best for cordage production

Extracting nettle fibres

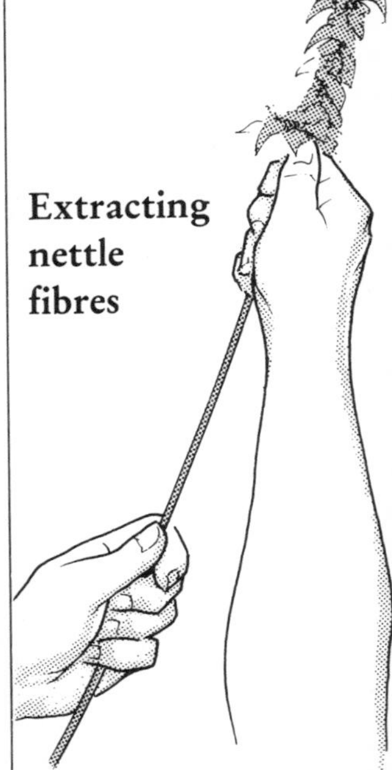

1 Cut nettle from ground. Strip off leaves with one smooth hand action, moving towards nettle top. Repeat to get rid of stinging hairs.

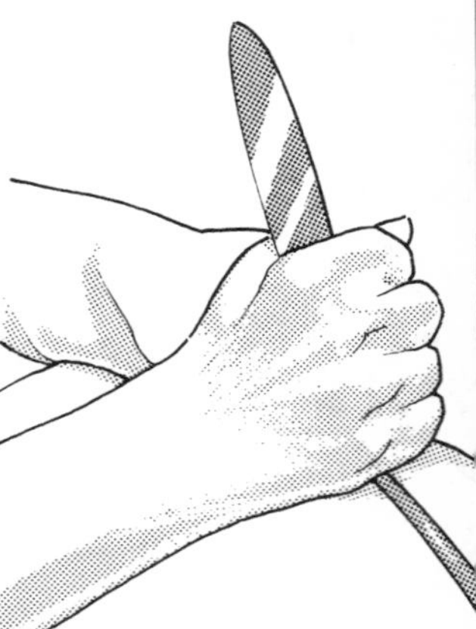

2 Squash stem flat by squeezing between fingers or gently pounding with knife handle.

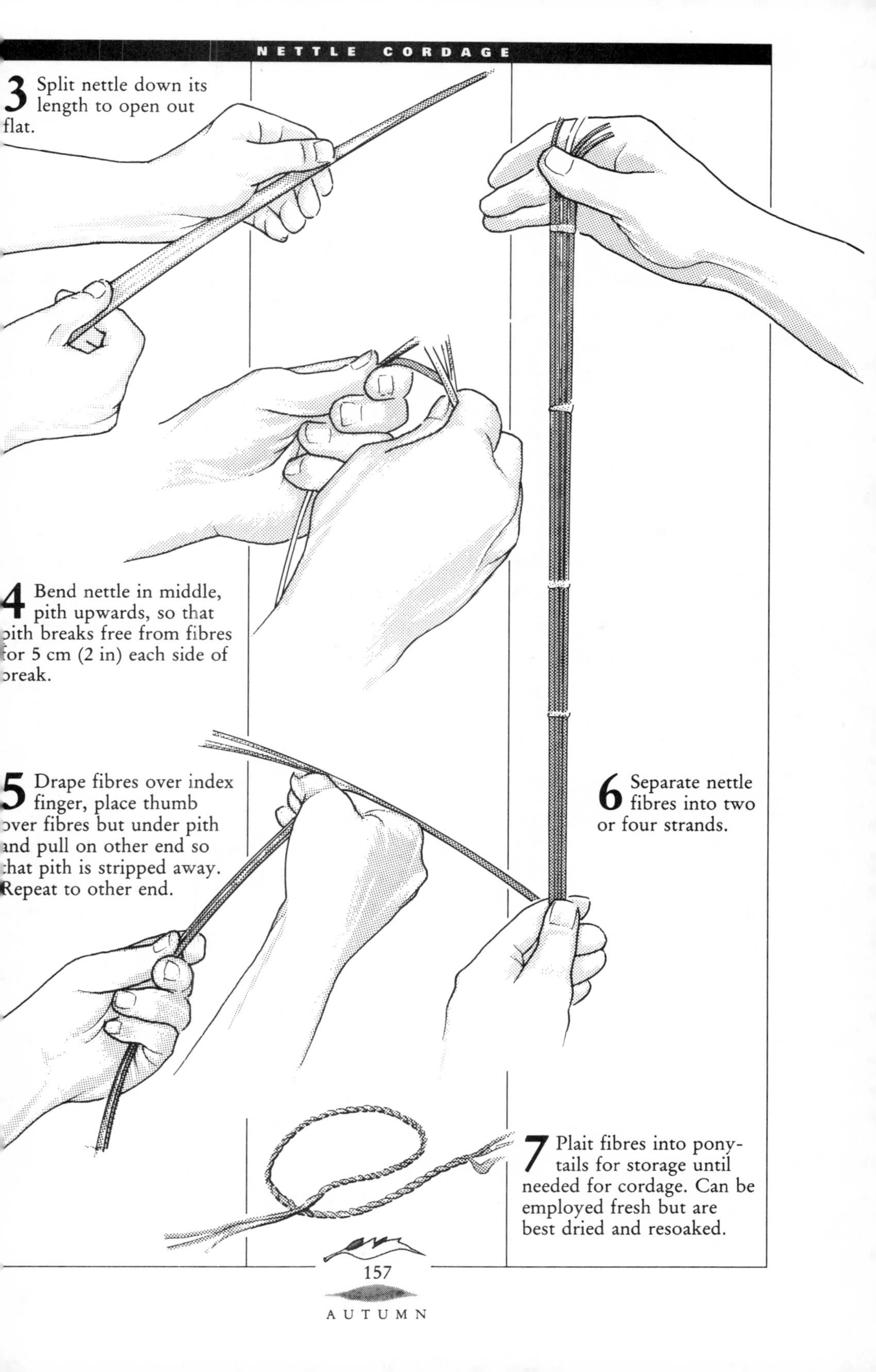

3 Split nettle down its length to open out flat.

4 Bend nettle in middle, pith upwards, so that pith breaks free from fibres for 5 cm (2 in) each side of break.

5 Drape fibres over index finger, place thumb over fibres but under pith and pull on other end so that pith is stripped away. Repeat to other end.

6 Separate nettle fibres into two or four strands.

7 Plait fibres into pony-tails for storage until needed for cordage. Can be employed fresh but are best dried and resoaked.

The pursuit of food

For our ancestors, just as for the animals, autumn was a time of gathering and preparation. All the family would have been involved in some way in bringing in the wild harvest. We can repeat many of the same seasonal activities today.

Competing with the squirrels, we gather up the protein-rich nuts; these then have to be stored in dry, airy conditions to prevent mould. Fungi can be gathered too, sliced thinly and dried for seasoning soups and stews throughout the year. Herbal teas can be prepared for the coming winter, and even some roots can be stored away.

Autumn is the last opportunity to preserve some medicinal herbs by drying them for use during winter and early spring. It is also a time to shore up your shelter in preparation for the coming damp weather – and it is the occasion of the year's last feast before the quiet family evenings of winter.

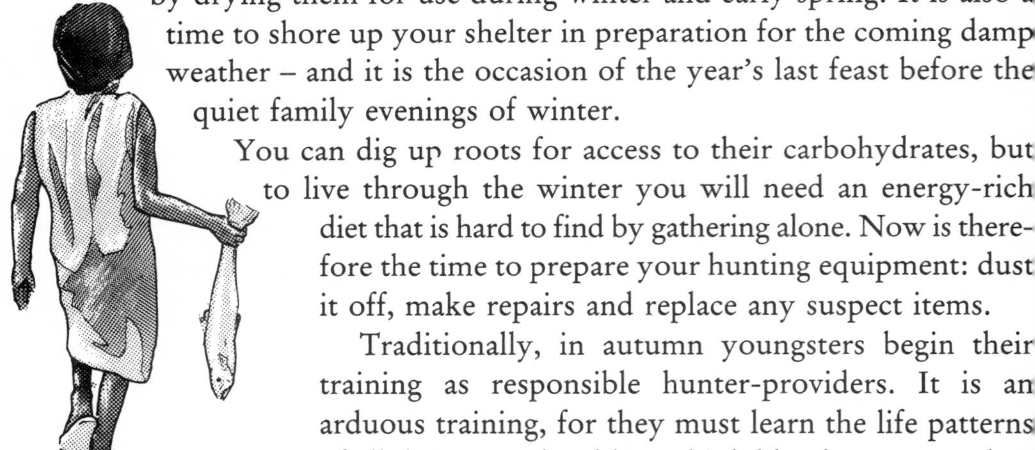

Youngsters learn to catch fish

You can dig up roots for access to their carbohydrates, but to live through the winter you will need an energy-rich diet that is hard to find by gathering alone. Now is therefore the time to prepare your hunting equipment: dust it off, make repairs and replace any suspect items.

Traditionally, in autumn youngsters begin their training as responsible hunter-providers. It is an arduous training, for they must learn the life patterns of all their prey, be able to think like the creature they are stalking and know how that animal will respond to changes in weather and food supply.

The best hunters know their prey well and have the greatest respect for the animals. In the past, hunters sometimes learned so much from one animal that out of respect they vowed never to hunt that species again.

Hunters who have to take their food from a limited area face a conflict of interests: while relying on hunting for their food, they also depend on the well-being of their prey. In some regions of the world, native hunters to this day pass down through their family the vital knowledge of how many animals of which species and from which territory they may take and in which season.

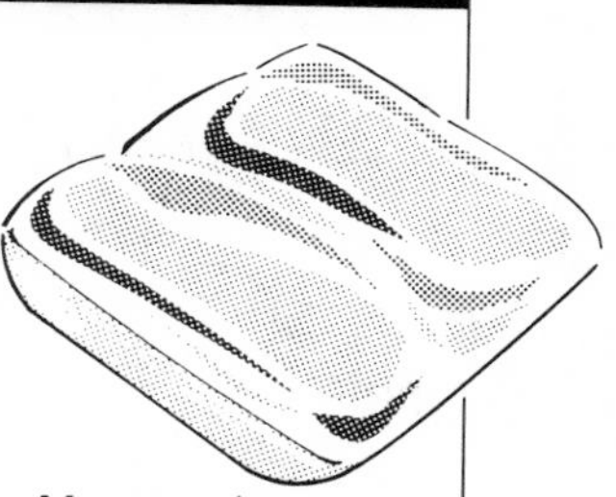

Meat: an important source of energy for late autumn and winter

Thus the hunter is bound by necessity to be at the same time a conservationist. Hunters who have learned this ancient respect will tell you that their aim in life is not to impose themselves upon nature but instead to find an understanding of and harmony with nature, for the long-term well-being of nature, family and tribe.

This deep-seated philosophy is often overlooked by those who criticise all forms of animal hunting without understanding the wisdom of traditional food hunters. If more people were to experience this form of learning, more respect would perhaps be accorded to wild creatures and their habitats. (Modern hunting for sport is, however, a much more controversial subject.)

All this about hunting may seem irrelevant. But you may one day find yourself out in the wild without food, when a basic knowledge of primitive hunting may prove useful.

The hunter's Way is exemplified by this old Cherokee teaching, related by Forrest Carter in *The Education of Little Tree*:

> The quail rose in a rush and sped into the trees – but one was slow. The hawk hit. Feathers flew into the air, and then the birds were on the ground, the hawk's head rising and falling with the death blows. In a moment he rose with the dead quail clutched in his claws, back up the side of the mountain and over the rim.
>
> I didn't cry, but I know I looked sad, because Granpa said, 'Don't feel sad, Little Tree. It is The Way. Tal-con caught the slow and so the slow will raise no children who are also slow. Tal-con eats a thousand ground rats who eat the eggs of the quail – both the quick and the slow eggs – and so Tal-con lives by The Way. He helps the quail.'
>
> Granpa dug a sweet root from the ground with his knife and peeled it so that it dripped with its juicy winter cache of life. He cut it in half and handed me the heavy end.
>
> 'It is The Way,' he said softly. 'Take only what ye need. When ye take the deer, do not take the best. Take the smaller and the slower and then the deer will grow stronger and always give you meat.'

Primitive hunting

The hunting weapons designed and employed by people through the ages show a staggering range and diversity. Their ingenuity marks the human species apart from the rest. Carefully used, these hunting implements enable us to live in balance with the other animals; but when abused, their effect has far-reaching harmful consequences.

For short-term feeding, simple rabbit-hunting equipment is all you need. For longer-term survival, it is essential to be able to kill larger game that bears heavier amounts of fat. Hunting these bigger animals requires more sophisticated – and harder-to-make – equipment. Many of the weapons featured here are still in regular use in remote regions of the world.

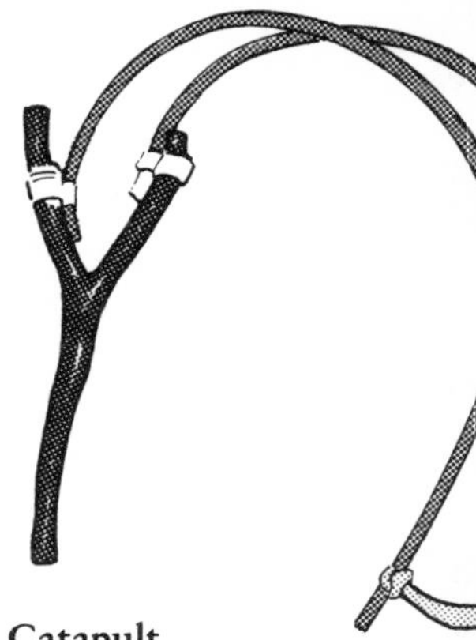

Catapult
A simple, pocketable weapon, in skilled hands one of the simplest and most efficient ways of taking small game.

Throwing sticks
Common to many parts of the world. With a little refinement in aerodynamic design, thrown sticks are swift and effective pot-fillers.

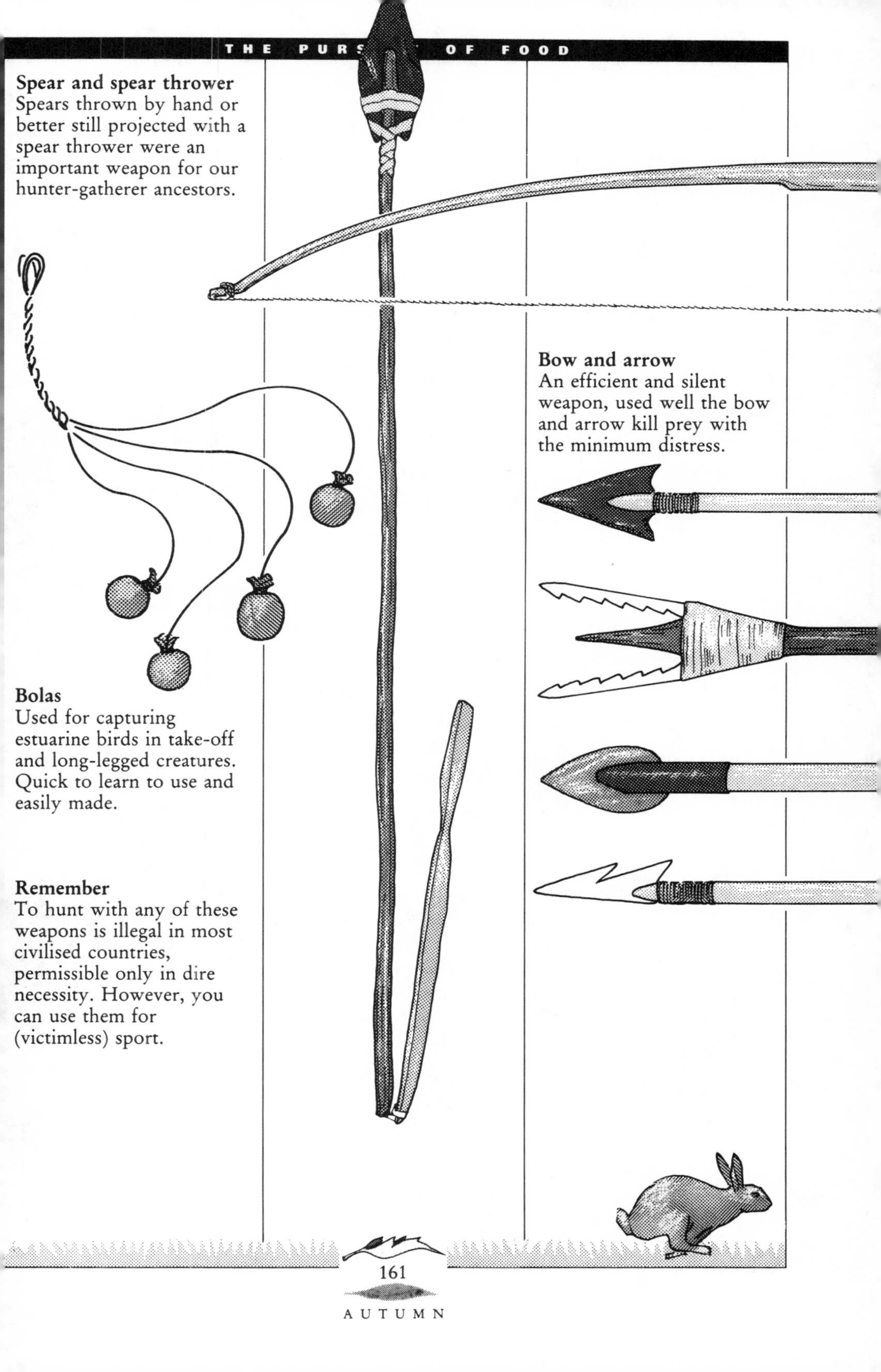

Spear and spear thrower
Spears thrown by hand or better still projected with a spear thrower were an important weapon for our hunter-gatherer ancestors.

Bow and arrow
An efficient and silent weapon, used well the bow and arrow kill prey with the minimum distress.

Bolas
Used for capturing estuarine birds in take-off and long-legged creatures. Quick to learn to use and easily made.

Remember
To hunt with any of these weapons is illegal in most civilised countries, permissible only in dire necessity. However, you can use them for (victimless) sport.

Skinning a small mammal

Once you have caught a rabbit, or perhaps bought one on your travels from a game shop, you need to know how to prepare it. There are many ways to skin a rabbit, determined mainly by what you intend to do with the skin afterwards. With practice, you should be able to remove the skin intact – feet, ears and whiskers. But the method shown here is simpler and can be used for most animals, small or large; naturally, it assumes that you want to save the skin.

Even though the animal is dead, it still demands respect in the way you handle it and its remains. Tribal traditions often attach importance to this. Young hunters soon learn that if they are unsuccesful this is likely to be because they failed to show due respect to their last prey.

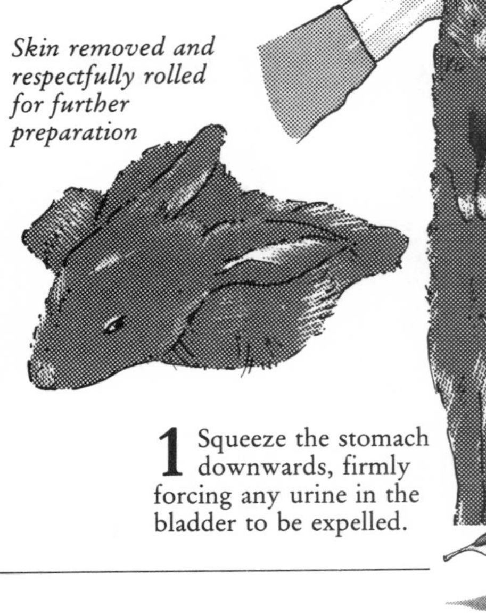

Skin removed and respectfully rolled for further preparation

1 Squeeze the stomach downwards, firmly forcing any urine in the bladder to be expelled.

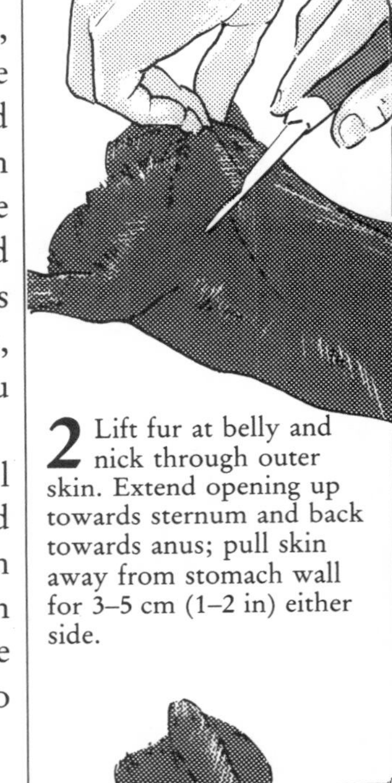

2 Lift fur at belly and nick through outer skin. Extend opening up towards sternum and back towards anus; pull skin away from stomach wall for 3–5 cm (1–2 in) either side.

3 Repeat process with stomach wall. Take care not to rupture internal organs.

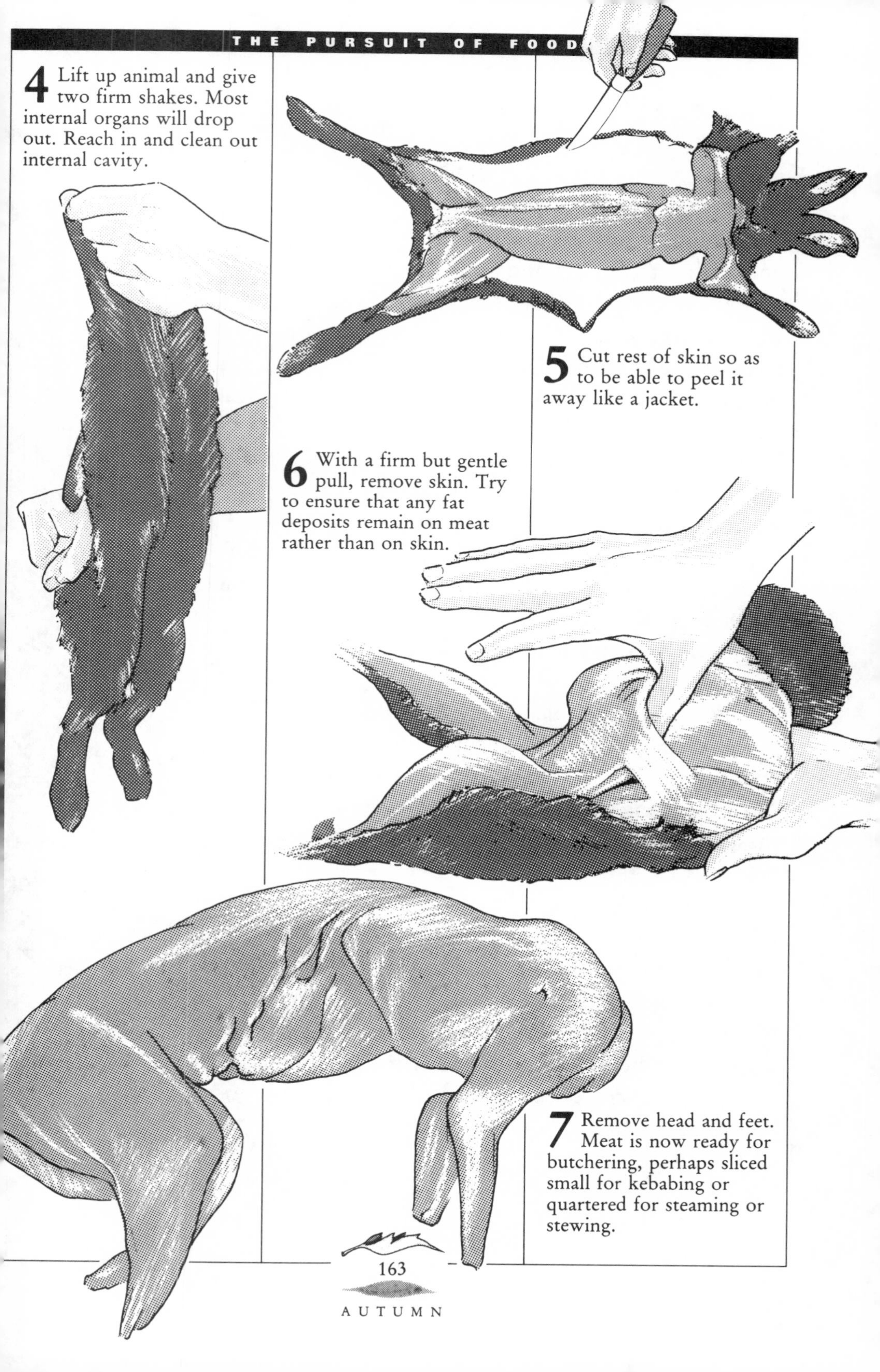

4 Lift up animal and give two firm shakes. Most internal organs will drop out. Reach in and clean out internal cavity.

5 Cut rest of skin so as to be able to peel it away like a jacket.

6 With a firm but gentle pull, remove skin. Try to ensure that any fat deposits remain on meat rather than on skin.

7 Remove head and feet. Meat is now ready for butchering, perhaps sliced small for kebabing or quartered for steaming or stewing.

Wasting nothing

The game of any region is a finite resource, and no part of it should be wasted. In fact, many important resource materials can be obtained from animal carcasses. Not wasting anything was traditionally part of the way people accorded respect to the creatures they hunted.

The North American plains tribes who followed the great buffalo herds on horseback were a fine example of the waste-nothing approach. Living as they did in a sea of grass, with less access to trees than other native Americans, the plains Indians made extensive use of the bison's bones and other by-products of their hunting.

They were completely dependent on the buffalo, and there was almost no limit to the applications they found for the animal's parts. Not surprisingly, the plains tribes worshipped these great creatures that provided them with the tools for life.

Although you are unlikely ever to need to use all the parts of your prey, an appreciation of the value of them will augment your understanding and appreciation of nature. Place the parts that you do not use somewhere respectful where they will return to the land again – for example, bury them. The rubbish bin is not a fitting way to dispose of these unwanted pieces.

Skin
Skin can be used for clothing, containers and coverings, prepared as rawhide or as buckskin (see p. 166).

Tendons
Dried and pounded to separate the individual fibres, tendons can be used to reinforce the backs of hunting bows and as thread for sewing together garments. They can also be used to make very strong cordage.

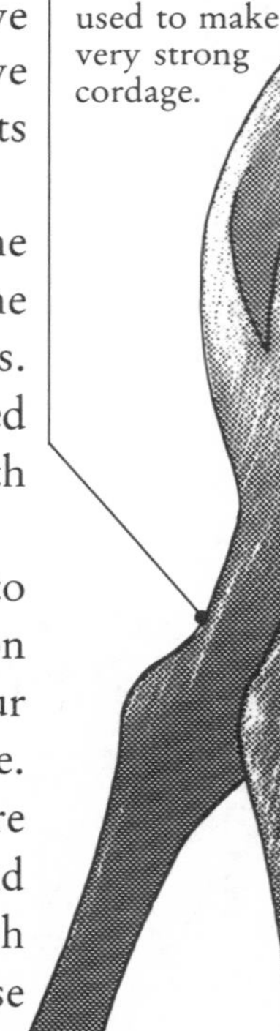

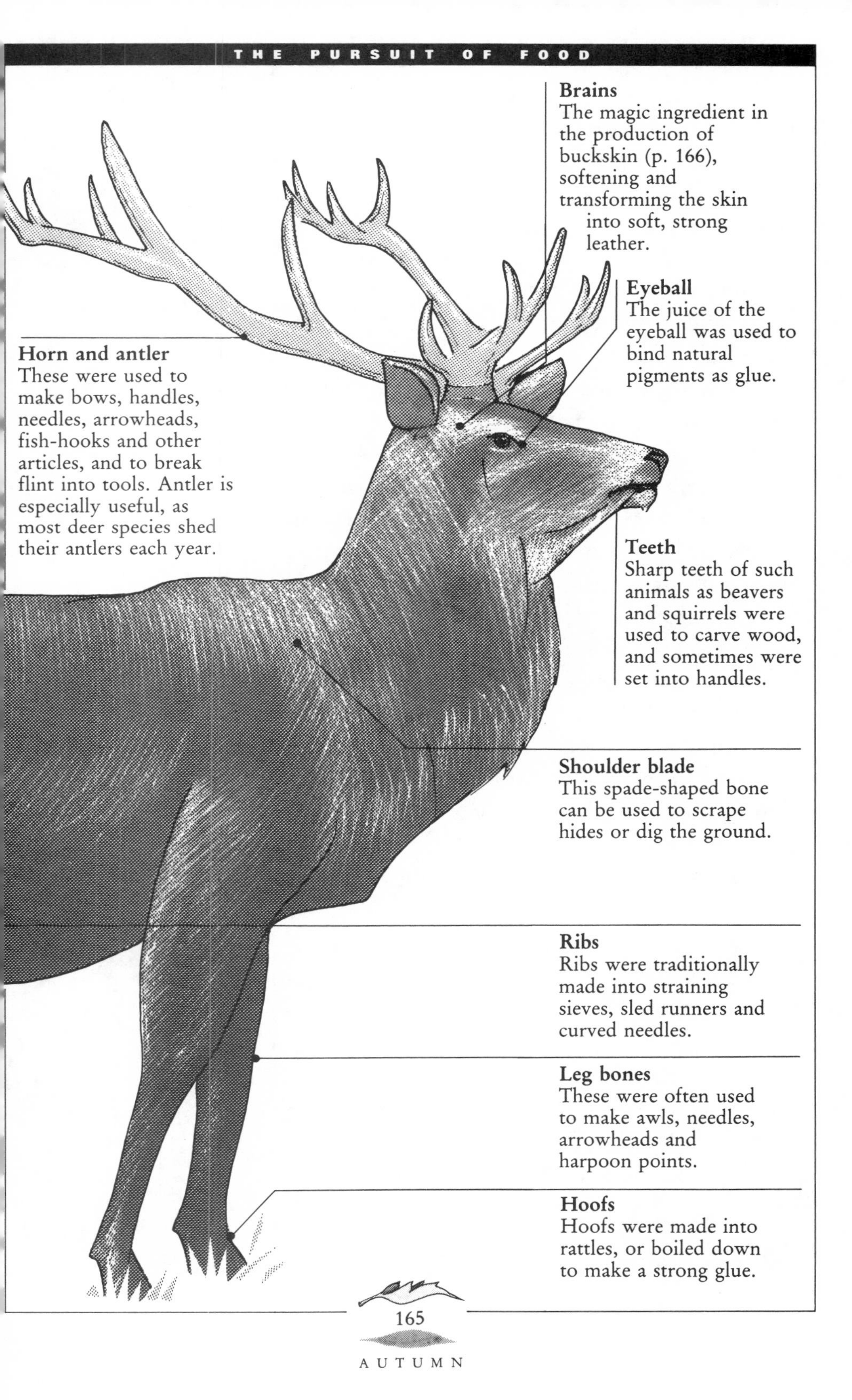
Brains
The magic ingredient in the production of buckskin (p. 166), softening and transforming the skin into soft, strong leather.
Eyeball
The juice of the eyeball was used to bind natural pigments as glue.
Horn and antler
These were used to make bows, handles, needles, arrowheads, fish-hooks and other articles, and to break flint into tools. Antler is especially useful, as most deer species shed their antlers each year.
Teeth
Sharp teeth of such animals as beavers and squirrels were used to carve wood, and sometimes were set into handles.
Shoulder blade
This spade-shaped bone can be used to scrape hides or dig the ground.
Ribs
Ribs were traditionally made into straining sieves, sled runners and curved needles.
Leg bones
These were often used to make awls, needles, arrowheads and harpoon points.
Hoofs
Hoofs were made into rattles, or boiled down to make a strong glue.

Preparing skins

Preparing and processing skins were once important activities, producing bags, cordage, shoes and clothing. Well-prepared hides are the result of hard work, but the satisfaction and benefit derived from the finished leather are more than adequate compensation.

Here we are interested in two basic products: rawhide and smoked buckskin. Rawhide is leather which has not been treated in any way by chemicals or other tanning agents. It dries stiff, shrinking slightly, and becomes soft in damp weather or after a soaking. This means that it can be made pliable by soaking before being used; once dry, it forms a vice-like grip. Rawhide is used in this way for drum heads, the tone of the drum changing according to local humidity. Buckskin is rawhide that has been treated with brains to soften the fibres and then smoked to help it resist stiffening after soaking. In feel it is much like chamois leather, but it is far stronger and suffused with the scent of woodsmoke. Buckskin is used for clothing, pouches and footwear.

Brains

Brains from the animal whose skin we are working are mashed finely into a slurry with some warm water. Soaked overnight in this solution, the hide takes on the texture, look and slippery feel of wet pasta. Theories abound as to what the brains actually do to the hide; but for our purposes it is sufficient to know that they soften it, producing buckskin.

Rawhide

1 Lay hide over a log, flesh side up. Use a bone or metal tool to scrape away fat and connective tissue.

Buckskin

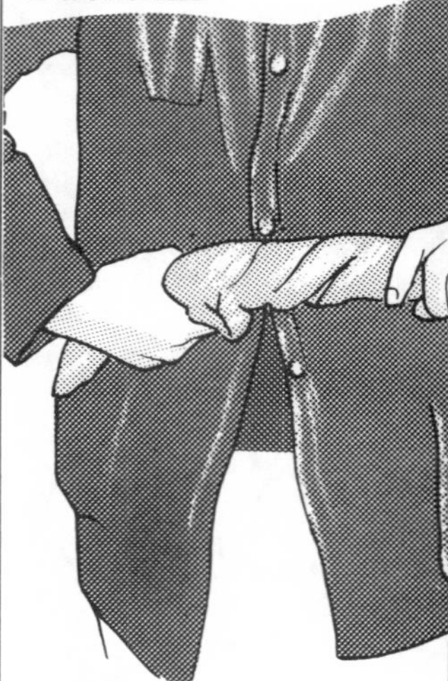

4 Take hide off rack, soak in water until soft and pliable, immerse overnight in brains solution, then wring out thoroughly.

2 Tie hide into a sturdy, well-lashed frame and allow to dry.

3 Use a tool with a rounded chisel-like edge to scrape away fur and outer skin layer below.

5 Re-rack hide and knead vigorously with blunt-ended stick until dry, soft and fluffy white. Use shade or water to prevent hide drying too quickly.

6 Take hide off rack, sew up loosely into a tube and arrange for smoking. Smoke both sides thoroughly until dark brown.

End-of-season treats

Early autumn sees the tail-end of the wild harvest, when the late-ripening fruits become available. Some of these become truly palatable only after the first frosts. Often, too, many summer delicacies can still be found. Once threatening skies have arrived, and the smell of decaying leaves fills the air, the edible nuts are ready for gathering. For our ancestors this was an important time; nuts can be stored over winter, providing much-needed fat and protein.

Acorns were and in some places still are a highly valued annual crop. The bitter acorns found in Britain are usually regarded as poisonous. But this bitterness – caused by tannin – can be dissolved out by boiling the kernels in repeated changes of water until the water ceases to turn brown; or by crushing them, placing them in a muslin bag and boiling repeatedly.

The cleaned whole nuts can be roasted and eaten, while the nut crush can be used as a gruel or damper (unleavened bread) mix.

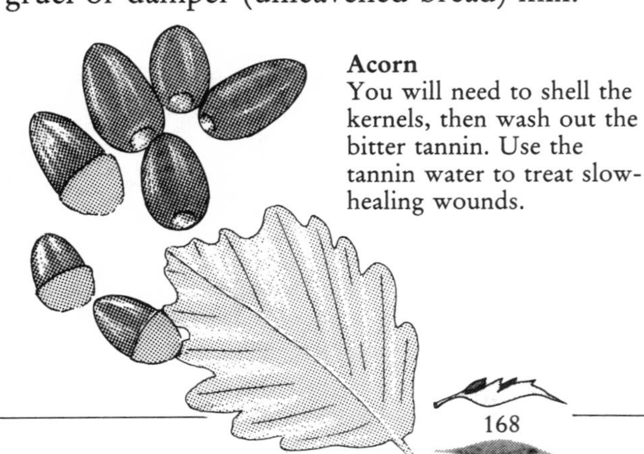

Acorn
You will need to shell the kernels, then wash out the bitter tannin. Use the tannin water to treat slow-healing wounds.

Sweet chestnut
A real delicacy. Remove from shell, pierce with your knife-point and roast in front of fire.

Hazel
Usually the first nut available and absolutely delicious. You will have to be quick to beat the squirrels.

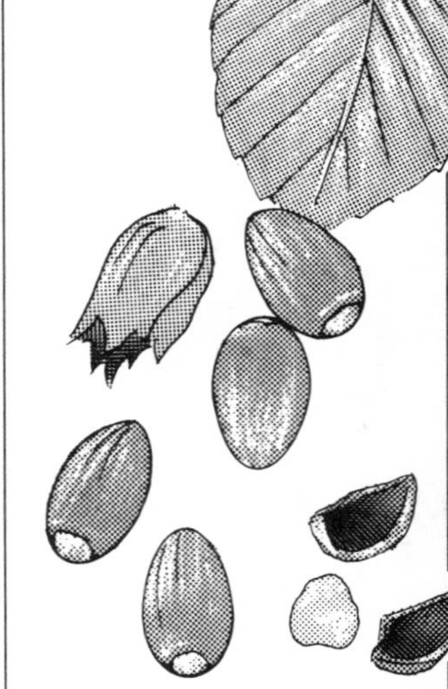

Walnut
Wild walnuts now rare, and few people today seem to recognise this forager's delicacy.

Whitebeam
Edible only once the red berries have begun to decay, when flesh is rich orange colour and soft.

Rowan
Berries are common on moorland but unpleasant raw. Make an excellent jelly when mixed with crab apples, whose pectin removes bitter taste.

Nutcracker

A simple nutcracker can be fashioned from a hazel branch. Cut just below a fork and 20 cm (8 in) above the fork, and you have a naturally springy U-shaped nutcracker.

Life out of death

Fungi help break down the debris of the forest. Without them, the woods would become choked with the undecayed remains of fallen branches. This breakdown is a vital part of the natural cycle, efficiently recycling the nutrients in the dead wood. Fungi are for the most part a grossly misunderstood resource; associated with death and decay, springing mysteriously from the ground and trees, they have a sinister reputation. Coupled with the fact that some species are fatally poisonous, while others induce hallucinations, it is no wonder that people kick them over in fear.

Not all fungi will do us harm, however, and many are useful for medicine, food or other purposes. In many parts of Europe, edible species are regularly gathered for sale in the markets. In many regions the fungi have been overcollected and are now endangered.

Fungi are more difficult to identify than plants. Their colour, shape, scent, habitat or host, and spore details are critical points of identification. Edible species often have very similar poisonous cousins, so care in identification is essential. If you are going to pursue an interest in wild fungi, you need to arm yourself with an excellent field guide. There is a problem, though. Your field guide will perhaps describe a certain fungus as possessing a particular scent – reminiscent, for example, of flour. Until you have smelled that species for yourself you cannot be certain you are correctly matching your scent descriptions with that of the book. By far the best way to learn about fungi is on a field course run by an expert.

Finding an expert

The study of fungi is called *mycology*. A local university should be able to put you in touch with its mycological society. Many nature-study centres run autumn fungi forays. The address of the Mycological Society of America is listed in Appendix 1.

Risks and dangers

The consequences of eating a deadly fungus are chilling. The most dangerous family is the *Amanita* genus which contains the death cap. Attacking the liver and kidneys, the symptoms of amanita poisoning – stomach pains, diarrhoea, vomiting – frequently show only after much damage has already been caused, sometimes only 24 hours after ingestion. THERE IS NO KNOWN ANTIDOTE, so it is essential to know the characteristics of this family and other poisonous species.

Danger signs

To identify any fungus, you need all parts of the specimen; if necessary dig it from the ground. It should be fresh and undamaged. The following are the characteristic signs of the amanita family.

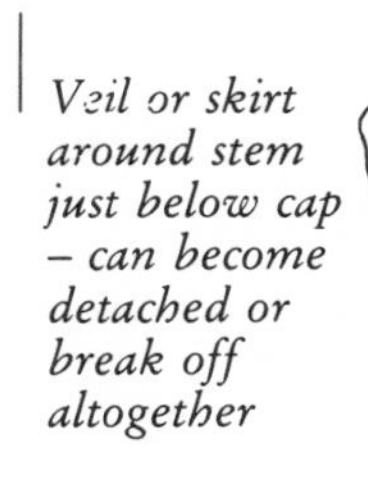

Veil or skirt around stem just below cap – can become detached or break off altogether

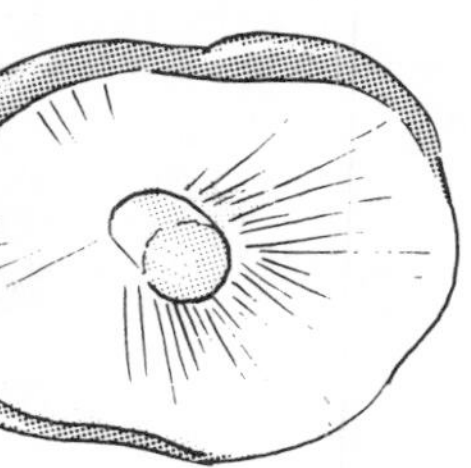

Pure white gills producing pure white spores

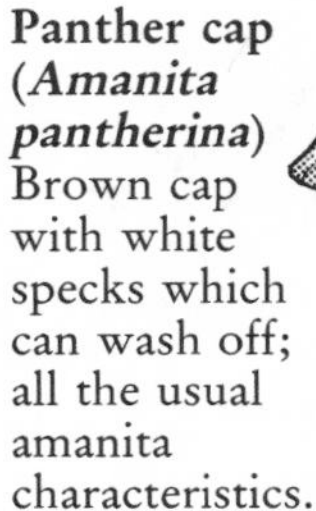

Volva or bulbous base, often with well-developed rim on stem

The egg stage

At first, an amanita resembles a small puffball. To avoid confusion, slice such egg-like fungi in half. Amanitas clearly contain the developing outline of cap and gills; puffballs are pure white throughout.

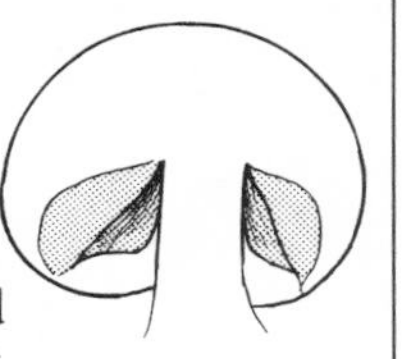

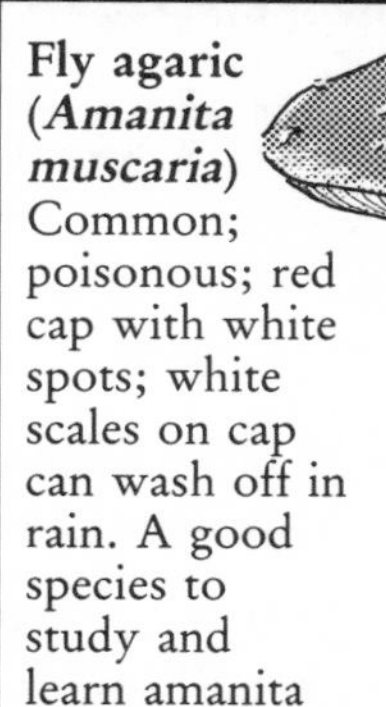

Fly agaric (*Amanita muscaria*) Common; poisonous; red cap with white spots; white scales on cap can wash off in rain. A good species to study and learn amanita characteristics.

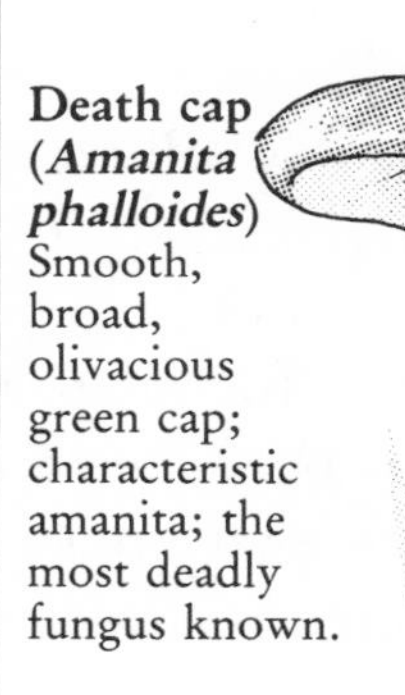

Death cap (*Amanita phalloides*) Smooth, broad, olivacious green cap; characteristic amanita; the most deadly fungus known.

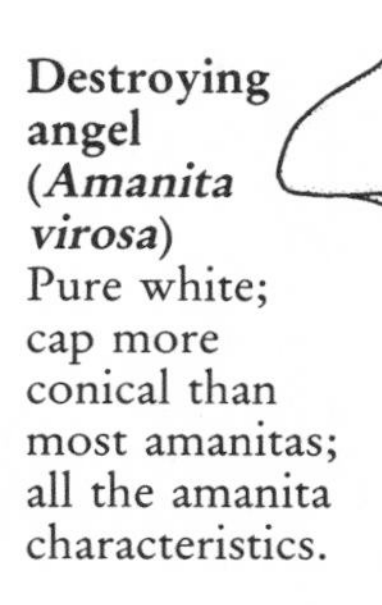

Destroying angel (*Amanita virosa*) Pure white; cap more conical than most amanitas; all the amanita characteristics.

Panther cap (*Amanita pantherina*) Brown cap with white specks which can wash off; all the usual amanita characteristics.

Edible fungi

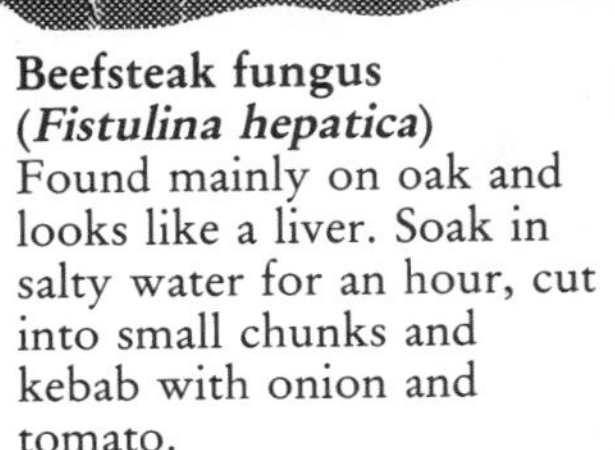

Edible wild fungi are far from nutritious, but they are wonderful flavourings for a host of cooking applications. The best varieties are to be found growing in woodland. Many species of fungus are edible; but if you are just starting out, my suggestion is to avoid any fungus that has gills.

While this will exclude some delicious fungi from your basket, it will also greatly reduce your risk of eating a poisonous species. Look particuarly for fungi with a mushroom shape but with pores instead of gills – that is, an underside that looks like a sponge. These fungi, often referred to as 'boletes', are especially tasty.

Beefsteak fungus (*Fistulina hepatica*)
Found mainly on oak and looks like a liver. Soak in salty water for an hour, cut into small chunks and kebab with onion and tomato.

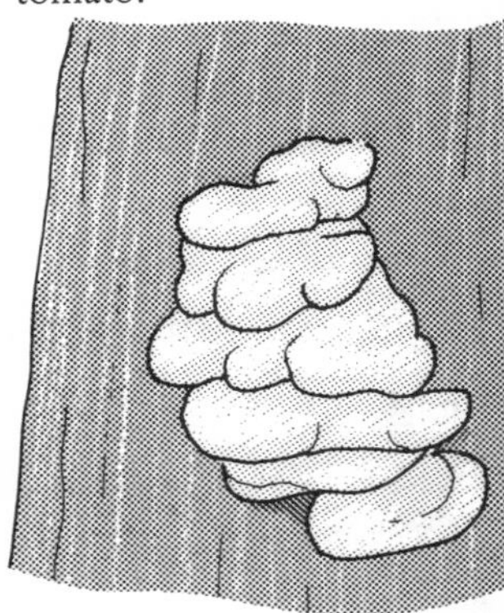

Chicken-of-the-woods (*Laetiporus sulphureus*)
Bright lemon yellow, prefers to grow on yew. Delicious when cooked in stews, sliced thinly like chicken breast.

Brain fungus (*Sparassis crispa*)
Found below scots pines, resembling a brain or coral. Clean carefully. Delicious with sauces. Dries well.

Some do's and don'ts

A handful of the boletes are poisonous, one seriously so. But fortunately these all have a distinctly unpleasant taste when raw, and in most cases they have orange or red pores or are flushed with orange or red on the stem. Therefore collect only those boletes that you know to be edible and that have yellow or cream-coloured pores. Avoid any specimens with orange on them. Also, cook all wild fungi before consumption – many contain substances that may upset you, unless destroyed by cooking.

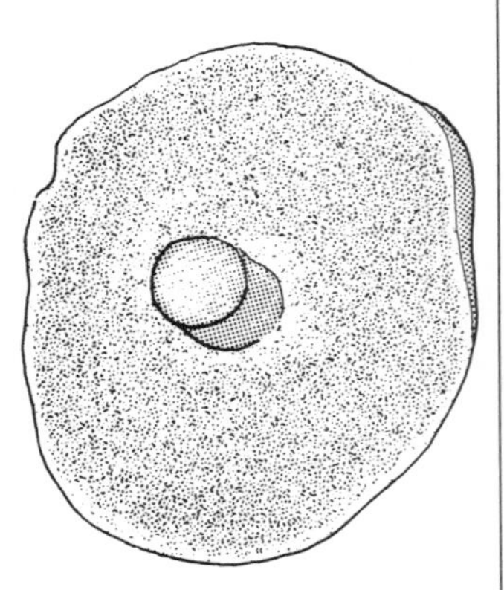

Cep or penny bun (*Boletus edulis*)
Delicious mushroom, especially when dried. Highly prized.

Bay boletus (*Boletus badius*)
Frequently overlooked; every bit as good as *Boletus edulis* when dried.

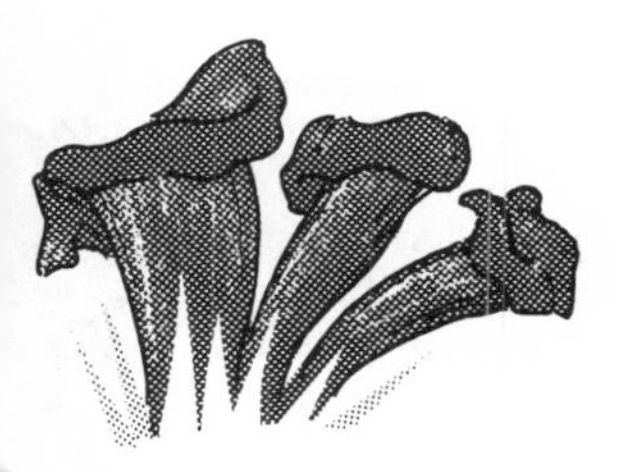

Horn of plenty (*Craterellus cornucopioides*)
Resembling little black crumpets, found in leaf litter. Delicious flavouring for any stew.

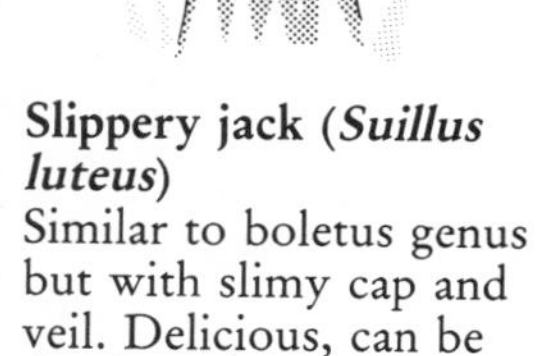

Slippery jack (*Suillus luteus*)
Similar to boletus genus but with slimy cap and veil. Delicious, can be dried.

Birch boletes (*Leccinum versipelle/L. scabrum*)
Grows under birch. Cream-coloured pores and scaly stem. Often ignored, excellent, especially when dried.

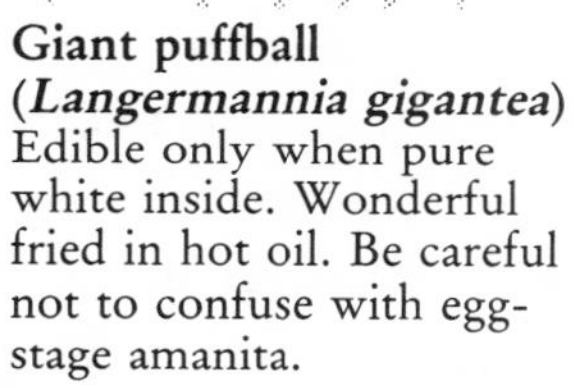

Giant puffball (*Langermannia gigantea*)
Edible only when pure white inside. Wonderful fried in hot oil. Be careful not to confuse with egg-stage amanita.

Hedgehog fungus (*Hydnum repandum*)
No gills or pores but spines instead. Small, likes coniferous woodland. Delicious.

Utility

Although we make little use of wild fungi today, they have a long association with people. More than just sources of food, fungi have traditionally provided a whole range of utilitarian services, such as dyeing, fire-lighting and materials for medicines and even blotting paper. Some varieties were once collected commercially, and some Australian Aborigines still use *Phellinus rimosus* to treat sinus problems. But in general the old folk-uses of fungi are gradually disappearing as modern alternatives replace them.

A knowledge of utility fungi can be a positive advantage for the backcountry traveller, as well as serving to keep alive hard-earned traditional skills. Here are just four of the best of these fungi and how they can be used.

Puffball

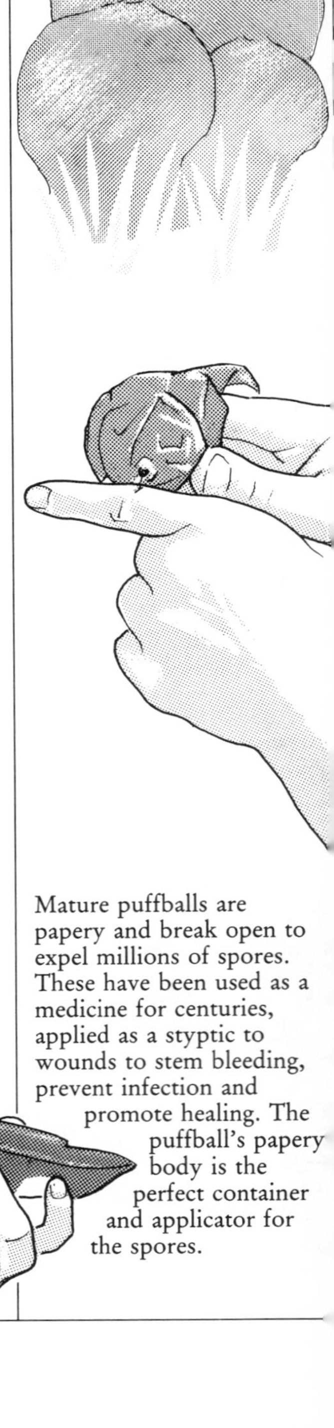

Mature puffballs are papery and break open to expel millions of spores. These have been used as a medicine for centuries, applied as a styptic to wounds to stem bleeding, prevent infection and promote healing. The puffball's papery body is the perfect container and applicator for the spores.

Birch polypore

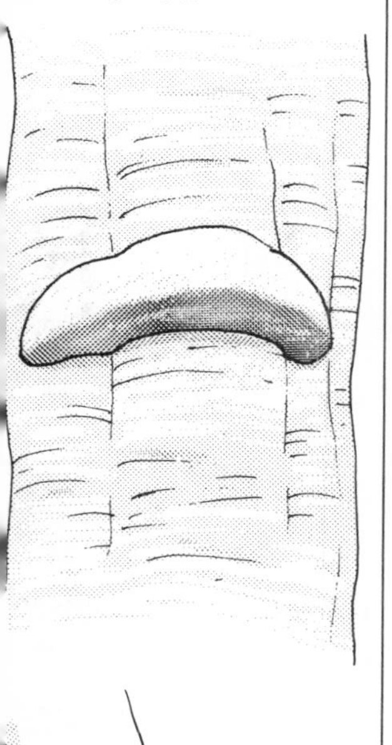

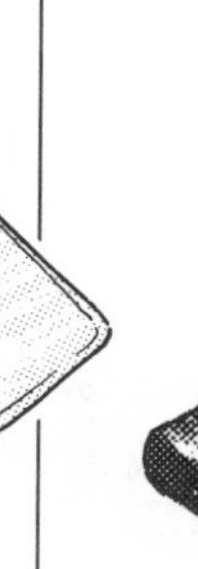

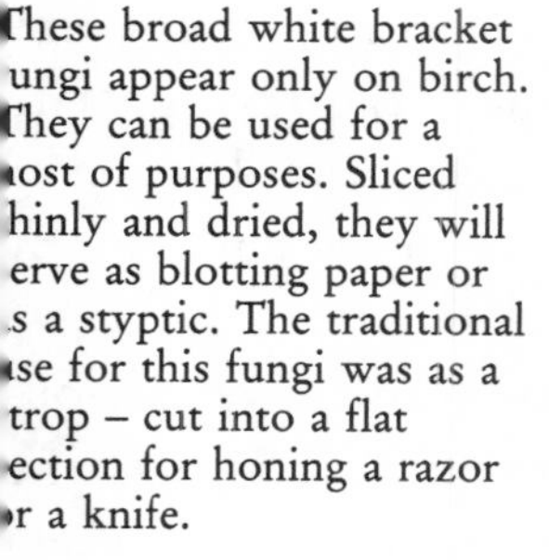

These broad white bracket ungi appear only on birch. They can be used for a ost of purposes. Sliced hinly and dried, they will erve as blotting paper or s a styptic. The traditional use for this fungi was as a trop – cut into a flat ection for honing a razor r a knife.

Cramp-ball

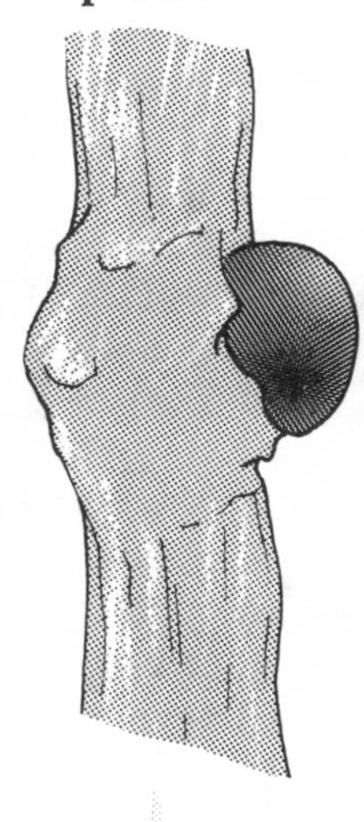

These tight, hard, brown-to black-coloured fungi are found mainly on ash. Broken open they contain concentric rings. We have already come across them for use as tinder (see p. 46). Several of them set alight will make an excellent substitute for charcoal for broiling meat. Cramp-balls also dispel insects.

Fomes fomentarius

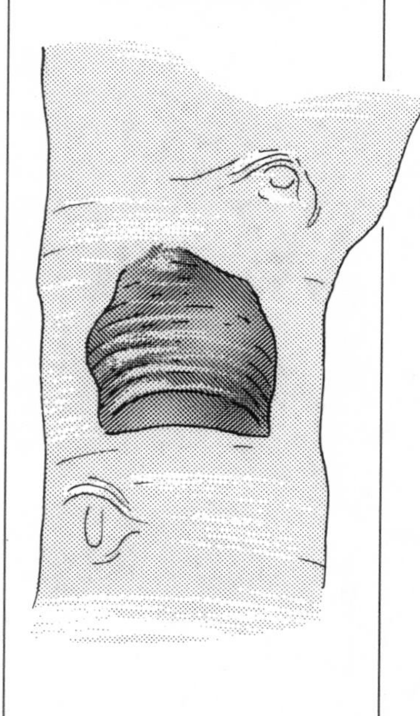

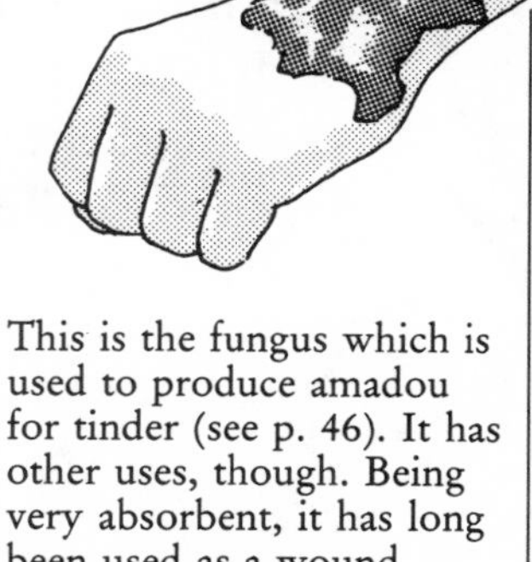

This is the fungus which is used to produce amadou for tinder (see p. 46). It has other uses, though. Being very absorbent, it has long been used as a wound dressing, a function it performs excellently. Anglers also use it to dry their fishing flies.

WINTER

In winter, Orion the hunter returns to a prominent position above the southern horizon. The weather turns dramatically colder, and the nights stretch out, shutting out the feeble sunlight. Winter is a season of extremes. It can be threateningly bleak or silencingly beautiful. On the trail, it is a time of severe testing, showing us whether we have learned our skills well.

Before venturing into the winter landscape, you should make a few preparations. Your clothing will need plenty of insulation with windproof and waterproof 'shell' layers. You will be using your torch hard, so give it a another good refit of bulb and batteries. If you are setting out into wild areas, go prepared with food, shelter and sleeping equipment.

Before setting off, estimate how long you expect to be gone for. Leave this information, along with your route plan, the number and ages of your party and details of the equipment you are carrying, with someone responsible. This precaution has saved many lives when parties become cut off by sudden changes in the weather.

Even simple excursions can have serious consequences at this time. Someone I know who lives in Yorkshire went skiing in the first decent winter snowfall one year – nowhere dangerous, just to the local hills. His rusty skiing legs failed him, and

Long shadows and bare trees are winter's hallmark

he fell awkwardly down an obscured depression, suffering a severely broken leg. Not having left a single word of his planned outing, he nearly froze to death within a mile and a half of his home. He was eventually found by a person walking their dog who summoned the local mountain rescue.

Few sights match the grotto-like beauty of a frozen landscape

Play-safe wisdom is far better than misplaced machismo.

For a long while on every winter excursion I have put a can of Heinz tomato soup in my backpack. It is one weight I don't mind carrying. At the end of the day's activity, with the fire just lit, the can is quickly opened, the lid bent back and creased to form a handle, and pushed into the edge of the fire. It then needs only the occasional stir while I see to the other camp chores. By the time camp is set, my favourite canned soup is ready for consumption.

Many people prefer to avoid camping out during winter, making day-hikes from accommodation instead. But winter camping has a magic all its own – to say nothing of ironing out wrinkles in your technique. The long nights seem made for camaraderie. There is no better time for exuberant groups of teenagers to go bivouaking, especially if they are able to construct a group shelter (see p. 186). While the shelter keeps out chilling drafts and falling rain or snow, everybody inside can sit snugly around the camp-fire.

For interesting short day excursions, head for the coast. Winter is an exhilarating time to be on the beach or among the rock-pools. The shore foods are now at their safest for eating; dangerous algae are greatly reduced, and sewage outfall is more effectively dispersed by the mighty winter seas. But be careful not to be caught by the tide.

Wherever you go in the wild at this time of year, the animals become bolder as they struggle to find sufficient food. They are also easier to track on the soft ground or, better still, in the snow. Follow a fox's trail for several miles in snow and you may find a kill site or places where the fox has cached its food. There is no better time to gain an insight into the way these creatures live.

Animal kingdoms

Winter is the harsh season, the time of cleansing. Bundled up in our centrally heated dens, it is easy to forget its real significance for the natural world. This is the time when icy cold sanitises the countryside, and rains wash every branch and twig. Gales blow away the remaining dead leaves on the deciduous trees. The animals must now struggle hard to find their food, and any weak, exhausted or old animals that cannot keep pace with the season's demands simply do not survive.

To understand winter well, you must learn how the wild creatures cope. Next time you come indoors to that dry cosy warmth and feeling of security, gaze out of the window and ask yourself what the deer or the weasel is doing. Most native wild animals are, in fact, far better adapted to being out in the cold than we are. I have watched a fur-clad fox sleep in the open, curled nose-under-brush, during a snowstorm until it was totally encased save for the ears which twitched at every strange sound.

Foxes are very active hunters during the winter months

Most fur-clad creatures develop a winter coat distinctly different from the summer one, with more downy under-fur protected by longer barrier-fur well endowed with natural oils as weatherproofing. In roe deer, for example, the winter coat loses its sheen and ruddy colour and turns a more subdued grey with more of a matt finish. Some animals totally alter their fur colour for better winter camouflage – the classic example being the arctic hare, which changes its coat from brown to white which blends better with snow. In Ireland it does not turn white, due to the less frequent snow; but in the Arctic itself this hare may wear its white coat all year round.

Preening of feathers or grooming of fur takes up a considerable part of any creature's day in winter, for careful tending of this insulative coat is essential to its full efficiency. The same principles apply to human cold-weather clothing. We need a weatherproof shell protecting insulating layers which trap air warmed by body heat. This must be oiled to repel insulation-destroying moisture, and carefully cleaned and maintained for full efficiency. It's simple, really!

The majority of smaller mammals hibernate or semi-hibernate for the winter in warm nests. Hibernation is a neat trick of natural adaptation that I have often envied on cold nights. Although well insulated in a nest of dry grasses, the animal's body temperature falls to a dramatically low level, and the body's vital functions slow to the verge of stopping. In this way the body's stored food reserves are eked out until the early-spring thaw.

Dormice disappear to their winter nests

The squirrel is an example of a creature that only semi-hibernates. If you are a seasoned woodland explorer in winter you will have encountered squirrels at this time, out searching for their stored food. They can be totally absent the next day. This is because their winter is interrupted by periods of activity when they must eat.

One small mammal that stays awake is the bank vole. This industrious little creature constructs tunnels under the snow, trapping the warmth from the soil. Travelling through a network of tunnels, the voles create depot-like stores of foods and deposit neat piles of their droppings. Watch for a fox listening intently to their activities, trying to locate their exact position for a pounce.

One of the most fascinating things to watch is a bird I like to call the water wren after its similarity of posture to the land-dwelling wren. More usually called the dipper, it plunges into the icy torrents of a fast-flowing winter stream in search of food. Its well-adapted claws enable it to walk over slippery rocks against the current. Where there are dippers there are almost certainly also kingfishers nearby. But of all the winter creatures the shrill-voiced and flashing red-breasted robin is my favourite. It can often be tempted into the campsite for tidbits; once fed a few times, the camp robin will be your regular companion.

The robin's song will cheer your camp

Winter trails

With its soft ground and snowy covering, winter is an easy time for tracking. In good conditions you can read trails with ease. Like a single note of music, each track joined with its neighbour reveals the life song of the animal that left them. This is an important training time for the tracker, for now you can learn the patterns of animal movements in relation to their activity. In other seasons when the terrain is less favourable, you will then have a better idea where the hard-to-distinguish track is likely to be.

Fox
In snow often places hind feet directly into forefeet tracks, leaving a trail as if walking upright.

Rabbit
Larger hind feet land in front of the forefeet. Forefeet placed diagonally apart.

Squirrel
Larger hind feet land in front of the forefeet. Forefeet placed beside each other.

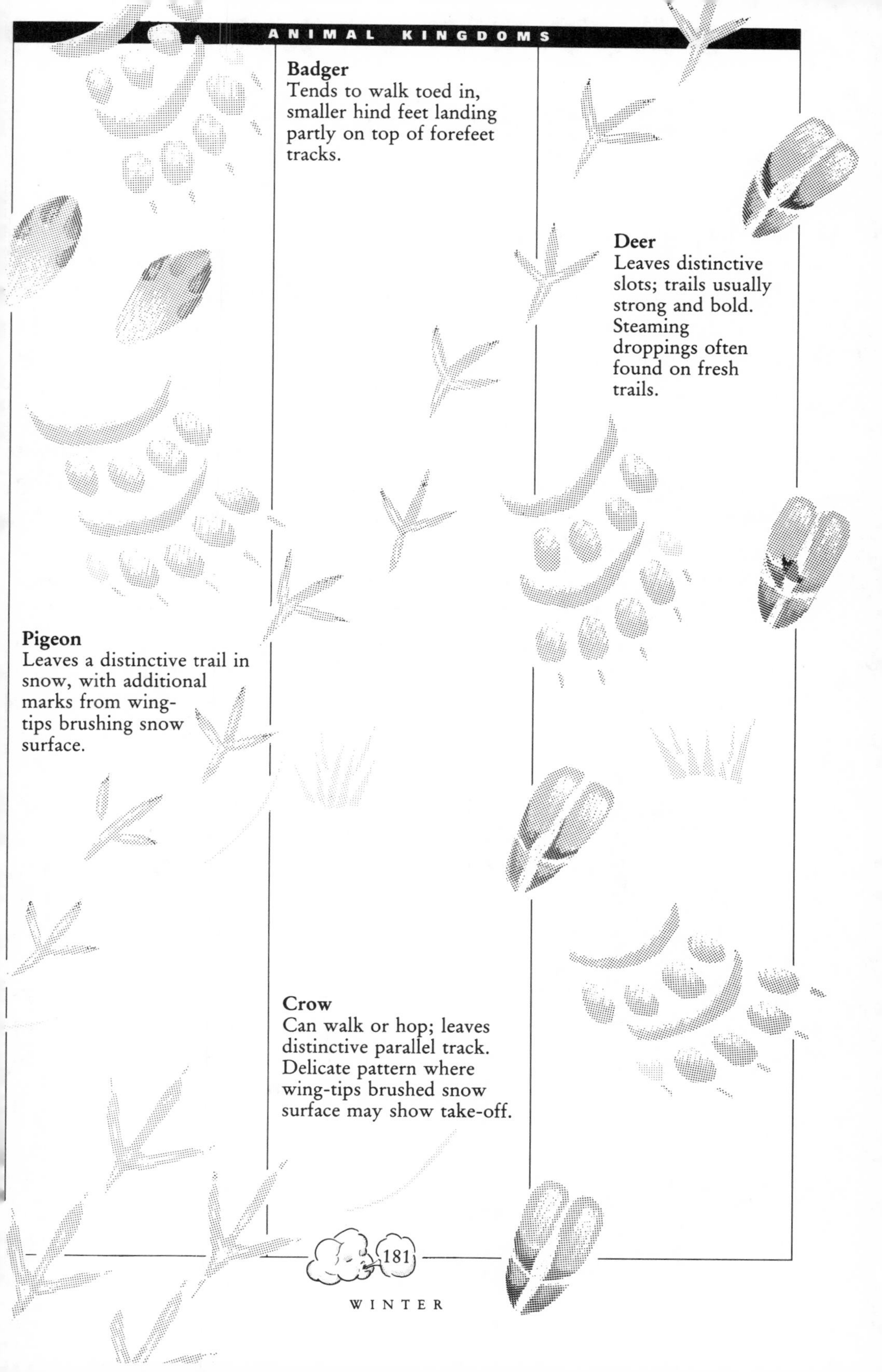

Badger
Tends to walk toed in, smaller hind feet landing partly on top of forefeet tracks.

Deer
Leaves distinctive slots; trails usually strong and bold. Steaming droppings often found on fresh trails.

Pigeon
Leaves a distinctive trail in snow, with additional marks from wing-tips brushing snow surface.

Crow
Can walk or hop; leaves distinctive parallel track. Delicate pattern where wing-tips brushed snow surface may show take-off.

Winter shelters

Finding or constructing a shelter in winter conditions is a serious business. With cold, damp and wind to contend with, your life could depend upon it. Every year people die of exposure in the British mountains. They may be ill equipped, unfit or poorly fed; they may be lost and over-extend themselves searching for the way home; mostly they have underestimated the potential hazard.

On our barren, exposed hillsides, the weather can change from pleasant to angry very quickly. So even day-hikers in these regions should carry some food, insulation (perhaps a fibre-pile sleeping-bag liner) and shelter – a tent or bivvy-bag, or at least an orange polythene survival bag.

A winter shelter must exclude wind, wet and cold. In snowy conditions the snow itself may be the only available material. The most commonly used snow for shelter construction is crusty snow that can be easily cut into blocks. Deep drifts of this snow can also be excavated to form snow holes and caves. Even only a 15 cm (6 in) depth of powder snow can be fashioned into a snow house.

When making shelters from snow, the shelter must always be well ventilated to prevent the build-up of poisonous gases, and the door-well must always be lower than the sleeping platform for adequate insulation. Try to remain dry while building the snow hole; you may need to strip off warm insulative clothing to prevent excessive perspiration. Always improvise an insulating layer between yourself and the snow platform on which you rest or sleep.

Using a polythene survival bag as an emergency shelter: cut breathing hole near bottom and pull bag over you; use climbing rope for insulative seat; tuck feet into knapsack

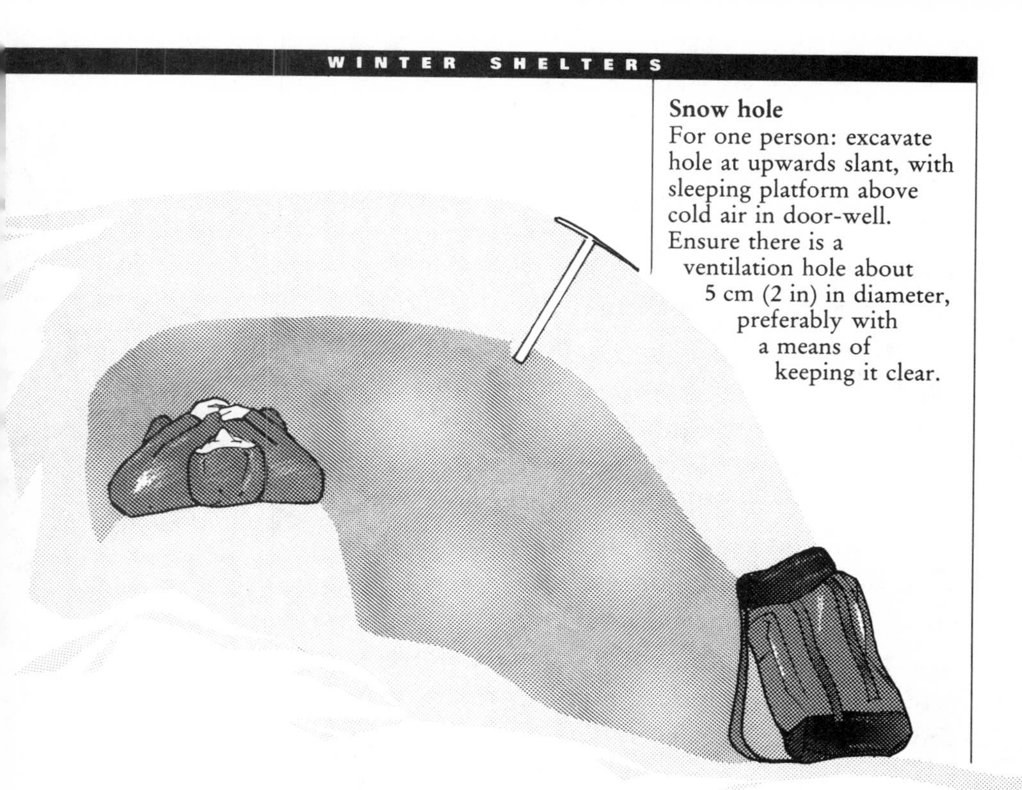

Snow hole
For one person: excavate hole at upwards slant, with sleeping platform above cold air in door-well. Ensure there is a ventilation hole about 5 cm (2 in) in diameter, preferably with a means of keeping it clear.

Snow cave
For two or more people: excavate through a large opening, quarrying the snow in blocks. Once completely excavated and bedding safely stowed, wall up entrance using blocks; finally, cut out entrance hole. As always, provide ventilation and raised sleeping platforms.

Quinze

The adaptable Athabascan people of north-central Canada developed the technique of building quinzes from powder snow. The secret in building a quinze (pronounced quin-zee) is to allow the snow to recrystallise in colder air as you pile it up to form the mound which will be excavated to form the shelter. This recrystallisation is essential, serving to bond the snow particles together.

As with all snow shelters, there must be ventilation, and the sleeping platform must be above the entrance level. The quinze's shape and size will depend upon how many people it will house. The walls must not be less than 30 cm (1 ft) thick and for strength should follow a graceful arch.

Domed quinzes will house three people, although two is probably the optimum number

More elongated (coffin-shaped!) quinzes are a cosy fit for one person

1 Using knapsacks or inflated survival bags, create a core for quinze, reducing volume of snow needed.

2 Cover sacks or bags with a large pile of snow, allowing snow to mix together as it falls.

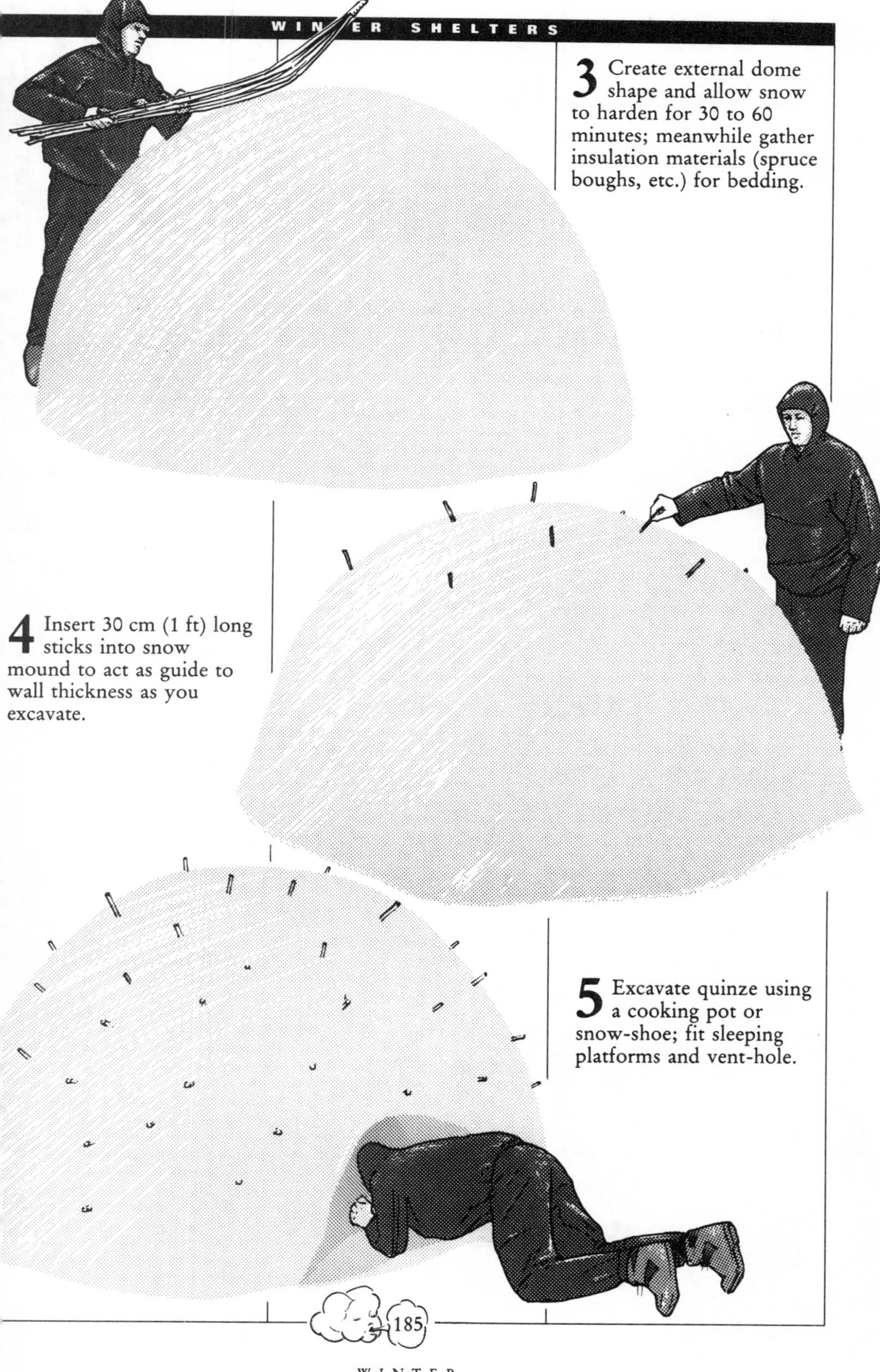

3 Create external dome shape and allow snow to harden for 30 to 60 minutes; meanwhile gather insulation materials (spruce boughs, etc.) for bedding.

4 Insert 30 cm (1 ft) long sticks into snow mound to act as guide to wall thickness as you excavate.

5 Excavate quinze using a cooking pot or snow-shoe; fit sleeping platforms and vent-hole.

Group shelter

Winter is often a time when youth organisations work indoors, but what an experience they are missing out on! The group shelter offers comfortable winter woodland camping that no tent can ever match. Here you can recline, listening to the wind howling and watching it swaying the trees, but not feel its bite, as you are comforted by the warm flicker of your fire. Being circular, the shelter encourages social dialogue and friendship.

The shelter should be as small as possible to save on materials and to keep in the warmth. The diameter of the central opening must be small enough to trap the heat of the fire without becoming a safety risk: usually this opening is made too large. A doorway is important to make the shelter function like a chimney, drawing the smoke straight upwards. Either side of this entrance, set in a good store of wood to keep the fire fuelled through the night; and work out an all-night watch rota to ensure the fire is maintained. Your shelter will provide a good home for weeks if need be.

What you need

Six forked uprights 1.5 m (5 ft) long

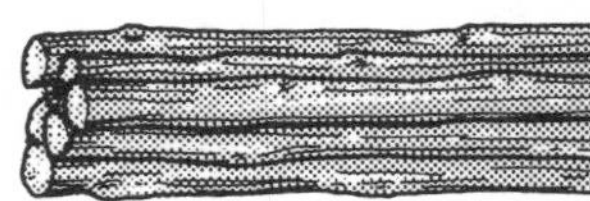

Six major diagonal supports 2.4 m (8 ft) long

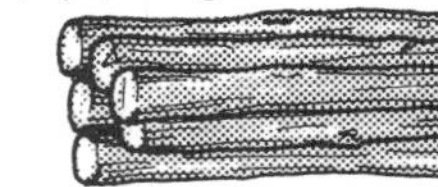

Six 2.4 m (8 ft) ridge-poles

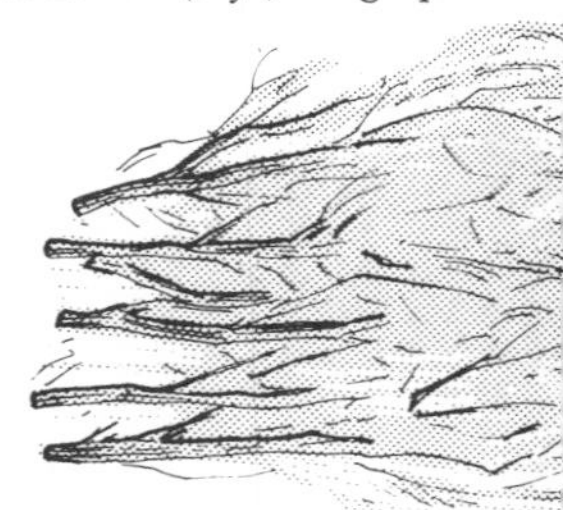

Rafter brushwood

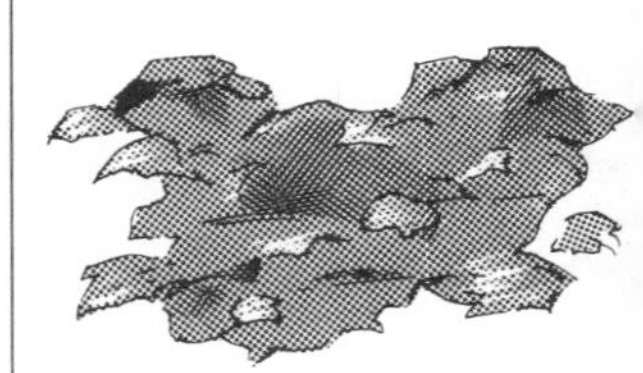

Leaf litter or similar for thatching

The group shelter gives you the warmth and comfort of a cabin for a fraction of the effort

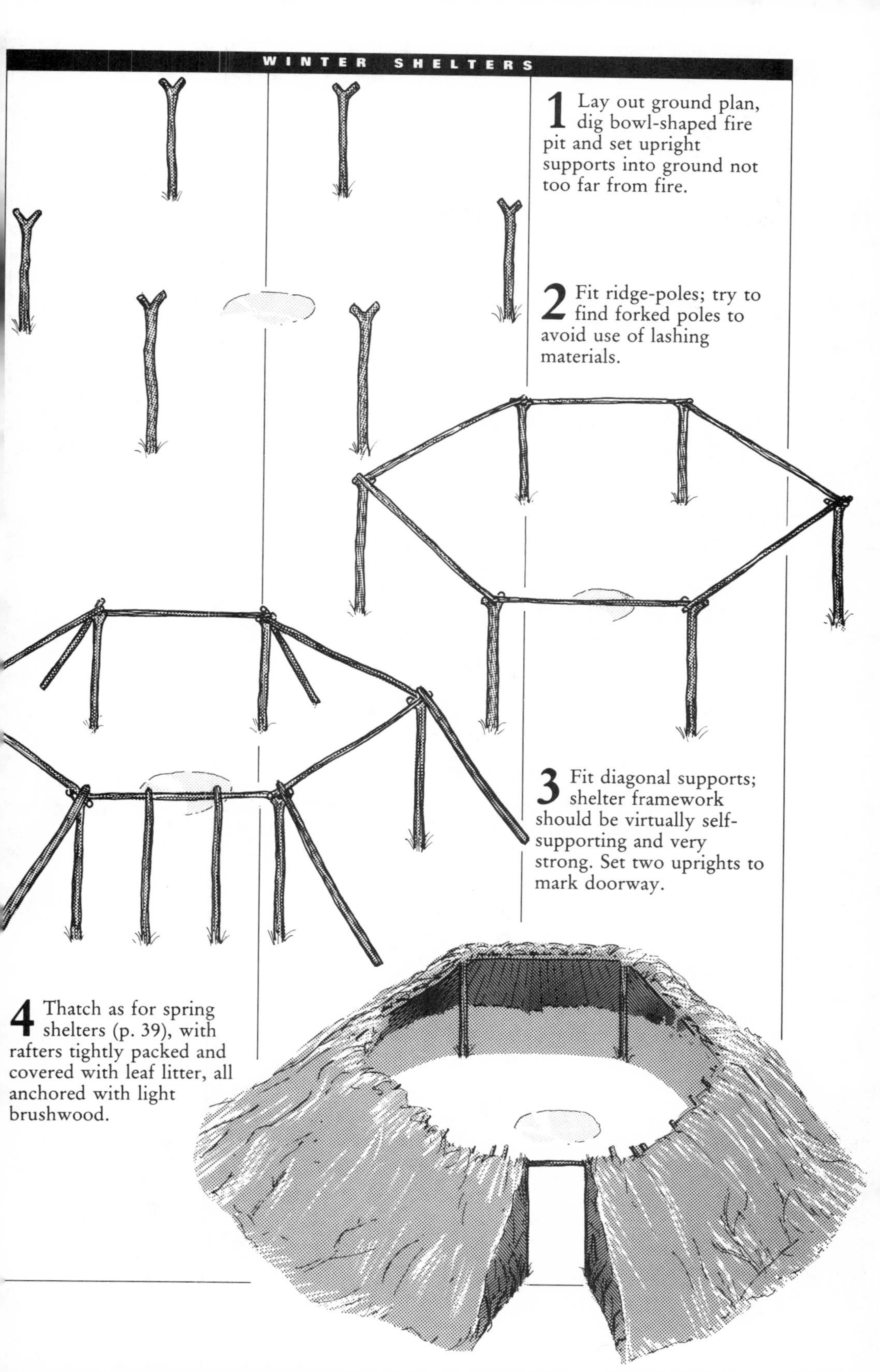

1 Lay out ground plan, dig bowl-shaped fire pit and set upright supports into ground not too far from fire.

2 Fit ridge-poles; try to find forked poles to avoid use of lashing materials.

3 Fit diagonal supports; shelter framework should be virtually self-supporting and very strong. Set two uprights to mark doorway.

4 Thatch as for spring shelters (p. 39), with rafters tightly packed and covered with leaf litter, all anchored with light brushwood.

Organising a bivouac

The experienced winter camper knows that organisation is the key to comfort and safety. In primitive circumstances this is doubly so. With daylight hours against you, and the weather making excessive demands on your energy reserves, careful planning can make a vast difference to your level of well-being. In snowy conditions, just moving about can become strenuous; how your bivouac is organised can make all the difference in such circumstances.

Start out by assessing the situation: isolate the problems and formulate your plan to eliminate them. Aim to achieve a camp so well organised that your routine almost runs itself without any conscious effort. I find that the secret is to get well set up from the outset. Good intentions to get set up the next day rarely work out as well as they sound.

Wind direction
Set lean-to (p. 148) with wind behind and at slight angle – to keep shelter warm but smoke-free.

Cooking fuel
Stacked within easy reach of fire ready for morning; try to keep in a dry place.

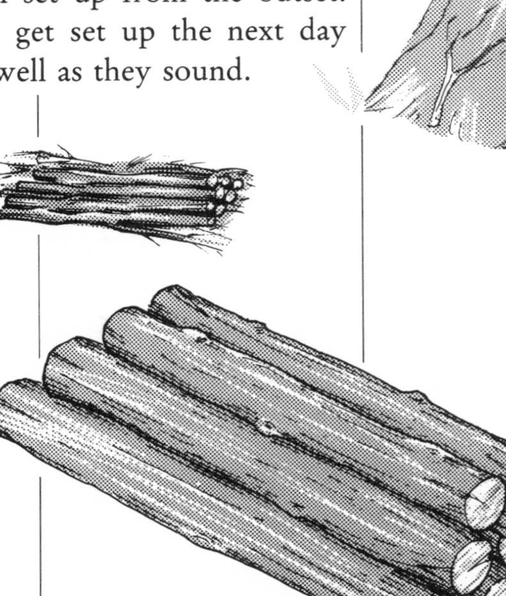

Fuel for the fire
Stacked near to fire – ensure there is more than enough for the whole night.

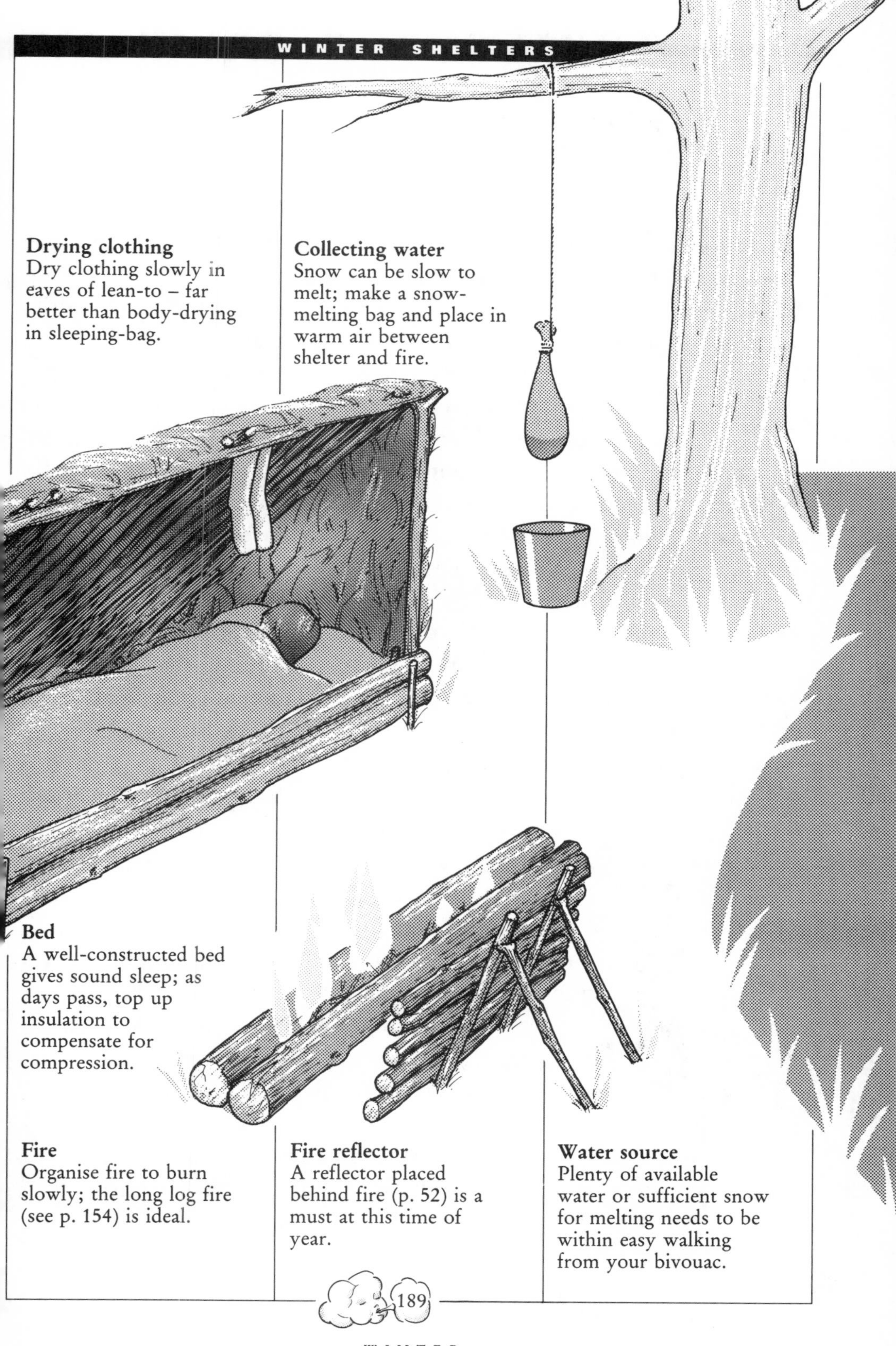

Drying clothing
Dry clothing slowly in eaves of lean-to – far better than body-drying in sleeping-bag.

Collecting water
Snow can be slow to melt; make a snow-melting bag and place in warm air between shelter and fire.

Bed
A well-constructed bed gives sound sleep; as days pass, top up insulation to compensate for compression.

Fire
Organise fire to burn slowly; the long log fire (see p. 154) is ideal.

Fire reflector
A reflector placed behind fire (p. 52) is a must at this time of year.

Water source
Plenty of available water or sufficient snow for melting needs to be within easy walking from your bivouac.

Insulation

Insulation is the key to staying warm. Think of your body as a machine that gives out heat as a by-product of its activities. Your body core is the boiler, your hands and feet the radiators. Unless these extremities are properly insulated, you will lose heat faster than it can be generated. In these situations your body's response is to reduce the flow to the radiators by narrowing the vessels carrying warm blood (your heating fluid) to them. If you are dehydrated, the effect is more pronounced; this prevents the proper maintenance of the muscles and causes inefficiency of action and even frost-bite. Exposure or, more correctly, mountain hypothermia occurs when the loss of heat from your body continues to the point where the core itself becomes chilled.

To prevent this heat loss you must be well fed, hydrated (check the colour of your urine: light straw is fine; dark yellow suggests dehydration) and well insulated. Choose clothing that meets the demands of the worst weather you are likely to encounter. Your head and neck are a critical area for heat loss, so always make certain you have a woolly hat with you. All of my outdoors jackets are equipped with integral hoods, not just my cagoule. Hoods trap the warmth around your neck and head.

Always wear a windproof outer layer. The jacket I usually wear is made of a tightly woven cotton called Ventile. This is virtually waterproof, and makes a comfortable bush-shirt or jacket in summer and a windproof outer layer over pullovers when cold.

In cold-weather emergencies people often forget that they can greatly increase the insulation of their clothing by stuffing their clothes with dry grasses or mosses. This is what northern native peoples have done for hundreds of years. It may be a little itchy if you have to use the less soft stuffings, but it may keep you alive.

Mukluks were stuffed with sedges in place of socks and are still preferred footwear among some Inuit (Eskimo)

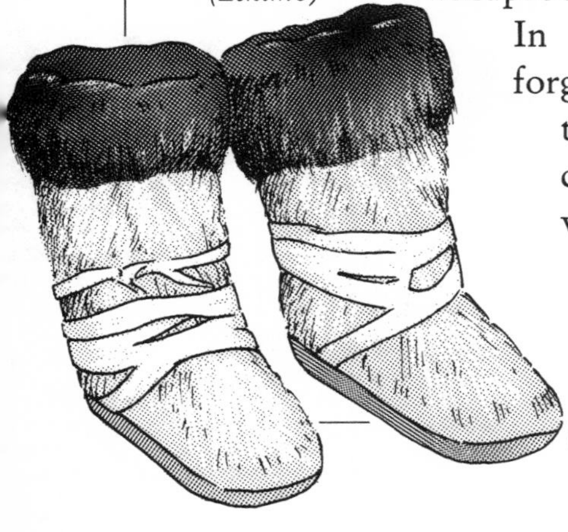

1 Sedges are better than grass, being less absorbent; cut sedges from beds and allow to dry.

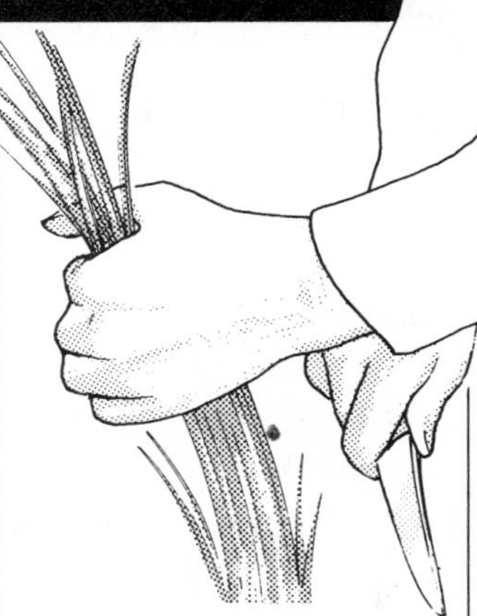

Stuff every gap where cold may seep in. You will be astonished at how effective this can be. Air the insulative stuffing each day

2 When dry, pound sedges with a malet to soften and break out fibres into a more fluffy mass.

Alternatives

Plant downs, particularly cat's-tail which is waterproof, make an excellent filling equally as good as modern sleeping-bag fillings.

Sphagnum moss is soft and springy when dry but will absorb moisture given the chance.

Pine needles – prickly but effective.

Dead bracken – good when dry.

Beech leaves – excellent.

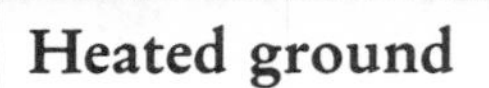

Heated beds

In the far north in winter, where the temperature can drop a long way below freezing, being caught out without a sleeping-bag or shelter is no joke. However, for the native hunters and trappers of these regions this happened from time to time; and these hardy, adaptable people had a solution.

If you have ever slept on the bare ground you will know that the heat seems to be sucked out of you to the cold earth. Hence the need for good bedding. In sub-arctic conditions hunters – by necessity masters of fire-lighting – would heat the ground on which they were to sleep. Done correctly with a covering of springy bedding boughs, this provides a toasty bed which is more often too hot than too cold. Surround this bed on three sides by a wind-break and on the fourth by a reflecting fire, and you can sleep without a sleeping-bag.

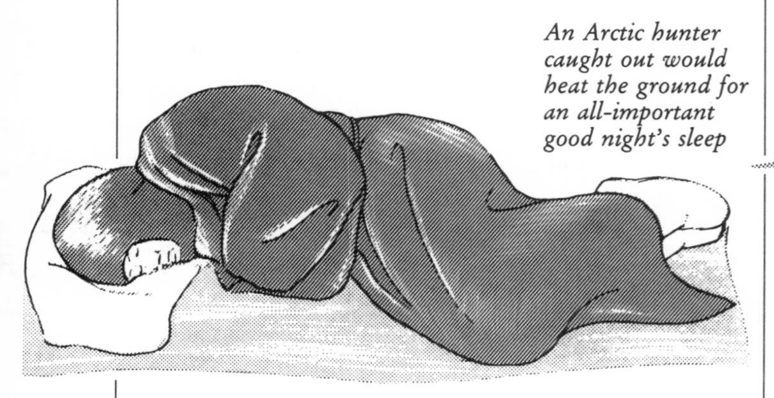

An Arctic hunter caught out would heat the ground for an all-important good night's sleep

Heated ground

1 Clear patch of ground to bare earth; a flat area on raised ground is best – cold air sinks into low ground.

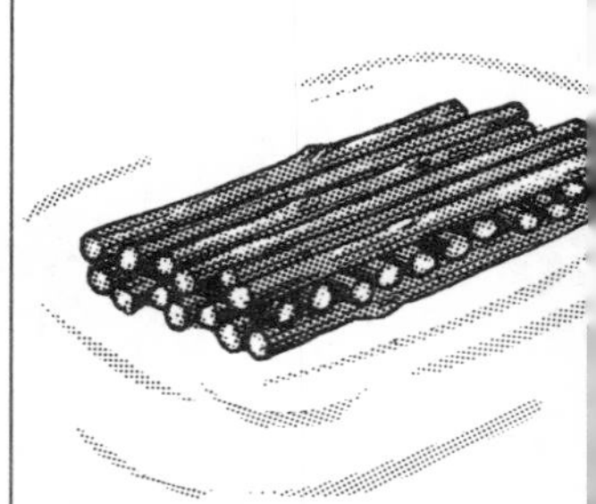

2 Lay large criss-cross fire over cleared patch and let burn furiously for at least two hours.

3 Move fire to side and brush ground clean of embers; lay bedding on top.

Hot rocks

1 Dig out bedding area to depth of about 25 cm (10 in); again, choose flat, raised location.

2 Lay criss-cross fire over hole and lace with grapefruit-sized rocks suitable for heating (see sweat lodge, p. 94).

3 When fire has burned to ash into hole, bury in with soil you removed; allow steam rising from replaced soil to dissipate before placing bedding on top. This method is more elaborate but also more effective than the previous one.

Fire

The condition of your fire can be crucial to your level of morale. If you cannot get your fire to light in bad weather, you are going to feel a whole lot worse having failed than before you started. During the milder seasons it may be enough simply to wait for more favourable fire-lighting conditions, but not now. Go out and test your fire-lighting skills in the worst weather conditions you can find. Keep at it until, come what may, you can make fire – and can do it quickly. In really cold weather the ability to light a fire fast in adverse conditions can be a life-saver.

Practise searching for tinder and drying it out on your thigh and in your pockets. Make a point of looking for as many reliable sources of dry tinder and fuel as you can find. Try splitting some suspended dead timber with your tomahawk; is it dry inside? Could it be shaved for kindling? Leave no leaf unturned in your search for fire-lighting aids. Improvise little shelters under which to start the fire, and know how to protect your fire from wind, rain and snow. If necessary, go back to the basics (p. 52) and recap on this skill. Winter weather will help to train you in a way no mortal teacher ever could.

You may have to build a little roof from bark to light your fire under

Double-platform fire
On very cold or damp ground, build fire on double-thickness platform; fire will then have stronger heart during early stages and resist cold and damp better.

Raised fire
In boggy ground, raise fire up on large platform covered in at least 5 cm (2 in) depth of soil or clay to avoid platform itself burning.

Pit fire
Cooling drafts increase fuel consumption; to make fire more fuel efficient, build it in shallow bowl-shaped depression, concentrating heat of embers.

Enclosed fire
In strong winds, enclose fire in 600 cm (2 ft) high windbreak; this will trap fire's heat and prevent embers blowing into surrounding bush.

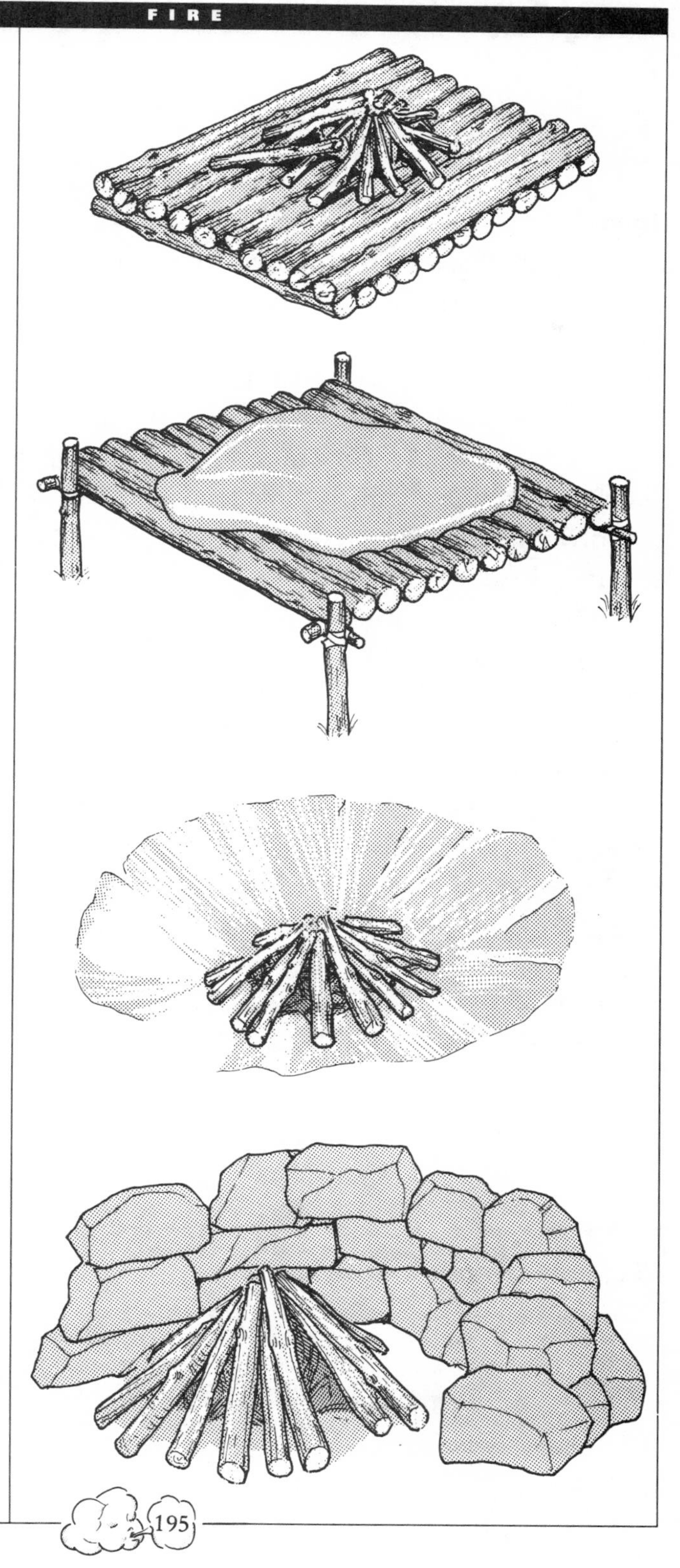

Transporting fire

Having managed to start your fire, it is also possible to carry it with you as you travel about. There are several methods that have been used by tribespeople in different parts of the world, ranging from the Aboriginal method of carrying a burning log and swinging it to keep it alight to wrapping a coal in a fireproof leaf, a practice that is favoured by the African Pygmies.

A carried fire usually helps to keep you warm as you go about your tasks. It can be made to smoulder and thereby keep away insects. Most important of all, it is a portable morale-booster when conditions are harsh.

The best material for keeping a fire smouldering is dried bracket fungi like those used to make amadou (p. 175). Failing that you can make a giant tinder cigarette which smoulders slowly.

If you also carry two fist-thick bundles of fine kindling wrapped up in fibrous grasses, you have the makings of an instant fire as and when you need it.

Smouldering bracket fungus

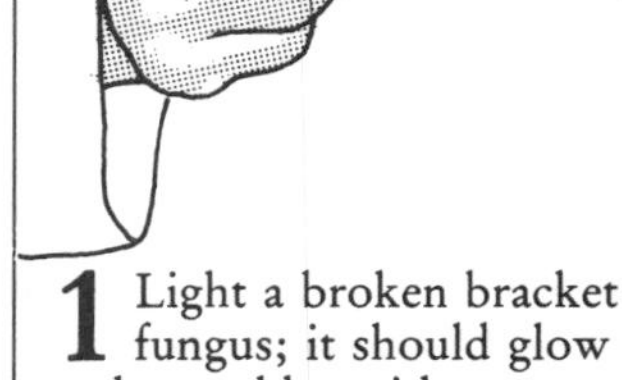

1 Light a broken bracket fungus; it should glow and smoulder with a pungent aroma; try e.g. *Ganoderma adspersum*.

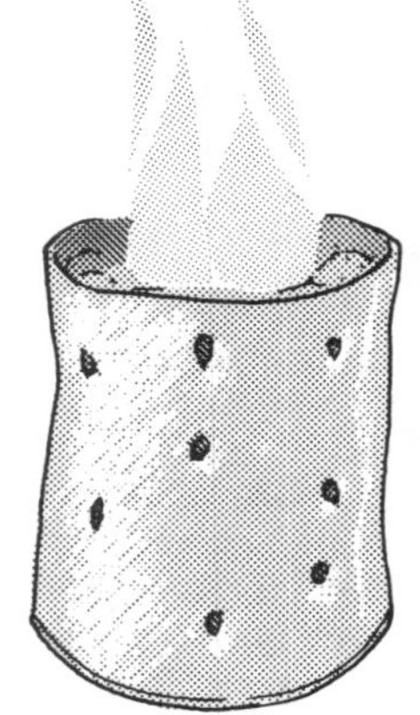

2 Carry smouldering fungus in improvised bark or wood container or old can punched with holes; surround tinder in moss to give insect-repelling smudge.

Faggots (Bundles of Branches)

Collect two fist-thick bundles of fine kindling broken no shorter than 30 cm (1 ft) in length. Wrap these bundles with dried grass or bark. When you need a fire, prepare a small platform, place your bundles together on top of it with a small amount of tinder beneath them and ignite. The whole operation need not take more than a minute.

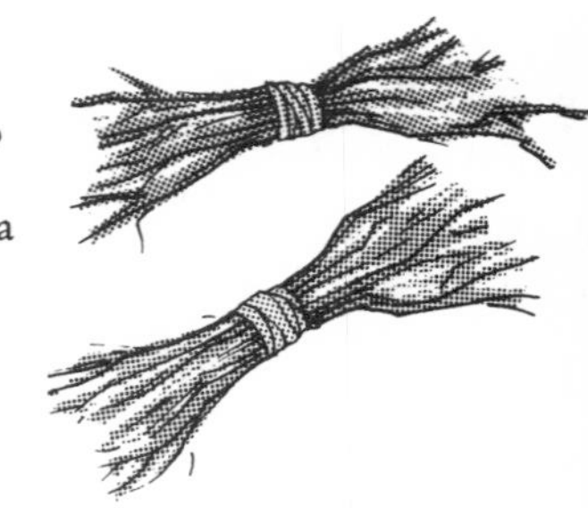

Smouldering fire tube

1 Take piece of long sheet of bark and lay finely teased grass or other fibrous tinder down middle.

2 Roll tube up and secure with ties every 8 cm (3 in) or so down length.

3 Drop large enough ember into end to start tube smouldering.

4 As you travel, keep tube pointing into breeze; manage smoulder by observing density of smoke; if it catches light, stamp out or spit on it to regain control.

Water

Water is as vitally important when the weather is cold as when it is hot, for in cold conditions water keeps you warm. Especially when you are bundled up in insulative clothing, it is easy to misjudge how dehydrated you are becoming.

As the temperature falls below freezing and the water itself freezes, the sound of running water is silenced. Now we must use our ingenuity to obtain our daily needs. In these situations without a fire or a stove, providing yourself with water can be a surprisingly difficult task. To melt ice or snow you need fuel, which must be carried or collected.

Ice is more compact in volume than snow and is therefore your best bet for melting. Snow is such an effective insulator and absorber of moisture that aluminium billycans (cook pots) stuffed full of snow have been known to burn through before the snow melts.

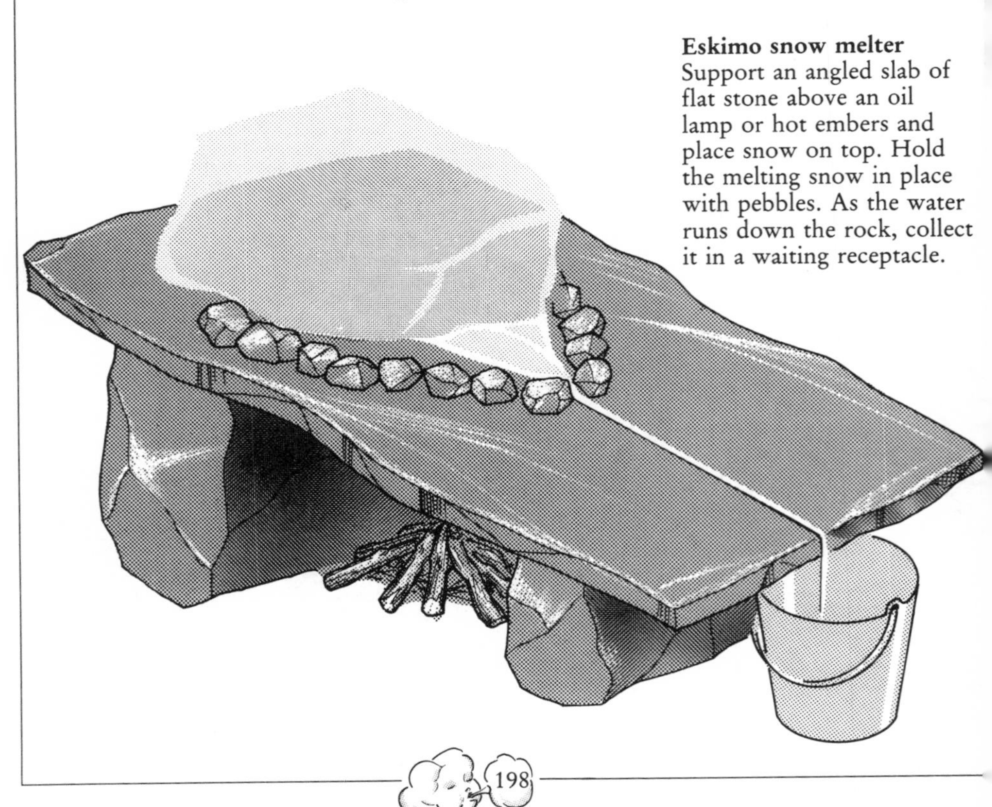

Eskimo snow melter
Support an angled slab of flat stone above an oil lamp or hot embers and place snow on top. Hold the melting snow in place with pebbles. As the water runs down the rock, collect it in a waiting receptacle.

Hot rocks
You can unfreeze frozen puddles with hot rocks. Collect, filter and purify the water before consumption.

Slow snow melter
Traditionally a sealskin bag, improvise using a T-shirt with sleeves tied. Fill with snow and suspend in warmth of shelter; as snow melts, water drips into receptacle below.

Melting snow over stove
Invert lid of pot and melt snow on this makeshift double boiler as you cook other meals.

Billy can
Melt snow in pot a little at a time; when half-full with water, add larger lumps. As long as added snow floats freely, pot will not burn through.

Cordage

In winter, cordage materials are generally less available than at other times of year. Most barks are locked tight to the trunks of dormant trees, and the majority of fibre plants are woody and brittle. Our native ancestors would certainly have stored cordage materials from other seasons to weave with through the long winter nights. However, there are still one or two cordage resources that we can make use of.

Finding cordage materials in winter more than in any other season teaches you to be adaptable – to use your eyes to search out fibres and your hands to test them. Many of the lifeless woody plant stems will still yield cordage if soaked in warm water and carefully and patiently worked. Take a hike to see what you can find.

Withes
Young shooting stems of trees, often found as suckers rising from roots of a mature tree, are easily gathered now the undergrowth has died back. A strong cordage resource with a variety of applications: ash and willow are exceptionally good.

Withes make excellent cordage for sewing together basketry and birch-bark canoes

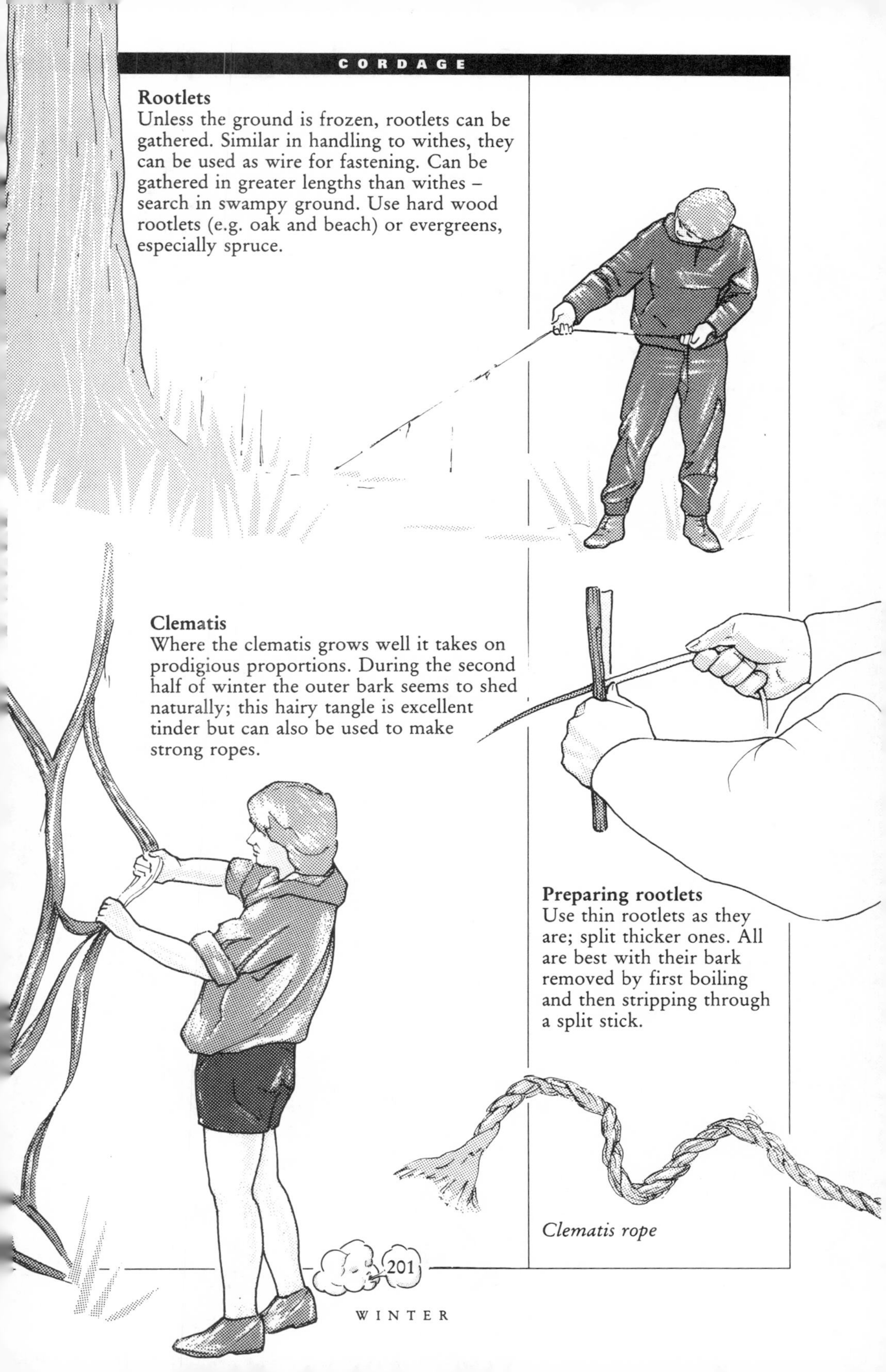

Rootlets

Unless the ground is frozen, rootlets can be gathered. Similar in handling to withes, they can be used as wire for fastening. Can be gathered in greater lengths than withes – search in swampy ground. Use hard wood rootlets (e.g. oak and beach) or evergreens, especially spruce.

Clematis

Where the clematis grows well it takes on prodigious proportions. During the second half of winter the outer bark seems to shed naturally; this hairy tangle is excellent tinder but can also be used to make strong ropes.

Preparing rootlets

Use thin rootlets as they are; split thicker ones. All are best with their bark removed by first boiling and then stripping through a split stick.

Clematis rope

Withes cordage

Withes and rootlets are slightly different in their handling characteristics, as you will discover. However, they can be prepared in the basic same way. You can use both whole or split, and both are made pliable by boiling, although this is particularly true of rootlets, which benefit from soaking in a concentrated wood-ash solution. In a hurry, simply steam them under your fire for a few minutes.

1 To split a withe, start split with knife and continue by hand.

Some of the ways withes can be split.

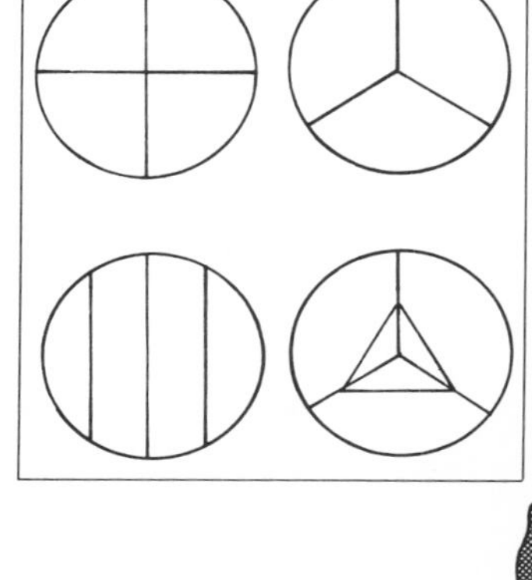

2 Control split and prevent it running off to one side by bending thicker side to greater degree. With practice you can split withe in three using teeth as a third hand.

Twisting
Withes used for quick bindings have fibres loosened by twisting while still attached to the ground; this increases pliability.

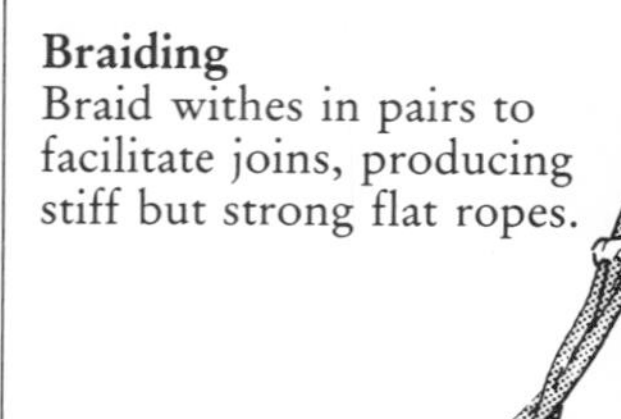

Braiding
Braid withes in pairs to facilitate joins, producing stiff but strong flat ropes.

Clematis cordage

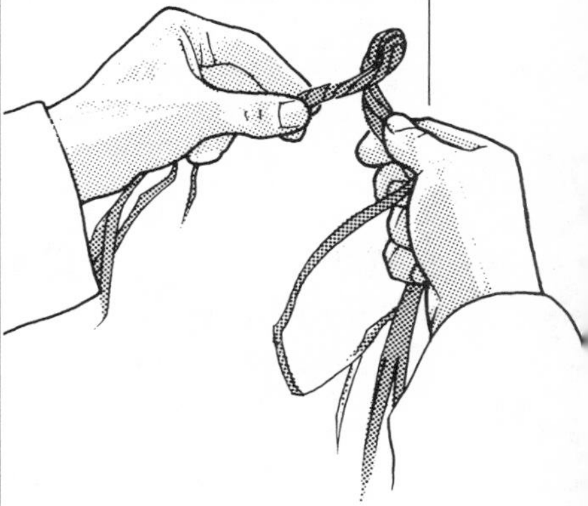

Clematis needs little more preparation than hand-separation of the fibres. It tends to be a somewhat messy material to work with but produces excellent cordage. The beauty of this material is the speed with which it can be gathered in quantity.

1 Twist up fibres until they kink into a strand about 2.5 cm (1 in) in diameter.

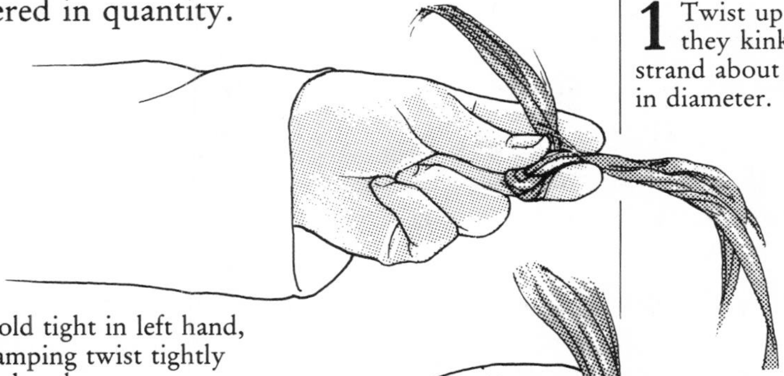

2 Hold tight in left hand, clamping twist tightly under thumb.

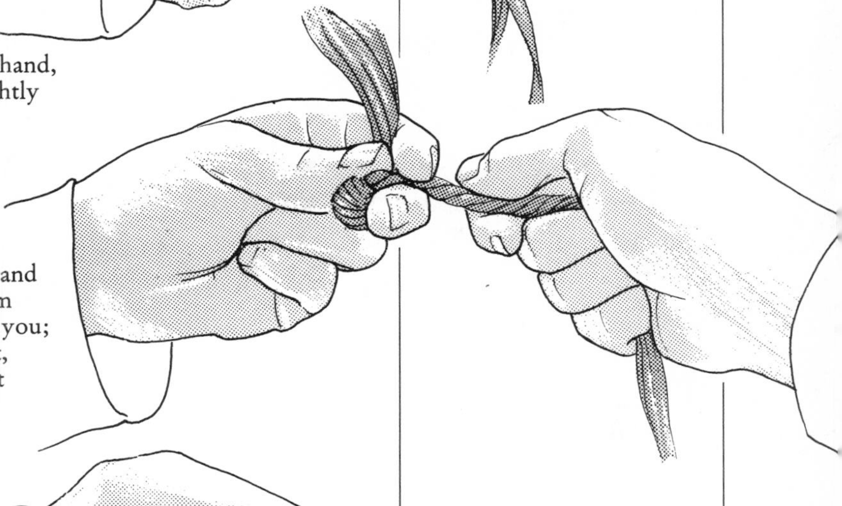

3 Twist fibres of strand furthest away from you twice away from you; at end of second twist, hold strand to prevent unravelling.

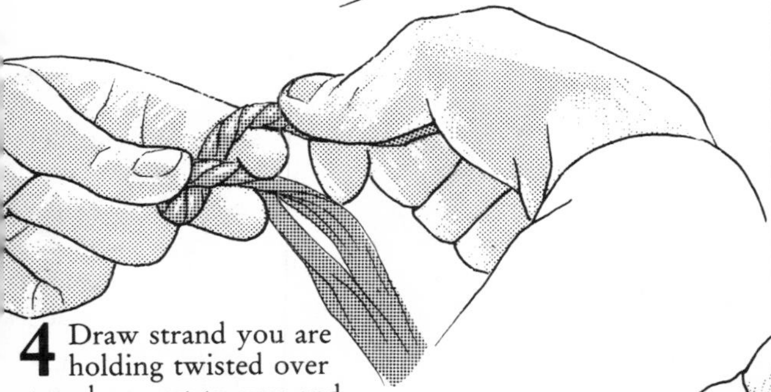

4 Draw strand you are holding twisted over strand nearest to you and interchange them.

5 Repeat and continue until rope is of desired length. Add new fibres as for thigh-rolled cordage (p. 58).

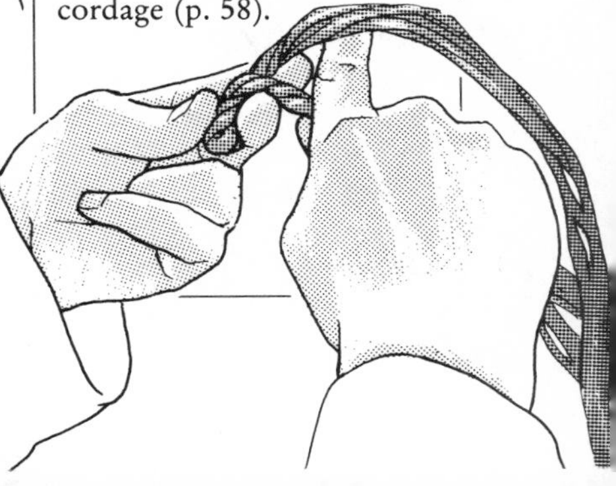

Carving

The long winter nights bring the ideal opportunity to repair and refurbish equipment and to replace what is worn out. Traditionally during this season, everyday items were embellished, carved or incised with intricate designs. Illuminated by the firelight, carving takes on a special beauty, the flickering shadows inspiring designs and patterns. With the sap no longer rising in the trees, this is also the best time to gather wood. There is almost no limit to what you can carve – from hunting tools and eating implements to totems and figurines.

Part of the appeal of carving is that once you have started a project you can work on it during those tranquil moments after meals or whenever the mood takes you. Carry small carvings in your pocket and whittle them whenever you get an opportunity.

The tools you use for carving need not be elaborate; the cutting tools already mentioned are more than adequate. A gouge, some sandpaper in grades from coarse to extra-fine, some wire wool and boiled linseed oil will enable you to smooth off your work-pieces. Linseed oil especially will help to preserve the wood and accentuate the natural beauty of the grain. If you want to carve in the really primitive way, use the edge of broken flints and smooth the work with sand and buckskin.

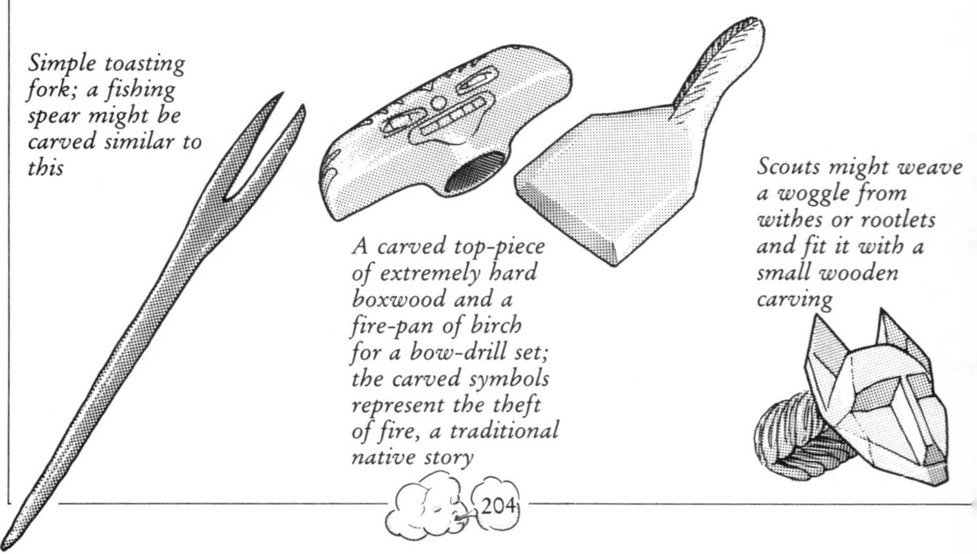

Simple toasting fork; a fishing spear might be carved similar to this

A carved top-piece of extremely hard boxwood and a fire-pan of birch for a bow-drill set; the carved symbols represent the theft of fire, a traditional native story

Scouts might weave a woggle from withes or rootlets and fit it with a small wooden carving

Liberating the object

One of the most important aspects of all carving is understanding the strength and qualities of the wood you work with. In time, you will find that as you look at a piece of wood you can see an object lurking within it. Your task, then, is to liberate it. Carve spoons and ladles, for example, from a large piece of wood where a branch attaches; the branch becomes the handle. In this way the strength of the grain is harnessed in the object itself.

Old scars on some trees can be sawn off and hollowed out to make vessels. Where the outline of the object follows the grain, this helps to make it more water resistant. Even with the driest wood, moisture can be transported along its grain; so if the grain goes across the vessel, it may leak. Look for unusually shaped branches with shapes you can make use of. To carve and whittle effectively it is important to read the grain patterns in the wood – pay attention to this as you carve.

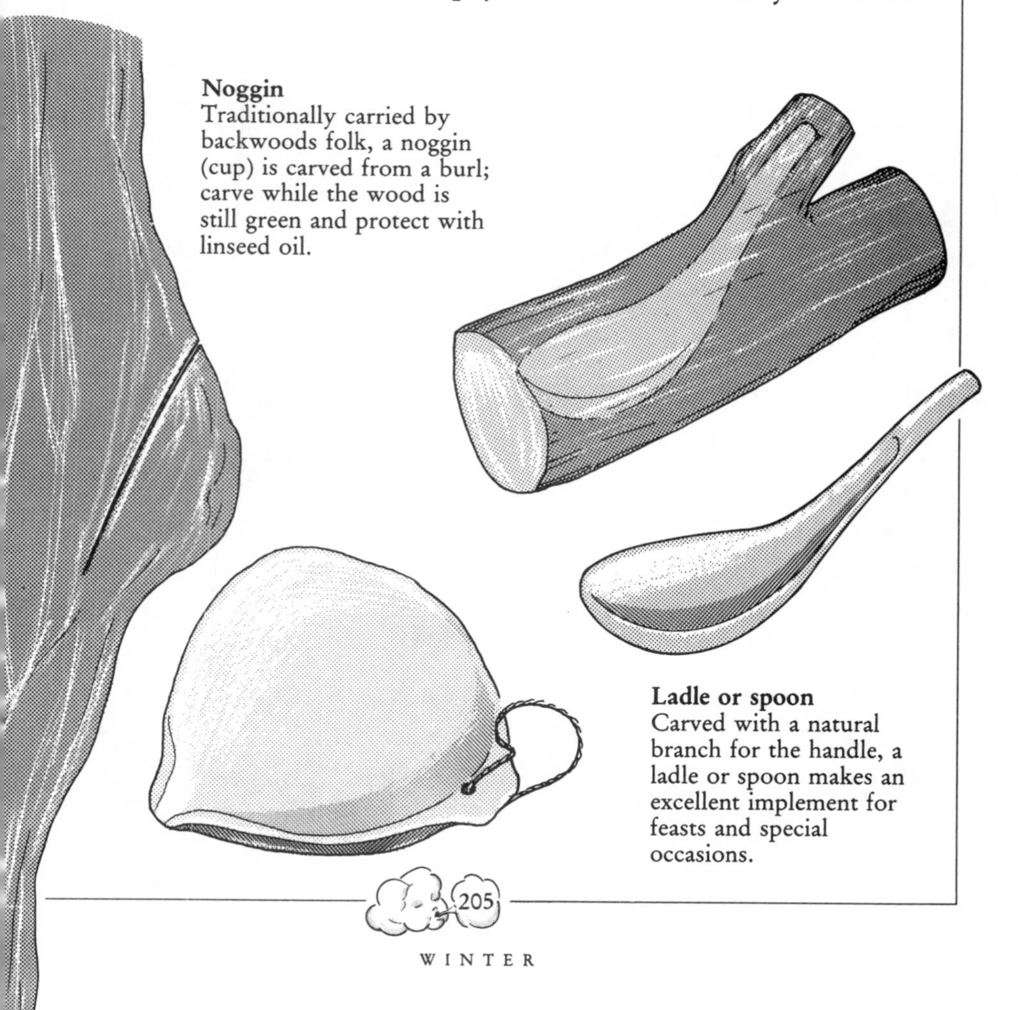

Noggin
Traditionally carried by backwoods folk, a noggin (cup) is carved from a burl; carve while the wood is still green and protect with linseed oil.

Ladle or spoon
Carved with a natural branch for the handle, a ladle or spoon makes an excellent implement for feasts and special occasions.

Carving techniques

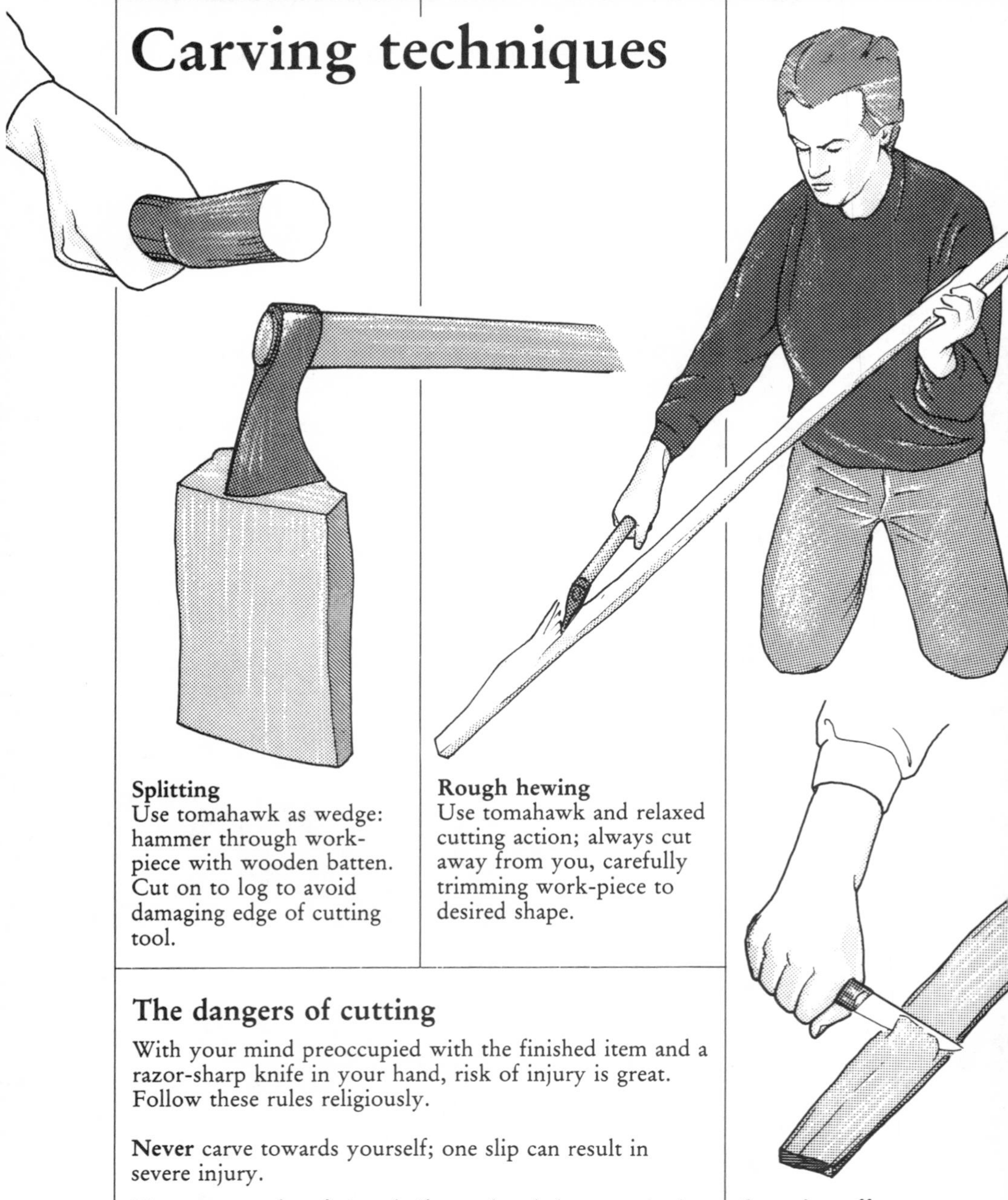

Splitting
Use tomahawk as wedge: hammer through work-piece with wooden batten. Cut on to log to avoid damaging edge of cutting tool.

Rough hewing
Use tomahawk and relaxed cutting action; always cut away from you, carefully trimming work-piece to desired shape.

Squaring off
For heavy carving and squaring off work-piece, use strong all-arm carving action; as always, work away from you and towards empty space.

The dangers of cutting

With your mind preoccupied with the finished item and a razor-sharp knife in your hand, risk of injury is great. Follow these rules religiously.

Never carve towards yourself; one slip can result in severe injury.

Never carve when fatigued; if your hands become tired while carving, take a break.

Never carve with a dull knife; a dull edge needs greater force to cut and tends to slip.

Never rush or hurry your carving; make every cut a deliberate pre-planned action.

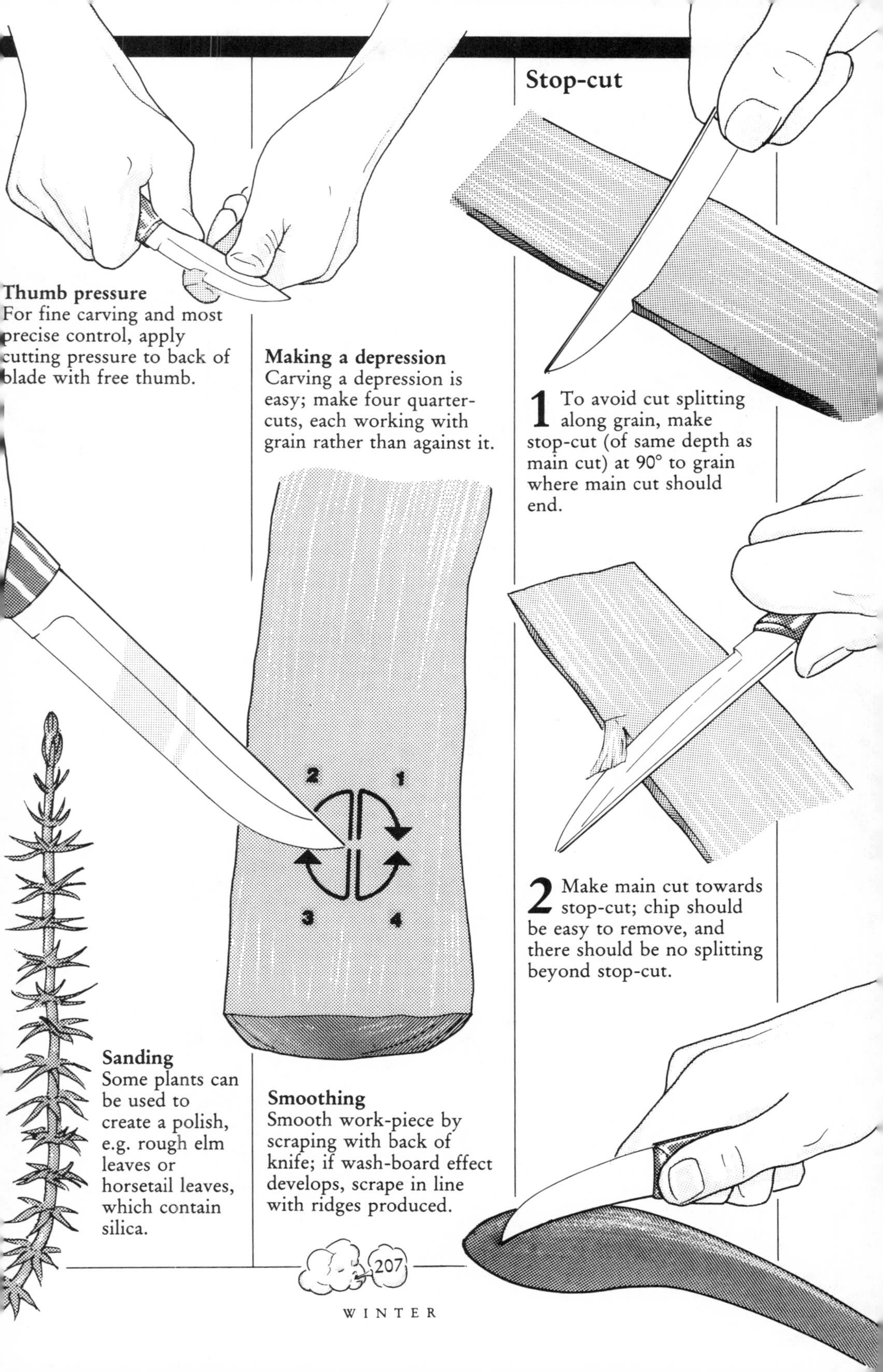

Thumb pressure
For fine carving and most precise control, apply cutting pressure to back of blade with free thumb.

Sanding
Some plants can be used to create a polish, e.g. rough elm leaves or horsetail leaves, which contain silica.

Making a depression
Carving a depression is easy; make four quarter-cuts, each working with grain rather than against it.

Smoothing
Smooth work-piece by scraping with back of knife; if wash-board effect develops, scrape in line with ridges produced.

Stop-cut

1 To avoid cut splitting along grain, make stop-cut (of same depth as main cut) at 90° to grain where main cut should end.

2 Make main cut towards stop-cut; chip should be easy to remove, and there should be no splitting beyond stop-cut.

Carving projects

For your first carving projects, try something simple – a spoon or a bowl is ideal. In their manufacture you will learn about carving with the grain and will end up with useful things to take with you on the trail. You can even carve at home. Five minutes' carving daily, and you'll soon have a finished article; but don't rush it.

A simple bowl

1 Split a section of 10 cm (4 in) diameter log; carve a shallow depression in the flat side.

2 Take a marble-size ember from your fire and place it in the depression.

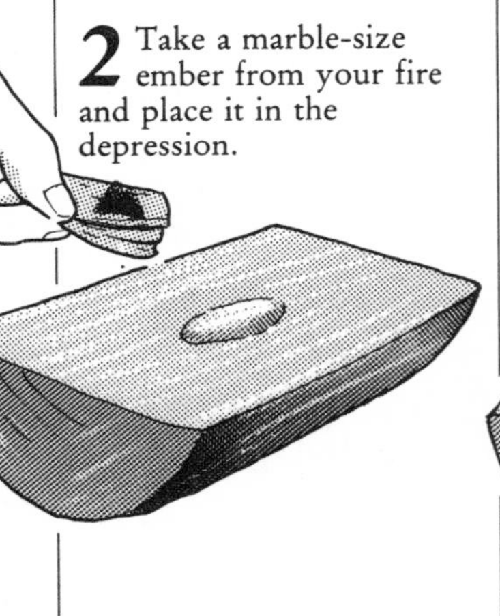

3 Use section of reed as straw to blow on coal to encourage it to burn into surrounding wood; work slowly to avoid splitting wood.

4 Scrape out the charred wood and continue until you reach the desired depth.

5 Finish the bowl by shaping the outside to your satisfaction.

A simple spoon

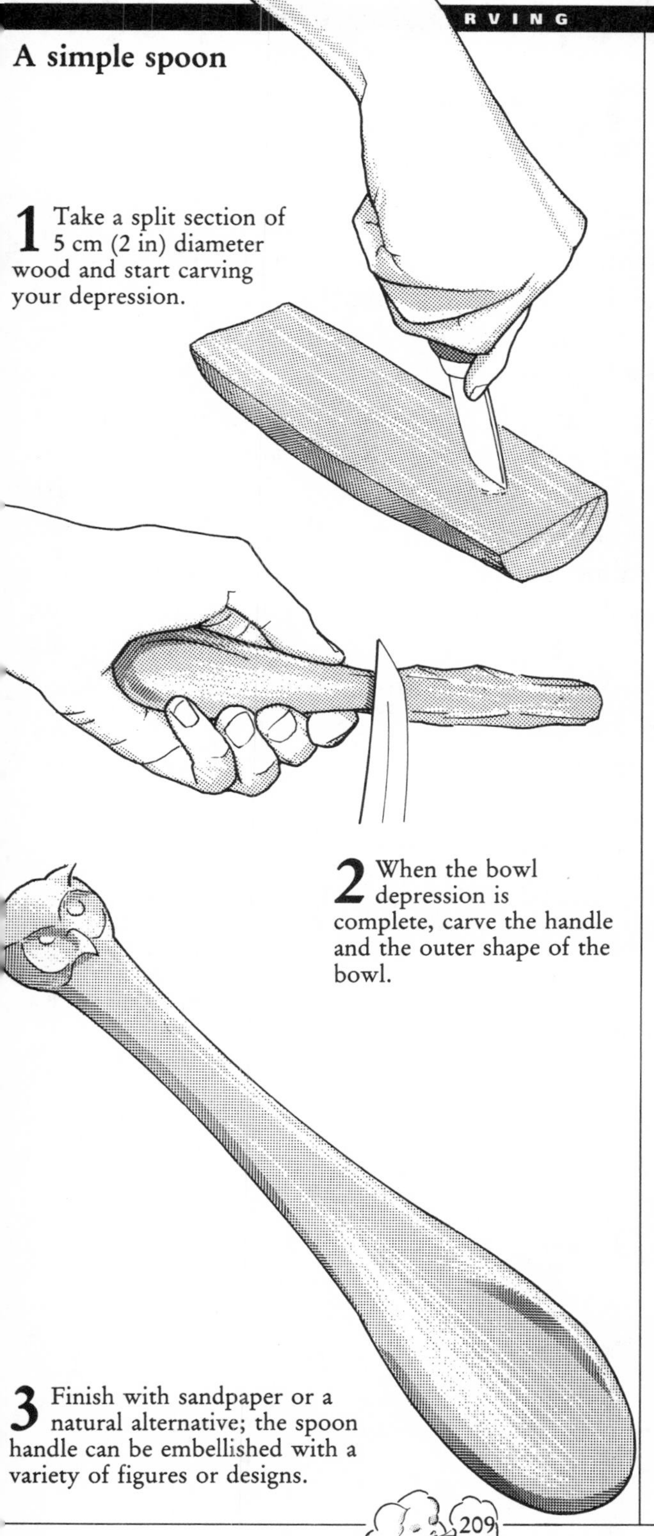

1 Take a split section of 5 cm (2 in) diameter wood and start carving your depression.

2 When the bowl depression is complete, carve the handle and the outer shape of the bowl.

3 Finish with sandpaper or a natural alternative; the spoon handle can be embellished with a variety of figures or designs.

Which wood?

Every wood has unique carving qualities, and you will learn which to use for each purpose.

Sycamore
A soft, easily carved wood, ideal for spoons and eating utensils.

Beech
A hard, tight-grained wood, ideal for carving fine detail. Not suitable for beginners.

Hazel
A stringy, pliable wood, easily carved, but tends to split easily; good for forks and spoons.

Ash
Hard to carve but makes excellent tool-handles, bows and weapons, e.g. throwing-sticks. White with a beautiful straight grain.

Horse chestnut
Underestimated. Outer surface under wood has lovely gnarled appearance.

Birch
A beautiful wood for carving spoons and bowls, easily worked and quite strong when finished. Decays easily, though.

Lime
Light, soft, easy and quick to carve; ideal for beginners.

Yew
Very hard and springy, with beautiful red heart-wood; makes excellent bows, spoons and bowls. Not for beginners.

Winter lights

The dark nights of winter will soon deaden the batteries of your flashlight. So it is useful to know how to improvise illumination from natural materials. There will certainly be times when you need illumination more portable than your camp-fire.

If you need an extra blaze of light around the fire, throw on some strips of birch bark. Filled with oil, they quickly burn to brighten the fire's surroundings, but the effect is short-lived. You can also use birch bark to make simple portable torches for travelling with. Failing that, you will need to use animal fat rendered down by heating – not as complicated a process as many imagine it to be. If you are lucky enough to come across a bees' nest broken open by other animals you may even be able to obtain wild beeswax and produce a primitive candle.

With all these lights and lamps making use of a naked flame, you must take great care with them.

Birch-bark roll
A tight birch-bark roll 60 cm (2 ft) long and 5 cm (2 in) in diameter makes an excellent torch. Invert briefly to re-establish dying flame.

Birch bark folded
Birch bark folded and fitted to a split stick is a traditional northern night-fishing torch. Fold accordion fashion so that finished fan is 8 cm (3 in) wide and as long as you can make it.

Cat's-tail
Dip cat's-tail seed-heads in rendered fat and leave near fire so that fat seeps in. Burn like a large candle when lit.

Mullein
Treat knobbly old seed-heads of mullein with rendered fat in same way as cat's-tail, to burn like a candle.

Lamp

Simple oil or fat lamps have been used for centuries to provide illumination, even in the tunnels of Stone Age flint-mines.

1 Carve out the bowl-shaped lamp from the lump of chalk, with a short spout-like protrusion to support the wick.

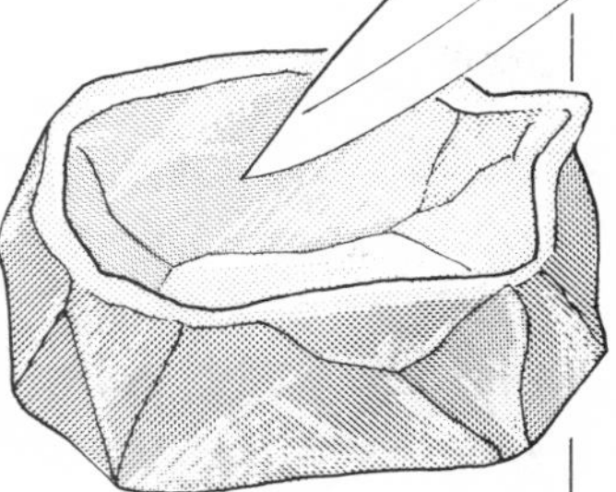

What you need

Large piece of soft, easily carved stone, such as chalk

Wick made of moss or other plant materials

Some rendered fat

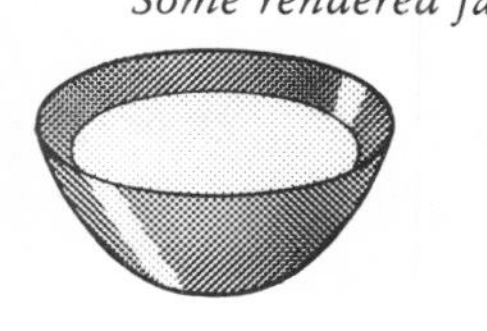

2 Add the rendered fat until the lamp is half-full.

3 Fit the wick and light. Lamps such as this can be used to heat well-ventilated snow caves, to cook food and to melt snow or ice.

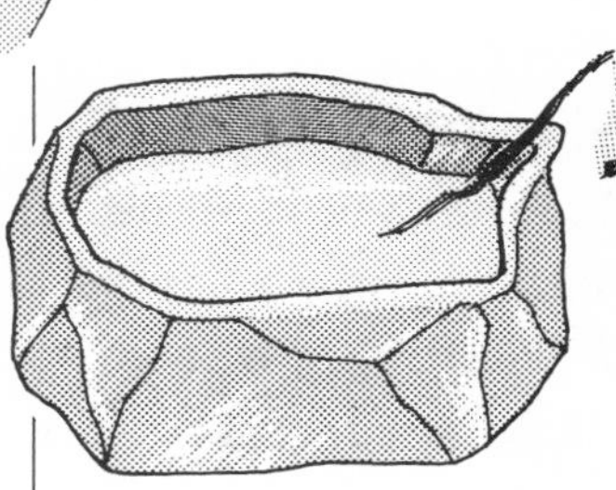

Wicks

You can improvise wicks from a variety of materials, ranging from cotton from your clothing to natural materials such as sphagnum moss. Some plants with pithy stems can also be used.

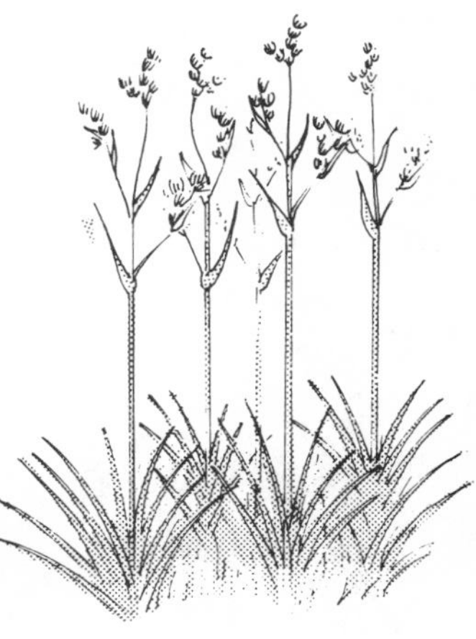

Elder

You can use the pithy stem from elder stalks for a wick, although it tends to consume itself when the level of fat runs low.

Soft rush

The pithy centre of the soft rush was once dipped in tallow and sold commercially as cheap rush-light candles. You can use the same pithy centre as a wick for your lamp.

Special equipment

Winter in northern regions requires an adaptable approach to mobility. The highly versatile native inhabitants of these regions invented tools to help them cope with the harsh conditions. Where frozen lakes were reliably solid, skates and sleds replaced canoes for transport. In the snow-clad hill country, skis were invented to enable people to follow game and reindeer herds easily.

The sun shines dazzlingly off the white snow. So our northern ancestors invented the first 'sunglasses' to prevent snowblindness. These strips of hide with a narrow slot cut in them evolved into the wooden snow-goggle, still favoured over sunglasses by some today because they do not steam up. Designs varied from a simple two-piece hinged version similar to swimming goggles to the solid type often incorporating a small peak.

Where powder snow was deep and obstructive, snow-shoes were invented to spread the human weight wide enough to prevent sinking. Here again, designs varied, often according to region. Good snow-shoes require the investment of considerable labour; but every trapper needed to know how to improvise emergency snow-shoes, such as the Roycraft, made quickly from easily accessible materials.

Snow-goggles

Snow-goggles are easy to carve from a solid block of wood. Use an easily worked hardwood such as birch. Make a good job of the carving so that the goggles fit comfortably, and carefully polish the inside to remove all splinters. Don't make the eye-slots too wide. Once completed, darken inside with black paint or soot mixed with linseed oil or fat. Fit the goggles with a buckskin thong to hold them on.

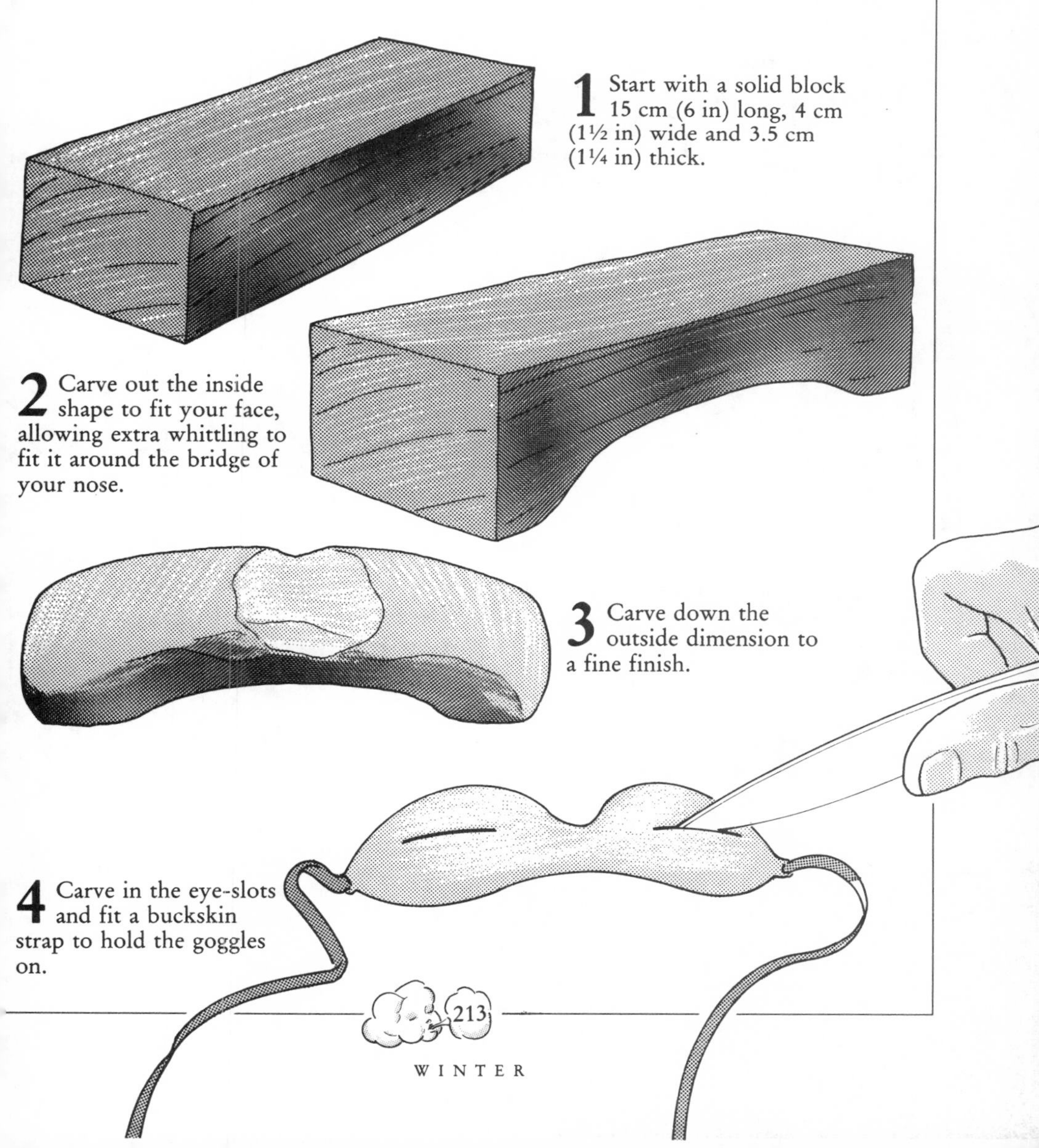

1 Start with a solid block 15 cm (6 in) long, 4 cm (1½ in) wide and 3.5 cm (1¼ in) thick.

2 Carve out the inside shape to fit your face, allowing extra whittling to fit it around the bridge of your nose.

3 Carve down the outside dimension to a fine finish.

4 Carve in the eye-slots and fit a buckskin strap to hold the goggles on.

Snow-shoe (Roycraft pattern)

What you need per shoe

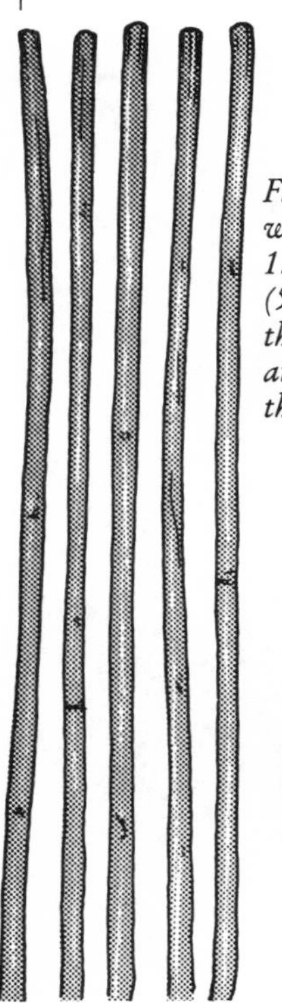

Five straight wands 1.5–1.8 m (5–6 ft) long, thumb-thick at their thickest end

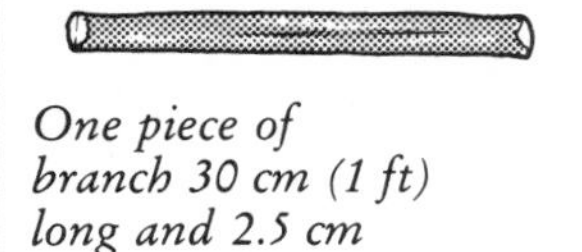

One piece of branch 30 cm (1 ft) long and 2.5 cm (1 in) thick

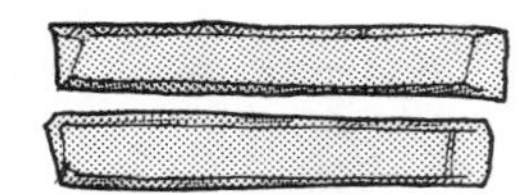

Two flat boards 30 cm (1 ft) long, 5 cm (2 in) wide and 2 cm (3/4 in) thick

Plenty of strong cordage 30 mm (1/8 in) in diameter

1 Taper the narrow ends of the wands to a point on two sides; the taper should be 7–8 cm (about 3 in) long.

2 Lay the flat sides of the tapers together and bind securely for at least 8 cm (3 in).

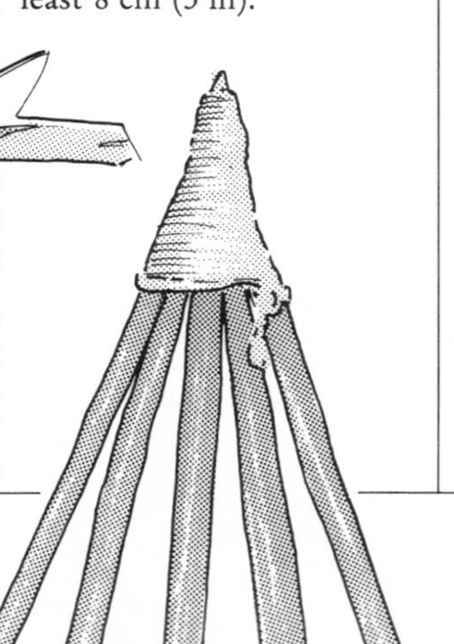

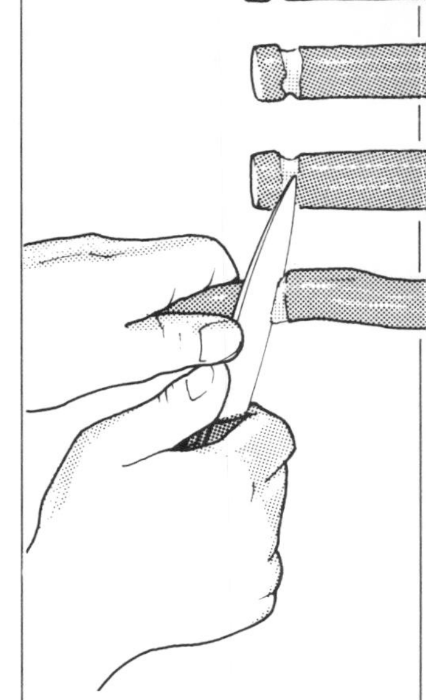

3 Trim the wands' rear ends so they are all of uniform length; encircle each with a groove 16 mm (1/16 in) deep.

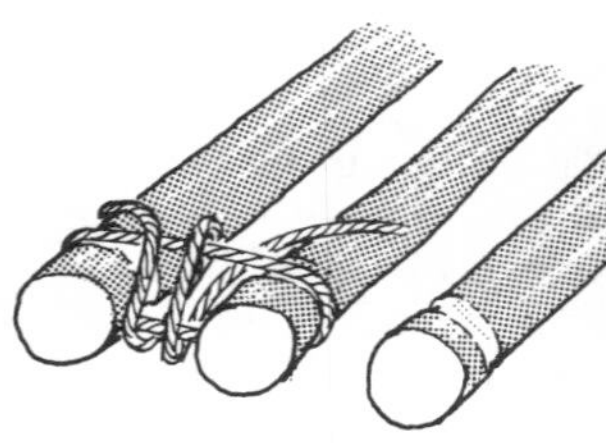

4 Bind all the ends about 2.5 cm (1 in) apart with cordage.

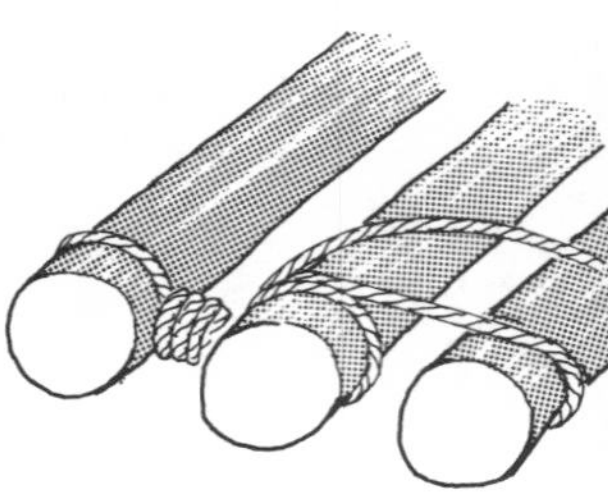

5 The binding between the ends must be tight and locked off with clove hitches so as not to unravel in use.

6 Bind on the batten about 60 cm (2 ft) from the blunt end of the snow-shoe. This bar holds and spaces the wands, so each must be lashed securely to it.

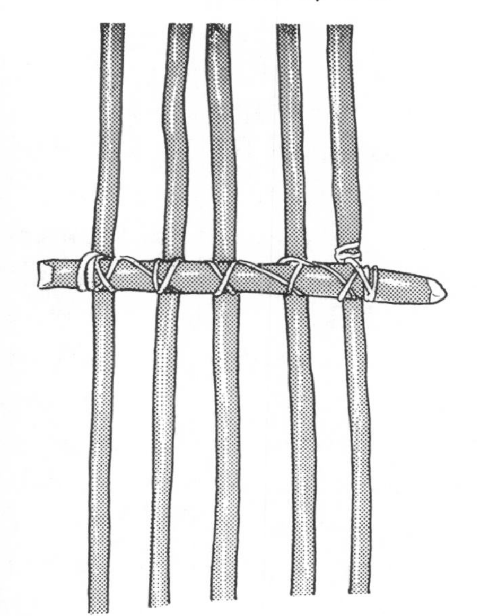

7 Position one board just behind the batten and the other behind that – with ball of your foot resting on forward board, rearward board should fit exactly under heel. Lash these only to outside wands.

8 Bend up the point of the snow-shoe and lash it securely back to the batten with doubled cordage.

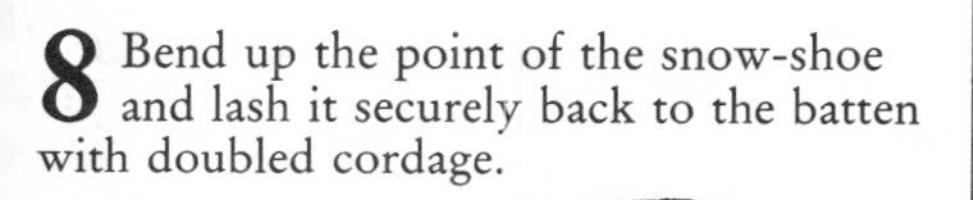

9 Arrange the boot binding as shown here, using trebbled cordage or rawhide strips. If too narrow, the cordage will cut into your foot.

The pursuit of food

Times are hard for all creatures that remain awake during the cold time. If we wish to rely upon the land to feed us in winter, finding wild food teaches us to be ingenious. Just to stay warm we must have energy-rich foods, carbohydrates and fats; to stay healthy we have to maintain our balance of vitamins and minerals. Early pioneers in Arctic lands frequently suffered from scurvy due to the lack of vitamin C in their meat-and-dried-cereal-based diet; but the natives they encountered thrived.

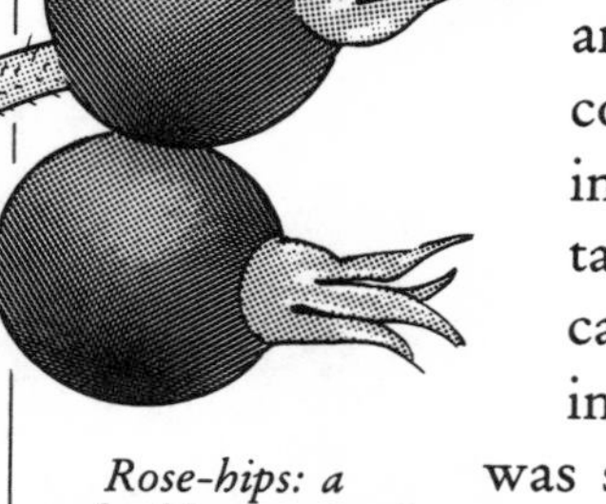

Rose-hips: a valuable source of vitamin C in winter

Maintaining a varied diet is of more importance now than at any other time. Many wild foods contain small quantities of poisons. These are insignificant as part of a varied diet, but when taken as a major feature of any eating regime they can cause serious problems. As mentioned earlier in the year, one of the traditional cures for scurvy was spruce-leaf tea – the spruce needles are steeped in water which has just dropped from the boil. (Boiling would destroy the vitamin C.)

Our distant ancestors relied heavily upon stores of the autumn harvest to supplement their winter diet. They probably followed the migrating herds of animals that they hunted, never straying far from their food supply. Fruits, herbs, meats and grains can all be stored during the dark winter months; without such provisions you will have to forage very widely indeed and become versatile in your approach to what is edible. You will also be competing with the other creatures for the limited food supply; so civilised sensibilities may have to be put temporarily to one side! The reward is tangible, though, for no meal tastes half as good as a winter meal foraged from the land.

You can find fat in the creatures you trap and hunt. This must not be wasted – add the fat into stews and avoid at all costs cooking techniques that destroy it, such as broiling.

You can obtain carbohydrate from the roots of dormant plants, so you need to develop a keen eye for the decaying leaves and stems of edible plants. If the ground is frozen, you may have to thaw it with fire to extract the root. The energy equation (energy gained v. energy expended to obtain it) then becomes a close-run thing. Look for roots that can be extracted from the ground without too much effort, and take advantage of mild spells when the soil is not hardened by frost.

Cat's-tails, arrowheads and other edible water-dwelling plants are easier to gather than roots. But take great care if the water has frozen over. Ice in ponds and lakes is a potentially lethal hazard.

Even in the depths of winter there are fresh out-of-season greens to be had. Keep your eyes peeled for them. Dandelion, dock and other hardy plants are often available, particularly in sunny locations sheltered from the biting winds. Don't let opportunities such as these pass you by.

You can still find rose-hips on the bush even when there is snow on the ground. Packed full of vitamin C, they are true winter treasure, well worth the effort of collection and preparation. Towards the end of winter, early spring flowers are sometimes tricked into the air, fooled by the occasional sunny day. In fact, during this period you may come across almost any of the spring and autumn foods we have learned about, so stay alert.

But you don't have to be subsisting from nature to be foraging for food in winter. Winter is by far my favourite time to go beachcombing. Washed by the season's storms, the beaches have a lot of interesting flotsam and debris to offer to those who take the trouble to look. But more important, now is the safest time to gather edible shellfish – some of the year's tastiest delicacies.

Coastlines are fascinating places to explore. What could be better for a winter foraging trip than a wind-swept rocky shore? I have many fond memories of such excursions, of watching the tide return to scour the beach clean as I head off to a cosy retreat with an open fire and a good meal to look forward to.

For the survivor even winter-killed creatures can mean food

Winter plants

In winter, plants are important, for they contain vitamins otherwise lacking in a winter subsistence diet. A few edible greens or roots are usually available for the observant forager. It really helps if you have made a careful study of two aspects of the plants' nature. First, you need to know exactly what sort of habitat each of the plants prefers. Coupled with observation of prevalent weather effects on the most likely plant habitats in your area, this will greatly increase your efficiency in searching. The other important knowledge is the ability to recognise plants as they emerge from the ground in spring; for even in the depths of winter some edible species can be fooled into germination by favourable conditions.

In general, midwinter to spring is the most barren time for gathering plants. If gathering water-dwelling plants, take care to avoid falling into the freezing water.

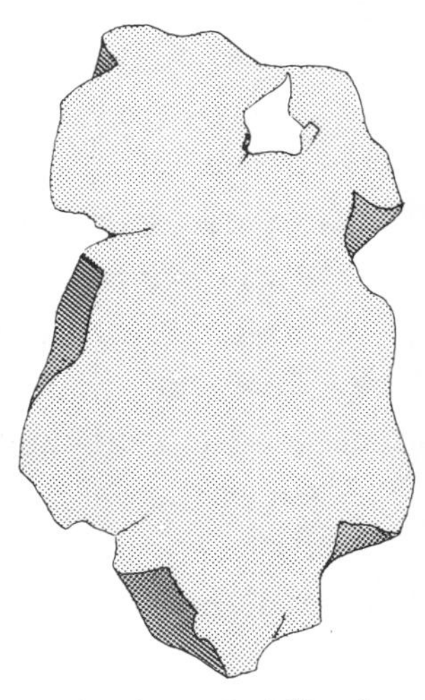

Rock tripe (*Umbilicaria* spp. and *Gyrophora* spp.)
Encrusts rocks in western Britain; less-than-pleasant taste on its own; soak before adding to soups and stews.

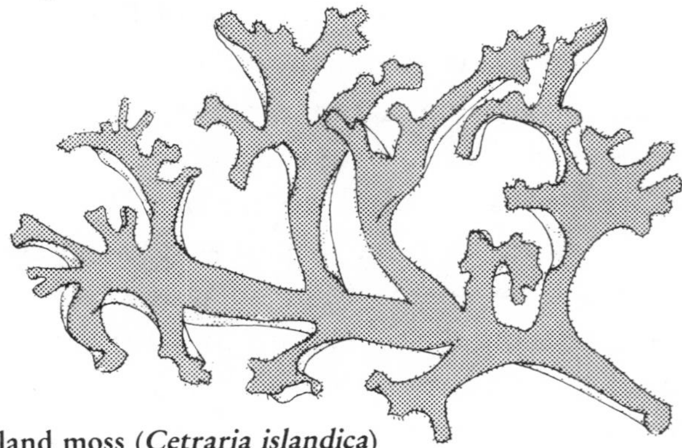

Iceland moss (*Cetraria islandica*)
Red-brown lichen of northern moors. Soak for 1–2 hours in several changes of clean cold water to reduce acidity. Use dried and powdered as a soup/stew thickener.

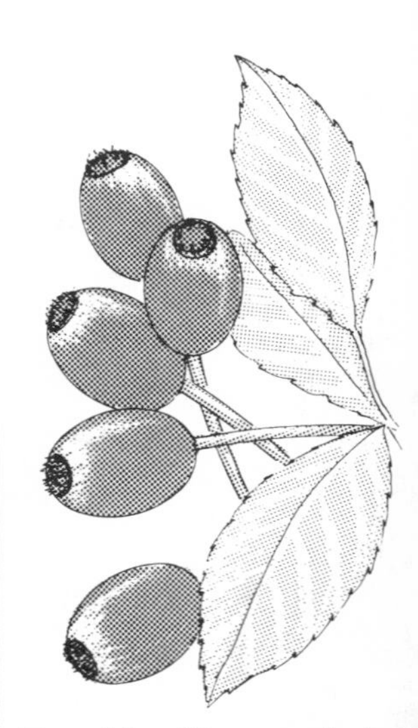

Rose-hips (*Rosa canina*)
Full of vitamin C and eaten raw; scrape hairy pits clean from every hip by cutting in half and using knife-point.

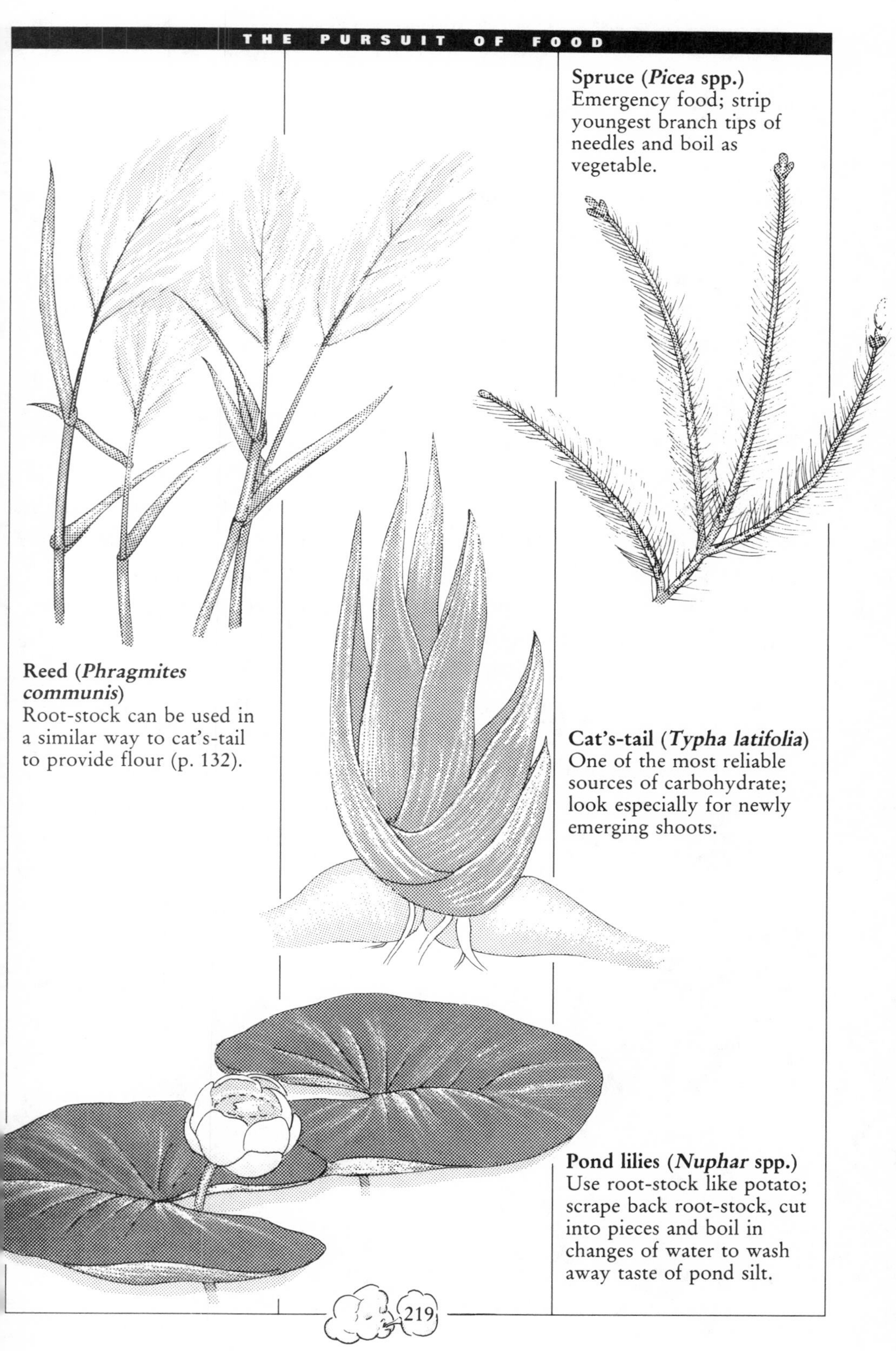

Spruce (*Picea* spp.)
Emergency food; strip youngest branch tips of needles and boil as vegetable.

Reed (*Phragmites communis*)
Root-stock can be used in a similar way to cat's-tail to provide flour (p. 132).

Cat's-tail (*Typha latifolia*)
One of the most reliable sources of carbohydrate; look especially for newly emerging shoots.

Pond lilies (*Nuphar* spp.)
Use root-stock like potato; scrape back root-stock, cut into pieces and boil in changes of water to wash away taste of pond silt.

Sea-shore foods

People have utilised the abundant resources offered by the coast from ancient times. On many of the Scottish islands large midden piles – ancient rubbish heaps – attest to the importance of shellfish to the islands' Stone Age inhabitants. Washed by the tides bringing in driftwood and flotsam from the ocean currents, coastlines are always interesting. Unfortunately today they highlight the way our species is currently abusing the planet.

If you investigate your local coastline, there is a high probability that you will encounter oil, sewage and refuse (even from overseas) and in extreme cases canisters containing toxic chemicals. The sea was once a great provider, but it has become the carpet under which we try to sweep so many of our problems. It is overfished and over-polluted: fishermen have to sail longer and further to fill their nets, bringing home smaller and less healthy catches.

There are many small islands around the British coast whose inhabitants have traditionally had an intimate dependency on their sea-shore. In the days before powered shipping, many of the islands were cut off by tempestuous seas for significant periods of time. The hardy inhabitants learned to exploit every possible source of food, frequently endangering their own lives in the process.

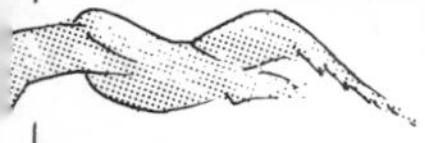

People used to fish from the sheer sea-cliffs with an apparently reckless disregard for the risks. The process involved swinging a weighted line around their heads and thereby casting it out into the ocean several hundred feet below. The angler then sat on the cliff-edge with one foot extended wearing a special shoe with the line passing over the reinforced toe. In this way the line could be hauled in clear of the cliff face.

In Scotland the islanders were just as daring in taking advantage of other sea-shore resources. They clambered on the precariously crumbly sea-cliffs to raid the nests of sea-birds for their eggs. All birds' nests are now protected by law.

You need not go to such risky extremes to enjoy foraging along the coastline, although you must take some precautions. Whenever you enter the inter-tidal region of the shore in search of foods, you must be aware of the local tide times. Every year holiday-makers are stranded on precipitous shorelines by rising tides. Ensure that you allow plenty of time to make it back to land.

You should also dress sensibly for the conditions. Wear warm oiled jerseys and a weatherproof shell. Choose old foot-gear that will not suffer from the salt water, but make sure that this will give you good purchase on slippery rock. I prefer old plimsoles or deck-shoes – if you fall into deep water you can swim in them, unlike wellingtons or waders, which fill with water. Rinse your deck-shoes in fresh water after your foray.

Shorline edibles

The inter-tidal shoreline is particularly rich in wildlife, much of which you can harvest for food. Many molluscs will provide a tasty and easily collected meal, although there are some important precautions which must be taken when gathering food of this sort to avoid intestinal upsets or really serious poisoning. As always, take care not to denude an area of its wildlife – gather instead from a wide area.

Gathering

The most important thing when collecting any shellfish is that it should be fresh, alive and healthy when gathered. Avoid any shellfish that you suspect is not in the peak of condition. Wash all shellfish before cooking and if possible store them overnight in fresh salt water, discarding any that have died during this time. Don't gather molluscs close to sewage outfalls; they may contain high concentrations of pathogenic bacteria which can make you very ill. Never eat shellfish raw; cook them by steaming or boiling at least for five minutes.

Filter feeders

Bivalves feed by filtering food from seawater. In the process they can become infected with harmful bacteria (usually destroyed by sufficient cooking) and a dangerously poisonous single-celled alga commonly called the red tide organism (not destroyed by cooking). This can cause shellfish poisoning, possibly fatally, with no known cure. The organism is most prevalent in the summer, but it is wise to be wary of all bivalves.

Limpets (***Patella vulgata***)
Can be hard to remove from rocks; relatively safe to eat; boil furiously, cut from shells and cut away internal organs, then consume orange flesh.

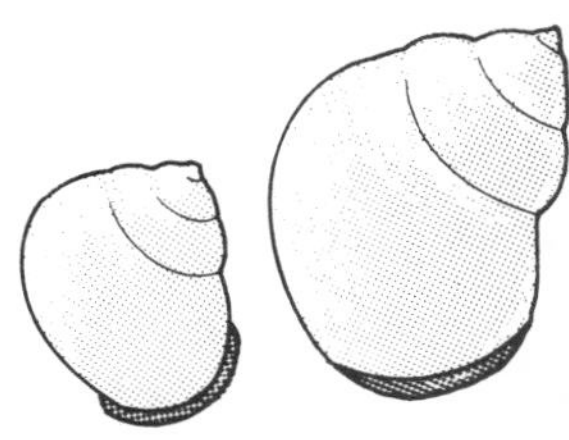

Winkles (***Littorina littorea***)
Still popular; boil fiercely in water for ten minutes; remove obvious shell flap (operculum) and weedle out with long thorn.

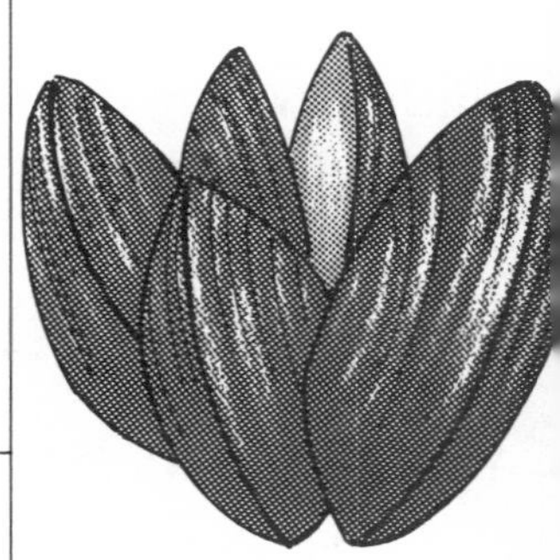

Mussels (***Mytilus edulis***)
Easy to gather from rocks; delicious; but probably worst transmitter of shellfish poisoning; only gather in winter – there is no safe way to tell if fit to eat.

Cockles (***Cardium edule***)
Small bivalves with beautifully shaped shells, found just below surface of exposed mudflats; look for bulges in mud and dig them out.

Sea urchins (***Echinus esculentus***)
Handle fierce sharp spines with care; once broken open, extract fat-rich meat and boil or steam before eating.

Razor fish (***Ensis siliqua***)
Burrows vertically in sand; look for feeding-hole and catch by sprinkling hole with salt; as they come to surface, grasp quickly and pull up firmly.

Clams (***Mya arenaria***)
Gritty shellfish; store alive in fresh seawater; usually tough – tenderise by pounding.

Seaweed

As the winter ends and spring begins to show through, many of the edible seaweeds are at their best for gathering. In many regions of the world seaweed is an important part of the diet. Rich in iodine and other minerals, it has a long-held reputation for healthfulness and medicinal value. Nearly all seaweeds are edible, but it is vitally important only to gather healthy seaweed that is still attached to the rocks by its holdfast. Avoid any that is smelly or that has started to decay.

To avoid destroying the seaweed you collect, harvest it so that you leave 50 cm (20 in) or more attached to the holdfast. An excellent way to use seaweed is dried and cut up for a seaweed stock or ground up and added to stews; you can even eat it deep-fried.

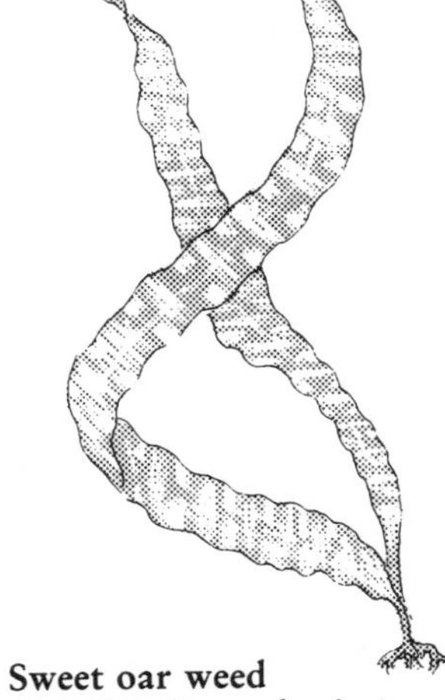

Sweet oar weed (*Laminaria saccharina*)
Very common; as the name suggests, frequently fouls oars.

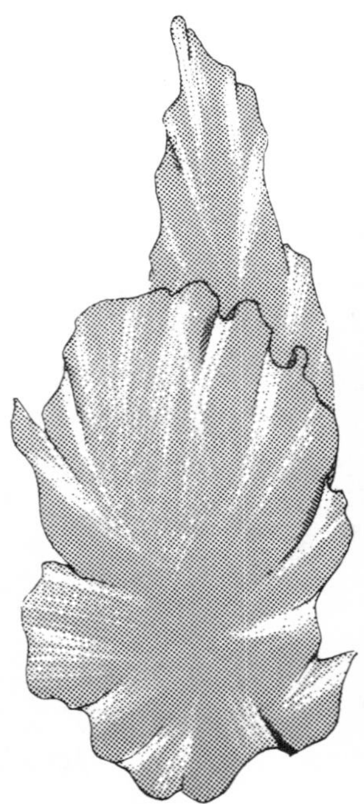

Laver (*Porphyra umbiliculis*)
Less common in the winter, more easily gathered from early spring; highly nutritious, packed with vitamins and well worth searching for.

Edible kelp (*Alaria esculenta*)
Difficult to reach, preferring to skulk under submerged rock outcrops; can sometimes be found in rock-pools.

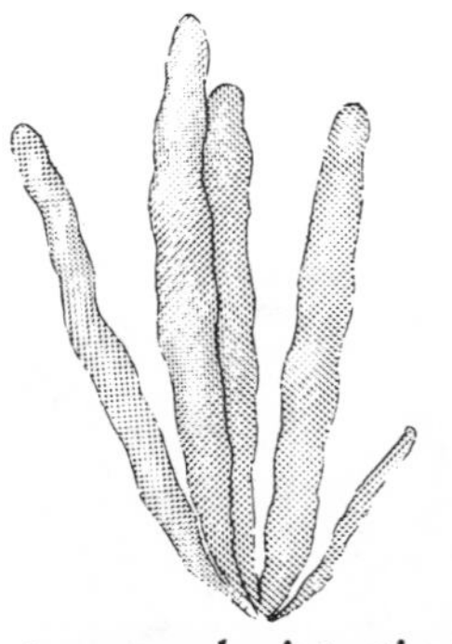

Enteromorpha intestinalis
Found in rock-pools above high-tide mark; easy to overlook; try frying like noodles.

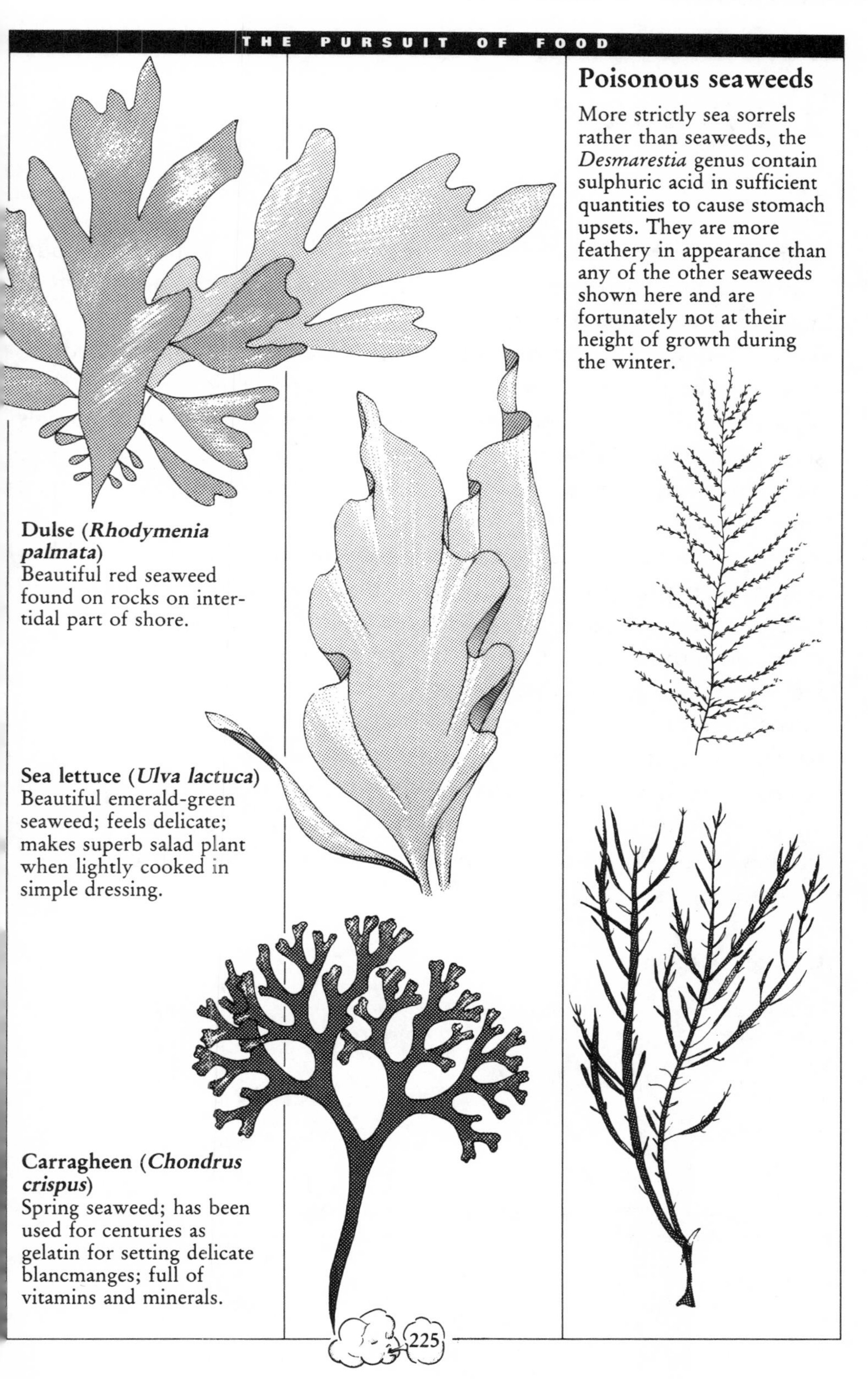

Dulse (*Rhodymenia palmata*)
Beautiful red seaweed found on rocks on intertidal part of shore.

Sea lettuce (*Ulva lactuca*)
Beautiful emerald-green seaweed; feels delicate; makes superb salad plant when lightly cooked in simple dressing.

Carragheen (*Chondrus crispus*)
Spring seaweed; has been used for centuries as gelatin for setting delicate blancmanges; full of vitamins and minerals.

Poisonous seaweeds

More strictly sea sorrels rather than seaweeds, the *Desmarestia* genus contain sulphuric acid in sufficient quantities to cause stomach upsets. They are more feathery in appearance than any of the other seaweeds shown here and are fortunately not at their height of growth during the winter.

Trapping

Trap designs, born out of detailed observations of animal behaviour, epitomise human ingenuity. I consider traps to be the birthplace of modern mechanics. For traditional northern hunter-gatherers they were – and still are – essential tools of the winter. A trap enabled the hunter to be in many places at once, hunting during the long winter nights; and if the trap was well constructed even dangerous animals such as bears could be taken with minimal risk to the hunter. There was, however, always the risk of injury from a wounded trapped animal.

Traps are illegal today – for very good reasons. The main problem is that, no matter how carefully sited, they are indiscriminate and will take any animal, regardless of whether it is the intended victim. While many primitive traps are cruel, causing distress and suffering to their victim, in emergencies their use is justifiable. Even today, therefore, a knowledge of how to trap can be useful. In the natural world life is harsh, with little room for sentimentality – a fact many people feel uncomfortable with and refuse to accept. The trapper, relying on his wits, has no delusions: his first priority is to catch food to stay alive. However, the skilled trapper should be able to be both successful and humane, by using traps that kill swiftly wherever possible.

Choke toss snare

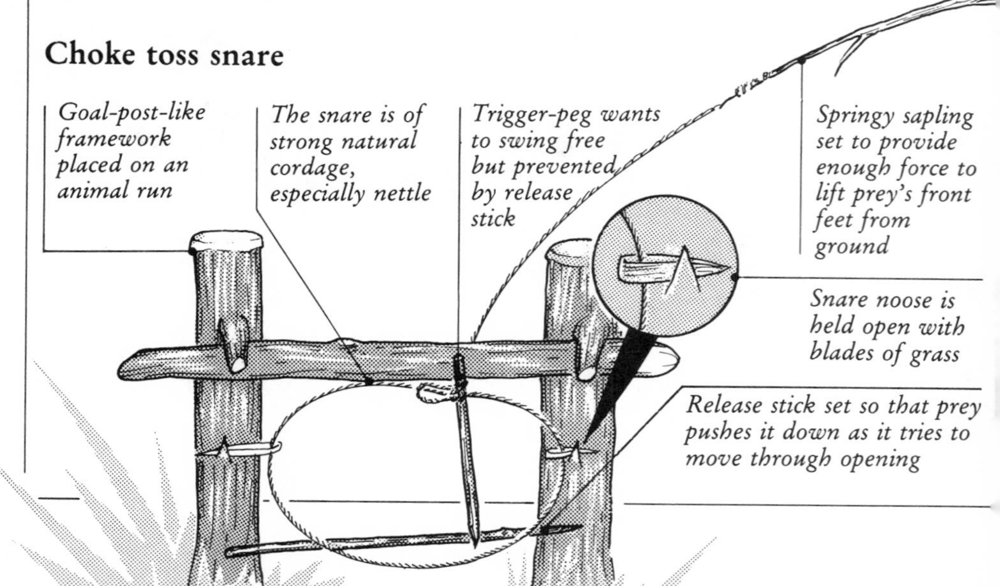

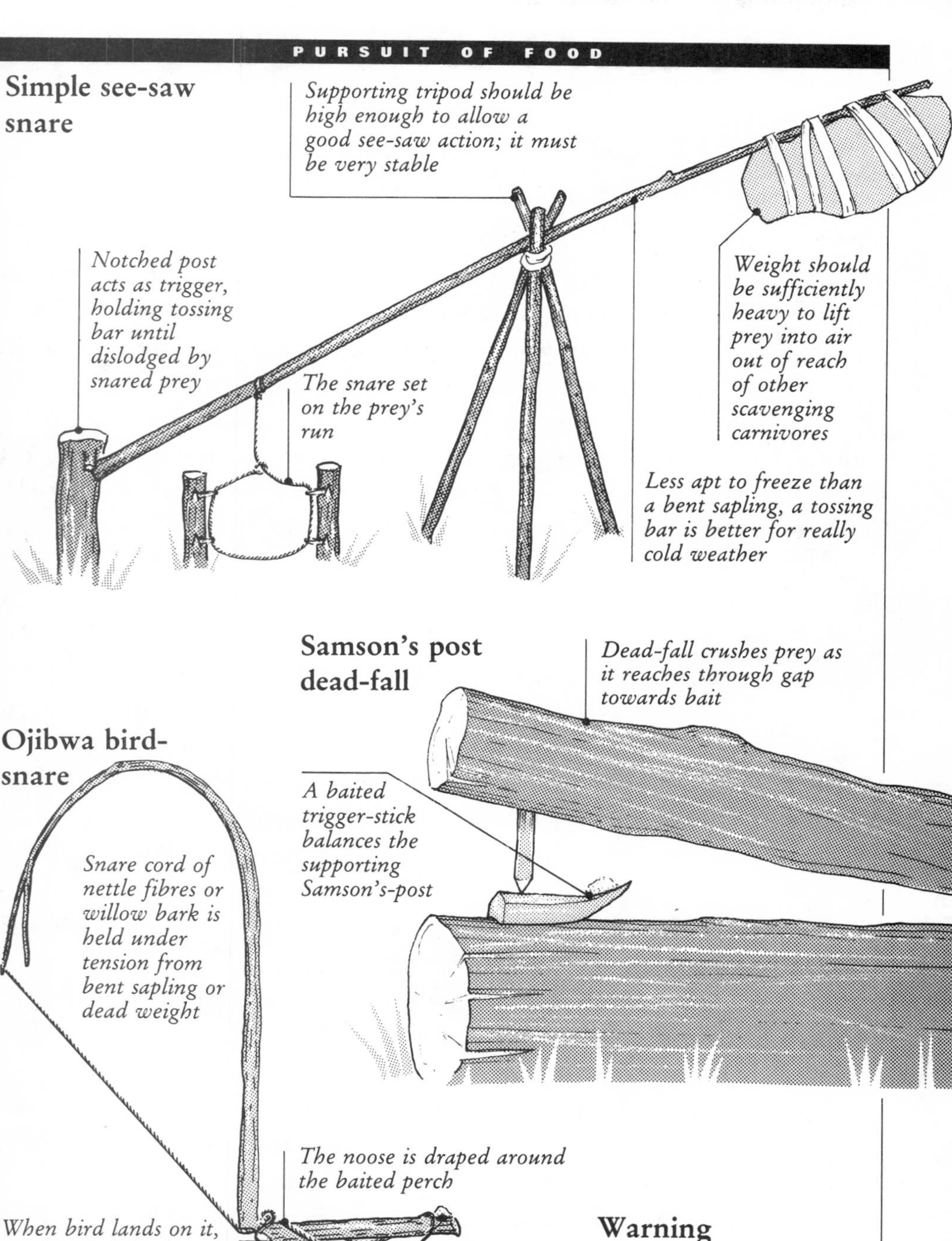

Warning

The traps shown here are illegal and shown only for completeness of content. I do not advocate their use in any situation outside a genuine emergency.

Story-telling

'Tell us again, Grandpa, oh, yes, do . . .' All draw near to the camp-fire circle as the elder gathers his thoughts and raises his face, now transformed into a many-mooded mask by the firelight. With the practice of his years the story-teller conjures images of heroes, legends and mythical beasts from the fire's smoke. The spirits of the forest sit there too, obscured by the shadows, tickling the listeners' spines with their chill touch in perfect synchrony with any ghost story.

Stories, jokes, tall tales, short tales, tips, advice, adventures, tricks and poetry: these are the ingredients that make for a good camp-fire. The long winter nights suit the story-teller best. For now, with a pitch-dark backdrop to the flickering firelight, they can entrance, intrigue and entertain their audience to the full. Yet how few they are who can do this! Spoiled by mass forms of entertainment in the electronic age, we are losing our ability to tell stories; self-consciousness stifles our voices and snuffs out the magic rising in the flames.

The camp-fire is probably the most addictive part of any outdoors adventure. I have many fond memories of the fragile glow from camp-fires in wild places. Friends of the camp-fire are bonded for life, and in a strange way the ground itself seems to retain the magic of the night long after the last dead ember has blown away.

But do not think that you can simply sit people down in a circle around a fire and say, 'Sing and make merry' – for around the camp-fire the audience are also the players. Never try to force or artificially create a camp-fire celebration; the spirit in the flames is shy, preferring to emerge at impromptu moments. To encourage the right atmosphere, lay in a good stock of fuel to avoid interruptions, and also set some water in a billy by the fire to heat for a warming drink. Keep the fire surround tidy and cosy, the fire not too large. Never discuss the atmosphere or how it can be improved. This is instant death to the spirit in the flames.

The best fires are always those where the circle members have each brought with them a contribution to the fire circle – a story, trick, song or other party-piece – to swap. Be bold when you tell your tale, and use the natural drama of the shadows to enhance the effect. If you can play a musical instrument, learn some popular songs; these need not necessarily be traditional camp-fire songs, but should be songs that your company are likely to know the words to. Sea shanties are good songs for the fire: try working your way around the circle, person by person, inventing verses as you go, with only the chorus length to create the verse and a forfeit for anyone who cannot keep up.

Well, I can see you've got the hang of it! Our year has come almost full circle. We have walked many trails these past seasons in search of the secrets our ancestors knew. We have learned to be more reliant on our own ability and nature's gifts, growing as individuals in the process. We have also seen much of the damage our kind are doing to the natural world. We have shivered and sweated together and bashed our thumbs occasionally; and there were those odd cuts and a few insect bites for good measure, but nothing to worry about. The important point is that you have mastered your fire-lighting and can find shelter and food, should you ever need them.

My job is done for the time being. In the appendices to this book you will find some tips on keeping your cutting tools sharp (p. 232) and notes on how to coppice green wood for your projects (p. 234); and there are also some useful addresses for advice and equipment (p. 230). Now, if you will excuse me, I will take my blanket from your fire, for I have a trail to explore and there is someone very special who I need to catch up with.

Useful addresses

Backpacks
Eddie Bauer, Inc.
P.O. Box 3700
Seattle, WA 98124

L. L. Bean, Inc.
Casco Street
Freeport, ME 04033

Lowe Alpine Systems, Inc.
P.O. Box 1449
Broomfield, CO 80038

Fungi
Mycological Society of America
Harvard University Herbaria
22 Divinity Avenue
Cambridge, MA 02138

Binoculars
Carl Zeiss, Inc.
1 Zeiss Drive
Thornwood, NY 10594

Camping Kits
Coleman Company, Inc.
P.O. Box 1762
Wichita, KS 67201

Finnish Knife
Iisaakki Jarvenpaa Oy
62210 Kauhava
Finland

Karhu USA, Inc.
c/o Merrell
P.O. Box 4249
Burlington, VT 05406

Rab Sleeping Bags
32 Edward Street
Sheffield S3 7GB
England

Ventile Jackets
Snowsled Ltd.
Steet Farm Workshops
Doughton
Tetbury
Gloucestershire GL8 8TP
England

Society of Primitive Technology
P.O. Box 3226
Flagstaff, AZ 86003

Outdoors Equipment
Survival Aids
Morland
Cumbria CA10 3AZ
England

Tents
Wild Country
624 Main Street
Conway, NH 03818

Author's Courses and Equipment
Woodlore
1 Beechcroft Avenue
Kenley
Surrey CR8 5DW
England

Outward Bound
National Office
384 Field Point Road
Greenwich, CT 06830

American Camping Association
5000 State Road 67 North
Martinsville, IN 46151

The Young Explorers Trust
Royal Geographical Society
1 Kensington Gore
London SW7 2AR
England

Sharpening a knife

A blunt knife is dangerous. It requires more pressure behind it to cut, and tends to slip on the surface it is cutting rather than biting in like a sharp knife. There is no point in buying any knife if you don't have the means to keep it sharp. You will need two sharpening sets: one for use at home or in camp and the other carried in your pocket on the trail.

At home the best set-up is a two-sided India oilstone, a two-sided novaculite sharpening stone (Arkansas) and a leather strop. The stone should be coarse on one side and fine the other. You start with the coarser India stone and then move on to the finer and harder novaculite and finally the strop. In the field, just take a small novaculite.

The following method is intended for the type of knife featured on p. 21, which has a flat bevel edge. This edge is ideal for cutting wood – the main activity you are likely to use your knife for. With a sharp and suitable knife you will have no difficulty butchering or carrying out other tasks as well.

At home

1 Lubricate stone with light oil or WD40 lubricant.

2 Lay blade with bevel flat on coarse side of large stone.

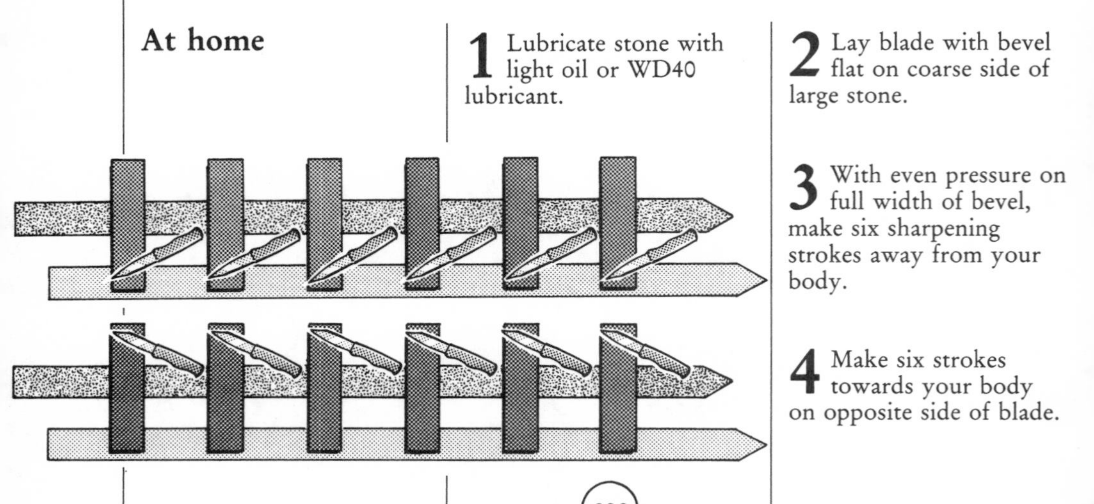

3 With even pressure on full width of bevel, make six sharpening strokes away from your body.

4 Make six strokes towards your body on opposite side of blade.

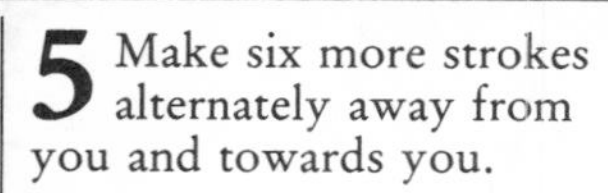

5 Make six more strokes alternately away from you and towards you.

6 Repeat steps 1 to 5 on fine side of stone.

7 Strop blade to make edge more robust. If this is not done, edge will tend to blunt more quickly. Stropping can be carried out on back of a 5 cm (2 in) wide leather belt. Drag blade away from edge, alternating direction each stroke. Fifty strokes will see job done.

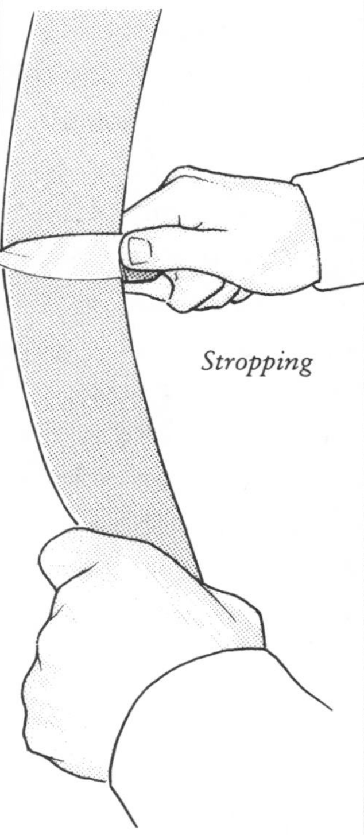

Stropping

Using the sharpening stone

Lay bevel flat on stone surface

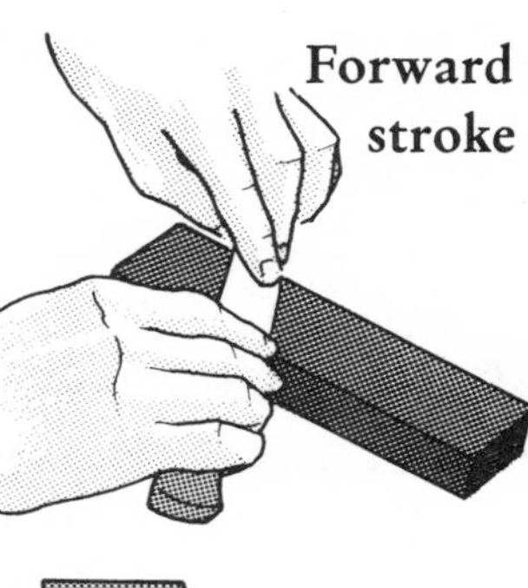

Forward stroke

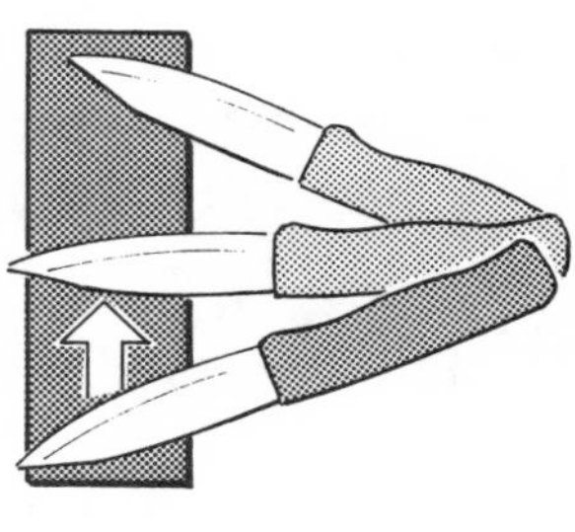

In the field

1 Steady blade on tree-stump. With small stone lubricated with spittle, stroke edge in sawing action. Always keep flat of stone in full contact with bevel.

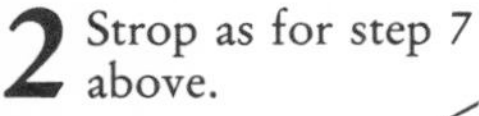

2 Strop as for step 7 above.

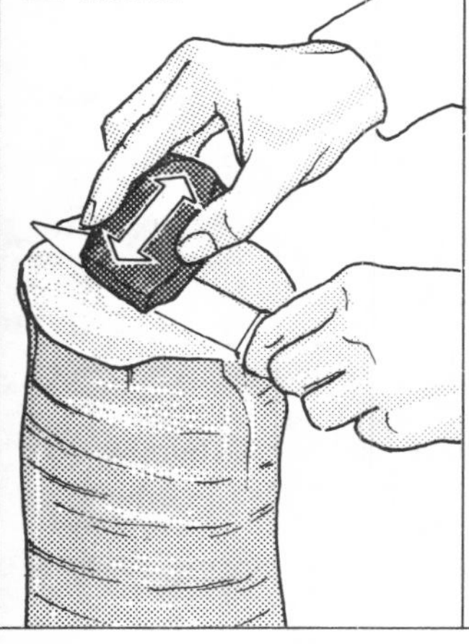

Rearward stroke

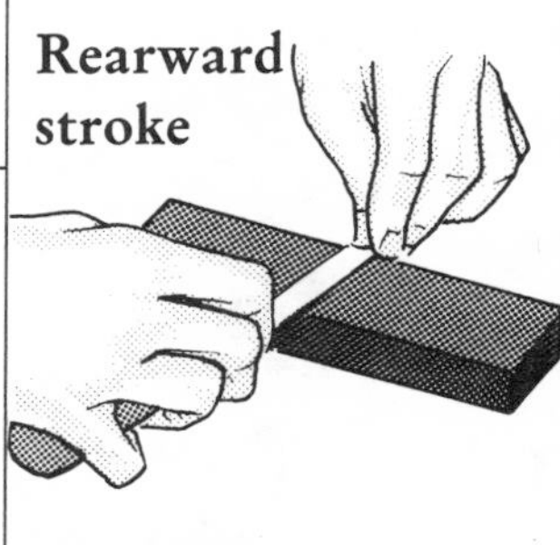

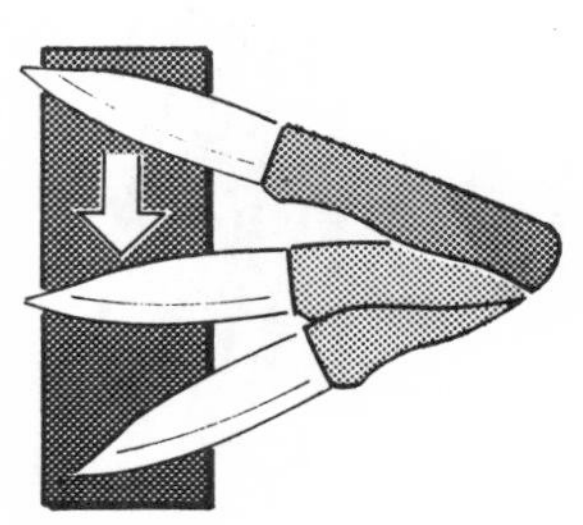

Care of sharpening tools

Never use stones without a lubricant, which prevents the pores clogging with metal particles. Clean your stones periodically with a strong soda solution. Keep your stone flat: you can flatten a stone that becomes hollowed by rubbing it on a sheet of glass with piston carborundum grinding paste and detergent sandwiched between.

Coppicing

For centuries, areas of woodland have been managed by coppicing. This involves cutting a sapling close to the ground. In the next year new shoots will rise from the stump. These are allowed to grow until of a useful size before they too are trimmed. As time goes on, the stump – called the coppice stool by foresters – grows in width, providing ever more shoots to harvest.

If you have to gather green wood for any reason, you should try to do so by coppicing. If you have to trim a branch, trim it close to the trunk, so that the tree will be able to grow bark over the scar and seal out the decay from bacteria. Recent research suggests that the bark at this point has special fungicidal properties.

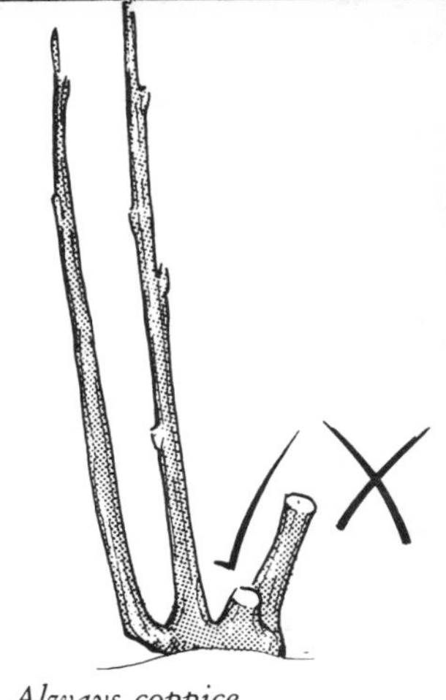

Always coppice close to the ground

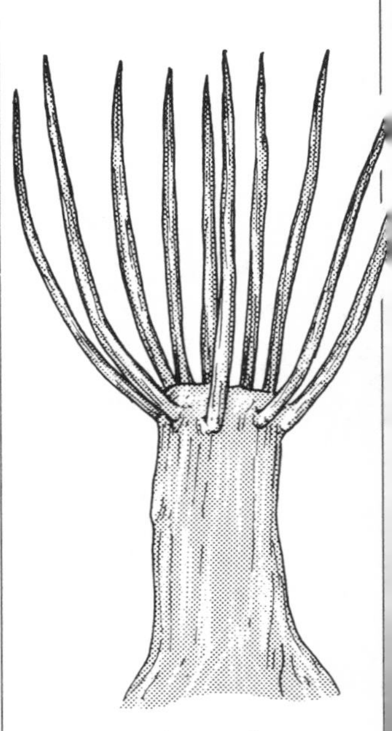

Coppicing leaves the new shoots at risk from browsing animals. So in areas grazed by domesticated livestock the coppicing was carried out 1.5 m (5 ft) above the ground, a variation known as pollarding. This is the method used to grow willow wands for basketry.

Coppicing

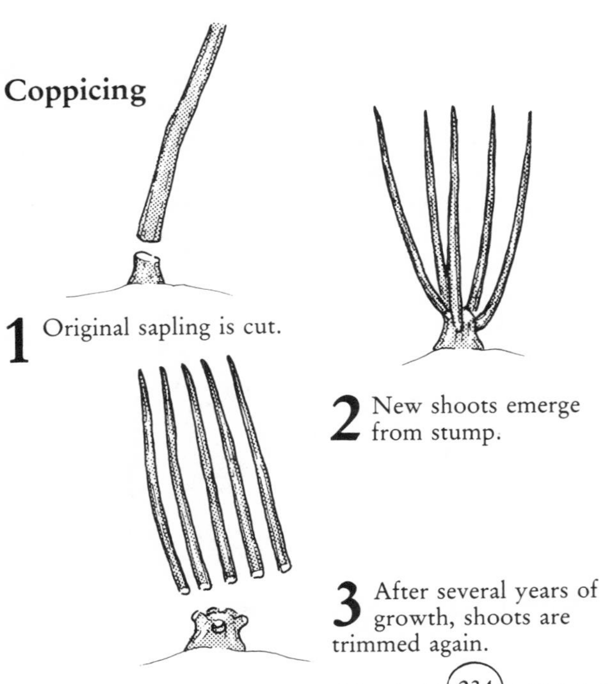

1 Original sapling is cut.

2 New shoots emerge from stump.

3 After several years of growth, shoots are trimmed again.

Trimming a branch

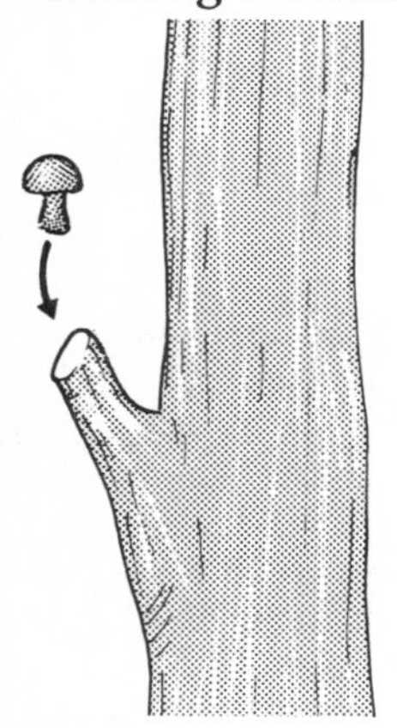

Trimmed like this, fungus can enter the scar and attack the tree.

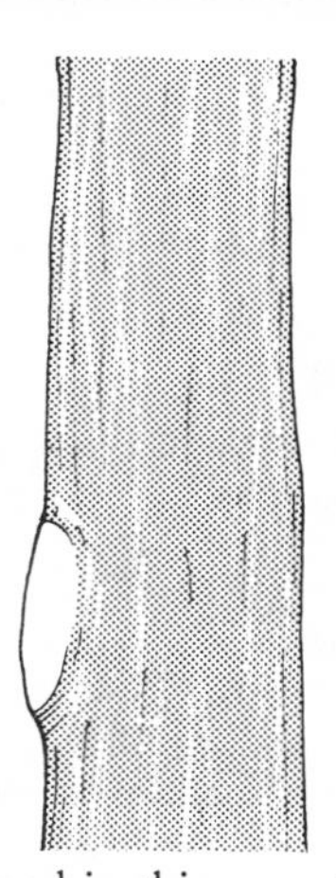

Trimmed in this way, the tree can begin to effect a heal by growing bark over the scar.

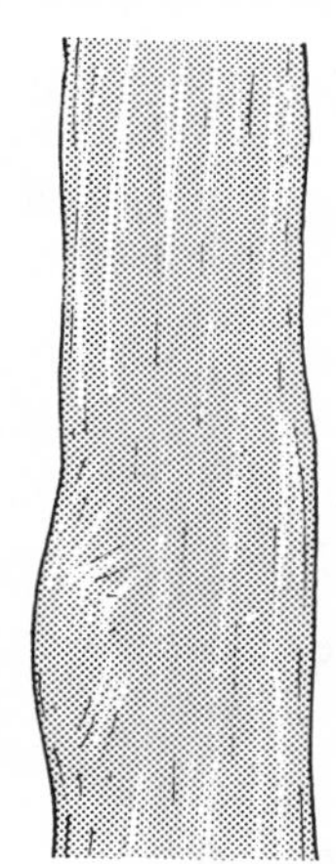

After several years the scar is sealed over by new bark.

Trimming branches

Whenever trimming branches with an axe or knife, use the grain in your favour to avoid splitting the wood.

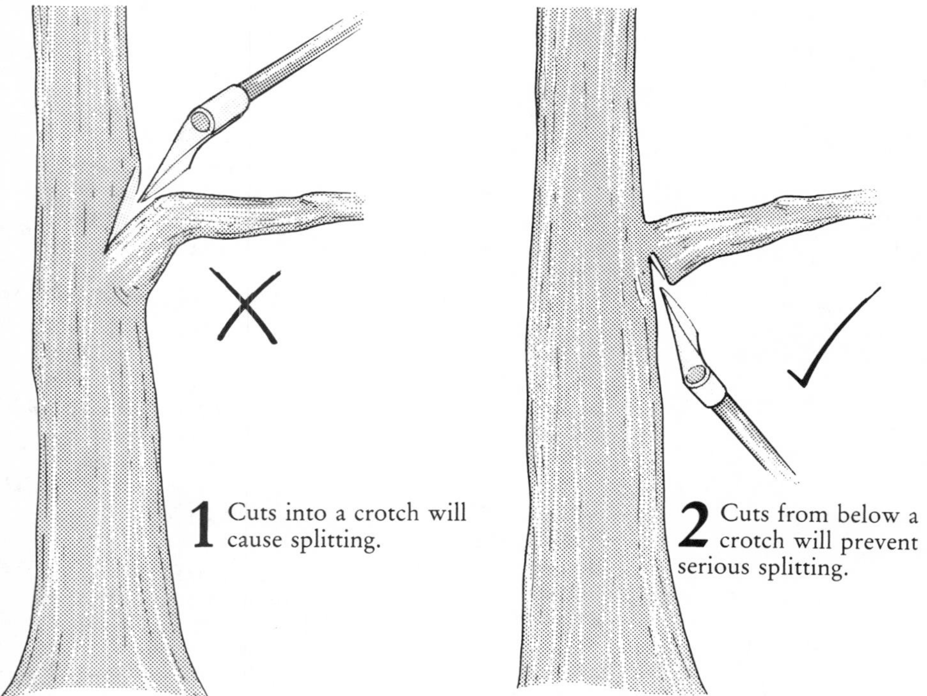

1 Cuts into a crotch will cause splitting.

2 Cuts from below a crotch will prevent serious splitting.

Any trimming or coppicing from living trees is best achieved with a saw or very sharp blade, to leave a smooth scar.

Index

N

O

P

Q

R

S

T

U

V

W

Y